# Sources for the History of Cyprus

Volume XII

## German Texts:

## Turkish Period (after 1800)

# Sources for the History of Cyprus

*Edited by*
Paul W. Wallace and Andreas G. Orphanides

# Volume XII

# German Texts:
# Turkish Period (after 1800)

*Selected and Edited by*
HANS A. POHLSANDER
(University at Albany, State University of New York)

Greece and Cyprus Research Center
2006

ISBN:          1-931226-12-1

ISBN set:      0-9651704-0-3

# TABLE OF CONTENTS

# PREFACE

Like preceding volumes in this series, this volume endeavors to make original source material on the history of Cyprus available in English translation, in this case to those who might have a serious interest in the subject but limited or no knowledge of German. Those who read German may find this volume a convenient first step in further research.

The texts selected for inclusion in this volume have been arranged in chronological order. The chronological parameters range from the beginning of the 19th century to 1878, when the British assumed control of Cyprus and initiated a new era in the history of the island. It is anticipated that subsequent volumes will be devoted to both earlier and later German-language sources.

Some of the German-language sources of this period are of such length that they could be represented by excerpts only. Translations are mine unless otherwise indicated. Author's footnotes have generally been omitted; where they have been included they have been specifically marked as such. On the other hand I have included many corrections and additions of my own, briefer ones in brackets within the text and longer ones in footnotes.

Readers will find much information on social and economic conditions, such as the living conditions, agricultural production, trade, taxation, means of transportation, and the status of the clergy. The Greek majority receives far more attention than the Turkish minority. Archaeologists will be interested in the beginnings of their discipline on the island, as it evolved from treasure hunting and touristic curiosity into a serious pursuit. The attitudes of the writers toward the island and its people will be of interest as well.

# ACKNOWLEDGMENTS

Kind assistance given by the following individuals and institutions is gratefully acknowledged:

Professor Virginia Aksan, McMaster University, Hamilton, Ontario
Dr. Traugott Bautz, *Biographisch-Bibliographishes Kirchenlexikon*
Dr. Sylvia Brehme, Staatliche Museen, Berlin
Professor Kemal Çiçek, Turkish Historical Society, Ankara
Dr. Nicholas Coureas, Cyprus Research Center, Ministry of Education and Culture, Nicosia
Lady Hunt, Trigraph Limited, London
Dr. Gunda Pfunder, Landesmuseum Joanneum, Graz
Ms. Rachel Rowe, Library of the Royal Commonwealth Society, Cambridge, U.K.
Professor Michael Toumazou, Davidson College, Davidson, N.C.
Frau Christine Weidlich, Universitäts- und Landesbibliothek Bonn
The staff, Niedersächsische Staats- und Universitätsbibliothek Göttingen
The staff, inter-library-loan office, University Library, University at Albany, State University of New York
The staff, Office of the Representative, Turkish Republic of Northern Cyprus, Washington, D.C.

# BIBLIOGRAPHY

Bergk, *Ansichten*  Bergk, Johann Adam. *Ansichten von der Türkei, hauptsächlich von Caramanien.* Leipzig, 1812.

Cobham, *Excerpta*  Cobham, Claude Delaval. *Excerpta Cypria. Materials for a History of Cyprus.* Cambridge, 1908.

Engel, *Kypros*  Engel, Wilhelm Heinrich. *Kypros. Eine Monographie.* Berlin, 1841.

Friederichs, *Reisebriefe*  Friederichs, Carl. *Kunst und Leben: Reisebriefe aus Griechenland, dem Orient und Italien.* Düsseldorf, 1872.

Gazioglou, *Turks*  Gazioglou, Ahmet C. *The Turks in Cyprus.* London, 1990.

Goodwin, Jack C. *An Historical Toponymy of Cyprus,* 2 vols. 5th ed. Nicosia, 1985.

Gunnis, *Cyprus*  Gunnis, Rupert. *Historic Cyprus: A Guide to Its Towns & Villages, Monasteries & Castles.* London, 1936. Repr. Nicosia, 1956 and 1973.

Hackett, *Orthodox Church*  Hackett, John. *A History of the Orthodox Church of Cyprus.* London, 1901.

Hadjiioannou, *Kypros*  Hadjiioannou, Kyriakos. Η ΑΡΧΑΙΑ ΚΥΠΡΟΣ ΕΙΣ ΤΑΣ ΕΛΛΗΝΙΚΑΣ ΠΗΓΑΣ. Nicosia, 1985.

Hammer-Purgstall, *Ansichten*  Hammer-Purgstall, Joseph von. *Topographische Ansichten gesammelt auf einer Reise in die Levante.* Vienna, 1811.

Hill, *History*  Hill, George. *A History of Cyprus.* 4 vols. Cambridge, 1949–1952.

Inalcik, Halil, with Donald Quataert. *An Economic and Social History of the Ottoman Empire, 1300–1914.* Cambridge, 1994.

Kotschy, "Reise"  Kotschy, Theodor. "Reise nach Cypern und Klein-Asien, 1859," *Petermann's geographische Mittheilungen* 8 (1862) 289–304.

Lullies and Schiering, *Archäologenbildnisse*  Lullies, Reinhard, and Wolfgang Schiering, eds., *Archäologenbildnisse: Porträts und Kurzbiographien von klassischen Archäologen deutscher Sprache.* Mainz, 1988.

Petermann, *Reisen*  Petermann, Julius Heinrich. *Reisen im Orient.* Leipzig, 1860.

Pococke, *Description*  Pococke, Richard. *A Description of the East and Some Other Countries,* 2 vols. in 3. London, 1743–1745.

Richter, *Wallfahrten*  Richter, Otto Friedrich von. *Wallfahrten im Morgenlande,* ed. Johann Philipp Gustav Ewers. Berlin, 1822.

Ritter zur Helle, *Vilajet*  Ritter zur Helle von Samo, Alfred. *Das Vilajet der Inseln des Weissen Meeres, das priviligierte Beylik Samos und das selbstständige Mutessariflik Cypern.* Vienna, 1878.

Ross, *Reisen*  Ross, Ludwig. *Reisen nach Kos, Halikarnassos, Rhodos und der Insel Cypern (Reisen auf die griechischen Inseln IV).* Halle, 1852. Translated by Claude D. Cobham, *A Journey to Cyprus, February and March 1845.* Nicosia, 1910.

Sakellarios, *Kypriaka*  Sakellarios, Athanasios. Τὰ Κυπριακά. 2 vols. Athens, 1890–1891. Repr. Nicosia, 1991. First published Athens, 1855.

Ludwig Salvator, *Levkosia*  Ludwig Salvator. *Levkosia, Hauptstadt von Cypern.* 1873. Translated into English by Ferdinand, Ritter von Krapf-Liverhoff, *Levkosia Capital of Cyprus.* Routledge and Kegan Paul: London, 1881. Reprinted by Trigraph: London, 1983.

Schröder, "Reise"  Schröder, Paul. "Meine zweite Reise auf Cypern im Frühjahr 1873," *Globus: Illustrierte Zeitschrift für Länder- und Völkerkunde* 33–34 (1878) 135–39, 152–56, 168–72, 183–86.

Seiff, *Reisen*  Seiff, Julius. *Reisen in der asiatischen Turkei.* Leipzig, 1875.

Seiff, *Skizze*  Seiff, Julius. *Skizze einer Reise durch die Insel Cypern.* Dresden, 1874.

Stylianou, *Cartography*  Stylianou, Andreas, and Judith A. Stylianou. *The History of the Cartography of Cyprus.* Nicosia, 1980.

Stylianou, *Painted Churches*  Stylianou, Andreas, and Judith A. Stylianou. *The Painted Churches of Cyprus.* London, 1985.

Unger, *Cypern*  Unger, Franz. *Die Insel Cypern einst und jetzt* (a lecture delivered in Graz, winter of 1866). Vienna, 1866.

Unger and Kotschy, *Cypern*  Unger, Franz, and Theodor Kotschy, *Die Insel Cypern, ihrer physischen und organischen Natur nach, mit Rücksicht auf ihre frühere Geschichte.* Vienna, 1865.

# ABBREVIATIONS

| | |
|---|---|
| *BBKL* | *Biographisch-Bibliographisches Kirchenlexikon,* ed. Friedrich Wilhelm Bautz, 1990 ff. |
| *BCH* | *Bulletin de Correspondance Hellénique* |
| *BMus. Inscr.* | *Collection of Ancient Greek Inscriptions in the British Museum,* ed. C. T. Newton, Oxford, 1874–1916. |
| Cass. Dio | Cassius Dio |
| Catull. | Catullus |
| *CIG* | *Corpus Inscriptionum Graecarum,* ed. A. Boeck, Berlin, 1828–1877. |
| D. L. | Diogenes Laertius |
| Euseb. *Praep. Evang.* | Eusebius, *Praeparatio Evangelica* |
| Euseb. *De Laud. Const.* | Eusebius, *De Laudibus Constantini* |
| *FGrH* | *Fragmemte der griechischen Historiker,* ed. F. Jacoby, 1923 ff. |
| *FHG* | *Fragmenta Historicum Graecorum,* ed. C. Müller, 1841–1870. |
| *IGRom.* | *Inscriptiones Graecae ad res Romanas pertinentes,* eds. R. Cagnat et alii, Paris, 1911–1927. |
| *JHS* | *Journal of Hellenic Studies* |
| *Kl. Pauly* | *Der kleine Pauly,* 1964–1975. |
| Max. Tyr. *dissert.* | Maximus Tyrius, *dissertationes* |
| Müller, *Geogr. Gr. Min.* | Karl Müller, *Geographi Graeci Minores,* 3 vols. Paris, 1855; repr. Hildesheim, 1965. |
| *Od.* | *Odyssey* |
| *OGI* | *Orientis Graeci Inscriptiones Selectae,* ed. W. Dittenberger, Leipzig, 1903–1905. |
| Paus. | Pausanias |
| Pi. *N.* | Pindar, *Nemean Odes* |
| *PIR* [2] | *Prosopographia Imperii Romani Saeculi I, II, III,* 2nd. eds. E. Groag, A. Stein et alii, 1933 ff. |
| Plin. *HN* | Pliny the Elder, *Historia Naturalis* |
| Plu. *Cat. Minor* | Plutarch, *Cato Minor* |
| Plu. *Cim.* | Plutarch, *Cimon* |
| Plu. *Demetr.* | Plutarch, *Demetrius* |
| Ptol. *Geog.* | Ptolemaeus, *Geographia* |
| RE | A. Pauly, G. Wissowa, and W. Kroll, *Realenzyklopädie der klassischen Altertumswissenschaft,* 1893 ff. |
| Sen. *Q. Nat.* | Seneca the Younger, *Quaestiones Naturales* |
| Serv. *Ad Aen.* | Servius, *Ad Aeneidem* |
| SHC | *Sources for the History of Cyprus,* eds. Paul W. Wallace and Andreas G. Orphanides, Altamont, New York, 1990 ff. |

| | |
|---|---|
| Strab. | Strabo |
| Strack | Max Lebrecht Strack, *Inscriptiones Graecae Ptolemaicae,* Chicago, 1976. |
| Suet. *Tib.* | Suetonius, *Tiberius* |
| Tac. *Ann.* | Tacitus, *Annales* |
| Tac. *Hist.* | Tacitus, *Historiae* |
| Thuc. | Thucydides |

# GERMAN TEXTS OF THE NINETEENTH CENTURY

## von Hammer-Purgstall—before 1811

### [Plate 1]

Freiherr Joseph von Hammer-Purgstall (1774–1856) was an Austrian civil servant and scholar, with a special interest in the Near East. The following excerpt is taken from his *Topographische Ansichten gesammelt auf einer Reise in die Levante* (Vienna, 1811) 121–55, and 176–84. He has adorned his account with numerous quotations of Greek and Latin poetry; these have not been included in the translation. Mythological and other digressions have also been omitted.

Anchor was cast at Limassol . . .

A traveler who inquires in Cyprus about noteworthy ruins is referred to two places where such can be found. Both of them are on the southern coast, on the shore; one at Baffo (Paphos), fourteen hours east [west] of Limassol, the other at Maussa [Maghusa] (Fama augusta) [Famagusta], sixteen hours to the west [east].

As far as can be learned from inquiries made, the former has medieval remains mingled with ancient remains, and the latter buildings from the days of the rule of the Lusignans. The most remarkable thing about these cities, people say, is the large number of churches with icons of the Saints, and from this one can deduce the earlier size of this city. In both places one can see, supposedly, the remnants of 365 churches, i.e. one for each day of the year . . .

In addition to these noteworthy ruins people also mention some others in the area of the monastery of St. Nicholas[1] and on the site of old Limassol.[2] The former are on the side toward Paphos, three hours to the east [west], and the others on the side toward Fama augusta, three hours to the west [east] from Limassol.

A short distance out of Limassol on the way to St. Nicholas the beautiful countryside breaks off. The whole terrain between the sea and the chain of mountains which runs an hour distant parallel to the sea is a barren steppe of sand and salt. In the winter rain water collects here, and, in the summer, when it evaporates, salt crystals. The monastery and the cultivated land around it lie on a tip of land, like a fertile oasis surrounded by salty floods and steppes.[3] It is a medieval building built of ordinary stone. The large marble columns which lie in front of it undoubtedly belonged to a splendid ancient building on the foundations of which the monastery rises. In front of the main facade one can still see the places where the columns stood, which here formed a hall. Chicken are cackling in the cells of the monastery, pigs are grunting in the cloisters, and donkeys are braying in the hall. The whole building is inhabited by a single kalogeros (καλόγερος), who is monk, custodian, and abbot at the same time.

Old Limassol is located on the opposite side, three hours distant from the modern city of Limassol. The way there is as varied and charming as that to St. Nicholas is monotonous and barren. It leads through fertile fields and bushes just high enough to prevent

---

[1] This must be a reference to the Monastery of St. Nicholas of the Cats, which is located on nearby Akrotiri peninsula, hardly three hours distant.

[2] This is a reference to Amathus, only c. five miles to the northeast of Limassol.

[3] In a footnote the author confuses the location of the monastery of St. Nicholas with that of Curium [Kourion].

one from seeing the sea, which is only a few hundred paces away. One travels through planted fields and clusters of trees; one does not see or anticipate the sea, and yet one continually hears the sound of the surf. The chain of mountains in the interior now approaches the path, and where they meet the city of Amathus, the favorite haunt of Aphrodite, stood in the earliest times. The distance from Larnaca is not seven miles (as given in Pococke,[4] presumably by a slip of the pen), but fourteen miles.

The sea here once formed a bay, now filled in by sand, and the mountains form a large arc, the base of which, the seashore, is about an hour long. In the middle of this large basin a single steep hill rises, completely separate from the arc of mountains, the ends of which stretch to the sea. In this awkwardly described setting old Limassol and formerly Amathus lay on the seashore. On the western, inner side of the arc, close to the sea, there are two large grottoes carved into the rock, and one of them has a subterranean entrance, which was filled up with stones. According to the guide the path supposedly continues under ground and on both sides of it grottoes and vaults are carved out.

On the opposite side of the basin, namely the eastern, inner side, there stand the walls of a Christian church with its paintings of saints still almost completely preserved. Individual columns and fragments of walls, the work of later times, are the only ruins which one finds after a long search; otherwise there is no trace of old temples or other buildings of classical times. But a Turkish peasant from the village of Ayios Tychonos [Tykhonas] assured me that there were stones with old inscriptions in the area.

An hour before reaching old Limassol and turning inland from the usual route, one comes to a beautiful, romantic valley. It is limited on the land side by continuous mountains, which sometimes follow a straight line and at other times form protruding roundings; on the sea side it is limited by a number of separate oblong hills. These stand there like the pieces of ruined ramparts, each one separate from the next; their forms are sharply delineated like the sections of gun bastions, and where they do not block one another the view is open toward the sea. Aromatic herbs cover the walls of the hills; olive trees and cultivated fields the floor of the valley. After one has crossed the plain for an hour and climbed up on the eastern wall of hills one reaches the village of Ayios Tychonos [Tykhonas].

This lies at the far end of a small valley, about half an hour from the sea, the blue inlet of which fills the opening of the rocks. At the exit of the valley the traveler sights the walls of the church just mentioned and realizes that he has circumvented the basin in which old Limassol and Amathus lay from behind. From here the Turkish peasant from the village of Ayios Tykhonas acted as my guide and led me through a defile into the basin of old Limassol and to the lone-standing hill. One climbs this hill delayed first by the difficulty of the ascent and then by a pleasant amazement. The natural rock is at the height of several fathoms in its entire circumference cut by human hands, sometimes vertically like a wall, sometimes carved out in small grottoes and arches. This view vividly brings to mind the carved rock wall of Mt. Bisutun [Behistun] in Persia, and just as there so here a depression carved into the rock with an inscription attracts attention. It is located on the west side of the hill and has suffered great damage by the passing of time

---

[4] Pococke, *Description; SHC* V 35–56.

and the rough weather. It gives the name of the man who had the carving done.[5] The devastation and destruction of the rock wall is explained by the softness of the stone.

On the platform of the summit, where perhaps a large temple stood, one still finds two huge temple vessels of marble, in which presumably water for purifications was stored. One of these is let into the ground and broken, but the other is still almost completely intact.[6] The largest bulge measures seven paces in circumference; its height is that of a man. It has four handles, on the outer sides of which an animal is carved out in low relief; this appears to be a horse. Like a new Hans Nord[7] the traveler climbs into the large vessel, and his voice sounds like a constant echo in the stone cavern. In vain one looks for the remnants of a building to which these huge vats must have belonged. On the way back to the village one meets a colossal fallen column with its base; this column presumably bore the statue of a deity or an important man.

In the village of Ayios Tykhonas there are the other inscriptions which the Turkish peasant Hassan had promised to show me. The first thing which one notices is the large number of round stone altars and sacrificial tables of various sizes. These are partly in Hassan's house, partly scattered through the other houses of the village. All of these carry inscriptions, but only a few of these are still legible.[8] On the front they bear the name of the individual who dedicated them or in whose memory they were dedicated. These altars, in the course of time almost completely eroded, give ample evidence for the presence of an old temple in this area. Then there is a large piece of ancient sculpture, of which it is now hard to judge whether it was the torso of a statue or something else.

Everywhere there are traces of the temple. From the sacrificial tables and from the column capitals it can be learned that this temple was of the Ionic order. All these stones are eroded, and from the kind of work one can see that they belong to the infancy of art.

Everywhere there are the ruins of a sanctuary! Where was it located? Seek and ye shall find. In the village itself the foundation walls of the temple still stand, unharmed and built of squared-off blocks of stone which have been turned green by age. These walls differ greatly from those in the plain of old Limassos by their beauty and firmness. In the half-round of the front part there stands a great stone table, which perhaps served the statue of the goddess as altar or pedestal. Outside of the walls there lie another three, their inscriptions totally ruined. Within the walls of the temple a Turkish peasant has put up a barn. The main side of the temple faces east; the entrance is from the south . . .

The temple stood in the middle of the hill at which the two arms of the chain of mountains meet, and between these it offers a view of the sea . . .

Larnaca is called Tuzla, i.e. salt mine, after the nearby salines. It consists of the harbor and the city proper, which are less than half an hour distant from each other. In that part of the city which is situated toward the harbor the buildings of the consuls are topped by poles with the various flags of their nations, so that, when all the flags are flying, the consular quarter is like a fleet on land.

---

[5] For this inscription see below, "Inscriptions from Cyprus," no 48, and *CIG* II 2644. It hardly merits comparison with the Behistun monument.
[6] It was removed by French explorers in 1866 and is now in the Louvre. See the selection from Franz Unger in this volume.
[7] Hans Nord, a character in the *Fabeln und Erzählungen* (Leipzig, 1746–1748) of Christian Fürchtegott Gellert (1715–1769).
[8] For these inscriptions see below, "Inscriptions of Cyprus," nos. 44–47, and, correspondingly, *CIG* II 2648, 2652, 2649, and 2643.

The small Catholic church is divided into three aisles in the old Greek manner. In the central nave there are some pews, which the consuls fill with their families, not without quarreling about rank. The two aisles are provided for men and women separately, for they are segregated in Oriental fashion. The men have an unobstructed view of the altar; but on the women's side the view is not only blocked by a grate but covered with a curtain, so that the women see nothing of the church service. Only on the Saturday of Holy Week do they see the priest when he blesses the water, for the baptismal font stands, as is proper, in the women's aisle.

This strict separation and covering-up is limited in Larnaca to church. On the street and in contact with the public the women, even those from Aleppo (of whom a number are living here), enjoy far more freedom than anywhere else in the Orient. Their manner is freer, less constrained, and more given to conversation; in short, social relations have, thanks to the large volume of commerce in the city, become more like those of Europe.

A day's journey from here, namely in Limassol, the women veil themselves very strictly; here, even on the street, they veil only their headdress[9] . . .

An opportunity to see all the women in full dress is provided by the Easter festival, when for three days the residents of the city visit one another. From early morning until late evening people meet one another every few moments in church, on the street, or in a home in the course of a reciprocal visit. Every visitor is offered toast and coffee, and coffee lovers can in this manner afford twenty or more cups a day.

Larnaca would be a paradisaical place to live if the nearby swamps and salines did not spoil the air. Hence the many and persistent fevers, the generally pale color of the inhabitants, the physicians, and the many graves. The Catholic community alone has four physicians, and, since the church is served by four Franciscans, the number of those who tend to the needs of the body equals that of those who tend to the needs of the soul. Also the climate is so mild that there is no winter, but the heat of summer is doubly felt. Throughout the year there is an abundance of roses and mosquitoes.

Of the walls of Citium [Kition], which was close to Larnaka, nothing remains to be seen. Of a tomb which was found some fifty years ago in the same area legend has made the tomb of a mummy of the Prophet. The governor at the time favored the miracles and visions which were claimed. Long ago, so said the sheiks, imams, and dervishes, it was at Akri [Acre?], whence it was carried by angels across the sea to Cyprus. Since then the mosque built on the spot has become famous and rich by worship and superstition.[10]

Old and New Paphos once counted among the most preferred cities of Cyprus. The former was in earliest antiquity the principal and favorite abode of Aphrodite, also her birthplace and sanctuary. The latter was in later times famous as a port city and the capital of its own kingdom.

The memory of New Paphos [Kato Paphos] is preserved in the good-size pile of stones and in the name of Baffo (Βάφω).[11] Travelers confuse it with Old Paphos [Palea Paphos], which was situated sixty stadia, i.e. about three hours, distant on a height where the Turkish village of Kouklia[12] now stands.

---

[9] A detailed description follows, but has been omitted here.

[10] This is a garbled reference to the Hala Sultan Tekke. See Gunnis, *Cyprus,* 119–20, and Gazioglou, *Turks,* 278–80.

[11] The author consistently refers to it as Baffa.

[12] The author consistently refers to it as Kukla.

The remains of the temple of New Paphos are preserved in the pile of rubble that is Baffo, and the foundations of the old temple of the goddess at Kouklia, which so far has not been explored by travelers.

Pococke describes very accurately all that could be seen in the ruins of New Paphos. But he bypassed the ruins of Kouklia without exploring them; he was content with the mere notice and the conjecture that Old Paphos might have stood here. This conjecture pointed the way to the discovery of the old temple.

Notwithstanding the fact that New Paphos flourished in Roman times as a commercial center and the capital of the entire west side of the island, the site of the old temple thereby lost none of its fame and honor. The world-famous oracle maintained its reputation in full splendor and even strengthened it when Titus Vespasianus inquired of it and found the omens of the entrails of the sacrificial victims and the pronouncements of the high priest Sostratos according to his wishes, whether by coincidence or collusion.[13] Under Tiberius the senate examined and decided upon the rights of places of refuge, the claims of peoples and cities to sanctity and inviolability, the good deeds of their ancestors, the treaties of their allies, the decrees of their kings, and the honors due to their deities. On that great and illustrious day the Cypriots, on account of their temples at Amathus, Salamis, and especially the oldest one at Paphos, were granted the right of sanctuary.[14] Every year the nations flocked to the sacred place in festive processions; every year the inhabitants of New Paphos made their way in a joyous pilgrimage to the old temple. Let their route be ours.

We will first spend some time at Baffo, i.e. among the ruins of New Paphos. Then we will wander to Kouklia, i.e. Old Paphos. Along the way on this classical ground we will pause at every object which deserves our attention and at every resting place which offers some protection against the burning heat of the sun, for which Cyprus is rightly known.

The ruins of New Paphos stretch out for half an hour along the seashore; they are noteworthy for their ancient splendor as well as for their size and vast extent.

Three man-made hills rise with the remnants of three ancient temples from the common pile of rubble, like the ruined grave markers of the great from the wide-spread confusion of the common burial ground. The first and most prominent one rises almost behind the back of the small castle which is washed by the sea. Large foundations and subterranean vaults can be seen under the accumulated layers of soil and the wild bushes. Twenty-one column shafts of gleaming grey granite are scattered about, lying, standing, or imbedded in, above, or under the ground in oblique, horizontal, or vertical direction[15]...

This temple was, as evidenced by the stones which are spread over the neighboring fields, surrounded by buildings, but was outside of the walls of the city, at least those walls which were erected in later times; these, too, are already ruined, and only the foundations and the city gate are still extant.

First within the walls we encounter the high, ruined walls of a Gothic church, and not far from there the ruins of a Greek church which is built on the ruins of an ancient temple but is falling into dust. Four columns of gray granite and from early times are ex-

[13] See Tac. *Hist.* 2.3–4, and Suet. *Tit.* 5.
[14] Tac. *Ann.* 3.60–63.
[15] This area is known, with some exaggeration, as "Forty Columns" or "Saranda Kolones." Subsequent excavations have shown it to have been not an ancient temple but a Frankish fort.

tant in the hall of the front. They are partly submerged in the ground and are sinking deeper yet.

A quarter of an hour further to the south there stands a low Gothic chapel with half of its pointed arches, open tracery, and pendants preserved. On the opposite mound there are the remains of the third temple, consisting of splendid granite columns. Several of these, partly with and partly without fluting and shafts, lie scattered about; two others, each measuring three shoes in diameter and three fathoms in height, stand in proud isolation amidst the ruins of their mates . . .

On the hill behind the ruins of the city just described one finds the walls and vaults of a single large building. This may have been a public council house or a private palace and is distinguished from the vast pile of rubble of the others by the well-cut blocks of stone of which it has been built. The rock quarries which Pococke mentions and from which the stones for the building of the city presumably were obtained are not far from there. Several chambers cut into the rock leave the observer wondering about their original purpose: were they chambers for the living or for the dead, granaries, or cisterns? Two of them served as churches and a kind of catacombs, as one can see from their murals.

One of these was was dedicated to the Seven Sleepers,[16] the other to St. Salomone.[17] About half an hour to the north from here, close to the seashore, the rocks are formed so regularly both from the outside and from the inside and cut into chambers, that from the distance they give the appearance of the ruins of an old city with gates and windows of the houses. Therefore the ignorance of the inhabitants calls them the ruins of the old city, τὸ παλαιὸν χαλασμένον. On close inspection they appear to be a home for the dead, entrusted to the rocks on a height, following the ideas held by the most ancient peoples about burial and the examples of Upper Egypt, Palestine, Palmyra, and Persepolis.

On the outside the rocks have lost for the most part the regular shape given to them by the chisel; this destruction is due to the passing of time, which has eaten up the easily corroded stone. From the sharp cuts and the remaining steps one may surmise that the tombs, from the outside, rose sometimes in the shape of cubes and sometimes in the shape of pyramids, not unlike the form in which Wood[18] has described and sketched the tombs of Palmyra.

The interior arrangement of the small tombs follows no particular rule, and the tomb niches are cut out sometimes one next to another, sometimes one above another, in different directions. But the larger tomb structures, which must have belonged to kings or the leaders of the people, are all arranged in the same fashion.

The entrance leads into a rectangular forecourt that is cut into the rock and was surrounded on three sides by a colonnade of the Doric order, as one can tell from the remaining moldings and pedestals. This forecourt is cut into the surface of the rock downward, so that it has the open sky for a roof, and the entrance leads straight down through a

---

[16] The original cave of the Seven Sleepers is still shown at Ephesus. Their feast day is 27 July. See Butler's *Lives of the Saints*, eds. Herbert Thurston and Donald Attwater, 7 (London, 1932) 375–80; also see *Lexikon der christlichen Ikonographie*, 8 (Freiburg, 1974), cols. 34–48.

[17] Also Salomonis and Solomone. One of the Maccabaean martyrs, reportedly put to death, together with her seven sons, at Jerusalem under Seleucus. Her feast day is 1 August. See Butler's *Lives of the Saints*, eds. Herbert Thurston and Donald Attwater, 8 (London, 1933) 5–7; also *Lexikon der christlichen Ikonographie*, 8 (Freiburg, 1974), cols. 343–44.

[18] Robert Wood, *The Ruins of Palmyra, otherwise Tedmor in the Desart* [sic] (London, 1753; repr. Westmead, Farnborough, Hants., England), p.17 and pls. XXXVI–XLII and LIII–LVII.

small passage cut into the rock. On the right side and the left side the entry into two or three chambers is open, and each of these contains a larger or smaller number of burial niches of the appropriate length and breadth to contain a human body. Facing the entrance to the forecourt there is the entrance to the main chamber, on both sides of which the same number of burial niches have been cut out. One of these, presumably the place of honor, lies opposite the entrance into the chamber and thus also opposite the main entrance into the forecourt; it differs from the other niches only by the size of the room and the entrance. Here, presumably, lay the head of the family, surrounded by his offspring, the solemn court of death.[19]

These tombs are neither Roman nor Greek (although the Doric order of the columns seems to argue for the latter). They cannot be ascribed to the days of the Franks nor to the times of the Egyptians (for neither of these peoples placed its dead into such resting places). They are the work of the Phoenicians, the oldest inhabitants and rulers of the island. This assertion, which for now may be represented as a mere probability, will soon be elevated to the rank of evident truth by the announcement of a discovery made not far from Old Paphos. Right here nothing remains which might indicate Phoenician origins, other than the form [of the tombs], which in spite of all destruction can still be observed and is similar to the exterior of the tombs of Palmyra. Everything else has been destroyed by time and human hands. The columns (still seen by Pococke) are broken, and the cornices have collapsed in earthquakes. The steps leading in from the outside have been corroded by wind and weather; the tombs have been broken into from curiosity and greed; the epitaphs have been smashed; the sarcophagi have been carried away; and the ashes of the dead have been mixed with litter and dust, desecrated by the cattle which have their shelter in these rooms.

The ruins of New Paphos carry even now the name of Baffo, and scattered among them are a few occupied houses and a few cultivated gardens. Half an hour further inland, on a height, lies the principal town along the coast, called New-Paphos by Pococke. But the inhabitants do not know it by that name. They call it Κτῆμα or Μητρόπολις, because it is the seat of the Turkish and Greek authorities, the seat of the Agha and of the Despot, i.e. of the Turkish commander and of the Greek bishop. There are no old buildings to be seen here, and of newer ones but two or three, which were put up entirely in the Italian style two or three centuries ago.

Sixty stadia, i.e. three hours, distant from Ktima, near the seashore rises the village of Kouklia. In this place, according to the data given to us by the ancient geographers, stood Old Paphos with the original holy temple of Aphrodite. The noteworthy places which the traveler encounters on his way there are the following:

Half an hour outside of Ktima, on a low hill, lies the hamlet of Agiostibi. Its church, dedicated to Ayia Paraskeve, rests on the foundations of an ancient temple, the columns and cornices of which lie scattered about. A few grottoes, cut into the rock nearby, once were, so it seems, connected one with another and with a subterranean aqueduct, now destroyed, like the limbs of a body. An earthquake, which caused the collapse of New Paphos in the days of Augustus and left its traces behind especially here in the craggy rocks and cleft chasms, presumably destroyed the columns and foundations of the temple, smashed the aqueduct, and filled in the connections between the grottoes . . .

---

[19] These tombs are commonly but erroneously called the Tombs of the Kings.

Half an hour further along the way the hamlet of Pollona deserves to be mentioned for its Gothic church and large stone water basin. At the same distance from Ktima as Pollona, only further inland, lies the hamlet of Ayia Marini, surrounded by shady groves.

After another half hour, i.e. at the half-point between between Baffo and Kouklia, one finds the hamlet of Archelia on the ridge of a promontory which is called Zephyrion and stretches far into the sea, amidst springs, shade, and luxuriant fields of cotton and groves of pomegranate trees.

There are three well-preserved Gothic arches of a lofty aqueduct, of which more traces can be seen on a line extended toward the sea; a large ruined building, the ruins of which are leaning against the rock; and a Greek church, the exonarthex of which is held up by a single beautiful column of white marble. That is all the creations of human hands that can still be seen and might attract attention. Everything else time has destroyed.

The same is not true of the natural beauty, which has especially graced this place for millennia. Long ago the sacred gardens tended by priestly hands flourished here; today everywhere meadows, cotton bushes, and vines grow in luxuriant abundance. For the same simple reason today as in antiquity: running water, the vital spirit of the gardens, protects the soil from the scorching rays of the sun, which burns the neighboring fields, and fructifies them with the blessing of moisture . . . The promontory of Zephyrion received its name from Zephyrus, the husband of Flora . . .

Another half hour along in the plain the village of Timi lies along the way, and in the mountains to the left the village of Anarisi can be seen in the distance. Near by the former, the herds of the whole area are grazing around the shaded estate (Mandria). In a straight line from here, at the seashore, which is half an hour away, there are the ruins of several houses and of a Greek church called Ayia Avgona by the local inhabitants, and next to that some stalactite grottoes, which seem to have been inhabited by hermits. The largest of these, which has entrances both toward the land and toward the sea, is of visual interest, when one first enters it, by the uncertainty of the exit and by the manifold refractions of the rays more than by the form of the stalactites, which are rather common.

This grotto and the ruins spread about nearby lie next to the sea on a small, rocky height, in the middle of a bay formed by two promontories. The promontory on the right is Zephyrion and the one on the left is, as Pococke assumed, Arsinoe. On the east side of the latter there used to be the harbor of Old Paphos, which the sea has silted up. But the fields, with building stones scattered all over, show on land what the sea has covered up. Two large and very ancient stone pillars, with rectangular openings, which seem to have been windows, serve to direct the curious visitor looking for the location of the harbor. In front of these is a large pit, the depth of which cannot be determined because of the immovable pile of stones with which it is filled. There are squared stones, parts of a cornice, pieces of columns, and a huge sacrificial table of marble. Presumably these are the remains of an old and ancient temple in which the pilgrims offered their first sacrifices to the goddess. For this was the landing place of the priestly delegations of the nations and of the embassies of the cities . . .

From here people ascended to the height on which the temple stood. The distance is less than half an hour. The route led, as it seems, not along the seashore but further inland on a paved road which leads there even now. Presumably the buildings of the harbor spread as far as this road and perhaps even further. Small streams, which murmur on both sides of the way among the bushes, give to the area an uncommon freshness and charm . . .

The little streams mentioned are branches of a small river of many branches, which was called Barbaros by the ancients, but is called Dhiarizos today, because two of these little streams, which nearly always have water, can be considered the two sources of the river. The broad main bed of the river is crossed by a beautiful and large bridge of stone, the donors of which are named by a Turkish inscription. On the far side of the bridge there is a height on which the wide-spread ruins of the ancient city and of the temple and the wretched houses of today's Kouklia, as if deposited from above, appear to the eye at the same time.

How different is that which is there now from that which once was there! The whole surface of the height, half an hour's walk in every direction, is covered with ruins. At the highest point there are thick walls, which once surrounded a large building. They consist of huge blocks of stone, two to three fathoms long, more than one fathom high, and three feet thick. They enclosed a rectangle 150 paces long and 100 paces wide. This space is filled by an uninterrupted pile of rubble: broken blocks, bases, beams, cornices, eroded sculptures and inscriptions. Two large and walled-in openings, which are lowered into the ground nearly in the middle of these ruins and now are filled with rubble, seem to have been wells. From one of these a marble column sticks up, about three feet in diameter.

These walls, these ruins, their location, and their nature justify at first glance the conclusion that these are the ruins of the old and famous temple of Aphrodite; these huge remains of walls formed its sacred enclosure. The sanctuary itself stood on the eastern side of the walled district, there where the height is the steepest and where the huge blocks of the enclosure tumbled down into the valley.

Entire, well-preserved inscriptions of red marble and grey granite, dedicated to Aphrodite and found in this place, make the conclusion expressed above a certainty.

Several other stones lying about, on which only single words, or only the name of the goddess, or only the name of the city is legible, offer the same testimony with evident clarity.[20]

In several places of the area, where the debris has been cleared away and the earth stirred up, the old mosaic pavement of the temple is still completely preserved in its original glory. It consists of small stones, half an inch square, mostly gray, sometimes green and red, which are laid into a layer of cement, four to six inches deep, sometimes in simple rows and at other times in different round forms and spirals.

Another peculiar feature can be observed at the entrances or gates to the great enclosure, of which four or five can be made out. On both sides of these entrances large round holes have been cut through the stone pillars, from the outside to the inside in a curved line. Thus, through these channels, some communication could be maintained. Perhaps this was to receive gifts and requests from the outside or to pass out oracular responses and grants from the inside.

Other ruins rise behind those of the temple on the height and stretch down into the valley.

There is a jumble of collapsed houses and churches which may be dated to the days of the Greek emperors: works of ignorance and of the approaching darkness, raised from the ruins of monuments of better times. Pieces of columns and blocks of marble support spread-out walls, and stones with eroded Phoenician letters and broken Greek inscriptions are built into walls of rough stones.

---

[20] For the inscriptions see below, "Inscriptions from Cyprus," nos. 49–53.

In the middle of this cemetery of antiquity stands today's Greek church, wretched and poor, noteworthy for nothing but a few old inscriptions which name the goddess of the ancient city and the person who erected the statue.

Further down in the valley stands another Greek church, built of squared blocks in the Byzantine style; today it is deserted and ruined. The cupolas have collapsed, the entryways are obstructed by rubble, and with difficulty does one descend through bushes and rubble into the sacred halls. At the place of the altar lies a splendid block of granite, once, as the inscription tells, dedicated to Aphrodite of Paphos by Marcia, the aunt of Augustus.[21]

Anything else in the area worth seeing consists of the ruins of Englistro, one hour distant in the mountains, and of an underground grotto, barely a quarter hour distant from Kouklia.

The ruins of Englistro are those of a Greek monastery and of the church belonging to it, which once must have flourished. It is situated lonely among rocks and bushes. A few caves have been cut into the mountain, apparently to serve hermits as an abode.

The place which lonely reverence and contemplative piety have chosen here is more remarkable than the ruins of the monastery and of the church . . .

The grotto already mentioned is less than a quarter of an hour to the northeast of the ruins of the temple cut into the rock. It is a burial place of the same sort as that which I have described at New Paphos or Baffo. The conjecture expressed there, that this is the work of the island's earliest inhabitants, namely the Phoenicians, becomes a certainty here. The large block of marble which closed the burial chamber is leaning against the wall in the antechamber, and a Phoenician inscription with letters a span long carved into it renders any explanation and any proof pertaining to the originators of this burial chamber superfluous. In the sidechambers of the antechamber nothing has remained but dust and worms.

The forecourt of of the tomb, cut into the rock, like the tombs of New Paphos, and surrounded by colonnades, is blocked by sand and dirt. Only the smallest of openings has been left open; through it one can slip from the top down to the bottom of the tomb, sliding over the sand. And, if the curiosity of the visitors does not from time to time clear away the accumulated sand, even this small opening will soon be totally obliterated. This has happened with many other grottoes which still were accessible in living memory and in which, if they were opened again, several Phoenician inscriptions presumably could be found. Now the accumulated earth has hidden even their traces, and time has buried the markers of the tombs.

From the evident proof that these burial chambers are the work of the Phoenicians it follows incontrovertibly that the Doric order, in which the forecourts of the burial chambers are decorated, originally belonged not to the Greeks but to the Phoenicians. The sons of Cadmus were the first to bring art and science, commerce, and divine worship to Cyprus . . .

---

[21] For this inscription see below, "Inscriptions from Cyprus," no. 51, and *CIG* II 2629.

## Inscriptions of Cyprus[22]

41. On a stone in the house of the English consul in Larnaca.
To Zeus the Thunderer, to Aphrodite, to the city, to the people, and to civil peace Aviana and Avianos [have dedicated] these stoas and everything in them at their own expense.
[*CIG* II 2641.]

42. On a stone located in the same house and excavated near Larnaca.
[This statue of] Berenice, wife of King Ptolemy [I] [has been placed here] by Posidippos, commandant of Kition, and Boiskos, his fellow general [?].
[*CIG* II 2614. *OGI* I 20. Strack, no. 3.]

43. [Parian marble from Larnaca, now in the British Museum]
Crete was my country, wanderer. Niko was my mother and Sosyanax my father. Proxagoras was my name among men. The lord [Ptolemy I] the son of Lagos appointed me commander.
[*CIG* II 2613. *BMus. Inscr.* II 389. Strack, no. 8.]

44. On an altar of the temple of Amathus.
Demetrios, son of Philodoros, good friend, greetings to you.
[*CIG* II 2648.]

45. On another altar in the same location.
Pindar, son of Pindar, good friend, greetings to you.
[*CIG* II 2652.]

46. On the smallest and oldest of the altars.
Kalinetes, good friend, greetings to you.
[*CIG* II 2649.]

47. Built into the wall, before the door, of the house of the Turkish peasant Hasan.
From the Heraion to the paved road Aisimos has planted the trees and dedicated the shrine to the gods. Whoever destroys any of this . . . may the gods be no protection to him.
[*CIG* II 2643.]

48. On the heights of the mountain road near Amathus.
Lucius Vitellius Kallinikos has built this approach with the vault.
[*CIG* II 2644. *IGRom.* III, p. 364, no. 975.]
Presumably the Roman governor of Syria, of whom Tacitus says, "L. Vitellius was in charge of all things which were done in the East." *Ann.* 6.32.[23]

---

[22] Inscriptions 1–40 are from places other than Cyprus. The author's reading of these inscriptions and hence the English translations here offered are not necessarily correct in every case. Readers are urged to consult the epigraphical collections cited.
[23] On Lucius Vitellius see *Kl. Pauly* V (1975) 1306; he was the father of the later emperor Vitellius. Tacitus refers to events transpiring in A.D. 35.

49. On a piece of marble brought from the ruins of Old Paphos to the imperial collection of antiquities in Vienna.
King Ptolemy [VII] Eupator the deified [in the accusative case], to Aphrodite.
[*CIG* II 2618. *OGI* I 126. Strack, no. 101. Rudolf Noll, *Griechische und lateinische Inschriften der Wiener Antikensammlung* (Vienna, 1962), no. 26.]

50. On a stone from the same location, now in England [British Museum].
The city of the Paphians [has appointed] Kallippos the son of Kallippos, who has twice served as secretary of the council and of the people, as priest of the city and as secretary of the craftsmen serving Dionysus and the deified Euergetae [Ptolemy III and Ptolemy VIII]; previously he had served as secretary of the city and as gymnasiarch.
[*CIG* II 2620. *OGI* I 166. *BMus. Inscr.* II 385. Strack, no. 119.]

51. On the altar plate of the ruined Greek church amidst the ruins of Kouklia or Old Paphos.
The council and the people of Paphos [have erected this monument] to Marcia, the daughter of Philip, the aunt of the deified Caesar Augustus, and wife of Paullus Fabius Maximus.
[*CIG* II 2629. *IGRom.* III, p. 356, no. 939. On Paullus Fabius Maximus see *PIR* 2 III, pp. 103–105, no. 47.]

52. In the wall of a ruined house of Kouklia.
To good fortune.
[*CIG* II 2642.]

53. On a stone built into the wall of a still standing Greek church.
Of Aphrodite, Zeus of many thrones, and Hera.
[*CIG* II 2640.]

54. Amidst the ruins of Baffo or New Paphos, on a stone.
[The city of] the Paphians to Herod.
[*CIG* II 2628. *IGRom.* III, p. 355, no. 938. Herod the Great or Herod Antipas? Or Herodes Atticus?]

55. In the same location.
To Ptolemy [I] Soter [?] . . . of Asia . . . at his own expense.
[*CIG* II 2615. Strack, no. 2.]

56. On a stone built into the outer wall of the Greek church still standing in Kouklia.
I praise Aphrodite of Paphos. [This statue of] Gaius Umidius Quadratus of the Terentini, high priest, also [called] Pantauchianos, son of Gaius Umidius Pantauchos of the Terentini, the high priest and gymnasiarch, [has been set up by] Claudia Appharia, daughter of Teukros and high priestess of the temples of Demeter in Cyprus, to please her sons.
[*CIG* II 2637.]

# Bergk—before 1812

Johann Adam Bergk (1769–1834) was a "Privatgelehrter" (independent scholar) in Leipzig. The passage below and two illustrations are taken from *Ansichten von der Türkei, hauptsächlich von Caramanien* (Leipzig, 1812) 11–15. See further *Allgemeine deutsche Biographie* 2 (1875) 389.

## CYPRUS

This beautiful and rich island has been famous for many things since the earliest times. When, in the beginning, it was visited by the Phoenicians, it was densely covered with forests. The Phoenician seafarers used these forests in part to smelt the metals, of which an abundance was found on the island, and in part for ship-building timber. But since these two ways of consumption did not suffice to thin the forests and to render the island inhabitable many trees were cut down and destroyed. Those who cleared the land in this manner received it as their property. Perhaps it was then, when not much progress had been made yet in bringing the land under cultivation, that the island was considered unhealthy; for some more recent travelers give a rather different description of it. Pococke,[24] on the other hand, still regards it as unhealthy and attributes this to the extraordinary heat, because, he thinks, the heat of the sun is reflected by the high mountains and, especially, because little soil covers the white stone. But some of these mountains are covered all winter long by snow, which makes this island at that time of year colder than any other part of the Levant and frequently causes long and heavy rains.

However that may be, in antiquity this island was famous for its devotion to Venus, who, supposedly, had here her favorite abode, and for its wines, which are renowned to this day. But not all of its wines are equally good; that which is grown in the so-called district of the Commandery is the best. This district derives its name from the fact that it comprised part of the great Commandery of the Templars and of the Knights of St. John of Jerusalem [the Hospitalers]. When this wine has been properly aged and is properly handled it attains a quite excellent taste.

"The southern part of the island was Aphrodite's favorite abode; for here it is as hot," as Herr von Hammer (*Topographische Fragmente*, p. 121)[25] asserts, "as the flame which she kindles in the soul, and the soil as fertile as the embraces of lovers. In seeing the enchanting reality one forgets the magic of poetry. There are blessed fields of wheat and flowery pastures, crossed by low walls and stone-built country houses and dotted with fig, almond, palm, and sycamore trees. In one place there are vineyards in which the Cypriot's spice is ripening. In another place there is a chain of low mountains with many peaks which gets closer and closer to the sea, until it ends in a promontory which limits the view. The romantic effect is hightened by the white-clad figures which move through the green fields, like apparitions from a golden age. The women of this country not only veil their faces, but are covered head to toe by a long white shirt. And the covering of the face is stricter on the island of Cyprus than it is in Constantinople; the women leave only their eyes uncovered."

---

[24] Pococke, *Description.*
[25] The correct title should be *Topographische Ansichten.*

## A colossal vase at Limassol on the island of Cyprus
## [Plate 2]

The city of Amathus on this island was once famous for a temple dedicated to Venus and Adonis. In this temple there was kept, so the story goes, a necklace of gold and precious stones, a work which Vulcan had created as a gift for Hermione.[26] On the ruins of this city rose another, named Limisso or Limassol, which is now also destroyed and distinguished by the by-name "Old" from today's Limassol. The latter is a wretched place in its area, built of unbaked bricks and filled with ruins and debris, although its harbor is much frequented and occupies the place of the former Nemosia. In the area of this city Herr Mayer discovered an ancient vase, of which I here offer an illustration;[27] its circumference measured thirty feet and its thickness nine inches. It is of stone and its outer surface is very hard, while on the inside one can easily with one's fingers break off small sandy parts. These emit an odor which is like that of stone oil [petroleum], as is generally the case with stones on this island. This vase is located in a very deserted place, where people come only occasionally to hunt for game. The bull which one sees in the recess of one of the handles has served at times as a target in competitive or practice shooting.

A few more specific reports on the antiquities of Amathus or Limassol are provided by Herr von Hammer, who in general has made many an interesting discovery in Cyprus. Old Limassol is, so he says, three hours distant from the modern Limassol[28]. . .

"In this way one finds the temple of old Amathus, that is the temple of Aphrodite, the ruins of which travelers have tried in vain to find further down in the valley. The name of a saint has displaced the name of Aphrodite of Amathus, and her temple has been converted into a barn. The temple stood in the middle of a height, where the two arms of the mountain chain meet, and from there overlooks the sea, once crowded with ships carrying pilgrims who [then] made their way to the top with festive song."[29]

## Old fragments at Limassol
## [Plate 3]

Not only today's inhabitants of Egypt are lacking in knowledge and taste of architecture, but also today's Greeks seem to be no better in this regard, although they have the advantage of having more perfect models before their eyes. On the island of Cyprus as well as on the coasts of Africa one finds, heaped one upon another, fragments of columns which are the wonderful work of skilled artists of times past; capitals of any order, one next to another, and a piece from the smooth shaft of a Doric column which carries, or is carried by, another fluted piece of the Corinthian order, either of a larger or a smaller diameter, to extend something called a column; in short, everywhere there lie scattered about the fragments of the stonecutter's work. One would think that more recent

---

[26] Hermione was the daughter of Menelaus and Helen of Troy.

[27] The painter Ludwig Mayer visited Cyprus ca. 1780. The engraving offered by Bergk is the mirror-image of Mayer's painting. For the vase see further the selection from Unger in this volume.

[28] Bergk now quotes Hammer-Purgstall, *Ansichten*, 125–30, at length, with only minor changes.

[29] This is taken from Hammer-Purgstall, *Ansichten*, 130.

builders, having such models, would have been able to erect symmetrical buildings if they were not so extraordinarily ignorant and lazy.[30]

# von Richter—1816
## [Plate 4]

Otto Friedrich von Richter, *Wallfahrten im Morgenlande*, ed. Johann Philipp Gustav Ewers (Berlin, 1822) 298 and 301–26 and 566–69. In 1815–1816 he traveled widely in the Near East and died in 1816 in Smyrna. His diary and letters were edited and published in book form by his former tutor, Johann Philipp Gustav Ewers, professor at the University of Dorpat.

On the evening of 10 March [1816] I sailed again [from Latakia[31]] and bedded down in the back of the ship, although the night was damp and cool. At sunrise I sighted the coast of Cyprus, specifically the promontory of St. Andreas (Dinaretum). D'Anville's map[32] places a Mt. Olympus in its neighborhood. However, I did not see a high mountain, and the land gradually rises from the sea to steep limestone cliffs, the peaks of which seem to be of the same height. They are covered with low trees or, for the most part, barren. This Mt. Olympus is probably the high mountain which is located in the interior of the country and terminates the eastern mountains of Cyprus in the west. Then comes the large plain, which separates the eastern mountains from the western mountains,[33] as well as rows of low and flat limestone hills. On the southern coast [of the Karpas peninsula] the mountains terminate in flat promontories. One of these is Ras Bellur (Elaearum arca).[34] Here we were delayed by a calm which lasted almost through the night. The sea was so calm and so clear that by the light of the moon I could make out the stones at the bottom.

## Famagusta (Arsinoe) and Larnaca

At sunrise of 12 March [1816] we were in the harbor of Famagusta (Arabic Magusa), the entry of which is very narrow and is protected by a fortified tower close to the land. The width of its basin, enclosed on one side by the old walls and towers of the fortress and on the other side by a mole of rock, surprised me. The much-decried shallowness cannot be too bad, either. A large Danish ship lay at anchor, but, although loaded, did not dare to set sail for fear of the Barbary pirates. Other than that I saw only two boats and no life or activity anywhere. Since my Reis [captain] wanted to stay here for one day, I decided to leave my heaviest baggage on board and to take a ride to Larnaca. While the mules necessary for this trip were being hired I took a walk and inspected the city of the Ptolemies. It lies, for the most part, in ruins, among which about three hundred Turkish

---

[30] Bergk then offers more excerpts from Hammer-Purgstall, *Ansichten*, 134–35, 142, 150–51.

[31] The ancient Laodicea in Syria.

[32] Jean Baptiste Bourguignon d'Anville published a map of Cyprus in Paris in 1762. See Stylianou, *Cartography*, 142–43, no.183, and fig. 173. Also Christos G. Zacharakis, *A Catalogue of Printed Maps of Greece*, 1477–1800 (Nicosia, 1982) 11, no. 98.

[33] The Mesaoria, the Pentadaktylos Mountains, and the Troodos Mountains respectively.

[34] Cape Elea, Elaea, or Akrotirion Elaias.

inhabitants slink about. Even these have not been able to eradicate all traces of medieval splendor.

In a round tower there is a beautiful gate of white marble with the name of the builder, the year, and the Venetian lion, who is resting his right paw on a book.[35] Immediately behind the ironclad wings of the gate one can see the portcullis, which is held up by a low support erected below it. Near the tower, within the city, there lies a colossal lion, quite intact. The main street offers a strange sight: as far as the eye can see an abundance of green grows in the deserted ruins; only occasionally is there a building. The graceful Gothic arches of ruined churches and monasteries compete with the slender growth of palm trees; spreading fruit trees and all kinds of bushes give shade to their foundation walls.

To the left is the Church of St. Sophia, now converted into a mosque,[36] a masterpiece of Gothic architecture. As one enters the yard of the church one faces a facade of three pointed Gothic portals with many flutes, columns, etc., one above the other, as is customary. One can still see the bases of the images of saints which once stood in the niches and in the flutes of the doors but are now missing. Above each portal there is a triangular tympanum with very rich decorations, and above these in the middle a beautiful row of windows. At each corner of the facade a square tower with richly decorated pointed windows rises up, but the spires and the pointed roof which the church probably had are missing. The winding stairs which led to the top form a small round tower at each corner of the facade. On top of one of these [the northern one] a minaret was erected, but the tip of even that has already collapsed. Through the open door I observed the interior. Two rows of splendid, slender piers divide the nave into three parallel sections, and a strange, subdued light shimmers through the windows. These are closed with artfully carved wooden shutters, which are comparable to filigree work and admit sufficient light through their net-like openings.

The old buildings which surround the yard of the church are in ruins. On the side toward the street a Türbeh [mausoleum?] has been built; this seems to be new, and its windows are framed in beautiful marble. The poor columns have been placed on square ancient capitals with acanthus leaves; these probably belonged to white marble columns of the Corinthian order. In the facade, for decoration, two beautiful granite columns have been left standing; these do not carry a load and rise above the facade like two minarets. Their bases are of white marble, as are the capitals of the Doric order, and they have a high pedestal. In front of them rests an ancient sarcophagus of white marble. Genii in high relief hold up garlands of flowers and fruits which frame it; above these there are masks. Not bad work.

The entrance of the church yard meets the main square of the city. Exactly opposite there is a gateway decorated with four columns and Doric triglyphs; above these there is a coat of arms (black chevrons, oblique, one against the other, in a white field)[37] and the Roman eagle in another relief. This doorway leads to the court of a large rectan-

---

[35] The Sea Gate, or Porta del Mare, built in 1492 by Nicolao Prioli.
[36] The Lala Mustafa Pasha Mosque.
[37] The arms of Giovanni Renier, Captain of Cyprus in 1552. The Venetian governors of Cyprus were called "Captains."

gular building with many doors; it is now ruined and deserted, but probably was once the government palace.[38]

I followed the main street, saw the ruins of a few Gothic churches and of several [formerly] respectable houses, once the abode of knights and now of donkeys, and then climbed up on the wall. The dried-out moat is cut into the rock, and the wall and counterscarp rest on this rock. From here one has a view of the wide, mostly waste plain, in which only flocks of sheep alternate with burial grounds. The view is limited only a little by the two mountain ranges of the island, and on the other side the sea, inviting to life and activity, forms a sad contrast to the ruined towers and green ruins of the dead fortress.

For the ride to Larnaca I obtained an excellent, well-bridled mule. I thought it peculiar that the feedbag was tied to the animal's front. But I did not mind at all: the thick bulge keeps a careless rider from slipping onto the neck of the animal.

The trip almost surpassed the impression which I had already formed of the wretched conditions of the land. When I had the monastery and village of Ayios Loukas, not far from the city, behind me, an almost endless plain stretched out before me; only seldom did a village appear, with poorly culivated fields and gardens. Flocks of sheep with long, silk-like wool and fat tails, and also goats of three colors, roam about in the far-spread desert; they probably leave it during the summer, when everything is dried up, and move into the mountains. No tree is to be seen, only a small bush now and then. More frequently there are traces of former settlements: single, half-ruined churches with piles of stones lying about, and nearby the pits from which the building material was taken. In many places the naked rock crops up from the ground. A few flat, low-lying areas show a floor of limestone and once may have contained water; but of rivers, which D'Anville's map indicates, I have seen no trace.

For the trip from Famagusta to Larnaca one allows eight hours. Before I had completed half the distance I came upon the wretched Greek village of Agura,[39] in the vicinity of which I saw many pigs, which do very well in Cyprus. The houses are built of sod. At the half-point Ormidhia lies in a small valley. Here one descends, through stony gorges of limestone and conglomerate, passing many quarries, down to the sea and then rides along the shore to Larnaca. The ships on the wharf were already clearly to be seen. The road here is as good as the best road in Livland [Estonia]; it consists of fine gravel. The ground is thickly covered here with small juniper bushes (if I am not mistaken). Then I passed a ruined village, the church of which is still standing, and, close to the coast, a kind of log-house, once occupied by cannons. Now everything is deserted.

I rode straight to the marina (Scala) of Larnaca. It is built of clay tiles, like Damascus, but the houses here are much poorer than those there and of one story only. But their location on the quays gives them a pleasant character and fresh air. Mr. Peristiany, the Russian consul, received me hospitably . . .

At noon of the next day (12 March) I rode with Mr. Peristiany in a two-wheeled carriage to the city of Larnaca, which is in no way different from the marina. But it is strange that the city, although further inland, is situated at a lower elevation than the port. Its name supposedly derives from *larnax*, a hollow or grave.[40] This is not unfitting, for it

---

[38] The Palazzo del Provveditore.

[39] The author is probably referring to Avgorou.

[40] The derivation of *Larnaka* from *larnax*, although often repeated, is erroneous. See Μεγάλη κυπριακὴ ἐνκυκλοπαίδεια (Nicosia, 1988) 254–55.

is in part surrounded by salt marshes, which during the dry season, from May to October, spoil the air. The irregular streets are narrow and unpaved. Nevertheless the city holds about 5000 inhabitants, mostly Greeks, and engages in trade so important that all major European states maintain consuls or vice consuls here. Cotton, silk, wool, wheat, salt, and wine are the most significant export commodities, which are exchanged for a variety of manufactured goods and food stuffs . . .

The nearby rubble heaps of Tschitti (Citium) do not merit a visit. Of greater interest to me was the salt lake of Taslar, which is situated toward the west and the perimeter of which must measure several miles. The sandy soil and the surrounding heights are saturated with saltpeter and take on a yellowish color. During the winter the area fills up with rain water, which evaporates between May and July and leaves behind a very pure and white salt. This is carved out in August, piled up on the bank, and protected with sand against the winter rains until the whole supply is gradually moved away. At the bank there is the wretched hut of a Turkish supervisor and opposite it a Turkish mosque.[41] But on its northern bank are the deserted monastery of Ayios Georghios[42] and the aqueduct of Bekir Pasha,[43] which supplies good spring water to Larnaca and the marina. Nevertheless people usually filter the water before drinking it.

For the European traveler returning from Asia, Larnaca has its own charm. This is due to the various traces of European ways which he can here observe in people's dress; the list is headed by the hat which crowds out the turban. The women are for the most part dressed in the usual Greek style, but they wear above the skirt a camisole with a cutout in front and gathered together under the breast; this pushes the breast up and gives it a fullness but not a graceful appearance . . .

Nicosia and the Monastery of St. John Chrysostom

After I had, in the morning of 15 March, received a visit from the English consul, Mr. Palaziano, I undertook a ride into the interior, having gotten onto excellent mules, together with my servant and a janissary from our consulate, Hussein.

Soon I left the plain and rode up the barren limestone mountains, which descend here [into the plain] and have mostly flat tops. The stone is of the same kind as in Latakia, white and yellow. Occasionally one spots hardened clay, containing metals, and in some places I thought I could see traces of mining. Apart from that the ground lies almost completely waste, and the country folk slink about as pitiful figures. For transportation they employ two-wheeled carts drawn by two oxen. These may go back to the days of the Italian rule over the island; and so may the local windmills, which are like round towers and have a wooden roof with eight wings.

The stream beds which we followed were for the most part dry, and I found only a single running spring in this sad land which offers pretty views only from the distance. Here it offered the two mountain ranges. The western one [the Troodos range] is higher, but the eastern one [the Pentadaktylos range] is wilder and more jagged.

---

[41] The Hala Sultan Tekke or Tekke Umm Harram.
[42] Ayios Georghios Makris or "St. George the Distant," to be distinguished from Ayios Georghios Kontou or "St. George the Near." The former is two miles west of Larnaka, the latter right in Larnaka.
[43] Built in 1747 by the Turkish governor Ebubekir Pasha. See Gazioglu, *Turks*, 97, 144 and unnumbered illustration.

On the way I gradually joined a traveling group which consisted of an English dragoman, a Greek cleric, a Turkish Aga,[44] and their servants. After sunset we descended on the far side of the hill and reached the village of Katirdshy Koy, called Athienou by the Greeks,[45] where we stayed overnight in the house of the muleteer. My roommate in the same clean and spacious room was the Aga . . .

My hostess measured up to the reputation of Cypriot women and brought honor to the island of Venus . . .

The houses consist of lumps of clay and have on their roofs numerous small, square openings in which countless pigeons are roosting. The yards, gardens, and fields are enclosed by hedges, which must please the eye when they are green. The household furnishings are more European in style than Asian. Cane chairs and broad benches, which serve as bedsteads, are the most important. The dining table, which is made of palm branches in Egypt, of leather among the Arabs, and of tin-clad copper among the Turks, here is very well woven of cane.

We started out again at sunrise and rode for the most part across a plain, which, however, now and then is interrupted by flat hills. The village of Pyroi on the like-named little river, which is crossed by a bridge of several arches,[46] lies in a beautiful, soft valley of palm trees and blossoming fruit trees in green fields. But even here one notices the shortage of water, and this little river is almost dry. Nearby there is a church, right against the rock, and in this rock there are several grottoes. Further along, to the right of the road, there is the village of Margo, and further along yet, on the left of the Tschiftlik (country estate) is Athalassa, and there are several others. Then we descended the last row of hills and saw Nicosia (Levkosia) before us in a green plain.

The city makes a favorable impression from the distance by a combination of several factors. First one notices the far-flung works of fortification, which are only a little lower than the houses. They are built of sod, and the many palm trees remind of Egypt. But the cypress trees mingling with the palm trees and the lofty white minarets remind even more of Constantinople. The latter rise on Gothic churches, which transfer the viewer again to Europe. The two minarets of the Ayia Sophia mosque shine above the whole city and area. The works of fortification have round bastions, a double talus, one above the other, and many rooms; on the inside they are dressed with earth. One sees neither a moat nor a counterscarp.[47] The gate is in a large round vault which receives light through a round barred opening.[48] All the walls seem on the inside to consist of well-lined casemates, but are now dark and filled with rubble. There are only a few artillery pieces of small caliber. Right at the gate and beyond there is an aqueduct on many round arches of the Turkish kind.

I went to the monastery to call on the Archbishop, to whom our consul had recommended me.[49] His name is Kyprianou,[50] and he is independent of the Patriarch in Con-

---

[44] An Aga is a high-ranking officer, or an officer of janissaries.
[45] This was known as the "Muleteer Village," because the men of the village handled much of the island's transportation, especially between Larnaka and Nicosia.
[46] The river is actually the Yialias; the bridge is Venetian.
[47] But the original Venetian design included a moat, with a drawbridge at each of the three gates.
[48] This must be the Famagusta Gate; the other two gates are the Paphos Gate and the Kyrenia Gate.
[49] The monastery of Ayios Ioannis served as the archbishop's residence. Having been replaced by a new Archbishop's Palace in 1961, it is now known as the Old Archbishopric and houses the Folk Art Museum.

stantinople (autocephalous), which much enhances his standing. He currently competes for rank with the Mutesselim [governor], who is appointed annually by the Kapudan-Pasha (grand admiral) and in important matters pertaining to the Greeks can do nothing without the Archbishop. The latter is elected by the clergy of the island and must be a native. On festive occasions he has a large staff with a silver orb and a golden crown carried before him. The next one after him is the archimandrite of the monastery.

I was kindly received, but with much to-do and ceremony, as the Greeks generally like it. I conversed in Turkish[51] with the old ecclesiastic and thought that I could detect in him as much self-consciousness as intelligence. His annual income is reputed to amount to 30,000 piaster; enough to finance his princely lifestyle.

I also owed a visit to the archimandrite, but he is deaf and was not feeling well. To have myself introduced to the Mutesselim [governor], who lives in the old royal palace, I considered unnecessary, since the archbishop had already given me permission to visit all noteworthy sites at my pleasure.

The spacious monastery is built around the yard of the cathedral, which, like all Greek churches on the island has a triple, half-round, tower-like extension in the back, in which the holy of holies is kept. The style of the former Church of Ayia Sophia[52] is a mix of Gothic and neo-Greek, as once was fashionable with the Venetians. It has two large side portals, one on each long side; these are in part blocked by Turkish graves and poor huts. The facade has an exonarthex of three cross vaults.[53] The place of towers is taken by two minarets of different style. Since the floor is covered with mats and the walls white-washed it is not possible to see what might be left of tombstones, mosaics, or paintings. On the other side stands the ruined Church of Ayios Nikolaos; some of its vaults have collapsed, while silk is spun in others.

Several buildings in the city consist wholly or partly of old Venetian houses. I found many coats of arms, among others, not far from Ayia Sophia, the French fleur-de-lis, and another with a papal crown or "Degenkrone."[54] The foundations of the palace are old, and so are the gate in the tower and the interior stairs. In front of it, in the Turkish burial ground next to a mosque a granite column with a marble capital (of the Doric or Tuscan order) stands upright on a high pedestal. Its Latin inscription, at the very bottom of the base, is covered over by masonry except for a few non-continuous words. Next to it we find a sarcophagus of grey marble; it has the form of a simple rectangular box and is used as the enclosure of a fountain. It has two Greek inscriptions, on the same side and enclosed by the same line. The first one and half of the first line of the second one are deliberately destroyed; hence I could with difficulty make out only a few letters.[55] Near a tekke a stone with a Latin inscription marks the grave of a Cypriot minister, Agostino Canali, from the year 1554.[56]

---

[50] He was in office during the years 1810–1821; he was hanged in 1821 by order of the Turkish governor Küchük Mehmed. See Hackett, *Orthodox Church*, 226–29.

[51] The archbishops of Cyprus generally spoke Turkish as well as Greek, and von Richter may have felt more comfortable with Turkish than with modern Greek.

[52] Now the Selimiye Mosque.

[53] Also known as the Galilee.

[54] Richter is not clear on this "crown of sabers" or its relationship to the papal crown.

[55] See inscription XXIII below.

[56] See inscription XXIV below. There is no listing for him in the *Dizionario biografico degli Italiani*.

The population of Nicosia surely exceeds 16,000. More than half of these are Turks, the others are Greeks, apart from a few Armenians and Maronites. Their unattractive houses rest on old foundations and form narrow, dirty streets. The otherwise well-equipped bazaar is not even vaulted and is protected only by mats during rainy weather. Locally manufactured goods are limited to good cotton and silk cloth and colored leather.

The villages of Kaimakly and Omorfa are located not far from the city.[57] Further along I found a long bridge across the dry bed of the River Chatsirga, near the village of Neamylia.[58] The bridge is made up first of six low round arches, then three high pointed arches over one arm of the river, followed by two low round ones, another three high pointed ones over a second, dry bed of the river, and finally four more low round ones, all-in-all eighteen arches.[59] The ground in the dry stream beds is of grey marble.

Now I reached barren mountains consisting of clay-like stone. Its strata are at an angle, almost vertical, and run in long, parallel ridges from the main mountain into the plain, from east to west . . .

At the foot and steepest slope of the highest faces of the mountain lies the large and massive monastery of St. John Chrysostom [Ayios Khrysostomos].[60] From the outside it appears like a fortress. On the inside galleries, which lead to halls, and a small garden surround the yard. In it there is a church, built of especially long and smooth bricks and featuring a double iconostasis. The old main entrance is now on the side of the garden and is usually closed. After one has entered through the main portal into a vault which serves as a vestibule, one finds three carefully worked doors of grey and white marble. These lead into the nave, facing the iconostasis, which is completely covered with darkened icons and golden carvings. Next to and above the three doors, as well as on the floor, one can still see remains of old mosaics. The mosaics here are made not of glass tesserae but of colored stones . . . Many other traces of early times may have been wiped out by repeated whitewashing. Whether the pictures of saints on the ceiling are painted or mosaic I could not decide because of the darkness. The cupola rests on the walls of the church; half-round columns are attached to the walls. To the left of the main nave there is a second one, roofed by a smaller cupola . . .

## By Way of Buffavento, Kythrea, Timbos, and Larnaca to Karamania[61]

After I had (on 17 March) made a hurried sketch for a drawing of the Monastery of St. Chrysostom I rushed to the top of the mountain which towers above it and bears the ruins of Buffavento Castle . . . On a steep and difficult path, where olive trees and all manner of bushes grow among masses of fallen stones, Hussein and I courageously rode uphill. The muleteer and a guide accompanied me. The lazy Kirkor [the servant?] I had left, at his request, behind with my things at the monastery. The almost vertical face is broken up by fissures and cracks between which crippled pines and cedars are growing. At the foot of this face we dismounted and continued the climb on foot, sometimes on all four, following the trace of an old footpath. Thus we finally reached the upper edge of the

[57] Kaimakli and Omorphita, just to the northeast of Nicosia, now suburbs.
[58] The reference seems to be to the river Pedieos and to Mia Milea, on the road to Kythrea.
[59] A new bridge of iron girders was built here in 1883.
[60] It is also called the "White Monastery" and belongs to the Orthodox See of Jerusalem.
[61] The coastal region of Asia Minor, facing Cyprus and comprising Caria, Lycia, Pamphylia and Cilicia.

rocky ridge, where, on the other side, a rich and splendid view suddenly opened up. The mountain, one has to know, is very narrow, and on both sides the cliffs are very precipitous. On both sides one looks down into deep and dark hollows. Toward the northeast one enjoys a far view of the mountainous coast as far as the Karpas Peninsula, while on the opposite side the mountains of Karamania appear in the blue distance. On the other side, toward the southwest, the low slopes which I had crossed in the preceding days disappear almost completely and blend in with the wide and green plain [the Mesaoria] which separates the two mountain ranges of the island. The snow-clad heights of Olympus and Monte Croce and the sea in the north and south of the island form the horizon. It is worth the effort!

But from here to the castle we still had to climb a considerable distance, and when we reached it it gave me little satisfaction. A few vaulted cisterns are best preserved. Walls and towers hang at the edge of immense precipices. But the very top, although buildings have been put up there, I could not reach, because there no longer was a path between the precipitous cliffs. I returned to St. Chrysostom.

In the afternoon I rode over the same barren and curiously formed mountains as on the day before, but in a more northern direction. Above and below the monastery of St. Chrysostom the ruins of churches and houses indicate that the surrounding area once was densely populated. Now there are only a few peasants on a farm, engaged in tending olive trees and raising pigs.

At the foot of the mountain, in the plain, the village of Kythrea lies spread out among groves of olive and mulberry trees and well-watered fields of grain. Poplar trees, mixed with palm trees and cypresses shade the bank of a stream which emerges from a nearby strong spring and winds its way through the village in several branches.[62] The buildings are large and clean, built of clay bricks; and all around the gardens were more than full of ripe lemons. This property is divided into Ano Kythrea, Kato Kythrea, and Palaeokythrea. It belongs to a rich Greek by name of Petraki, by whom I was splendidly received, upon recommendation of Peristiany. His furnishings were beautiful and valuable; they combined European chairs and chests with Egyptian mats, and the sofas were covered with the well-known calico from Nicosia, the color of which never fades. I was given a tasty supper, while my host ate only meagre lenten fare. My bedlinens were of the finest muslin. In Turkish this lovely place is called only Deghirmenlik, i.e. place of the mills, because the stream which I mentioned powers several mills.[63]

Not far from the home of my hospitable host there are the ruins of an old Greek church, the ceiling and walls of which still show crude but apparently old frescoes. Nearby in the grass I found a rectangular block of marble, occasionally crossed by veins of quartz (of which the highest mountain ridge here consists); it bears a slightly damaged Greek inscription, which I added to my collection.[64]

Petraki, who speaks excellent Turkish, told me of the various chicaneries which the government makes him suffer, and how recently, at the slightest objection, he had been thrown into prison, from which the Frankish consuls rescued him. After the distribution of the head-tax he alone must pay 1000 piaster, not counting the other payments. The usual amount is two-hundred piaster, and even the poorest day-laborer has to pay no

---

[62] The stream is the Tengelis, which also supplied water to Salamis by means of an aqueduct.

[63] The water-driven flour-mills numbered as many as thirty-five.

[64] See inscription XXV below.

less than eighty piaster. In the past the Muhassil (the collector of government taxes, which here is the same as the Mutesselim) paid annually 150 purses;[65] recently this amount has been increased to 1,200 purses, although the Greek population of the island is declining every day. The land itself is rapidly heading for complete devastation. Lack of order and shortsighted greed destroy the forests, and thus the springs dry out; rains occur less frequently and the fields, scorched by the sun, do not produce; the peasants, who on top of everything else are always exposed to exploitation by the government, escape; wasteland and unhealthy marshes take the place of previously flourishing villages and gardens.

For the return to Larnaca I chose the route by way of Timbos, an estate of the archbishop, where I dined (18 March). A strong storm during the preceding night finally had accumulated some rain clouds over the sighing island, and these now brought some showers, accompanied by thundering. Thus the procession to the Madonna della Cheengna [?], to which the archbishop had invited me, had not failed to have its effect on the land and consequently on the faithful. The route was boring. The same desolate heath as between Famagusta and Larnaca and mountains so barren as had made me yawn on the ride to Nicosia. In good time I was back in the marina.

The next day, together with the consul, I paid a visit to Mr. Bernard and to Michael Karady, elderly members of an old Cypriot family, and to the bishop of Citium in Larnaca. The residence of the latter, situated in the yard of the Church of St. Salvatore [the Cathedral of Ayios Khrysotiros], is called the Metropolis. At its gate I found a stone and a badly damaged marble slab with Greek inscriptions.[66] The former refers to Cleopatra and Ptolemy Philometor. The dwellings of the rich are not lacking in expenditure or comfort; but the residents seem to me to live a life of boredom, which I would not want to share any longer.

Much to my relief a three-mast commercial ship out of Trapezont [Trapezus] had just arrived from Beirut. With the captain of this ship I negotiated passage to Attalia for 50 piaster, and it was up to me to continue the journey on land or to wait until he had there taken aboard his load of grain for Constantinople. He played the hero and seemed to want to defy the storms of the equinox, which were announcing their coming with constant rain showers and covered the horizon with thick clouds. In the end he remained quietly at the wharf of Larnaca, where he had nothing to do, until the dreaded feast of the Forty Martyrs (9 March, old style[67]) had passed. To pass the time I looked for something to read and was more than a little pleased when I was handed Voltaire's historical writings. Thus I escaped the harsh talkativeness of the people around me, who, in turn, accused me of being as taciturn as a Turk.

Late in the evening (on 21 March) the captain sent his boat for me, in utter darkness, so that I could see neither the ship nor the city . . . But there was a calm, and the ship would not budge. The cabin was occupied by the chief shipper, a feeble old man, and his little Georgian slave; the other one and the clerk occupied the berths at the rudder. Thus there was nothing for me to do but to make my bed with the sailors in the open room, and there I spent a very poor night. In the morning the anchor was lifted, and then

---

[65] A purse, at one time, was the eqivalent of £62.5.

[66] See inscriptions XXVI and XXVII below.

[67] The Julian calendar was at this time lagging 12 days behind the Gregorian calendar; thus 9 March by the Julian calendar was 21 March by the Gregorian calendar.

the entire day was spent maneuvering the ship within sight of the wharf of Larnaca. At one time the ship hit a sandbank, but was quickly loosed by changing the sails.

The second night brought favorable wind, and in the morning we were facing Limassol. Through the telescope I could clearly see the houses and the minarets, in a long row along the shore, the plain in the west, and the high, forest-clad mountains in the back. This area, which, as is well-known, is the only one that produces the excellent wine of Cyprus, seemed well cultivated. Churches, monasteries, estates, and villages alternated. In the afternoon we passed Baffo (New Paphos). A part of the city lies on an extended rock; another part lies at the foot of that rock, is mixed with gardens, right down to the sea, and includes an old harbor fort. In the evening I sighted the western cape of the island, [Cape Arnaouti]. During the night another calm came up, but a fresh morning wind finally took us into the channel between Cyprus and Anatolia; it lasted the following day. Then the Taurus mountains appeared through clouds and fog.

## Inscription XXIII
On a sarcophagus of grey marble in Nicosia.

The fate of death has overtaken me. The earth hides my body,
Taking back the gift which it had given me.
My soul has gone to heaven and the halls of Zeus,
But a law which cannot be averted has taken my bones to Hades.
This great gift I, Eulalios, have received from the gods themselves,
to be married, although I was single among mortals.
[An elegiac distichon. *CIG* II 2647, more complete.]

## Inscription XXIV
On a tombstone, built into a wall, at Nicosia.

To Augustino Canali, renowned senator, a man of the greatest devotion and piety toward God and Country, who had honorably held numerous offices at home and abroad in administering the affairs of the Republic of Venice, and finally was Counselor of the Kingdom of Cyprus,[68] his faithful wife Marieta and his son Gabriel have set up this stone, so that posterity may remember. He died on 11 October 1554.

## Inscription XXV
On a grey, rectangular block of marble at Kythrea.

Jason, son of Aristocreon, philopatris[69] and gymnasiarch, the students at the palestra have thus honored.
[*CIG* II 2627.]

---

[68] Under the Venetian system of governmemt in Cyprus the governor was assisted by two Counsellors.
[69] Literally "loving one's country," sometimes used as an honorary title.

Inscription XXVI
Before the gate of the city of Larnaca.

The city is honoring Agias, son of Damothetos, the Cretan, the chief of the body guards and guardian of the city, for his excellence and for his service to the divine Philometores King Ptolemy [VI, 180–145 B.C.] and Queen Cleopatra [II], his sister, and to their children, and for his service to the city.
[*CIG* II 2617. *OGI* 113. Strack, no. 97. Since 1821 in Berlin: Staatliche Museen, Antikensammlung, Inv. Nr. SK 1181; information courtesy Dr. Sylvia Brehme.]

Inscription XXVII
On a badly damaged marble tablet in the same location.

[This inscription is too fragmentary to permit translation. *CIG* II 2645.]

# Ross—1845

[Plates 5, 6]

Ludwig Ross, *Reisen nach Kos, Halikarnassos, Rhodos und der Insel Cypern (Reisen auf die griechischen Inseln*, IV, Halle, 1852) 83–209. Translated by Claude D. Cobham, *A Journey to Cyprus, February and March 1845* (Nicosia, 1910).[70] Cobham's text is here given with a minimum of editorial changes. See further *Deutsche biographische Enzyklopädie* 7 (1998) 404.

## Preface

*Ludwig Ross was born in 1806 on a farm in Holstein, and died at Halle, by his own hand, in 1859. He was a scholar and archaeologist of some note, who wrote several valuable works, but his* Travels *(published 1852) are not often quoted, and perhaps not very well known. Fifty years ago there were very few Englishmen interested in Cyprus, and few enough who read German. I have before expressed the wish to see at the command of the future historian of Cyprus in a handy form the material he will most care to use, and this book seemed to me one which an idle man could do no harm in translating: it gives a simple and scholarly account of a journey in Cyprus, made by a route which a visitor today, with a month or six weeks at his disposal, might profitably follow.*

*The main object of his search, though his success was not conspicuous, was inscriptions in Greek and Latin. He is not attracted to medieval traditions and remains. He spoke one of the languages current among the peasants, made light of fatigue and discomfort, and described the natural features of the island with some spirit.*

*The Piastre seems to have been worth 2½ d: the Prussian thaler three shillings, the* gulden, *two.*
*Villa Claudia, Larnaca.*

---

[70] A microfilm of this rare title exists in the library of the Royal Commonwealth Society at the University of Cambridge and has been made available by the kind assistance of Ms. Rachel Rowe.

*April, 1910.*

# I
## Departure from Smyrna. Rhodes. In sight of Cyprus. Landing at Larnaca. The Marina. The old harbour. Medieval ruins. Statistics. Population. Revenue. Locusts. The Salt Lake. Kiti. Beccafichi. Wine. Turkish administration. Antiquities in Kition.

*12–19 February, 1845.*

After a stay of some length in Smyrna I found at last an opportunity of getting to Cyprus. At 5 p.m. on February 12 the s.s. Archduke John, of the Austrian Lloyd Co. sailed for Beirut, touching on the way at Rhodes and Larnaca. The weather was raw and windy, so that I soon retired to the saloon where there were but very few passengers. At dawn the next day we were under the steep western slopes of Kerketeus in Samos, with Icaria on our right, the barren islands of Korassia (Furni) and further ahead Patmos, near which lay Leros and Calymnos. On our left the vague outline of the low coast of Ionia, stretching from the promontory of Mycale, by Miletus. After mid-day, as the vessel glided onwards, we saw clearly the villages on the West side of the peninsula of Halicarnassos, in the neighbourhood of the ancient Myndos, and descried further off the ruins of a fort on a steep cliff between Zephyrion and Halicarnassos. The town and green coast line of Cos lay bathed in sunshine, no less green was the soil of the ancient Cnidos, which we passed at sunset, after doubling C. Triopion, Nisyros rose, steep and volcanic on the right, and further ahead rocky Telos. I had visited all these islands and shores before, some of them more than once, and rejoiced to see the well known outline of their hills, which were soon lost in the twilight. The evening was warm and soft, the moon flickered behind vaporous clouds. Shortly before midnight we anchored in the inner harbour of Rhodes.

The steamer stayed here only until the next morning, to deliver goods and letters, to land some passengers and take on others. I hastened to look up Hassan Pasha of Cheshire, Professor Hedenborg, and other acquaintances; about mid-day we were off again. We had a fresh breeze against us, growing towards evening to a storm, which maintained its violence through the next day and night, and brought thunder, lightning and heavy rain. On the morning of February 16 we were to the S. of the S. W. coast of Cyprus, under C. Bianco, for so is called the high and steep cliff which dominates the coast between Palaipaphos and Kurion. The N. wind shifted now to W. and we steamed in quieter weather along the S. coast of the Island. Fresh snow was gleaming on the top of Olympos (now Troodos) which lifts its huge bulk to about 6000 feet, (6406) and as well as my eyes could judge, is at least 1000 feet lower than Ida in Crete (8057 feet). The peninsula Kurias (Capo delle Gatte) stretches its long level to the S. On the east side lies in a corner the town of Limassol, called more properly by the natives Lemessos. The coast from this point eastward is lower, the beach broader. Then comes a group of whitish hills, which rise round the ancient Amathus, and above these again the second highest mountain in the island Aoos (now Machaira, 4674 ft.) with several peaks. The range ends to the East in the isolated and pointed hill Santa Croce (Σταυρὸς ὁ Θεοκρέμμαστος). About 2 p.m. we rounded the low tongue of land called Kition (C. Citi) and an hour later anchored on its eastern side in the broad but ill-sheltered bay of Larnaca (Λάρναξ) now the principal port of the island.

A dozen merchant-vessels, mostly French and Ottoman, lay here at anchor, but at some distance from the land, for the coasts are low. A couple of hours were wasted in the formalities of quarantine before we could land. A big boat at last took us on shore. A not unpleasing row of houses, overtopped by a minaret and a few hundreds of scattered palms, stretches along the beach; this is the so called Marina of Larnaca. The town itself lies five or ten minutes inland, divided from the Marina by some open fields.

I went up at once to the town to find the Prussian Consul, Signor Giacomo Mattei, a R. C. native, who received me in a very friendly way, and got me a lodging in the Marina in the house of one Michel Béraud, a Frenchman born in Cyprus. Béraud kept a kind of restaurant for French and other ship-captains: I found here a fairly furnished room which opened on a wooden gallery, and overlooked the general sitting room. Tired with my stormy journey I soon lay down to sleep.

The next morning (Febr. 17) the mild and pleasant weather was a surprise, and a contrast to the quite unusually raw cold which I had left in Smyrna. To orient myself I took a walk through the fields to the beach. Wild hyacynths and other flowers were in bloom, and swallows and butterflies were on the wing. I went round the small salt pan which lies between the North end of the Marina and Larnaca, obviously a bit of the old artificial harbour, to a great heap of earth rising on the West of the pool. Men were digging out of it squared stones and other material for the new church now being built in Larnaca. In this mound which is still 20 or 25 feet high are seen the remains of old cisterns and the vaults of cellars. I could not consider the work to be really old, and fancy I had before me the ruins of a strong fortress of medieval date, built out of ancient material. The Italian Friars Minor who watch the spiritual interests of the local community, and are carrying out the building of the church, assured me that neither inscriptions nor works of art have been unearthed.

In the afternoon I visited Cesare Mattei at the Marina. He has some good coins, and fine engraved gems; then I went to Larnaca to the Austrian V. Consul, Signor Caprara, and spent the rest of the afternoon with him and his chancelier, Signor d'Altina. From the conversation of these well informed men, I learned much about the island and its condition. They reckoned the present population of Cyprus (the figures were confirmed by my later researches) at 110 to 115,000 souls, including some 5000 negro slaves brought over from Egypt, and employed by the Turks on their farms: Some of them however were maintained in the richer Latin families, for it is difficult here to find other servants. Among the Christians there are about 1000 of the Latin rite, of whom 500 live in Larnaca and Scala, a few in Nicosia and Limassol, the rest belong to the Maronite villages. Formerly there were a good many villages of these Christian-Arabs, chiefly on the east coast of the island, but they have gone over gradually to Islam or to the Greek rite, and therewith assumed Ottoman or Greek nationality. The revenue is made up of the poll tax, the tithe, and customs' duty, 3% on imports and 12% on exports. The gross sum accruing to the Porte is put at 4,500,000, the net revenue at 3,000,000 piastres, making at the present rate of exchange 272,000 gulden £31,650. This sum includes P. 350,000 (25,333 Prussian thalers) from the farmers of customs in the five ports of the Island, Larnaca, Limasol, Paphos, Keryneia and Ammochostos, and 100 to 200,000 P. from the yearly farming out of the Salines at Larnaca. The customs are let this year to the young Mehmed bey, who will make about 100,000 P. profit on the deal.

My informants told me also of the plague of locusts which visits particularly the Eastern half of the Island, the broad plain of Mesaoria, and the promontory of Carpas. These insects, which are hatched from the egg generally about March 9 (new style 21) are often met with in clouds which literally hide the sun. They lay their eggs for the most part on uncultivated strips of land, preferably on the Southern slopes of stony hills from which the rain runs quickly off. The female bores a hole in the soil, and fills it with a glutinous matter. Herein she lays her eggs, and then stops the hole with the same stuff. The present Pasha, in order to extirpate the locusts, has ordered these eggs to be collected and destroyed. The shepherds and peasants are used to observe where the locusts lay their eggs, they then scrape the soil lightly with a rake or hoe, and thus easily find the egg-cases, which they shake in a sieve to free them from earth. In this way during last autumn in the whole island there were gathered and delivered 200,000 okes (466,666 lbs) which the Pasha had thrown into deep trenches, and covered with earth well stamped down. On cultivated stretches of land the danger of the multiplication of the locusts is less marked, for when the plough has once cast up the egg-cases from their place, they are easily affected by damp, which destroys the brood. The more widely then the Island is cultivated, the sooner the plague will be stayed. But in certain years the loss is very severe, and if the grain crops, the young cotton plants and vines, are still small and tender when the insect is hatched out terrible devastation is wrought; and when the locusts die off in late summer, and their bodies, swept together by wind and rain, get massed in the beds of the mountain-streams, they poison the air far and wide, and bring in autumn disease into the lowlying lands of the neighbourhood.

On February 15, I began my excursions with a ride to the village of Kiti lying a good German mile S. W. of Larnaca on the further, Western, side of the low spit of land, which is called by the medieval writers C. Salines, but now generally known as C. Kiti. A quarter of an hour S. of Larnaca begins the remarkable Salt-lake, which with its little creeks has a circuit of two hours. On the Southern side, towards the cape on which stands a medieval watch tower, there is yet another string of salt-lakes and pools. This lake, which has no visible communication with the sea beyond it, gets filled in winter by the rain: This water is congealed in spring and summer by the intense heat, and leaves in the middle of the basin a crust of the finest salt, about a span and a half thick, which is broken up, brought out in blocks and piled up in great heaps on the border of the lake. On a little mound to the west of the lake stands a Turkish mosque or tekye with two slender minarets, which are seen from afar across the level plain. The inexhaustible riches of this salt-lake, and the fine quality of its yield were not overlooked by the ancients, and probably the salt was already an article of export in the time of the Phoenicians. In the days of the Lusignan Kings, and later during the Venetian rule, many ship-loads were sent to Italy, and the Turkish Government, as we said above, farms out the salt for 100 to 200,000 piastres yearly.

From this point my road took me over bare little-cultivated plains. The village of Kiti covers a long stretch of ground on the western shores of the peninsula. At its northern end lies a church of some size, probably of Gothic style, and so dating from Frankish times, called the Panagia Angeloktistos; and not far from this the ruins of a knightly castle of the middle ages, whose last owner must have been the brave Hector Podocatoros, who distinguished himself in the defence of Levcosia against the Turks. Of ruins of a higher antiquity there are none, and it is instructive that the venerable old name of Kition was only transferred in the early middle ages, at a time when what is now Larnaca had not yet arisen from the ruins of the ancient city, to this then larger village.

I returned at mid-day to dine with the Prussian Consul who gave us delicate preserved *beccafichi*, and good old Cyprus wine. The *beccafichi* (more than one species of little birds, especially of the genus Sylvia) pass under this name, are caught here on limed twigs in late summer and in autumn, from August to October, in incredible number, chiefly in the vine-bearing districts. They are then very fat, and when carefully plucked are dipped for a bit in boiling water, and then preserved with various herbs in very strong Cyprus wine. In the days of the chronicler Lusignan (*Chronografia*, 1572) they cost nine Venetian ducats the thousand; Many hundreds of thousands were exported to Venice and other parts of Italy, especially as presents, and still very large quantities are pickled and sent as gifts to business-friends in Smyrna, Alexandria, Constantinople, Marseille, Genoa, Triest and other ports.

Cyprus wine is no longer so important an item of export as it was in earlier days, before the wines of Madeira, Spain and Sicily drove it from the European markets. The wine districts lie almost exclusively on the S. spurs of Olympus and Aoos (Machaira), and Limassol, not Larnaca, is the centre of the trade. Cyprus wine, as is well known, is when new darkred, almost black. The older it gets, the lighter it grows, until at last it takes a brownish-yellow hue. The best kind, and this only goes to Europe, is called Commanderia, because the district whence it is won was originally a Commandery of the order of S. John. Commanderia of two to three years old is sold on the spot at 20 to 25 piastres the *couza* (eight *okes*, or 14 to 15 bottles): when it is ten years old and over, the price rises to 160 piastres (10⅔ Prussian *thaler*) and more: even to a Spanish dollar the bottle. The most precious quality of Cyprus wine is that, when it gets over the first year, it never, like most of the other Greek wines, suffers a change for the worse: probably careless treatment accounts in their case for the speedy deterioration. The flavour of goat and tar is owing to the pitched goat-skins in which it is brought from the villages to the towns: there is no question of a mixing of tar with the wine, as is often done in Greece. The inferior kinds are exported to Alexandria, Beirut, Rhodes, Castellorizo and other neighbouring ports. It is remarkable that the cultivation of the vine in Cyprus is confined to the districts above mentioned, and that the other parts of the island, with few exceptions, do not produce as much wine as would supply their own wants. Towards evening I received a visit from M. Caprara, who told me a good deal more about the Turkish administration. At the time of the Greek war of independence the Pasha was a very cruel man, one Kuchuk Mehmed. Although the Cypriot Greeks kept quite quiet, and even did their best to prove their loyalty, and to excite no suspicion, the Pasha notwithstanding denounced them to the Porte as rebelliously disposed, enticed the most prominent and richest citizens to Nicosia, caused the five bishops to be beheaded, and executed one by one the other notables. Their property was confiscated, and the Pasha reserved for himself as much as he could. It is reckoned, certainly with exaggeration, that in these years he had amassed about two millions of Prussian thalers (£300,000). An Armenian, who, as dragoman, was under French protection, was at the same time imprisoned at Nicosia. The Consul's complaints remained unnoticed, and when shortly after Kuchuk Mehmed Pasha came to Larnaca, and the Consul did not, as was usual, greet his arrival by hoisting his flag, the injured savage sent at once a messenger to the capital, and had the Armenian hanged, affixing his patent on his back as a further insult. Such outrages on the part of the Turks were then allowed to pass unavenged.

I could relate other stories of the same kind, but I resume the account of my journey. To get quite clear about the localities I went next morning round about Larnaca. Of ancient Kition, the city of the Phoenicians and Greeks, this seems to have included the whole space on which stand both the present towns—on a second look I should call them villages—with the fields between them, and a further longish stretch of land to the South West—no surface remains are visible beyond some foundations and plenty of old potsherds, and even the foundations are disappearing daily, for they get built over, or the stones are dug up and used in new buildings. The ancient harbour, now quite filled in, I have mentioned already. On the western edge of Larnaca, and again farther to the W. and S. many old graves occur in the fields, most of them mere plain holes, lying just under the shallow crust of gypsum. But Signor Baltazar Mattei, brother of our Consul, took me to a very ornate tomb, built of squared stone, under the courtyard of a house in Larnaca. One descends through a narrow passage into an outer chamber eight feet square with a roof of smooth stone slabs resting on three very carefully hewn stone beams, a door leads into a second longer room, covered by a vaulted roof of hewn stone, and at the farther end is seen at last a niche, with its tomb. The monument, when again exposed to view some few years since, had been plundered at some unknown date, and unfortunately no inscription remains to show if it is Greek, or Phoenician. But it corresponds with other tombs in Kition, which I shall describe later on, which in the main features of their plan I must hold to be Phoenician. In the Western quarter of Larnaca are often found smaller grave-chambers just scooped out in the solid soil, or the crumbling rock, containing three, four or even six sarcophagi of gypsum; but these coffins are entirely plain, without inscription, carving or other ornament. No small number of them is scattered up and down the town, for they are used in the courtyards of houses as drinking troughs or washing tubs. White or even blue marble (the first is called by way of distinction Κιόνιν, from Κίων) is very scarce in all Cyprus; yet the Phoenicians used it for inscriptions and pedestals, as well as in their buildings.

Two of the Phoenician inscriptions I found are on white marble. The contents of such graves are generally of small interest. I was shown some bronze mirrors, without figures or ornament, such as occur in Greece, and big common bowls with Phoenician-Egyptian decoration, in the style of those found in the island of Thera. I saw too the remains of two gold garlands of olive and ivy leaves. I received too from Signor Caprara a charming present—three pretty alabaster figurines, of female sex, and about three inches high, on a common base, which were found in a grave here. The result of my search for inscriptions was very poor. I found only some epitaphs and the pedestal of the statue of a Gymnasiarch and Agoranomos, who also had restored the theatre at his own cost.

## II
## Journey to Levcosia. Aradippou. Dali (Idalion). Ruins. Phoenician Statuettes. R., Satrachos. Earthquake. View of Levcosia. Visit to the Pasha, and to the Bishops. The Archbishop. Government. History of Nicosia. Venetian fortifications. Churches. Population and Industries.

After I had made myself acquainted with the site and surroundings of Kition, I determined to start on my first excursion into the island: I was to go first to the capital, Levcosia (Nicosia) and to the districts in the North and East. I hired some mules at a much lower rate than I had been accustomed to pay in Greece, and even in the lonely parts of Southern Asia Minor, or in Rhodes and other islands, and as I had brought no servant with me my host lent me his negro for the journey. Rashid, as he was called, was much pleased about it, and although he was living in a Christian house, and was now lent for the service of another Christian, was determined not to forego his quality of Musulman, so he armed himself straightway with a pair of mighty pistols stuck in his sash in view of his peaceful duties of cooking a fowl, or getting me a cup of coffee. The negro spoke Greek fluently, for this after all is the current language in Cyprus, and spoken or at least understood by all the Turks born in the island. So at 9 a.m. on Febr. 20 in glorious weather I started with Rashid and the muleteer from Scala for Dali, where I was to find some antiquities.

I rode through Larnaca, then in a North-West direction over the sparsely cultivated plain which stretches round old Kition. In an hour I reached the considerable village of Aradippou on the Southern edge of the bare white chain of hills which runs East from M. Santa Croce to Cape Greco. Here I saw many old stones heaped together for use in the building of the new church of S. Luke, among them a base with an inscription nearly effaced of which the words ΤΙΕΩ... ΙΕΡΕΣ... (possibly τῆς—ἕνεκα) only were legible, and a small pedestal of white marble with a Phoenician inscription, which I acquired later: it is now in the Berlin Museum.

After a short halt I started again on my ride. Five minutes behind the village I passed the old quarries from which the squared blocks and sarcophagi, which one sees in plenty at Larnaca, seem to have been hewn. From this point the road runs for three hours always between the low denuded bleached hills of gypsum and sandstone, barren, treeless, untilled, which slope down from Machaira and S. Croce towards the South-West of the island to the capes of Pedalion and Throni. Even in the lowlands one scarcely finds a cultivated tract, so one's first impressions of Cyprus are lonely and sad. To my left lay the village of Goshi, and an hour and a half farther on I passed through Lourigina. Here we see again some cultivation, and get a glimpse between the hills of the river valley. I crossed more low hills, and in a[n] hour reached Dali, a pretty and important village, situated under trees in a richly watered plain: the river flows from Machaira (Aoos) on the West, behind M. S. Croce, in an easterly course to unite with the Pediaios.

Dali has preserved the name of the ancient Idalion. Here was the grove of Aphrodite, here her much-frequented sanctuary. The ruins of the old city lie only ten minutes S. of the village on the North slope of the chain of hills which encloses the valley on this side. Two peaks of the hills, which fall steeply to the South, form as it were two acropoleis. On the North their slopes run together, and sink into a table land over against the village. This space, of no great extent, was enclosed by a considerable wall of sandstone. But this wall, always of poor construction, is partly weathered by time, partly ruined and overthrown by constant digging for hewn stones to be used in the buildings of the neighbourhood, that its lines show out from the edge and slopes of the hill like low earthworks out of which protrudes here and there a squared block of stone. Towards the plain and the village one can no longer follow exactly the lines of the town; but it extended probably down to the river. The little plain which lies between the projecting acropoleis to the South bears the name of Paradise from a garden-grove which in happier times may have decked the spot.

Within the city one sees only unimportant fragments of stone, and a few broken potsherds, for the whole plain, and even the slope of the hills, is used for plough-land; but at no great depth under the surface are found everywhere foundations of sandstone, which the peasants, when they have no other work, keep digging out and breaking up, to sell as building stone, and at the same time to clear the fields. While at this work they find in incredible numbers little statuettes of the same stone, from one to two feet high, all female, and holding a flower or other object against the breast, with distinct traces of painting, blue, green and red. Among them are fragments of larger statues of terracotta, even of life-size. I acquired a few such figures for the Berlin Museum: after me, and my suggestion, a young French traveler, Mons. de Mas Latrie, found others and took them to Paris. Without hesitation I pronounce these statuettes to be Phoenician, yet their style affords no proof, partly because we do not yet know a particular Phoenician style, partly because the experience of the last five to ten years has shown us that the national differences in the treatment of works of plastic art (e.g. in Assyria and Syria, compared with the older works of Greeks and Etruscans) were less marked then we were inclined to assume. Hence it has happened, that the school which would allow to the Greeks only among the nations of antiquity an active taste for art has declared the figurines from Idalion, a Phoenician place of worship, situate in that interior of the island, where originally and from the earliest times Phoenicians only had settled, to be Greek images of Aphrodite.

I saw too in a house a bas-relief of sandstone, about three feet high, of a peculiar style, which I must also hold to be Phoenician: it represented a male figure in a long garment, facing one, and wearing on the head a tight-fitting cap, like the Egyptian *Kalantika*, and as in the other female figures, with one hand pressed to the breast, but the face and hands were entirely destroyed.

On a little eminence at the East end of the village, over the river bed, the peasants had found a few years since sarcophagi of gypsum, which they thought bore inscriptions: but they were broken up in the rebuilding of their church, and in the whole village I failed to get even a fragment of an inscription. The coins which I found here are chiefly of the Ptolemies.

Of the identity of Dali with the ancient Idalion, as indicated by earlier travelers, I have no doubt. The main proof is the retention of the name, for nothing is commoner among the modern Greeks than to discard a vowel at the beginning of a word, and the omission of the o in the last syllable happened frequently in the ancient tongue, as inscriptions show. So Dalin came from Idalion. The statuettes were offered by women in the temple of Aphrodite. I take the river to be the ancient Satrachos, which came from the hill Aoos, and joined the Pediaios; but Aoos, as we shall see, is now Machairas, and the Dali river rises in Machairas, and carries its waters to the Pediaios.

The next morning, February 21, I was aroused about five by a prolonged earthquake, which began with gentle tremors, and ended in a severe shock, the whole lasting quite half a minute. At the same time a slight breeze from the South-East brought over the island a thick damp mist, which lasted until about ten o'clock. These morning mists, as well as the copious night-dews are more frequent in Cyprus than in the districts known to me in ancient Greece.

About 7 a. m. I started from Dali for Levcosia, but the dust prevented me from seeing much of the country. I rode through the river, crossed some sandstone hills, then over some small streams all but dry, and open stony flats variously cultivated. After a ride of three hours, when I was only a quarter of an hour from Levcosia, the mist suddenly parted and the city lay before me in surprising beauty. The extent is considerable, the fortifications stately and well preserved, the cathedral of S. Sophia in the midst, and the whole view topped by a dozen slender minarets, and some hundreds of tall palms, their bushy crowns waving in the sunlight. I thought I really saw before me the city of some Eastern King, so fair and stately was the sight. But as soon as I had ridden thro the vaulted gate there appeared but poor houses patched against the still standing lower stories of stone buildings of the Turkish time, and narrow dirty lanes. I traversed the city in its greatest length, as far as the Franciscan convent on its N.W. side, and so passed through the considerable bazar. The Turkish women, who were in no small number on their way to the market or the baths, (it was Friday) made a better show then ever in their long snowy white wraps. They drape themselves in these wraps far more gracefully than Turkish women in Smyrna, for instance; and more than one, if the veil told true, gave promise of a lithe and well-formed body. The peasants too, of whom there were many in the market, wear but seldom, so mild is the climate, the heavy woollen or goatshair cloaks of Greece, but often carry only large square rugs, striped in blue white and red, of coarse woollen stuff, much as do the Arabs, drawing them round the neck and shoulders, as our women use their shawls.

The Franciscan Convent belongs to the great Catholic foundation which under the name 'Terra Santa' is maintained by contributions from Italy, Spain and France, and thus finds the means of providing for the spiritual care of Catholics in Jerusalem, Damascus, Aleppo, and especially throughout Syria, Palestine and Egypt.

This convent is occupied by Spanish monks, a Prior (padre presidente), another monk and a lay brother; while the Capucin Convent in Larnaca, another dependency of Terra Santa, has as many as nine Italian monks. The good fathers, strong handsome men in the flower of their age, received me hospitably and cheerfully shared with me their Lenten fare, including excellent brocoli from their garden. I had two little rooms on the first floor of the convent, in which I settled down, a Protestant and a Muslim negro as guests of Spanish monks.

In the afternoon I went to see Chelebi (*Junker*) Jancos Georgiades, the richest Greek in Cyprus, to whom I had an introduction. His father was beheaded in the Revolution, and he himself had lived nearly twenty years in exile at Tokat; but five years ago he returned to Cyprus and resumed his paternal property. He accompanied me in a visit to the Governor of the island Edhem Pasha, an elderly man who shortly before had injured a foot through a fall from his horse. His palace, in the Turkish fashion, a poor crumbling lumber chest with hanging doors, rotten floors and paper window panes, is built in the ruins of the palace of the Kings of the house of Lusignan, and later of the Venetian *proveditori*: of this there still survives a vaulted porch decorated on one side with the royal arms, on the other with the Lion of S. Mark. In a shabby room lay the Pasha, in rich furs, on a divan. I handed him a note of introduction from the Grand Vazir, and received a so called *buyuruldu*, a circular letter addressed to the local authorities of the island. I was annoyed by the cringing fashion in which Chelebi Yancos showed his subservience to the Turkish potentate, and was glad when our short visit came to an end.

We went thence to the archiepiscopal residence to visit the bishops there assembled, among them the bishop of Kyrenia, who two months ago was raised to the post from that of a secondary schoolmaster (in acquirements certainly far below the lowest Prussian Seminarist). The Archbishop of Cyprus is the independent head of this church, owing allegiance to no Patriarch. He is styled makariotatos, and alone of the Greek clergy wears purple robes, and signs his name in red ink (Vermilion, kinnabari, minium). These, in the ceremonial of the Byzantine Court, imperial privileges, were granted to his predecessors by the Emperor Zeno on the occasion of the finding of the Gospel of S. Matthew in the tomb of S. Barnabas, not far from Salamis. At the same time the Archbishop, under the oversight of the Turkish authorities, is to a certain degree the temporal Head of the island, in so far that with the advice of the other three bishops and a few lay notables he has to arrange what shall be the taxation to be paid by the Christian *ria'ya*, the general assessment of the country, when in times of scarcity to make advances, or in better seasons to collect them again. In this relation we see a close analogy with the old position of the chief priest of the Paphian Aphrodite, who was also in the earliest times a kind of theocratic head of the island: others have observed already the same likeness. So, in a sense, the Jewish highpriestly office has its counterpart in ancient Paphos and in Cyprus of today. But this makes the archiepiscopal purple an object of great envy and constant intrigue, and it is but rarely that an archbishop of Cyprus dies on the throne. An ambitious bishop or other member of the higher clergy conspires with the lay notables, the archbishop is accused to the Porte, is deposed and exiled, and the happy victor takes his place. So the present bishop of Kition was many years since archbishop of Cyprus, then banished to Prusa and the Mysian Olympus, and now restored as simple bishop of Kition. He has doffed the princely purple and resumed the black cowl, and of his former dignity nothing remains to him but the empty title makariotes (he is styled ὁ μακαριώτατος πρώην Κύπρου). His successor fared no better. He was hounded out by the present archbishop (Joannikios) who at the time of the Greek insurrection fled as a young deacon to France, spent twenty years there, and gained in Paris the friendship of Fethi Pasha. To the influence of this Turkish noble he drove four years ago the aged archbishop from the throne, and set himself thereon. His fallen predecessor is since dead: but, if present signs prove true, the days of his reigning Blessedness are already numbered.

The talk with the archbishop and bishops turned on the earthquake of today: it has alarmed the Turks not a little. The severe shock threw down the crescents from both the shaky minarets which they have built on the towers of S. Sophia. They consulted their prophetic books, and found that this event portends a bloody war, and the death of many brave men.

Straightway they took thought to replace one of the crescents; the roof of the second minaret was two rickety to allow anyone to venture thereon. The naiveté of the Turkish ideas about earthquakes is still great, most of them believe that the earth rests on the horn of a buffalo, and when the beast is tired of the weight, he shakes his head and tosses it on to the other horn. Hence earthquakes. Should one ask on what does the buffalo stand, one gets the frank answer that 'God knows.' With more show of sense these Muslims explain that God holds in one hand a bundle of nerves or threads, which start from different countries of the earth. If the Lord is dissatisfied with any one region he pulls at a string to give it a sign and to rouse the inhabitants from their indifference. This causes an earthquake in their land.

The next morning, with Dr. Laffon, a Frenchman who lives here, I had a walk through the town, and along a part of the walls. But before I speak of Gothic churches and Venetian fortifications, I must touch shortly on the history of Cyprus in the middle ages. When the quick-tempered Richard Lion-heart, who was a good deal more of a Frenchman than an Englishman, wrested the island in 1191 from the Greek duke and usurper Isaac, and sold it to the Templars, Levcosia seems to have been a considerable, but unwalled town, protected only by a castle. When the King had defeated the Greek in sundry fights, and captured his person, he took Levcosia and destroyed a part of the town. The Templars installed themselves, but soon the people rose against them, and they were compelled to take back what they had paid of the purchase-money and restore the island to its conqueror. Richard then sold the island again to Guido, of the house of Lusignan, who had been driven from his kingdom of Jerusalem (1192). The Lusignans made Levcosia their capital, and under their rule the city grew considerably in size and prosperity. The commerce of Europe—Venice, Genoa, Pisa, the Hanse towns—with India and the East, which centred, as long at a part of the Holy Land remained in the hands of the Franks, in Tripoli, Tyre and especially in Akka or Ptolemais (S. Jean d' Acre), just as the commerce of Europe with further Asia was concentrated in the days of the Phoenicians at Sidon and Tyre, betook itself, after the final loss of Palestine, across the sea to Cyprus. Here the harbours of Ammochostos (Famagusta) and Limassol (which took the place of the ancient Amathus), were the places of export, while the mart and industrial centre of the island was at Levcosia. So it befell that at the end of the fifteenth and the beginning of the 16th century Levcosia had about 250 churches and chapels, and some 50,000 inhabitants, a mixed crowd of Latins, chiefly Italians and French, Greeks, Armenians, Copts, Maronites, Indian Christians, Nestorians, Jacobites and Iberians or Georgians: while the circuit of the city extended to three hours or one and a half German miles (6 $^9/_{10}$ E. m.), so scattered were its buildings, and so many its gardens and squares. And so it remained under the rule of the Venetians, into whose possession it came from the last Queen Caterina Cornaro, widow of the bastard Jacques, in 1489. The Dominican monk Etienne de Lusignan, a descendant of the old Kings, describes with astonishment the variety and pomp of the processions in Nicosia on the feasts of Corpus Christi or S. Mark. In front was borne a Greek cross, followed by the Greek folk in motley array, then the Greek priests with a picture of the Virgin and behind them the women. Next followed the Latin Mendicant Orders, and the Indian priests with strange headgear of skyblue, among them their bishop: and again the Nestorians, Jacobites, Maronites, Copts and Armenians with their priests and bishops. Then appeared the Latin clergy, as the most distinguished and dominant, while the civil officers with the troops and nobility closed the train. The good father Stephen ends his sketch with this exclamation bursting from his patriotic and pious heart. "O, but it is a fine thing to see so many sects and classes of Christians of many rites and names." Many a Venetian painter up to the Turkish conquest may have gleaned something for the pictures in which Eastern raiment, negros and other rarities so often figure.

In 1567 Venice, foreseeing the approaching war with the Porte, for Selim II was continually spurred by the ill-famed Jew Miquez, in 1580 Duke of Naxos, to the conquest of Cyprus, decided to fortify Levcosia, and it was found necessary to reduce the circuit of the walls to one hour. To this end the straggling suburbs and about eighty churches were pulled down, and therewith the citadel built by Jacques I, in which was the royal castle and the stately cloister of S. Dominic. Of the castle a little corner was preserved, as we have said above, to form the entrance of the present palace of the Pasha, but the convent, with the graves of Kings Hugues the great and the little (Ughetto), *Perrin,* Jacques, Janus and Jean, with their consorts and children, the Princes of Antioch and Galilee, Prince Louis of France; the seneschals and constables of Jerusalem and Cyprus, and many Counts and Barons of Tabor, Sidon, Toron, Caesarea, Beirut, Tripoli, Jaffa, and others, as well as those of sixteen Patriarchs, Archbishops and Bishops, were levelled with the ground, leaving never a trace.

The Venetians fortified in the manner of the period, with banks of earth, faced without with squared stone, with seven projecting bastions, and three vaulted gates, called now, Ammochostos, Paphos and Kyrenia, but the walls had not reached the height it was intended to give them, nor were the fosses below dug out when the storm that was expected burst over the island. On June 25, 1570 Mustafa Pasha landed at the Salines (Larnaca) with 100,000 infantry, 10,000 cavalry and 10,000 campfollowers and other indisciplined levies from Caramania, and marched at once to Levcosia. The Venetians, although they had long foreseen the war, either through their own dilatoriness, or especially through the carelessness, bordering on treachery, of the general in command, one Dandolo, were ill prepared to meet so huge a force. The Turks began forthwith to besiege and bombard the city, in which were shut up 56,500 souls, and after a struggle of 45 days, during which two attacks in force were repelled by the despairing garrison, captured it, and left it for ten days at the mercy of murderers and robbers. More than 10,000 were killed. With the surrender of the other fortresses—the siege of Famagusta gained undying glory from the heroic defence maintained by its Commander—the conquest of the island was completed in this and the following year, 1571. Since then Cyprus has remained under Turkish rule and is steadily sinking in population and wealth.

We visited first in our walk the Palace-square, where near a small mosque, a relic of the Venetian lordship, an ancient column carrying the lion of S. Mark, stands on a tall base. At the foot of the pillar is an ancient sarcophagus with inscription in Greek verse [already published, C.I.G. 2647. cf. Engel, *Kypros* (1841) 1.152.] We then went with one of the Pasha's qavasses to the mosque of S. Sophia, a fine and (at least outwardly) well preserved Gothic Church. It lies nearly in the middle of the city, and here the old Kings of Cyprus assumed their crown. Within, the church is, in Turkish fashion, stripped of all the altars and ornaments, and coated with white wash: the floor is paved with broken slabs of marble from ancient tombs, but the inscriptions are so mutilated and worn as to be no longer legible. Against the facade two minarets are reared upon the substructions of the old bell-towers. I mounted one of these by 170 steps (more than 100 ft.) to the highest gallery. One saw therefrom the greater part of the broad central plain (Mesaria): to the N. the long mountain chain, with well shaped peaks, which runs from the promontory Crommyon (now Cormakiti) in the W. along the N. coast of the island to the further point of the north-eastern promontory of Carpas for twenty German (92 English) miles: to the S. M. S. Croce, rising over the low Idalian hills, further westward Aoos or Machaira, with its many peaks, and in the S. W. the broad top of great Olympus or Troodos, which, on its N. side falls steeply to the plain, and still kept a good coat of snow on its summit. On the distant S. E. horizon I could descry the spires and minarets of Ammochostos or Famagusta.

After S. Sophia the largest and most important church is that of S. Nicholas which lies a little to the S of the first, and now serves as a grainstore. The third is S. Catherine, built by the Templars, and now a mosque. Not far from S. Sophia are the remains of the former Palace of the Latin Patriarch of Jerusalem, and of other structures of Lusignan and Venetian times, built like the churches of squared blocks of a brownish-yellow sandstone.

These poor relics of ancient grandeur did not detain me long, and we started to walk round the walls. They are still decked with about a hundred Venetian field pieces and bronze guns, but most of these lie without carriages on the ground, and such carriages as remain could scarcely bear a discharge: and further the defences generally are in such a state that one company of German musketeers or grenadiers with two storming ladders could capture the fortress in less than an hour. In front of the Kyreneia gate are buried the Turks who fell in the siege, and within it, in a row of shabby Turkish chapels with domed roofs, lie the Pashas and other superior officers.

Leaving aside the remains of the Frankish magnificence the interior of the city, as I remarked before, is dirty and wretched, and a little water channel running from W. to E. which catches all the filth of the place, spreads in summer unhealthy exhalations. Levcosia has now twelve to fifteen thousand inhabitants, mostly Turks. It has an industry of its own, the dyeing and printing of moderately fine cotton stuffs, which are known in commerce as 'Indiennes de Chypre,' and are in request at Constantinople, Smyrna and other Eastern places as covers for divans; but this is now only the shadow of a business formerly of great importance. Another branch of trade is the tanning and manufacture of a quantity of boots with thick wooden soles, not only for Island-use, but for export to the coasts of Caramania and Syria, for the peasants of these parts, on account of a venomous kind of snake, are obliged to wear some such stout covering for their feet.

## III
**Journey to Famagusta. Athiainou. Muleteers. Tremithus. H. Sergios. S. Barnabas. Prison of S. Catherine. R. Pediaios, Ammochostos or Famagusta. Arsinoe. History. Salamis or Constantia. Livadia. Cultivation. Mesarian Plain. Fertility. Cattle. Price of Land.**

*February 22–24, 1845*

At mid-day on Feb. 22 I left Levcosia, and rode in a southerly direction along the road to Larnaca, over a hummocky dry hilly tract, with few villages and little cultivation. I noticed particularly the want of olive trees, which are planted usually everywhere.

Two hours later I crossed on a stone bridge the river that flows from Idalion, and which bears today the unseemly name Koprisi, really the ancient Satrachos. Beyond the bridge lies the village Piroi, and a little distance away on the left the farm or *chiftliq* Margos. Then I rode for a good hour over a well-tilled plain to the big village of Athiainou.

All the inhabitants of this village of 150 houses ply the trade of muleteers (Greek agogiates, Turkish, Kiraji—the Turks call the place Kiraji-Keuy). According to a unauthenticated tradition these *Kirajis* are of distinguished ancestry, for they say that at the capture of Famagusta, after all the principal Venetians had been executed by the Turks, there were still a number of poorer nobles, to whom the victors, tired of bloodshed, granted their lives. Helpless and poor, without the means to return to Venice, to which their families were now for several generations strangers, these patricians turned to the calling of guides and muleteers, and to this end settled between the capital and the chief port. Anyhow, be their origin this or other, the villagers of *Athiainou*, whose business brings them into touch with people of all kinds, and with strangers too, are far more wide awake and handy than the other Greek peasants of the island, who seldom wander far from their village, or to the nearest town, and to whom the proverbial taunt 'Cypriot oxen' (*bous Kyprios*) is still applied. On the other hand the Cypriot villager is comparatively better housed than the peasant of the Greek mainland, and has by way of furniture what we do not find there, a bedstead, a few shabby cane chairs, and perhaps, even a table. But this luxury, as well as the use of a two-wheeled cart drawn by a pair of oxen, where the condition of the ground allows it, are legacies of European origin, dating from the days of the Franks. I sought in vain for ancient ruins in the neighbourhood of the village, though some years ago the peasants found quite close while clearing a little hill ancient graves containing some earthen vessels of poor quality.

The next morning I set out to ride in an easterly direction to Famagusta. An hour later I passed a small Turkish village Melusia, and came to Tremithusia. Here to the right lies a little chapel with a Corinthian capital and some grave-altars of sandstone; on the left the monastery of S. Spyridon. I was shown too a small plain sarcophagus as the original grave (Ciborium) of the famous bishop, whose bones were translated to Corfu, where they still rest in a silver coffin, for S. Spyridon enjoys very great reverence as the patron and protector of that island. The presence of this convent and the remains of ancient foundations and graves in the village prove that here was Tremithus, of which the saint was bishop. What is now a poor village was reckoned in the middle ages as a small town, which was destroyed by Richard Lion-heart in 1191. The similarity of name would not by itself be sufficient proof, for the cultivation of the Terebinth tree (Cypriot *Trementhos* for the late form *Terebinthos*) was widely spread in the island, so that there are still half a dozen villages and hamlets called Tremithia and Tremithousa. In this older Tremithus a sand stone statue was found a few years since, but before a merchant in Larnaca, to whom I owe this notice, could acquire it the Turks had broken it up.

From Tremithusia I came through the small villages Lysi, Contea and Couklia to Calopsida. Behind this the plain which was so far hummocky gets flatter, and begins to show marshy pits (*bolistra*) which are generally throughout the year under water. Owing to the long drought I found them all dry. Round about grows a herb [sonchus oleraceus] from the ashes of which soda is extracted. It was a ride of an hour and a half from here to Trapeza, a ruined village with two large decayed churches. Here I left the direct road to Famagusta, and turned northwards up the dry river bed to Styli: the name attracted me, but I found nothing ancient there. Possibly there stood here in old days a few pillars from the great aqueduct built by Justinian to bring the water from Kythraia to Salamis, and hence the name. An hour beyond Styli is H. Sergios, a considerable village not far from the east coast, and close to Salamis, where I found quarters in a country house belonging to the Russian Consul. From its flat roof I saw, about two hours distance to the south, the towers and churches of Famagusta lighted by the setting sun.

The next day I rode with the steward of the little property to Famagusta. We visited first some remains of Justinian's aqueduct, ten minutes to the south of the village, built of squared sandstone set in mortar, with sharp-pointed arches. Four continuous arches are still erect. Some half-obliterated inscriptions of early Christian date, which I found in the village, appear to belong to this aqueduct [Sakellarios, *Kypriaca* (1890) I, 179, 150].

Ten minutes further on in the fields is the large Byzantine church of S. Barnabas, with many Corinthian capitals of poor work, brought from the ruins of Justinian's city of Constantia, which was quite near. The grave assigned to the Saint is in a little ruined chapel behind the church built over a mineral spring, whereof the holy water (agiasma) is credited by the people with extraordinary curative powers. The water has a faint taste of salt. The descent into the little hole from which it springs is unpleasant, because those who are healed here hang their rags on the walls. In front of the chapel lie some fragments of sarcophagi of sandstone. The grave of the apostle was discovered under Zeno, and on his breast lay the Gospel of S. Matthew: hence the high privileges with which the Emperor invested the Archbishop. Owing to the nearness to the Holy Land and the early reception of Christianity, Cyprus is full of Christian antiquities and legends of Saints, so there is shown between the church of S. Barnabas and the ruins of old Salamis the so-called Prison of S. Catherine. This is a half-subterranean sepulchral chamber of huge blocks of stone, lying North and South, with the original entrance on the east side, and an annex on the West. The main chamber is more than 10 metres long by 5½ broad, the side-chamber is 3 metres high, and covered with a pointed vault, built of five stones only, the middle stone extending the whole length of the room. The vault of the main chamber is formed of still greater blocks. The Phoenicians seem to have been fond of the use of such stones for their graves.

We left, for the present, the ruins of ancient Salamis on the left; and rode through the broad and marshy bed of the Pediaios, the Cyprian Nile, now quite dry, but which in due time enriches with its wide overflow a great part of the plain: The road led us over sandy soil to the famous fortress. As soon as we had crossed the river bed we saw on our right low stony ridges, which had served as quarries, and in which were hewn the rock-tombs of old Ammochostos.

The fortress lies on a slight eminence close to the shore. It is surrounded by high strongly-built walls, in front of which a broad and deep fosse is cut out of the natural rock; a bridge protected by a salient work leads over the fosse to the only land-gate, situate on the S. W. side. Within the town is like a desert, for it has really no inmates beyond the 100 or 150 Turkish soldiers (Topjis, Gunners), with half a dozen mechanics and small shopkeepers. We rode through the narrow silent lanes, between the ruins of old houses, convents and churches, to the barrack of the *Zabit* or governor of the District. He read my *buyuruldu*, and gave me a soldier as escort. Here, as in Nicosia, a large church of S. Nicolaos stands in the middle of the city, as well as a fine Gothic cathedral dedicated to S. Sophia: between the two comes the former royal residence, a long building with two wings, built of squared sandstone: two stories are still preserved, the windows and doors are set in dressed blocks. It only wants floors and a roof, window frames and doors to restore the palace as a spacious and fitting princely dwelling. The King of Greece and his consort had for six years a far smaller and less conspicuous residence. Between, the palace-court and the front of [S. Nicolas] was formerly a small square with a pillared passage of ancient granite columns, with a fountain: judging from what remains of it, it could bear comparison with the most beautiful market places of the medieval towns of Italy. Now there prowl about it men who have no notion of the dignity and grandeur of these buildings. Even the expression 'prowl' is too refined: in shoes down-at-heel, in torn breeches, the sons of Islam, bowlegged from their perpetual sitting and squatting, slink and waddle though the ruins.

The cathedral of [S. Nicolas] is rather smaller, but its facade is more ornate than the cathedral of S. Sophia at Nicosia. Here the Kings of Cyprus, surrounded by their barons, received the crown of Jerusalem: on the same spot a tattered *dervish* in a foul loathsome nightcap was saying his prayers. In the forecourt of the church stands a Corinthian frieze of white marble, 42 cm. high, with stags, horses, oxen, lions and other animals intermixed with the curves of the acanthus leaves. It came doubtless from Salamis or from the ruins of old Famagusta, and now serves as a bench. There is a sarcophagus too with festoons of flowers and *genii*. From the flat roof of an aisle I counted the ruins of more than thirty churches.

From the cathedral to the Water-gate. Just within it lies a colossal lion of poor work, on the walls are still seen in several places the arms of Venice, and over the door without the inscription Nicolao Priolo Prefecto MCCCCLXXXVI. The harbour of oblong shape is roomy, enclosed with skilfully made moles and jutting rocks. It proves that the Ammochostos of the middle ages, called by Europeans Famagusta, stood on the site of the old city of the same name (though known under the Ptolemys as Arsinoe): while the name which it took from its condition, Ammochostos (buried in sand, the sand-heap) has survived for more than a thousand years in the mouths of its inhabitants. Unless the name, which appears in Ptolemy too as a gloss, and is mentioned by no other author, took its rise in the middle ages. It is a pity that the artificial harbour has become through neglect pretty well blocked with sand, so that only small trading vessels of light draught can get in. The entrance to the basin is protected on the N. side by a projecting citadel, a Genoese work, which forms a part of the fortress, though divided from it by a fosse of its own.

It was this harbour, into which, after the loss of the Holy Land, poured the largest share of what was then, before the discovery of the sea-route to the East Indies, the immeasurably rich and important trade of Syria. The Venetians and Genoese had here their store houses, which, as in earlier days at S. Jean d'Acre, were under the jurisdiction of their respective Consuls, and their mutual rivalry was often the cause of bloody conflicts. In an outbreak of this kind, on the occasion of the coronation of Peter II as King of Jerusalem, all the Genoese in Famagusta were slaughtered: a conference which Pope Gregory XI caused to be held in the interest of peace at Thebes in Boeotia failed of its aim, and in 1373 the Genoese in revenge captured Famagusta, plundered Nicosia, and laid waste a huge part of the island. The efforts of the King and his successor to win back from them this important city had no success: the fortress withstood many a stubborn siege, and only the last King of the house of Lusignan, the adventurous and vigorous Bastard Jacques II was able to regain it. But the Genoese lordship saw the decline of the rich commerce of the city, and the Venetians and Cypriots transferred their activity to the bay of Kition (Larnaca) and to Limassol.

On my way back from the harbour I visited another bit of the fortifications: the solidity of the work and its excellent preservation attest the skill and patience of the Genoese and Venetian engineers, and insure their fame. The strongest bastion is at the highest point of the West side, pointing inland, and under it are huge vaulted passages and chambers, which served some warlike purpose. And this city, once the centre point of the interest of Europe, stands empty, and is destined to certain ruin, unless it fall quickly into other hands.

Half an hour S. of the fortress lies a straggling Greek village Varosia, where live also a good many Turks, with large gardens of lemons and oranges. Somewhere here must have been the harbour which Strabo calls Leucolla, and the cape (Greco) which lies behind the village includes the two promontories known to the ancients as Pedalion and Thronoi.

On the return journey to H. Sergios we visited the ruins of Salamis, on the site of which, from the time of Constantius Chlorus or Constantine the Great, stood the Roman city Constantia. They lie in heaps along the shore, stretching northwards from the mouth of the river. But the building material was sandstone only: it is all dug out and broken up, and one sees the merest ruins, for the remains of the ancient city have not only supplied material for the fortifications, churches and palaces of Ammochostos, but serve even to this day as a quarry for the neighbourhood. Even the inhabitants of Levcosia & Larnaca (as did lately the *Capucins* for the building of their church) get squared stones from here. The only monument I saw proved the ruins of a large reservoir (castrum aquae) into which ran the water of Justinian's aqueduct: on another spot lay on the ground some thirty monolithic granite columns, of two to two and a half feet in diameter. The number of these columns, which came probably from Egypt, must have been immense, since for more than a thousand years so many have been carried off to Ammochostos and to churches in the neighbourhood, while others have been broken up, and yet new ones are continually found in the ruins. They were certainly imported, for there is no granite in Cyprus. Most of them seem to have been used for the inner courts of dwellings, as at Delos.

Between Salamis and the church of S. Barnabas, and again westward of Salamis, one notices two fairly large tumuli. The sages of the country have satisfied themselves that on the one nearest Salamis the Persians (!) planted their engines of war wherewith to besiege the city. They fail to explain its fellow. The contents of these hills deserve investigation, for they seem to be the oldest monuments in the island, where so far I have observed no other tumuli.

The shore from Ammochostos, and northward again for some hours distance beyond Salamis, is formed of low sand-dunes, thrown up by the South and East winds. These dunes the peasants clear away in patches parallel with the sea, and close up to its edge, down to the virgin soil, and so win a stretch of land, whose natural moisture resists the summer's most scorching heat, and which lends itself well to the culture of madder, cotton, onions, melons, beans, greens and garden produce generally. These little gardens set between the sand dunes are called here meadows (*libadia*) and are the most valuable lands in all the island; a scala of such, a land measure forty paces each way, that is 1600 square paces (the *scala* of plough-land measures 60 paces each way, or 3600 square paces) sells for 1000 to 6000 *piastres* (90 to 540 *gulden*) and never fails to give a rich return. The same form of cultivation holds along the South coast, at Larnaca, Kiti, and Episcopi (Kurion) and on the N. W. in the district of Morphou, at Lapethos and other places, but the meadows between Ammochostos and Tricomo are the best and richest.

I stayed what remained of the afternoon at H. Sergios, where I found an inscription of the Ptolemaic epoch. H. Sergios, so called after a local Saint, the proconsul Sergius Paulus, is now only a village of eighty houses, with about twenty gardens or plantations of fruit and mulberry trees: in the time of the Kings and the Venetians it was large and flourishing, with some eight hundred gardens, and on account of its healthy situation on a dry plain, cooled by the sea breeze, was the favourite summer refuge of the inhabitants of Ammochostos. To what wealth, what splendour and prosperity might these places not rise again, if instead of the crescent the Cross flashed from the battlements of Nicosia and Famagusta, and a German Prince set on his head in the cathedral of S. Sophia the crowns of Cyprus, Armenia and Jerusalem.

In the evening the consul's steward, an Italian born in Cyprus, talked to me of the economic condition of the island, especially of the great plain which he knew best. This plain, so far as a man unlearned in geology can explain it, seems to have been formed by a great flood which on the upheaval of the island was confined between two parallel chains of mountains, and then broke through the lower heights, tore them apart and washed them away, slopes from its watershed, a couple of hours West of Nicosia, Eastward and Westward to the sea: the Eastern half, called par excellence Mesaria or Mesaoria, is the larger, or rather comprises two thirds of the whole. The soil of the plain is somewhat broken and hummocky, here and there remain low hills, which have resisted the flood, mostly in the form of table-mountains (whence the common name Trapeza) or in that of small cones and pyramids; in other places the plain is broken by flat beds of limestone or gypsum, raised a very little from the surface. The two rivers Pediaius and Satrachos, which rising in Aoos or Machairas join their streams between Levcosia and Salamis, cross the plain; the Pediaios takes in several brooks which flow from the northern mountains. Those stony hills and plains here described by the common name *trachones*, or rough mounds, are, owing to the scanty population, hardly tilled at all, although most of the land is admirably fitted for the plough, or for the cultivation of olive, fig, almond and mulberry trees. On either side of the river beds the land is low, the soil heavy and clayey, overflowed in winter by the rivers, and some of it capable of being watered in summer by channels drawn from them. The dependence of the plain on the rise of the rivers gives one a foretaste of Egypt. Natural causes account for the differences of soil in the Mesaoria.

Arable land, not reckoning the meadow-gardens or Livadia along the seashore, which we have mentioned above, is divided into irrigable or cotton land and dry land. A scala, 3600 square paces, of the first may be worth 500 to 100 piastres, according to its quality, and its nearness to some bigger centre: the scala of trachona land sells at 50 to 100 piastres, the mean price is about 10 to 25 p. A pair of oxen works on an average a hundred scalas of irrigated land viz. 15 to 25 scalas with cotton or madder, another 15 to 25 with vetches for fodder, and 40 to 50 with cereals. Rotation is kept with grain and vetches. Where there is no irrigable land, a pair of oxen can well work 200 scalas of *trachona* land, 100 with grain, 50 with vetches, while another 50 lie fallow.

As for cattle—a pair of oxen costs from 200 to 1500 p., a horse from 100 to 1000, a mule from 200 to 2000, a donkey from 50 to 400 p. Camels are kept chiefly by Turks, although here it is not, as in Asia Minor, forbidden to Christians to possess the Prophet's favourite animal.

Swine are found nearly everywhere, except in the towns and in the villages inhabited exclusively by Turks: although a law now fallen into desuetude confines the keeping of this unclean beast to certain specified villages. As in Greece cows are kept only to breed oxen for the plough: milk and butter are won only from sheep and goats. A flock numbers 200 to 1000 head, worth 20 to 80 p. a head, a fat kid of a year old costs about 80 p. A ewe or she-goat gives yearly an oke of butter and ten okes of cheese. Then there is the goat's hair, and a sheep gives up to two okes of wool. The sheep are all of the fat-tailed race, and the rams have often three, four and even six horns.

To return to the breeding of swine—one need travel for no long time in these parts to convince oneself of the wisdom of the Mosaic and Mohammedan law which forbids as unclean the use of their flesh. Even in Greece it is recognised that pork is unwholesome in warm weather, and it is rejected accordingly. In Cyprus the peasants eat it freely, and prudent inhabitants have observed to me, that to this habit is to be ascribed the frequent occurrence of leprosy, while among the Turks who form a quarter of the population, and who live mixed with the Christians under the same social and climatic conditions, hardly a case is known: no doubt the more frequent use of warm baths must help to keep the skin of a Turk in a healthier state.

I close this chapter with some remarks on the price of land which I collected in different parts of the island. In Acanthou, just over the hills on the N. coast, a scala of arable land on stony soil is worth only 5 to 10 piastres, an olive tree (they grow well there) only 80 to 50 p. on account of the considerable distance (12 hours) from Nicosia, and the difficulty experienced in the transport of produce. On the other hand, at Kythraia, near the capital, with very rich soil and ample irrigation, an olive tree is worth 250 to 400 p. (16 to 26 Prussian thalers). At Dali (Idalion) one pays for a scala of unwatered but quite good arable lands 25 to 30 p.—the spot lies just between two District centres. At Mazoto, on the S. coast between Larnaca & Limassol, a scala of good arable land is worth 15 to 20 p. at Episcopi, near Kourion, a scala of the best cotton-land, irrigated from the river, costs 500 p.

A peasant with his family, living in the very frugal style of today, can maintain themselves with 40 to 50 scalas of grain (wheat and barley) and 20 scalas of cotton land, planted with cotton, madder or tobacco, selling the produce for ready money. If the land is unwatered he would want twice the amount.

Large properties, where the fields are not mixed up with those of other owners, are few. A farm (chiftliq) of 1000 scalas of bare arable land, without trees and buildings, but with some little water, at Jeri near Nicosia, was sold lately for 2500 p. or less than 250 gulden, such a property would suffice for the keep of two to three German families.

A garden at H. Sergios, with four scalas of fruit trees, which would give 15 okes of silk (a 100 p. the oke), another four scalas of untilled garden ground, small dwelling and a spring for irrigation, sold the other day for 5000 p. or not quite 460 gulden. A German gardener family would keep themselves comfortably on the produce of the silkworms and the trees, and in a few years lay up no inconsiderable savings.

Europeans pay a tithe (really about 25%) of all produce and 9% on all exports. They pay nothing for their flocks, and nothing for wood for building or burning from the forests. On the acquisition of landed property this must be kept in mind. If the proprietor dies without male heirs, the land returns to the Sultan as a pledge, which must be redeemed by the female heirs or the owner's brothers, unless they are prepared to renounce it, at two thirds or three fourths of its value. This process is called *tapuliq*. But the land is generally estimated below its real value.

## IV

**Karpasia. Journey through the Mesaoria. Avgasida. Levkonikon. The northern hills. Acanthou and the neighbourhood. Cantara. Achaion Acte. Aphrodision. Seclusion of inhabitants. Knodara. Artemi. Exo Metochi. Ancient Chytri. Return to Nicosia.**

*February 25–27, 1845.*

My original plan had been to visit after Salamis the promontory called Carpas, which thrusts its narrow length towards East and North-East. However the information gleaned at H. Sergios left me little hope of finding there many traces of antiquity. Pococke certainly saw the ruins of the city Carpasia, but did not find one inscription. So I gave up the idea, and am sorry I did so. It was just there, in sight of the Phoenician coast, that some memorials should be found.

I left my kind host of H. Sergios on Febr. 25 to return through the Mesaoria to Levcosia, for I was impatient to see the Western end of the island, and its more famous towns. My road led me through Alimia and Aloe to Avgasida, a small convent-farm: in the church here a medieval tombstone is let into the pavement. It shows in basrelief a man in Spanish costume, with a short slashed jerkin, short full breeches, a cap on his head, with the somewhat unorthographic inscription.

Ἐκοιμίθη ὁ δοῦλος τοῦ Θεοῦ Μισὲρ (messire) Τζόριζ (Γεωργιος—the surname I cannot read, it looked like Οὐσαλὰρχ) ἐν μινὶ Σεπτ]εμβρίου— the rest illegible] ΑΦ—1500. Probably this was a man of knightly rank (Messire) once the proprietor of the farm, and builder of the church. At midday I reached Levconico the biggest village of the Mesaoria, with about a hundred houses. The church has no antiquities. A commonly recurring feature in the later architecture of this neighbourhood is the transition of a square base to the cylindrical form of the column, while the sides of the cube are scooped out in half-circles, and the corners projecting between them are blunted, so that the upper surface of the basis, between the highest points of the four half-circles, make a circle.

I heard it again asserted in Levconico that at Acanthu, on the N. side of the mountain-range, there were old ruins. I determined to make a *détour* thither, and so to see also this bit of the N. coast. The distance from Levconico is four hours. The road runs N. to a pass which you see from the plain (cutting, *boghaz*), and in half an hour leaves the plain for the foothills. They are of sandstone and clay-slate, denuded and full of clefts. The vegetation is scanty, wild or dwarf cypress, pines, arbutus, lentisc and thorny shrubs unknown in Greece. On the clay-slate lie rounded blocks of lime stone, split off and rolled down from the peaks: for the mountain tops, 2000 feet and over, thrust steep, pointed, masses of limestone through the clay-slate. You see the same formation as in the N. chain (S. Elias range) in Rhodes, and this too stretches in a straight line from W. to E. In Cyprus this chain extends from the promontory Krommyon (Kormakiti) in the West, along the entire N. east up the E. extremity of the Carpas, where it forms the second or lesser Olympos. But we do not know any name in antiquity which covers the whole. Now the portion which lies over against the N. E. side of Nicosia is called after the peak Pentadaktylos.

As soon as one has crossed the watershed, you get a view through a narrow pass, with a small brook, of the sea and of Cilicia Tracheia. When the path has cleared the pass, it runs eastward for an hour and a half to the hills, over rocks of tertiary formation, much contorted, but fairly clothed with trees, and with here and there pretty little olive groves. Then I reached Acanthou charmingly situated, about three quarters of an hour from the shore, on a hill top near a stream. To the South there towers over the village the bare blue and red limestone masses of one of the highest peaks of the range, crowned with dark pines. The day was too far advanced to allow me to search for the ruins of which I had been told. I revelled in the beauty of the soft warm spring evening, as I strolled thro' the richly wooded outskirts of the little place.

The next morning I went on foot with a guide to the church of our Lady (Panagia Pergamou) following always the foot of the mountains in an easterly direction through olive plantations, and across deep gorges with little water. As we walked my guide told me that the storm of February 15 had washed some oxen into the sea on the Caramanian coast, and driven their bodies across to the shore below us. Probably a similar occurrence gave rise to the old poetic legend of the deer of Cilicia, how in longing for the juicy pastures of Cyprus they swam across the sea from the promontory of Corycus to Curion: a story which Strabo, seeing Curion lies on the South coast, is so eager to prove absurd. In an hour and a quarter we had reached our aim. The church, newly restored, lies in the plain, scarcely ten minutes from the shore, and contains nothing old. In a thicket close by lie the ruins of an ancient and small village, squared blocks, smooth pillars of sandstone, and many stones from a vault. On a low rocky rise a hundred paces to the North, are more old foundations, and bigger heaps of squared stones, broken sarcophagi, and fragments of tiles lying about the fields. At Levcosia I had been told of an inscription which was to be seen on the rocks, but the villagers of Acanthou knew nothing of it, and I could not find it. The small stony promontory which thrusts itself from the shore is called Hypsili. Half an hour farther E. stands the church of St. Charalampos. From this point one sees about two hours away the sharply pointed height of Kantara on the line of the range at the beginning of the Carpas. Upon it lie the ruins of a medieval castle, known to the neighbourhood as 'the Hundred houses.' We find the same name often in Cyprus, it is merely a version of the Turkish 'Yuz bir oda' (hundred and one chambers) a common name among Turks for similar medieval remains. I had already in Larnaca, Levcosia and H. Sergios collected sufficient information about it, to satisfy myself that I had nothing to find in the Castle of Cantara.

Ruins like those near the church of our Lady of Pergamo are found on the shore below Acanthou and on many points of this narrow but rich and charming slip of coast. But the peasants assure me there are nowhere to be found sculptures or inscriptions or even a fragment of marble, nothing but scattered blocks of sandstone, so that it was not worth my while to visit the spots. We have to recognise however in these ruins the remains of what were villages built by Achaians who settled on this shore, hence called Achaion Acte. On the same strip must have stood also one of the many temples of Aphrodite, the Aphrodision, perhaps near this very church of Our Lady, a very fitting site for an ancient temple.

I returned to the village, and struck off at once towards Levcosia. I had to traverse my path of yesterday through the same pass which connects the lonely village with its 40 or 50 families with the rest of the world. What isolation! The men, sometimes but seldom, cross the mountains into the Mesaoria, and even as far as the twelve-hours-away market of Nicosia, which is for them the centre of the universe. But women are born and die here without having seen more of the world than their village with its charming surroundings, the broad mirror of the Cilician sea, rarely enlivened by a sail, and the distant high coastline of Cilicia Tracheia, crowned by the snowclad peaks of Taurus. Such conditions, which we find again in the Southern half of Rhodes, partly explain the crass ignorance, the mere stupidity, the dark superstition, the distrustful repugnance to all that is strange and unusual, which mark the inhabitants of the smaller islands of Greece. The men at least live mostly on the sea and from the sea; and in Greece itself the Revolution and the War, and later the intermixtion of the people in the common affairs of the township, and in the elections, and for the younger generation schooling and conscription, and lastly the more frequent and wider intercourse with educated persons of their own nation, and with strangers, have shaken men up and roused them, developed their intelligence, and enriched them with many a new experience. But in the faraway valleys of Rhodes and Cyprus, where the Greek lives in the narrowest limits, takes no part in public affairs, and withdraws himself as far as possible from the view of the Turk—here indeed one is often tempted to ask oneself if the intelligence of which the Greeks are so keen to boast is really a prominent natural and inherited characteristic of their race.

I had left the pass behind me, turned S. W. and leaving the hamlets Mallountas and H. Nicolaos on the S. slope of the range to the right, had climbed in two hours over the wooded foot hills which stretch out far into the plain to Knodara. The country I had traversed was rich in game, several hares and foxes, many partridges and wood pigeons came out from the thicket right and left from the road. In the evening, when I was far away from the place, I first learned that in this wood lay a little village, inhabited by Turks, called Artemi. Here too probably stood a temple of the goddess of the chase, and the firwood was dedicated to her. Only too often a traveler first gets informations which would have been precious to him on the spot when he has already left the place which they concern. Just so I met here the priest of Tricomon, three hours N. of H. Sergios at the beginning of the Carpas, who told me that Greek graves and vases had been found in his village, and that in Syncrasis, in the church, was a Latin inscription. But I had left Tricomo and Syncrasis a day's march behind me.

Walled in on the N. side of the church at Knodara is a stout pillar of blueish limestone with a Latin inscription, from which it appears that a Roman castle stood here in which was quartered the seventh cohort of the Breuci: the old name of the place is unknown. The soil round Knodara is heavy and well watered. Then the road crosses a stony tract out of which deep layers of gypsum crop up. On the left one sees Marathobounos, on a hill over the river: on the left the road leads to Kythraia. The twilight was already closing round when I reached Exo-Metochi, situated in a rich and fruitful hollow, where I lodged with the priest. As the clergy in Cyprus are generally the most notable and well to do men of the village the reception of strangers commonly falls to their lot. Today I shared the priest's hospitality with a Turkish peasant from Artemi, who with his wife and child were on their way to the capital. The woman, though old and ugly, kept herself carefully veiled, and I dared not enter the part of the house where she was: but her little girl Aysha came willingly to me, and accepted sugar. It is a pleasing custom that in Cyprus the priest is not, as in other places addressed as Papa, Despota, or Geron, but with the biblical title Didascale (master). And because most of them, on account of the nearness of the Holy Sepulcre, have made the pilgrimage thither, they are greeted as would be any elderly pilgrim, with the Turkish title Hajji Baba.

Two short hours N. W. from Exo Metochi lies the large village Kythraia, on a rich spring; and again an hour to the S. W. on the brook which runs from this spring into the Pediaios, the hamlet Palaikythro. I traversed this place without finding a trace of ancient remains, nor were any more to be seen in Kythraia. Both places however have preserved the name of a city which was in ancient times long one of the chief Cyprian cities (Chytroi), until it became subject to Salamis, and fell into insignificance. Now the name of the ancient city is always written with the Greek *chi*, while the pronunciation of the names of the villages of today Citria and Palaicitron [with Italian *c*] requires the form to have *k*. This passage from χ to κ is easily explicable in Cyprus, because here too as in other Southern islands, *chi* before an *i* sound approaches to *sh*: and for the *sh* sound the people, who guided by an instinct common to all peoples, assimilate where it is possible their place names to an etymology which they can all understand, substitute the sound of the κ of Kitron, Kitrea—lemon, lemon tree.

From Palaikythron I rode without a halt across the plain to Levcosia, and was again kindly received by my Spanish hosts in the Franciscan Convent.

## V

**Pass to Keryneia. Abbey de la Paix. Buffavento. S. Hilarion. Keryneia. Ruins. Old graves. Notice of Cilicia. The Castle. Acheiropoietos Mon. Ruins of ancient Lapethos. S. Panteleemon Mon. Monkish life. Krommyon. Maronites. Palaiocastron near S. Eirene. Old statues. Negro slavery. Morphou town. Political rumours. English schemes. Palaiochora. Olympos. Petra. Villages of Solea. Ancient mines. Aipeia. Machaira. Politiko. S. Heracleidios. Copper mines. Pera. A bronze statue. Nesou. Idalion. Return to Larnaca.**

*February 28–March 5, 1845.*

I remained only one night in Levcosia, leaving the city on Feb. 28 to visit the country round Keryneia, Lapethos, Krommyon and Soli. The road strikes Northwards across the plain, and passes two arms or confluents of the Pediaios on stone bridges. After an hour's ride I reached the foothills, which consist here, as between Levcosia and Acanthou in low bare mounds of clay-slate and sand. An hour and a half later I came to the foot of the main range through a small plain in which lies right and left a couple of villages Vounos and Dikomon. Here begins the pass through mountains, which cover with bare and steep sides a core of hard limestone. In two hours we were through the pass, and before me lay a small but rich strip of coast, covered with olive and carob trees: half an hour away was Keryneia with its strong castle, and to the right on the slope of the mountain the ancient abbey to which the native Franks give a name which varies between Belpaese, Dellapais and other forms. I let my baggage go on to Keryneia, and pushed on with my negro to the abbey, which I reached in an hour.

I have scarcely seen in Germany or Italy more beautiful ruins of the middle ages than this abbey, which Hugues III, called the Great, built in the XIIIth cent. and endowed with many privileges: the abbot was adorned with the episcopal mitre, and might wear, when he rode forth in state, a gold sword and gold spurs, like the other feudal barons and knights. The building, situate on a spur of the mountain, leans against a rock, so that its northern walls climb to a dizzy height from the foot of the rock, while the main building with the church, which is on the S. side, rests on a natural rocky plateau. We enter from the west into a forecourt which leads on the right into the roomy church, and on the left, through a porch adorned with the royal arms of Jerusalem and Armenia into a stately inner court [the whole building is simply and solidly erected of squared blocks of yellowish sandstone.] This is surrounded by a lofty arched cloister, and adorned with a fountain constructed of two ancient marble sarcophagi, one of which is ornamented with genii, festoons of fruit and lions' heads in relief. To this court are attached several chambers on the ground floor, e.g. on the north side the large hall or refectory, 38 paces long and 12 broad, rising through two stories. In the thickness of the northern wall a secret stairway leads to a small pulpit, from which during meal times their teacher read to the monks. From the windows one gets a grand view over the plain and to villages well planted with fruit trees, and the sea with the shores and mountains of Asia Minor. From the inner court sundry steps lead to the upper stories, where were the cells, now destroyed. For unfortunately this glorious ruin serves as a quarry, and the village lying along side is chiefly built out of its remains. Yet so much still remains of the monastery, that in the hands of a wealthy and artistic European owner it could easily be restored, and form a noble property. As to the name, I noticed that the peasants of the country near said Baia or Alabaia, so that it was formed from la Badia, with the usual Cypriot rejection of the *d*. Some writers called the Monastery originally de la Paix.

At two hours distance above the abbey lies on an almost inaccessible peak a medieval castle, called by the Frankish historians Buffavento, by the Greeks of today *ta spitia tes rhegainas*, the Queen's houses. A second like it lies on a peak west of the pass which leads from Levcosia to Keryneia; this the Franks of the middle ages called "the castle of the god of love," the Greeks H. Hilarion, the Turks 'Yuz bir ev,' the hundred and one houses. One sees them first from Keryneia, to which I rode down from the Abbey. The barley in the plain was already quite tall, and in ear: it is generally reaped about the (15) 27 March.

Keryneia, it keeps its ancient name unchanged, is a poor place, situated close to the shore, on the site of the old town. The medieval castle, a well preserved oblong quadrangle, with round towers and a fosse dug deep into the rock, stands on the east of the town, on a jutting spit of land. On the western border of the space there are still to be seen remains of the boundary walls, with round towers; one of these at the S. W. corner near a projecting fragment of the wall is built of large sandstone blocks mostly cut into facets, and appears to be a Roman work. Still further west a couple of low rocky ridges run out into the sea full of ancient graves, some of them hewn out in the perpendicular face of the cliff, some of them with steps leading down under the rocky shelf as at Aigina and Melos. All of them were opened and rifled long ago. In one spot excavations were lately made to get building stone and a number of small smooth pillars were found. The fields close by are full of old sherds of tiles and coarse pots of a red colour.

At Keryneia in the evening I met a man from Levcosia who has a store at Kelenderis, now Cylindria, on the opposite Cilician coast. With this place there is communication generally once or twice a week, and before the establishment of a steamboat service the Tatars with despatches for Cyprus and Egypt usually traveled across Asia Minor and through Kelenderis. Cilicia Tracheia is now called by the Turks Icheli: Caramania proper begins further eastwards in Cilicia Pedia, but Europeans use the name for well nigh the whole of the south coast of Asia Minor: the eastern end, including the Syrian coast is called, one knows not why, by Greek seamen *ta parasamia*. My informant assured me that there were but few Christians in Cilicia, merely a few shopkeepers in the coast towns. Generally the population is very sparse, and consists only of Turkish nomads, Yuruks. Alaya only has a few vessels. The country is quite peaceable.

The next morning I went early to the Commandant, *Yuzbashi*, who lives in the town, and was accompanied by one of his soldiers to the Fort. It is a substantial building of considerable height. A draw bridge leads over the fosse, and vaulted steps and passages lead from the left of the gate through the great N. W. tower to a chapel with four columns of marble, then deeper within to vaulted chambers where three or four big cannon command the entrance to the harbour at the sea level. Above, along the stout walls, are some rusty iron pieces, and about thirty big bronze Venetian guns, mostly dismounted, their carriages unserviceable. To this strong fortress in 1460 fled Queen Charlotte and her husband Louis of Savoy, when her half-brother, the twenty years old bastard Jacques, late archbishop, landed at the Salines of Kition with Egyptian help, to wrest from her the crown. The new King began at once the siege of the castle; in the ensuing spring Louis and his consort fled to Italy: the Queen indeed returned to Kyreneia, only to leave it again, and after a two years' siege the fortress surrendered to Jacques. In 1571 it fell into the hands of the Turks. Since then it has stood yet another siege, for in 1765 the rebel Khalil agha shut himself up here, and stood out for a long while against the Pasha's troops, until by trick and treachery he was overpowered. The details of this insurrection are given by Mariti in his Travels in Cyprus.

The little harbour on the west of the Castle is eked out with moles of masonry, and in earlier times may have given good shelter to galleys: now it is pretty well choked with sand, and offers room to only a few small craft: Keryneia gives a title to one of the three bishops who are subject to the Abp, but the holy one of Keryneia does not reside here, but at one of the Monasteries of Acheiropoietos or Panteleemon. At eight I started from Acheiropoietos, which lies on the shore three hours to the west near the ruins of ancient Lapethos. The road keeps along the plain pretty close to sea, on the left lie the well-wooded foothills and a whole row of small villages, dominated by the steep summits of the range. The country is delightful, full of olive and carob trees and rich greenery so that Lapethos still deserves its old name *himeroessa*, charming. After a ride of three hours one leaves on a slope on the left the village of Caravas and the still larger village of Lapethos, a picturesque spot with tall trees and slender minarets, and turns down to the right and the shore to the Monastery. This consists of a large court with open pillared halls of some dignity but as it now stands of no great age. It takes its name from the fact that there is here preserved in an icon of the Virgin Mary a piece of the handkerchief which wiped the sweat from the Saviour's brow [the mandylion]. Beyond this, and a tombstone said to be that of the founder, the church presents nothing worth seeing.

The ruins of the ancient city, to which native savants give erroneously the name Lampousa begin directly behind and eastward of the convent with a rock squared and smoothed to be the support of some building. Similar blocks occur in the town which stretches for a good way along the shore, but like Salamis and all other ancient sites in

Cyprus is a mere heap of rubbish, for it has been used as a quarry. Ancient rock-graves, like those at Keryneia, are found on the eastern edge of the town.

I rode on in the afternoon and visited modern Lapethos. It is still one of the largest villages in Cyprus. Water runs in plenty through the place, irrigates the fruitful plain, and fills a streamlet of the same name. Yet it is but a shadow of what it was under Frankish rule, when it had 10000 inmates and its water meadows produced sugar cane. The whole village belongs to a Turk who lives at Constantinople. Then westward again across the plain, leaving Basili on the left—here I lost some time in stealing under the carob trees after a flight of wood pigeons. This tree (*Keratea. Ceratonia Siliqua.* "Johannisbrodbaum") is very common here, and many shiploads of its fruit are exported yearly from this and other points on the coast to Italy and France, to serve, as I was told, as fodder for cattle. An hour and a half from Lapethos I turned south and landwards through a gap down which a brook flowed to the sea, the rocky walls on either side seemed to contain copper. I emerged from the gap into a hollow and at last in the twilight climbed a steep slope towards the S. E. Here on a plateau some 800 or 1000 feet above the sea stands the monastery of St. Panteleemon, the usual residence of the bishop of Keryneia.

The bishop was with the Archbishop at the capital, but I found his clerical staff, the exarchos or vicar, his skeuophylax, and other poor and unlettered monks with like honorific titles, and as it was the last day on which the Orthodox eat flesh before the Lenten fast, this incredibly frugal folk made a high feast for their evening meal, serving three different dishes of meat, and a pudding. The next morning, March 2 I rode over stony hills planted here and there with firs, in an hour and a quarter to Kormakiti, a large village of a hundred Maronite families, which lies half an hour from the sea on the west of the promontory known to the ancients as Krommya or Krommyon Acte. The people were still in Church, I went in and heard the priest, standing before the altar in Latin vestments, deliver a sermon in modern Greek: he read the prayers and the Gospel partly in Arabic, partly in Syriac. When the Franks lost the Holy Land many thousands of these Maronites came from the Lebanon to Cyprus: at the date of the Ottoman conquest they had thirty villages, and Lusignan tells us that after the Greeks they were the most numerous stock in Cyprus. Originally there were many of them dwellers in the Carpas—the half Greek half Arabic name of the village Kome Kebir points thereto—but gradually some went over to Orthodoxy, others to Islam, and now only Kormakiti, four adjacent villages and a small convent belong to them. They number altogether only 500 souls; they still speak among themselves a bad Arabic, but they no longer understand the written Arabic speech, so that their priests, who have been educated in convents in Aleppo and Damascus, are obliged to preach to them in Greek. One may foresee that ere long these remaining villages will join the Orthodox church, an aim towards which the Greek priests work sedulously, and it really seems as though for Eastern folk, whose bent is to think little and feel little, Orthodoxy or Islam, which in their spiritual deadness centre all religious merit in outward and mechanical observances, are the fittest forms of faith. The Latin church makes too great claims on the heart and feelings; and as to Protestantism, since it possesses hardly any symbolism or commemorative practices, it hardly counts with Orientals as a religion.

The peasants of Kormakiti, to whose district belong the foothills, with their poor soil and their plantations of fir, assured me that they knew of no ancient remains thereon, but that three quarters of an hour to the S. W. I should find on the shore the ruins of the old town Palaiocastron, which were more completely destroyed than even Lapethos and buried in sand. I might learn more at H. Eirene, another hour and a half South of this. So I rode on there, and was shown in the church a badly carved sandstone column from a grave, with an inscription of Roman date, which was found quite lately, with other ancient but very poor graves, immediately behind the church. So the village itself stands on an ancient site. I was assured of the existence of Palaiocastron on the shore between this and Kormakiti, but was advised not to go there, as I should see only a few old blocks in the drift-sand. Some years ago two Egyptian (?) statues were found there. One of them, a female figure, I saw in a peasant's house. It is quite naked down to a small apron thrown round the hips, the end of which is drawn forward and just covers the middle: the left hand rests on the bosom, the right arm and head are missing. At the back is the squared pilaster usual in Egyptian statues, but there are no hieroglyphs on it. The other, a male statue, is now so walled into a building that one arm only is visible. But are these figures which I have called Egyptian, not rather to be described as Phoenician? It is insisted that no other statues or inscriptions have been found here, but the small amount of observation or interest shown by the villagers lends but little information. I bought here a coin with the temple of Paphos and a Phoenician legend. The town can only have been Kermia.

It took me an hour and a half to ride on to Syrianochori, first over a broad drift of sand, then along the beach between the sea and the so-called *Livadia*, where madder chiefly was grown. I have described these meadows in speaking of Salamis. The river of Morphou, which waters the Western half of the plain, forms here at its mouth marshy tracts, full of reeds and rushes. With these contends the drift sand which the westerly winds, which prevail for the greater part of the year, throw up into this open bight: the peasants by clearing off the sand down to the damp soil below, create their small but very productive gardens. Syrianochori, marked by its name as a former Maronite village, lies half an hour inland: a few small granite columns lie about its fields, and here as throughout Cyprus are linked with stories of hidden treasure. An hour later I reached the large town of Morphou, and slept in the convent.

I cannot leave untold something that happened today because it illustrates so well the better side of oriental manners. At Larnaca I had, as I have already said, borrowed from my host the French broker for my excursion into the interior a black slave as cook and attendant. For it is not only the Turks in Cyprus who own many black slaves, but the authorities are apt to wink at the keeping of such by Franks, and even by well-to-do Greeks. Today as the villagers of Kormakiti were coming from early service a peasant woman fell on my negro's neck, and clasped and kissed him, crying 'My son, my son!' I could hardly trust my eyes until I learned that she was the sister of his master's deceased wife. Yet she was a Christian while Rashid had remained a Muslim, and when I returned later to Larnaca, the whole household, the children particularly, ran with frank joy to meet the negro. Such is slavery in the East, against which our methodists declaim, while in their factories and workrooms they treat Christian children with greater cruelty and want of feeling than orientals do their black slaves, and these poor children cannot like the negros fly to the hills from the savagery of an inhuman master. Much that is blameable in theory is mitigated in practice.

Morphou, one of the largest towns in Cyprus, has 420 houses and over 2000 inhabitants, few of whom are Turks. The beautiful church of the monastery seems to date from Frankish times. Today was the Sunday next before the fast called *apokreos*, and in front of the coffee-house was merry making, music and dancing. I was pleased to see that the Governor of Solea, Levka and Morphou, a handsome young Turk from Nicosia, sat with the revellers, whose dances were none the less lively for his presence. Perhaps he wanted to allay the effect of a report which had been current for some days. The English Consul was just now claiming for one of his nationals a sum of money which this person had lent more than twenty years ago to the District, and this the bishop and leading lay-men disputed, and the common Turks, from misunderstanding or ill will, had founded on this a report that the Sublime Porte was inclined to meet the English claims arising out of the war in Syria by the cession of the island: and this was to give the Turks in the capital and other towns a pretext for a massacre of the Christians. I found as I traveled on that this fear was ripe among the Greeks in many villages, and at Larnaca could not forbear telling the matter to the English Consul, Mr. Niven Kerr. The rumour had reached his ear also, and he traced it to the following circumstances which he knew well being employed at Constantinople at the time in his father's business. In 1840 the Porte, at Rashid Pasha's advice, wished to get a loan from English houses of several millions sterling. The merchants declared themselves ready to find the money if Lord Palmerston would guarantee the integrity of Turkey, and they received a pledge. To this end the Porte offered them the entire customs dues of the Empire: the bankers found these revenues would sufficiently cover the interest, but finally declined the offer because the administration of so many custom-houses along so extended a coast-line would be too costly. Then the Porte which, enamoured as it was of its ideas of reform, was eager for the loan, proposed to give them in pawn the islands of Crete, Cyprus and Lesbos. But now the English government with-drew from the business, fearing that the occupation of these islands in a time of peace might prove a *casus belli* with the other Powers. Since then however, remarked the Consul, the rumour of an approaching occupation of these islands by England crops up from time to time in Turkey. In 1841 particularly we saw that the Cretan insurrection was only put down when it was clear that the insurgents wanted not the protection of England but union with the Hellenic Kingdom. At that moment this last solution lay without the English schemes and the instructions in the hands of their agents. But who knows what lies in the bosom of the future. The difference between the policy of England and that of the German cabinets rests chiefly on this, that the former does its work, and does it boldly, swiftly and firmly, where the latter at most allow themselves to nourish provisional ideas; and while in Germany the titles of Royal and Serene Highness are weighed against one another as so much gold, England sets up or pulls down kings whose realms are a bit big-ger than the possessions of the Princes of Reuss, Schwarzburg or Lippe.

Morphou has no antiquities. Half an hour to the north is the church of H. Sergios, near which Hellenic tombs have been found. Two hours to the N. E. not far from the vil-lage Kyra near the monastery of S. George the Royal there are Hellenic (partly only Frankish) graves, and yet another hour farther north, on the northern slope of the hills of Lapethos, near the little village Phloudi, Greek buildings occur. But these bits of infor-mation from a quite untrustworthy source reached me only the day after I had turned my back on Morphou and its neighbourhood.

Between Morphou and Levka, on the coast on the left bank of the mouth of the Xeropotamos, are the ruins of an ancient city called Palaiochora, which can only be Soli, the later town transplanted by Solon's advice from the heights to the shore: but the governor and others assured me that the remains are even less visible than those of Lapethos or Keryneia, and as I wanted to catch the Post at Larnaca on March 6, I gave up the idea of visiting the town, and turned south west to seek out the old coppermines of Soli among the villages on the N. slopes of Olympos. Olympos (now Troodos) rises on this side quite precipitously from the plain, showing to the North its snow capped head, which this year on account of the long continuance of the rain, and the early warmth, was less thickly covered than usual. In summer the peasants bring the snow to Levcosia and Larnaca. In an hour and three quarters I rode across the plain, through Nikita and Kokkinon Prastion to Elia, outside which village I crossed a dry river bed. Another half hour brought me to Petra, a large village, charmingly situated in a fruitful and well-watered hollow. Two Turks had recently found in the neighbourhood an ancient rock-tomb, containing only a few small glass vessels. The village church is remarkable for its very steep and crooked tiled roof, not unlike our northern roofs. Above Petra on the S. W. lies a group of hills separated from the main range and distinguished for its bright red white and green tints: they run from S. to N. and at the farther end are the ancient mines. The whole district is known as the villages of Solea. I rode round the N. end of the hill through the villages H. Georgios, and then along its west face. I had below me on the right the well tilled river bed of the Xeropotamos, with its many olive trees. It widens as it approaches the sea, and on the left side of its mouth the ruins mentioned above of Palaiochora or Soli are situated. At the S. end of the hill you first see great heaps of slag piled up into mounds, a long row of them stretches black and glittering along the foot of the mountain. On one of them stands the deserted monastery of our Lady of the Slag (Panagia skouriotissa), or in the vulgar speech skourgotissa. Here I dismounted, took a couple of candles out of my baggage, and climbed the slope with the priest of Petra, who had promised to show me the workings. Beyond the black slag came smaller heaps of red slag, and then we were at the entrance of the first workings. We found this however blocked by the half of the roof: this my guide assured me, could only have happened quite lately, probably through an earthquake. Before the entrance I saw a large quantity of broken pots, with very stout round feet, possibly smelting-crucibles, or only the cooking vessels of the old workers. Besides the main galleries, there are many other smaller adits equally blocked, and all on this side of the hill. A few years since a German mineralogist, Herr Kotschy[71], explored the mountains of Cyprus, and will have been able to give more satisfactory descriptions of the mines of the island than I could.

In another quarter of an hour we were at Kateidata where we had our mid-day rest. On a hill opposite on the West side of the river is the village of H. Epiphanios, with some few traces of an ancient site: tradition calls it the seat of a king, but nothing is visible but foundations. This might well have been Aipeia, the capital in pre-Solonian times of the kingdom of Soloi. Farther up the river are these villages of Solea, Lenou, Phlasou, Korakou, Evrychou, Nembria, Galatia, Mount Sinai, Kalliana and last of all, high up on the wild hills, Kakopetria. In the afternoon I started on my return to Larnaca. I rode from Kateidata round the other side of the slag heaps, leaving Petra in the valley below to the left. It took me a long hour to get to the river bed at Elia, and on to the plain again, and less than an hour more to cross a barren hummocky spur of the mountain to Astromerites, where I slept in a shepherd's hut.

---

[71] See the text of Theodor Kotschy in this volume.

March 4. It took me four and a half hours to get to Politikon by Peristerona, Menikon and H. Ioannes, villages lying at an average distance of an hour or a little more from one another. Peristerona has several ruined churches, and other medieval remains. It lies in a wide valley, on a branch of the Morphou river. The ground is hilly and I crossed several branches of the river on my way to H. Ioannes. On my right, or towards the south, I had all day at a distance of some hours the many-peaked mountain of Machairas, after Olympos the highest mountain in Cyprus.

On this side it is well wooded, and on a spur stands a monastery of our Lady (Panagia tou Machaira) one of the oldest and most important in the island. In these mountains, which with their northern spurs form the watershed between the E. & W. halves of the great plain, spring all the chief rivers of the island: the river of Morphou which flows N. W. into the gulf of Soli, the two arms of Pedieus, which fertilize the Mesaoria and fall together near Salamis into the eastern sea, and on the S. side the small streams which water a part of the coastlands between Kition and Limasol. Here must be the Aoos, "the hill of dawn," of the ancients; and as they make the Pedieus and Satrachos rise in the Aoos, and the Pedieus has but with little change kept its name to the present day, it follows that the stream next in importance, the Dali river, must be the Satrachos. From H. Ioannes I traveled for an hour and a half over sandy hills torn and denuded by the action of water, with a view to the left of the peaks of the northern range, then the path drops suddenly into the broad and fertile valley of the Pedieus. On its southern side, where the river leaves the hills, the little village Politiko stands on rising ground, above it is the Monastery of H. Heracleidios, on the other side that of H. Mnason. Politico, as witness the legend of H. Heracleidios, the firmly rooted tradition preserved among the villagers, and the name itself πόλις, stands on the ruins of the ancient city of Tamasos. As a matter of fact the ruins are so insignificant that even an observant traveler could traverse them, and take them to be nothing more than medieval rubbish-heaps. But I find irrefragable evidence in the ancient tombs carved out of the rock on the south side of the village. Some of them have been opened by chance, and disclosed only small and poor vases. When I had visited these few remains of old Tamasus, and sought in vain in the village for inscriptions, I turned to the monastery of H. Heracleidios some few hundred paces away. Here in a plain ancient sarcophagus, in a chapel adjoining the church, lies the Saint: You are shown the hole below in which the Apostles found him. On his left rests his sister Heracleidiana, on his right H. Theodoros, H. Mnason, H. Macedonios and others of his disciples. I wrote down this legendary lore as the abbot told it to me, without vouching for it. But pray do not think that the resting place of so many saints has anything imposing about it, such as you would find if it were of the Latin rite. It is all so plain and shabby, so poor and dirty as one can well imagine.

Tamasos was famous for its copper: the bare hills west of the village, behind the monastery of H. Mnason, have still the same yellow and reddish tint as the slag-heap of Kateidata. Yet I was assured that in the immediate neighbourhood neither workings nor slag are to be found, though such exist at Kepedes, a village at two hours distance in the mountains, where still ochre is extracted.

The main stream of the Pedieus breaks through a narrow gorge directly to the South-East of Tamasus. On its right bank ten minutes away lies Pera, and a quarter of an hour farther on Episcopion. These villages look old; they may have sprung up when Tamasos was still a city and bishop's see. It was only then that Pera could have borne the name of 'the village over there,' which corresponds to its position, and then too the bishop may have had a summer residence in the second village, Episcopion. It was between the two that in 1836, while digging for water in the dry river bed, that the peasants found a bronze statue of life size, another account makes it somewhat larger, and perfectly preserved. I asked the villagers all I could about this treasure, without being able to frame from their confused recollection and vague description an intelligible notion. The main traits were these: the head was shaved, this might describe a flat and close arrangement of the hair, as in the Apollo of Thera, which would remind orientals of their own custom of shaving the head, but might point also to the close-fitting headdress, common to the Egyptians and the figurines of Idalion: but it had curl or plats on the temples and behind the ears; the figure was entirely naked, the privities bare, but it had something tied round the hips, which they likened to their own cartouche-box, the *palaskais* or small silver case which Eastern men wear on a strap round their loins and let hang on their back. The left foot was a little advanced, the arms, as well as I could understand, hanging along the sides. The head, arms and legs were cast in separate pieces and soldered to the trunk, but as the statue was dragged over the gravel of the river bed they came easily apart.

And what became of this incomparable find? Partly from ignorance, partly from fear of the Turks, who when they hear of a discovery always dream of a treasure, and squeeze the unhappy finders, the peasants hacked the statue to bits and sold it gradually as old copper, about 80 okes of it, at five piastres the oke, making scarcely 40 *gulden*. The head only was preserved, and came into the hands of a M. Vondiziano at Larnaca, who sold it for 1800 piastres to M. Borrell of Smyrna. It is probably now in England, and would decide the question whether the statue were Egyptian Phoenician or Greek.

I hung about these villages for the rest of the day in hopes of lighting on a hand or foot of this statue, but in vain. All I could secure was a pygmy of bronze as long as a finger in the form of the Egyptian Phthah: with a little ring in the head, as though it had served as pendant to a lamp or other household utensil. I spent the night in a convent-farm (a metochi) as the guest of a priest, who kept a negro to do his field work.

The next morning, March 5, I rode from Pera over broken sandy hills and some small watercourses through a treeless tract, in three hours along the valley of the Satrachos, which the road strikes near the pretty and well wooded village *Nesos*, half an hour from Idalion. If the Satrachos gave its name to any town it must have stood higher up the stream, but I could hear of no ruins.

In Dali the villagers, stirred by my former visit, had dug again on the northern slope of the western acropolis, and found a number of the same kind of statuettes, of which I picked out the best. With them were fragments of terra cotta figures of life size. Perhaps on this spot had stood the temple of Aphrodite. In the afternoon I wended my way with my booty along the road already known to me back to Larnaca.

# VI

**Journey to Amathus and Kition. Aqueduct at Arpera. Mazoto. The Tetios. Pentakomon. Search for treasure. Amathus. Large stone vase. Old graves. Lemessos, commerce and industry. Kurias. Colossi. The Lycos. Episcopi. Graves and ruins at Kurion. Stadium. Temple of Apollo Hylates. Pissuri. Lacco Franco. Kuklia. Temple of Aphrodite. Phoenician grave and inscription.**

*March 5–12, 1845.*

On March 6 the Austrian steamer returned from Beirut (Berytos) bringing the news that owing to the return of the Muslim pilgrims from Mecca, Syria lay under suspicion of plague, and the vessel was in quarantine. I was cut off thus, unless some direct opportunity offered itself, from Rhodes and Smyrna as well. So I rested a day or two at Larnaca, and started on March 8 on a fresh excursion to Amathus and other towns on the South coast.

The road ran on the northern edge of the Salt-lake; the country is bare and scantily cultivated. In an hour I passed some arches of the aqueduct, and then Arpera, the garden with the springs from which a hundred years ago a banished Pasha brought the water at his own cost to Larnaca. The Phoenician inscriptions seen by Pococke must then, as I learned too late after my departure from Cyprus, have been built into the aqueduct. Possibly one or the other of them were still to be found about the place. At Arpera, formerly a convent-farm, I crossed the first small stream which rises at the foot of M. S. Croce and falls into the sea Westwards of Kiti. One has still a two hours' ride over a bare but cultivated plain to Mazotos, a village of fifty houses lying also on a stream. Aoos or Machairas as seen from here has three well marked peaks, running from S. W. to N. E.

Beyond Mazoto the plain is rather more fruitful and prettier. Half an hour further on the road are some traces of an ancient town: some foundations, scattered blocks of squared stone, a stump of a column and potsherds. Perhaps this was Strabo's Palaia? An hour later the track approaches the shore which it follows at no great distance, crosses several small brooks which rise in the foothills of Aoos, and leaves Maroni on the right. Four hours from Mazotos I reached the mouth of the Basilopotamos, perhaps the ancient Tetios, which flows in a wide bed from the mountains above Levkara.

The direct road to Amathus follows the shore, but half an hour in land up the bed of the stream lies the little village Marin. Although already on topographical and philological grounds convinced that this name, with its changed accent, could not represent the old Marion which one must seek on the N. W. coast, I still expected, since Lusignan and Mariti take the place to be Marion, at least to find some traces of antiquity, and struck aside to see it. But this little Turkish village has not the slightest claim to be the site of an ancient town, so I rode straight on, and in a little more than an hour, crossing broken copper-bearing hills clothed with brushwood and some solitary firtrees, and deep gullies to Pentacomo, a village of some five and twenty houses inhabited by Greeks and Turks. As its name shows it was once of greater importance. Here I stayed the night.

Although the impression that the search made by European travelers for ruins, inscriptions and other antiquities is directed merely to the discovery of hidden treasure, is one spread more or less among the peoples of the whole East, yet I have never found this illusion so general, so deeply rooted, and so offensive as in Cyprus. The reasons are of many kinds. It appears that more than once quite considerable sums of money have been found buried in Cyprus, and one can well understand that in the various sudden catastrophes which the island has suffered in ancient times, in the middle ages, and again at the Turkish conquest, treasures may have been now and then buried; it appears to be a fact only a few years since persons came from Italy, relying on the evidence of old family papers, and searched in Levcosia for treasures alleged to have been buried there in safe places. It is no less a fact that among some of the Consular Agents and other Europeans residing here exist the most exaggerated ideas of the treasures to be found here, and that some of these gentlemen have now and then gone out with divining rods in search of them. The worst is that one such agent, a native of Corsica living at Lemesos, who is constantly on the hunt for inscriptions in the parts about Amathus and Paphos, breaks up most of them—unluckily he understands nothing of their meaning—as he confides to his friends, under the superstitious illusion (I know examples of the same in Greece) that in the stones themselves gold is hidden. When persons higher placed and better educated than themselves thus supply food for their superstition one need not be surprised that this peasant-folk, whose fancy is lightly roused, and always inclined to the marvellous, invents the most ludicrous tales, spreads them far and wide, and believes them eagerly. Thus a man here related with great gravity that a villager had seen two Franks land at Amathus, go to an old stone and read from a book, whereon the earth opened before them. The man went down with them, and, lo, all below was full of gold! When he touches it it burned him, only the Franks took of the gold and went away. Then the hole shut of its own accord, and never afterwards could the Greek find the spot. To stories like this those present give full credence, without the least hesitation or doubt. If one asks seriously if the narrator had seen the occurrence himself, or had heard it from an eyewitness, he always confesses naively that he cannot name anyone, and that he got the story at third or fourth hand only. But such critical considerations will in no way shake his belief. So I, the negro Rashid, and the muleteer throughout our journeys in Cyprus had to be content with the reputation of treasure seekers and once when lending myself to the part, I pointed in joke to the heavy cases which carried our provisions, and said they were already full of treasure, a peasant-woman clasped her hands with an expression of envious wonder.

In Cypriot villages such houses as are built of mud bricks have generally flat roofs of *stamped* earth but to these, more wisely than in Greece, the builders for the most part give a slope to allow the rain to run off. Houses of a bigger scale have a blunt gable, and the roof slopes off towards either side. In the evening when I tried to relieve the perplexity of my negro by suggesting that he cook a pilau with ham, he laughed quietly and said. "But then, Sir, I shall not be able to eat of it." On March 10 I rode on from Pentacomo over the broken hills, getting a beautiful view of the higher summits of Aoos which lay further inland. Here too in ancient days were mines, and for the sake of these the Phoenicians founded Amathus close by. I soon returned to the ordinary road from Kition to Limassol, and then in an hour and a half to the shore: another half hour, and one reaches Amathus, (old Limassol). The ruins of the ancient city occupy an isolated hill, which falls precipitously towards the north, and slopes southwards to the shore, besides another low hill to the East. Where the ruins begin stands the large dilapidated church of H. Tychon, with some round grave-stones with inscriptions. Here I found a couple of shepherds, and leaving our mounts on the beach climbed under their guidance the hilly site. Quite at the top of the eastern side of the castle-hill, on a steep ledge of rock which crowns it as with a wall, is a quadrangular depression hewn out and bearing the inscription: Λούκιος Οὐιτέλλιος Καλλίνικος τὴν ἀνάβασιν ταύτην σὺν τῇ ἁψίδι ἐκ τοῦ ἰδίου κατεσκεύασεν, but of the buildings to which it refers I saw never a trace.

At the back of the Acropolis the shepherds led me to the famous colossal vase, which is half buried in the soil, half covered with the bushes growing about it. The depth inside is m. 1.60, the inner diameter of the mouth m. 2. The edge of the mouth is 0.40 broad, and from the edge to the handle 0.62.

From the outer circumference of the body project four massive handles or ears, each adorned with a bull *passant*. Each of these ears is m. 0.20 thick, the edge is m. 0.9

broad. The inner breadth of the back-ground is 0.48, height 0.88. Each bull is 0.28 long and 0.21 high. The ears run down to two *palmettes* reversed; the breadth of each of these is 0.25, the length 0.31. On the west side of this giant vase lie in the bushes the fragments of another like it: but one can find no traces of a temple or other large building. Whether the temple of Aphrodite, or some other shrine stood here could only be determined by examination. But I entertain no doubt that in the two huge vases we must recognise Phoenician work. Not only was Amathus from the beginning a Phoenician city, and in the earlier times a conspicuous one, but we have no example of similar objects in purely Greek temples. On the other hand, as Mueller has recorded, there were vessels of many forms in the Temple at Jerusalem, among them the brazen sea borne by twelve oxen. Sidonian *crateres* are mentioned by Homer, who notes the goblet of Nestor, which had four ears or handles on which were depicted golden doves, as bulls here. Nor would one question the use by the artistic Phoenicians of the *palmettes*, of which we find so many examples in Assyrian work. They must have stood quite aloof, taking no part in the great artistic movement which spread from the Nile and the Tigris to the Italian peninsula, learning nothing, imitating nothing—I cannot lend myself to the idea.

The upper surface of the hill, and where it slopes on the south to the sea, is strewn with broken stones. On the slope are still some remains of a medieval circle of wall. I found on the soil of ancient Amathus nothing but sherds of red pottery, and lots of glass, but not one fragment of marble, not reckoning the lid of a sarcophagus behind the church of H. Tychon, and a square pedestal of blue-black marble with an honorific inscription of Ptolemaean date. Generally, white marble is very scarce in Cyprus, partly because there are no rich veins of it in the Island, partly because such blocks as were imported were used up again in the middle ages or under the Turks for coats of arms, inscriptions and the like.

From the beach by Amathus I rode for another half hour up the dry bed of a torrent to the village behind the old town. On the road I found two or three illegible grave stones. The village has only twenty houses inhabited partly by Greeks, partly by Turks. Of the foundations of a temple and the remains of Ionic architecture, which Hammer-Purgstall thinks he saw here, I could find or hear nothing.[72] But I lighted on an old man who still remembered the Spaniard Ali Bey; the learned Turkish traveler (*mylordos tourkos*) as he called him. After a short halt I made my way back to Amathus, and then to Limasol. Between the village and the back of the old town I notice a row of pillar-bases, probably those of an aqueduct which brought water to Amathus from the higher hills which lie inland. Then I rode through the old town to some grottos which had been pointed out to me under an overhanging rock on the west. One of them is a small sepulchral chamber; in the others steps lead deeper down, but the entrance is blocked so that oxen may not fall in. The rock is of soft sandstone, all the soil in fact round Amathus is sandy so that the Greeks conceived the notion of deriving the name of this Phoenician town from their word *amathoeis*.

As I rode on towards Limassol I soon came on other traces, beyond Amathus, of ancient graves. Then the road runs westward through brushwood along the sandy beach: on the right stretches a dreary waste up to the foot of the mountains. In two hours I reached Limasol, where I lodged with M. Ianco Jasonides.

Lemesos, which the Italians call Limasol, is a town of 2500 souls, the second in commercial importance in the island. It stepped into the place of Amathus (the ruins still

---

[72] See the text of Joseph von Hammer-Purgstall in this volume.

bear the name of old Limasol) but the name seems to have come down from antiquity. It is the chief point of export for Cyprus wine, which is made on the southern slopes of Aoos and Olympos. Other products are exported as well, most of which go to Egypt. In the roadstead, which is protected against the South-East, lay a dozen vessels. A battery commands the port; in the town, which is built in a straggling, village fashion, is a small fort; from the platform you get a wide view. No ancient remains, a few grave stones lie scattered and smashed in the dry bed of the torrent which crosses the town, they may have been brought here from other sites. The chief church stands in the open on the land side of the town. The bay of Limasol is now so full of sand and so shallow that it serves as a salt-pan.

March 11. I left Limasol early, and rode in an hour and a half across the plain to Colossi, on my left I had the long flat peninsula Curias, which runs out for some six to nine miles. It is now called Akrotiri, by seafolk Capo delle Gatte. Kolossi, the main building, is a quadrangular tower, of great size and strength, ascribed to the Templars during their short reign, at any rate dating from the early middle ages. The ground floor still serves as a grain store. At one corner is a winding staircase. The first floor consists of two large vaulted halls, with fireplaces, and the tower ends in a flat roof, commanding a wide view. I saw from this point two convents on the peninsula, H. Georgios and H. Nicolaos (where Hammer says he saw ancient columns), and the village of Akroteri. In the tower are collected several shields of knights and kings, and there are more on the adjoining aqueduct. Nothing is known of the origin of the name Colossi; possibly a Colossus once stood somewhere near, the memory whereof is preserved in the name Colossi or Colossion. This important tract of excellent land, 10,000 scalas with a copious water supply, is granted by the Porte to a Greek, Haji Zacharias of Limasol, for 25,000 piastres (1666 Prussian thaler) cash, and 7500 piastres (500 thaler) yearly.

Another half hour and we reach the big village Episcopi. On the way I crossed a broad river-bed, which carried still a good deal of water, although the larger part was carried off by channels on either side, to irrigate the fields of Colossi and Episcopi. The stream rises in the gorge which divides Aoos from Olympos, and seems to be the ancient Lycos. Three hundred years ago, in the days of the Lusignans, Episcopi reckoned a thousand hearths; now it has about fifty Greek and rather more Turkish houses, and belongs almost in its entirety to the Mufti Efendi of Nicosia, who has much other property besides. I could hear nothing here of the tradition that, as at Lapethos and in most of the tracts on the coast, sugar cane was planted and sugar made by the Venetians: at any rate the sugar cane is no longer to be found here. After the colonisation of Madeira, which obtained vine-plants from Cyprus, and after the discovery of the New World the cultivation of sugar cane disappeared from Cyprus, and gave way to that of cotton, until under a wretched Turkish government as the population decreased this source of profit decreased also.

I made no long halt this time in Episcopi, but hurried back to Courion. The road crossed the shoulder of a hill on the edge of which the last heavy rain had laid open the entrance of an ancient tomb, hewn out of the soft rock, with steps leading down to it. But the floor within was covered with mud, and I found only a few sherds of large vessels with painting of a Phoenician type, in size and decoration just like those of Thera, and a few fragments of glass. Below this hill, where a small level tract opens on the sea, is the chapel of H. Hermogenes, with some old tomb stones, and above it to the West is the rocky height on which Courion stood.

The hill, composed of a whitish schistose sandstone falls, steeply to the south west, with two projecting walls, between which the path climbs among broken sarcophagi. On the top immediately to the right is the cavea of a small theatre which is built against the hill, with its opening to the sea: the projecting left wing is built of large blocks of sandstone much weatherworn. The whole surface of this rocky hill, the southwest side of which hangs directly over the sea, is strewn with ruins, but with the exception of the theatre, they are all smashed and weather worn beyond recognition: only at the north end, towards the land, are some small columns of granite, two to two and a half feet in diameter: also some spirally grooved pillars of blue marble. Close by is an open tomb-chamber.

This isolated hill is connected on the N. W. by a kind of isthmus, this too heaped with ruins, with a larger hilly tract which carries on the coast for a long stretch westwards. Only ten minutes from the town to the right of the road, is a stadion, well preserved throughout its length of about 222 metres: the open end faces west, the semicircle is on the east; the entrance is 2.22 m. broad. It is built entirely of sandstone blocks, resting on the surface of the plain, but not much of its height remains visible. The villagers of the neighbourhood call it the *hippodrome,* T. *at-meidan*, It. *carriera*, so preserving an idea of its original use.

A quarter of an hour hence I passed a small gully, and in another five minutes came to big heaps of ruins, to the right of the road at the back of the hill. They call these *ston Apellan* or *ston Apollo.* I found here plain drums of pillars, 0.50 to 0.70 m. in diameter, and Doric capitals with two very broad and flat bands, and a little higher the remains of a large building, with inscriptions on bases of the Ptolemaean era. The great ruins of the temple proper lie somewhat more to the west. On its southern side is a large cistern, underground. On the same side one can trace for some distance the foundations of the walls of the temple-court. These foundations are preserved on the north side also: the whole *peribolos* seems to have included besides the main temple four or five other smaller buildings. I came upon several fragments of round and square bases, but no more inscriptions. Nor was a single bit of sculpture to be found. There can be no doubt that we have here the ruins of the temple of Apollo Hylates. That it was a sanctuary of Apollo is shown by the tradition, which here, as in Naxos, and other spots in the Greek islands, has preserved the name of the deity. Hyla, with the temple of Apollo lay near Courion, not east of Colossi but west, exactly as Strabo says.

From Hyla I rode for another four hours over broken hills, on which wild cypresses were growing, junipers, wild olives, carobs, and here and there grafted olives. The edge of the hill, of a whitish sandstone, makes a steep slope down to the sea, forming the *Capo Bianco* of the charts. Landwards small deep valleys cut across the higher ground. About here we must look for the Treta and Boos-oura of Strabo. At Avdimou it was dark, and clouds hid the moon, but the air was as of spring, and the frogs croaked lustily. It was late and dark when I reached Pissouri, high in the hills, and after much fruitless knocking found a refuge in the priest's house. In the circumstances my lodging was comfortable enough, and the old priest and his wife very talkative. He told me that before the revolution he had helped a stranger at Paphos to bring down to the shore a square block of stone with inscriptions on three sides, but the ship that was to take it did not arrive, and when five years later they looked for it again, the stone could not be found; either it was smashed up, or buried in the sand. As we talked the name Afrodite occurred often, the priest said eagerly, "now they do not call her Aphroditissa, they call her now Chrysopolitissa." So their ideas get confused, and Aphrodite is but a title of the Blessed Virgin, who is called in Paphos Chrysopolitissa.

The raids of the Maltese live still in their memories. The priest's wife told me that she had heard from an aunt who lived over a hundred and twenty years, how the vessels of Maltese pirates had often fallen on their village by night, and cleared it of every thing portable. The women flew to the mountains, of the men of both sides several were left dead on the field. But she added, we hear that now Malta is a rich commercial port, and they don't do such things any more.

March 12. A fine fresh morning showed at what a height we were. Before we parted I had another chat with my hosts, whose confidence I had won. They were concerned about the rumours afloat concerning the hostile views of the Turks. In Levcosia twenty Turks tried to force their way into a church to rob it, and at Calavassos the Turks had threatened to fall on the Greeks. Here as in other places, the excuse is that they will not allow the Christians, who have no bells, to strike with hammers on a bar of iron, called a semantron, to call the faithful to church. As I knew what little weight was to be attached to the same sort of rumours in Rhodes and Asia Minor I tried as far as possible to comfort the good old priest.

The hills on which Pissouri stands are composed of a heavy white clay soil. The road wanders on up hill and down dale, leaving Alectora on the right. In an hour and a quarter I reached a place called the Frank's well, a church and spring, with some ruined houses in a valley. Here begins a long stretch of wild wood, olives, of which these may be 30,000, and some carobs. Half an hour later, on a hill, from which one sees the plain of Paphos, are some pillars and other remains of antiquity. Then the road turns down to the shore, to the mouth of the river which comes from the back of old Paphos, perhaps the Bocaros. With intense interest and like expectation I approached the famous temple of the goddess. The path swerves to the right up the low hills and brings one in a quarter of an hour to Kouklia (Palai-Paphos). But the site on which Phoenicians once established the throne of the Paphian goddess is now of sad aspect, a bare hill-shoulder with a few ruins, a medieval tower and a wretched village. Near the parish church are a few bases of statues, but walled in so that their possible inscriptions are illegible.

The importance of the ruins of the supposed shrine of the Phoenician Aphrodite has been greatly overrated by earlier travelers: from their actual condition few conclusions can be drawn. All attempts to reconstruct the plan of the temple by comparison with the well known Cypriot coins on which it is figured seem to me to rest on no solid ground. The blocks which compose the wall which is assumed to be the back-wall of the *cella* are of gigantic size, each of them is m. 2.11 high, 4.80 long and cm. 78 thick, of soft sandstone somewhat blackened on the exposed side: on the inner surface they have notches and holes where the tools have gripped them as they were set in position; one sees just the same thing in the Sicilian temples. Hammer has a wonderful notion that these openings were a kind of sound-holes whence the oracles were delivered. But at the S.W. corner only are found in more or less good preservation five or six such blocks, the remaining sides of the quadrangle are destroyed to the very foundations. Nothing more is left of the materials of the temple, all has been dragged away and used over again. On the north side of the shrine are the ruins of a small chapel of H. Paraskeve, and here is the coarse Byzantine mosaic. In the village are some shafts and capitals of Doric columns, of no great size, of yellowish limestone.

The hills about Palai-Paphos, especially on the East side are full of old graves, but most of them had been opened and plundered in the Frankish and Venetian eras, if not earlier. While my mules were eating their food I got taken to the so-called 'Queen's cave' which is a quarter of an hour from the village across a deep river bed under a rocky ridge. The entrance was built of squared blocks, and topped with large stone beams; it is now pretty nearly broken-up. Beyond is a chamber, m. 4 broad by 6 long, out of which on either side two smaller tombs open: on the same line is a second similar chamber, and again behind follows a third smaller room m. 3 each way. One of the passages was closed in ancient times by a large slab or door of sandstone, which now leans against the wall. Upon it is an inscription in large plain characters of many lines, which Hammer saw and copied. On the edge of the table land can be seen in several places graves hewn in the rock, and no doubt there are still other undisturbed tombs.

# VII
**Road to new Paphos. Seacoast, and plain. Hieros Kepos. Nea-Paphos, ruins and harbour. Ktema. Palaiocastron. Phoenician graves near Paphos. Acamas. Road to Kuklia. Enkleistron. Return to Kurion. Avdemou. Grave at Kantou. Statistics. Return to Larnaca.**

*March 12–18, 1845.*

In the afternoon I left Palai-Paphos and rode westwards towards Paphos. As I was leaving I met the archimandrite Theseus, a born Cypriot, who had lived long in Europe. He invited me warmly to visit him on my return at a place not far from Kouklia. From the foot of the hill on which Kouklia stands the plain stretches up nine to twelve miles towards Paphos and Ktema, with a breadth of four to six miles. On the left is the sea, on the right a rocky ridge, running out from Olympos to the promontory of Acamas crossed by sundry streams. In spite of the fertility of the soil cultivation is very deficient. I did not touch the shore, and can give no particular account of the villages and havens along it. Mandrika, with a church of H. Avgona lay on the left, Timi to the right at the foot of the hill. I passed through Aschelia and Coloni, and reached Hieros Kepos towards evening. Here lives a Greek, an English subject, to whom Admiral Smith was godfather, whence his remarkable name of Haji Smith! He was not at home, and I lodged with the priest.

During some days a south wind was blowing, and the heat was great: at midday and in the fall sunshine even oppressive. On February 21, the day of the earthquake, three strong shocks were felt here: this part of the island as far as Limasol is peculiarly exposed to earth-tremors.

The persistence of the old name Hierokepis as Hieros Kepos led me to expect antiquities, and the next day I searched the little village eagerly. But beyond a few fragments of pillars there was nothing worthy of notice. Below the church issues a copious spring from a channel hewn in the rock. The place may be taken to be the site of Hierokepis, following Strabo, whose account of Cyprus is so accurate that he must have seen the spot himself, or used some good authority.

From here to Paphos the road starts on a rocky tract, then falls again into the plain. Just before reaching Paphos it leaves on the right a bare quite low stretch of rock, with old quarries and graves hewn out of the hill.

Paphos, called also new Paphos to distinguish it from the earlier foundation, though the name was *even before this applied to the harbour*, whence the festal train set out on its march to the temple of Aphrodite, is a deserted ugly, largely ruined place with few inhabitants. For some hours I clambered grudgingly about these shabby ruins of medieval and later houses, to little or no profit. The ruins of the church of S. George contain a well preserved tombstone of a Chevalier de Charpigny, who stands in armour over his shield (two carps) round the stone is inscribed in Gothic letters *D. Rocardas de Charpignie miles, pa[t]er Petri P[ap]hen Episcopi cujus anim[a] requiescat in pace. Am[en].*

The site of the ancient temple of Aphrodite appears to be marked by the church of the Panagia Chrysopolitissa. Here two smooth columns of granite project from the soil, a metre in diameter, and three metres apart (from centre to centre 4 m.) also on the ground a fragment of a large badly carved Ionic capital of white marble. On account of the frequent earthquakes which visited old and new Paphos in ancient times one can only expect to find remains of temples restored by the Roman Emperors. Only a few interesting Greek inscriptions rewarded my toil.

Under the ruins of Paphos are many remains of fine Frankish churches. But in the days of the Lusignans the place was already in its decline and almost abandoned. On the northern edge of the town is a large cave in the rock, now a chapel of H. Solomone. The ancient harbour still remains, it is formed by two moles which run out at right angles towards one another: but the inflow of fresh water has choked it with mud, or filled it with reeds, making the place unhealthy. Intelligent and assiduous toil might clean the basin again. On the western mole stands a ruinous fort, the Cassaba. On the west and north side of the harbour are great heaps of debris, and some rock-tombs.

I rode northwards across the plain to Ktema, so they call a large village an hour from Paphos, set in the plain on the steep edge of a low hill. Here in the middle ages was the seat of the Bishop, and civil authorities. I passed on my way some small rock-tombs in the hill side. I had no introductions for Ktema, and took up my quarters in a cafe. The local archaeologist or cicerone soon found me out—a poor Turk, Deli Haji Samur, who spoke Greek fluently. He offers himself to any traveler who may stray here as a guide to Paphos and its neighbourhood. I saw first under his guidance what little there was worthy of notice in this big village, which runs for a good way along the rocky ridge, and has three mosques and a bath. In the Turkish graveyard he showed me the tombstone of a Frankish lady of the middle ages with an inscription in Gothic letters "Ici git dame Alis [fig]lie de Sire Says le Jenoeis que fu feme de Sire Nicolose Saoneis la quele arme vive in Christ l'an del incarnacion de nostre seigneur Ihu Crist MCCLXXIX a.XX Jors de Decembre. Pat . . . er. The rest was illegible.

In the afternoon I went with Haji Samur to the so called Palaiocastron. So they call a flat ridge of rock of considerable extent in the plain a little to the west of the ordinary road to New Paphos, pierced throughout with holes for graves. Their occurrence in a district distinctly Phoenician, the peculiarity of their plan, which departs widely from that of Greek work of the same class, and their close affinity with sepulchral monuments which are admittedly Phoenician, or at least Semitic (Hebrew) stamps them as Phoenician monuments. They have provoked the wonder of earlier travelers. Pococke, and with more marked naiveté Ali bey, took them for dwellings: Hammer recognized them to be Phoenician graves. The common feature in their plan is an open quadrangular court, surrounded with columns or pillars to a corner of which leads a passage hewn out of the rock, and also unroofed, resembling the unroofed halls with pillars round them of the Egyptian temples and palaces, and the *impluvia* of Roman dwellings. Behind the columns or pillars of the peristyle are the entrances to the tombs. This is the general plan, and herein consists the remarkable likeness to the tombs at Jerusalem or in North Africa. But most of these have suffered sorely from the fact that for more than a thousand years the herdsmen in heat or bad weather have gathered their cattle within these pillared halls, pitched their tents and lighted their fires there. One of the largest tombs forms an open court, on three sides are well wrought Doric columns with their entablature and frieze, while on the entrance side only square pillars: above the frieze the rock is cut out, so that here was superimposed an attic story or coping: possibly this recess was crowned with grave stones, as in the rock-tombs at Lindos in Rhodes. Most likely however the whole was roofed with huge slabs of stone. The diameter of the columns under the capitals is quite a foot, the interspace from centre to centre about four feet. Out of the pillared hall which surrounds the court on three sides and half of the fourth, open the entrances into the grave chambers, which are of different sizes and capacities. One door is well preserved, the section of its frame is as in Etruria of an Egyptian style. One of the passages extends in different branches well under the rock, the rest are mostly ruined, or filled with big heaps of sheep and goats' dung. Above one of the tomb niches a stout white fragment clings still to the wall with incised ornaments representing a door, like those mentioned above.

Close by is a second similar tomb, with the colonnade of Doric pillars well preserved on all three sides of the court. The entrance is at the S. W. corner, and on the west side are squared pillars. The plinth of the capital of the columns is of m. 0.58. The architrave 0.33, the frieze 0.37 high, the triglyphs 0.23, the metopes 0.37 broad. The depth of the peristyle, to the back wall in which are the entrances, measures m. 2.10. But the floor of the court is all covered with manure and earth, and the columns show only 3½ to 4 feet above the rubbish; the entrances to the tomb-chambers also are all but blocked. A third chamber of similar style but larger is worth special notice—there are several others—it has four Doric columns, (their shafts are broken) on each side, and on the east a covered passage, hewn into the form of a vault. The question may present itself, whether possibly these courts which are now open were originally covered with stone-slabs? whether the notch above the frieze does not point thereto? Otherwise could not the builders, in place of the covered court with its passages, (the roof of which in one case at least is preserved) have with less trouble have hewn out a facade in the rocks, and made their tombs behind it? That the Phoenicians handled huge masses of stone we shall see in the tombs at Kition; the monolithic chambers in Lycia show something of the same kind. And Lycia by position and kinship was in touch with Cyprus. I had unfortunately to content myself with no very strict survey of the chambers. Samur and my negro could help me but little, and in the passages which still remained open I found no inscriptions.

We returned in the twilight to Ktema. In the evening many Greeks and Turks of the village assembled in the café, and I gathered from them some information about the N. W. part of the island. Five hours to the N. W. of Paphos lies an island, visible from here, called Nesi on which is a round cistern-like building half under ground. On the shore opposite it are the ruins of a town which they call Palaia chora, with a church of S. George. But from the description I fancy there are medieval remains. The furthest point to the N. W. is the peninsula Acamas, which preserves its ancient name: there is plenty of wood, wild cypress, firs, oaks and lentisc and many springs: *stories* of wild asses and wild cattle, but no villages at all. On the road to Acama, three hours north of Ktema is a village, Baia with medieval ruins.

The next morning, March 14, we had again very soft warm weather. I wanted to visit some places behind Palaipaphos, concerning which my expectations had been roused, and took exactly the same road through Hieros Kepos (which they call sometimes Hierokepounta) Coloni, Aschelia, and Timi. Then before reaching Kouklia crossed the stream and turned to the left between the hills. I crossed another deep river bed an hour later on which the village Nikouklia stands in charming surroundings. Here is a quite deserted Metochi or Convent-farm belonging to Mount Sinai, and 8 to 9000 scalas of land, much water, two mills with sufficient olive and mulberry trees (350 of the latter) which the archimandrite Theseus, who in earlier years lived for a long while in Marseille, rents for three years at the ridiculous rate of 1500 piastres (100 Prussian thaler) a year. It is true he has to make shift with a wretched hut, which hardly deserves the name of a house.

I had heard in Palaipaphos of a grotto called Enkleistron in this neighbourhood, which was supposed to be of ancient date, and towards this in the afternoon we took our way. For half an hour we rode up the pretty river bed, under planes, willows and alders to the little village Susiu. Then we struck to the right over the high steep bank, and through a thicket of wild olive and carob trees to a ruined church. All round in the underwood are the remains of a village or convent of Frankish date. On the rocky wall which closes this valley on the East is a small grotto hewn in the soft stone, and adorned with the remains of Christian paintings of no very early style. This is the Enkleistron. The name is repeated in the convent H. Enkleistra six hours distant in the Olympos mountain.

A full hour N. E. of Palaipaphos, *stais palaiomandrais*, there should be ruins and inscriptions. Such was the information given me by a Turkish treasure-seeker, but it was unconvincing, and as I had been so often deceived in Cyprus I did not feel bound to visit the spot.

In the evening I dined with the Archimandrite in the open porch, carried on a few pillars, of his modest little house. The air was mild and fragrant, the frogs croaked merrily in the valley, and the francolin's shrill call was heard from far. Fruit trees of all kinds were in bloom: planes, willows, figtrees and pomegranates swelling with buds. The river has still plenty of water, though the rain has been scanty, and contains eels and big crayfish.

March 15, I rode hence over the hills to Kouklia, and after a short halt along the road by which I came back to Episcopi. In the wild olive grove I found on the road between the top of the hill and the Lakkos tou Frankou a limestone column, about two feet in diameter, with a Greek inscription of more than forty lines, very illegible, for the greater part of it lay covered up, and I and my attendants could not turn the stone over. I could here and there guess at, rather than read, some few words. The column seems to have been originally a Roman milestone, like others which have been found in other parts of the island. [A. A. Sakellarios, *Kypriaka*, 1.75.] Pisouri, where I had slept on my former journey, I left this time on its hill, and took the direct road to Avdemou. A Turkish peasant joined me on the way, who declaimed bitterly about the oppression exercised by his government, they leave neither Turks or Greeks unworried, every peasant, even the poorest, pays at least 800 piastres. 'Have you noticed the deserted villages,' he asked me, 'there used to live hundreds of men: where are they now?' At Avdemou, in the lower village, I found a ruined church of Frankish times, these were the only remains to be seen. Between Hyle and Courion the twilight overtook me, preventing my measuring the *Stadion*, and it was dark when I reached Episcopi.

March 16 was Sunday. A fine morning gave me a delightful view over the sea, the plain, the peninsula of Curias with its salt-lake, and the tower of Colosse. After church I went again with old Haji Chrysostomos to the foot of the hill on which Kourion was built, and crept into several rock-tombs, without finding any inscriptions. One gets nothing out of these graves but vases of the commoner kind, especially large pithoi, and small glass vessels. Meanwhile I had engaged some labourers to clear out the rubbish from the ruined church of S. George, where there are some Doric capitals of lime-stone, and in the floor of which one ought to find an inscription, but it was all in vain.

Then I mounted my mule and rode up the river bed for half an hour to the little village Kantou. Beyond it, in the bed of the Lycos, is a kind of weir or dam, of Frankish date, which divides the water into two equal parts; one goes in a channel to Colosse, the other to Episcopi. At Kantou I rested in the house of a peasant, who—a thing not common among Turks of the lower orders— was living with two wives. Some years ago, he had taken a second, a widow who brought with her a small property. She lived in a house apart, but came to that of her husband, out of curiosity to see the Frankish visitor. This villager had found some years back in the open field behind his dwelling a grave in stiff clay soil in which were several large *pithoi*, like those of Thera and Melos: the largest of them was over a metre in height, with ornament on the neck, and rings round its girth, in the same Egyptian or Phoenician style. He was using them for his store of oil, and could not part with them.

I passed Episcopi and Colosse on my way back, and stayed the night at Limasol with my former host. In our talks about the condition of the island it came out that the taxes used to give 3,200,000 piastres, including the Customs, and other sources of revenue. Now they bring in just as much, excluding the Customs which are farmed out for 4 to 500,000 p. There must be added again the revenues of the confiscated *Sipahiliqs*, so that the Porte gets in all about 7,000,000 piastres. As a matter of fact this increase is apparent only, because in the last twenty years the Greek, Russian and Egyptian wars have so much reduced the value of the piastre that, instead of 7 or 8, 23 to 24 go to the Spanish dollar. And as the population decreases so the revenue accruing to the Porte decreases too, and after all what is 500,000 Prussian thaler as the revenue of an island like Cyprus! Where in early days certainly a million, under the Lusignans 5 to 600,000, and at the beginning of the Venetian occupation 800,000 souls could be counted, we find now a population of 120 to 125,000.

March 17. In an hour and a half I reached Amathus again. Hence I rode along the shore between the low foothills, leaving Pentacomo on the left. About here were old copper mines; some bits of ore lay on the road. Further on the road keeps altogether to the shore, and runs under a low steep promontory of tertiary formation, behind which, at a distance of five hours from Limasol we reach at last the mouth of the Basilopotamos. I was now again on the old track, and slept at Mazoto in the house of a hospitable peasant who, in spite of the strict fast, offered me fresh milk. March 18. It took me four hours to ride through Arpera to Larnaca.

# VIII

**Importance of Larnaca. European Consuls. Greek chronicle of G. Bustron. Phoenician inscriptions. S. Lazarus. A new Turkish saint. Phoenician graves. Phaneromene. Excavation near Kition. English projects. Linobambakoi. Shipping and Trade.**

*March 6–8, and 19–24, 1845.*

As in ancient times Kition stood next in importance after Salamis and the religious capitals Amathus and Paphos, so on account of its commerce and its being the residence of the European consuls it is the real capital of the island. Between my excursions I made my longest halts here, and found kind and pleasant friends in the Prussian Consul, M. Mattei, and his brother; M. Caprara, an Austrian gentleman, the English Consul Mr. Niven Kerr, the Sardinian, Signor Cerutti, and the French M. de Fourcade. Besides what I have said already I will collect what they told me about Kition, with my own remarks, in a separate section. Especially my converse with Signor Cerutti was rich in interest; he entered thoroughly into the aims of my journey and all the more so because he had occupied himself with a chartographical study of the interior of the island, a work which he most kindly placed at my disposal. Also I found in his library Lusignan's oft-cited Chorography of Cyprus [Bologna, 4to, 1572] but I hunted in vain in monkish and episcopal libraries for the Greek Chronicle of Georges Bustron, which Lusignan used. I fancy it is lost. [Ed. by C. N. Sathas. *Bibl. Gr. Med. Aevi.* 8vo. Vol. II. Venice, 1873.]

When I was staying March 6–8 in Larnaca I tried to see something more of the neighbourhood. I owed to Signor Caprara the indication of two Greek inscriptions in his country house at Livadia, half an hour north of Kition, of a Phoenician inscription in the church of H. Antonios at Kellia, a village lying a little further away. The last is perfectly well preserved, engraved in large characters on a block of white marble about six feet long: but unfortunately it is built in across an arch within the church, so that all my negotiations carried on through the Prussian Consul with the bishop of Kition to get the stone were fruitless. [*Corpus Inscriptionum Semiticarum,* Part 1, Tom. I, p. 68, No. 47.] In the same church is also the fine front of a marble tombstone, adorned with elaborate palmettes of Attic elegance: the only one of this kind I have seen in Cyprus. All the Greek inscriptions found so far in the island do not appear to go back beyond the Macedonian era, while many of the Phoenician records must be earlier.

Another day I found myself in the company of M. Demetrios Pierides, a native of Kition, educated in England. He pointed out to me a few unimportant inscriptions, mostly on *Stelai* of sandstone, and took me to the Greek church of H. Lazaros, beneath which in a small narrow hole the supposed grave of the Saint is shown; a plain ancient sarcophagus, with two rosettes, of white marble. The Saint is said to have come here after his resurrection, and here to have died a second time in real earnest. His bones were carried off at some later time. The church, of considerable size, had formerly three domes, but Kuchuk Mehmed Pasha, the savage whom we have mentioned before, thought that such an ornamentation was unbecoming in a Greek church: by his orders the domes had to be reduced by a half, and the openings covered with wood: this gives the building a queer appearance. Close to the church is the little 'God's acre' of the Protestants.

The mosque in Scala, which is of some size, was built six years ago with stones brought in carts and on camels from Amathus and Salamis. Near it is the Turkish fort which commands the harbour, a small square tower with a few cannons, useful only to salute men of war on their arrival.

Six weeks ago the Turks discovered in their graveyard a corpse nearly incorrupt. The phenomenon is of easy explanation as the earth in a spot so close to the sea and the salt-lake is thoroughly impregnated with salt and saltpetre; and the body, in the opinion of people whose windows command the cemetery, cannot have been buried for more than 20 or 25 years. While the occurrence would have been held by the Greeks of very evil omen, and the corpse have been pronounced a vampire (*brykolakas*), the Turks have adopted it as a Saint without knowing its name, and as the busy mockers suggest, even its sex (*Sive tu deus es sive dea*—so too prayed the ancients.)

The old Pasha at Nicosia is delighted that the event happened during his term of office, and hopes that it will be a special recommendation for him at Constantinople: he has had a little oratory built at once in the graveyard over the body, and summoned a dervish to be its guardian. I went there one day with the English Consul to see for myself. We found a small whitewashed room, the unknown saint lay on a kind of catafalque under a green carpet, the dervish sat in a corner on his heels, smoking his pipe with the indispensable tray for coffee close to him. The cultus of the saint went no further.

I availed myself of my second and longer stay in Kition to examine closer some large and remarkable tomb-spaces on the rocky ridge, west of the Marina and south of Larnaca, which does not appear to have been included within the old Phoenician city. The ridge rises but a very few feet above the sown fields, on which the corn was already high.

In the first tomb one can now get into the first chamber only. It is an oblong: along the top of the walls the stones form the beginning of a semicircular vault, whereon rest big stone beams which make the roof. The section of the cornice is exactly that of the grave of Zacharias at Jerusalem. The chamber measures from cornice to cornice m. 2.02, the length is nearly twice as much. In the back wall a door leads to a second chamber, which is blocked with rubbish.

Another and better-preserved tomb has been used earlier as a Greek chapel, and keeps the name of the Panagia Phaneromene. It has consisted of two chambers and a porch but this last is all but destroyed, and of the walls of the chamber the corner to the right of the entrance is gone. The first chamber is m. 5.15 long and 3.45 broad: the side walls are built of blocks or slabs of stone 0.60, or nearly two feet, thick; and of the same height; the backwall is the live rock. The roof, still preserved, is arched, and of a single block, a monolith m. 6 long, 5.10 broad, and 1.50 thick. This makes one think it possible that the courts which I described at Paphos were covered with monolithic slabs. In the back wall is an entrance 1.25 wide, 1.74 high, 1.20 deep: it leads into a smaller chamber 3.14 broad, 2.86 long, 1.84 high, entirely hewn out of the rock. Its roof, like that formed by the monolith over the first chamber, is hollowed into a vault. The most singular point is that both chambers were closed, in default of doors, by great slabs of stone lowered from above, like portcullises, just as in the interior of the pyramids the passages to the tomb-chambers were blocked by portcullises of granite. The entrance from the first chamber to the second is furnished to this end with a groove on either side cm. 35 broad and 9 deep: but the portcullis, which must have been broken through to get across to the second chamber, is no longer to be found. Entrance to the first chamber was effected by breaking up the blocks at the S. W. corner. The door of this is still preserved, a stone 1.50

wide and 0.33 thick, it leans against its old place. Within there is no longer any trace of sarcophagi, ledges for bodies, or niches.

The archaeological booty which rewarded my tour in Cyprus, with the exception of the statuettes from Idalion, was little enough, but I had in the Phoenician graves in old and new Paphos and Kition obtained a clue to the art-history of this nation, which I should have been glad to follow up. I was encouraged to hope that in the fields west of Larnaca, between the town and the monastery of S. George, I might light on some still unopened graves, for a few years since a cavern was found with ten plain sarcophagi or coffins of gypsum. There was talk too of repeated discoveries of large amphorae painted with Phoenician ornaments, like those of Kantou and Thera, and many glass vessels. I saw too here in a Turk's house some fragments of such. On March 20 and 21 I had an excavation made in the fields which had been pointed out to me, and on the second day found under the layer of stiff soil two caverns adjoining one another, one with three raised ledges for corpses; the other had two chambers and seven ledges. But it was clear that both had been opened and robbed centuries ago, as Lusignan says often happened in the time of the Venetians, for I found no trace of bones, much less other tomb-furniture. All I carried away from my diggings was a few small black vases, and as Easter Eve fell on March 22 I had to give up the work.

Easter day I spent in Larnaca in the company of the Consuls and their families. Signor Balthasar Mattei, brother of the Prussian Consul, and perhaps the richest Catholic in the island, showed me a small deeply engraved stone with the head of a man surrounded by rays: between the rays is ΝΙΚΟΚΛΗΣ. Perhaps it is the portrait of the King of that name, who is here indicated by the rays as an *epiphanes*.

Among the European consulates the English certainly takes the most distinguished position, although the English commerce is quite unimportant. The English here as elsewhere in the East are at some pains to exact as much consideration as possible. There are in Cyprus at least two to three thousand souls, specially in some villages near Famagusta, who only outwardly and in appearance are Turks, but who really are Christians. They follow the outward forms of Islam but cause their children to be secretly baptised. They have the nickname 'flax-cottons,' *linobambakoi*. The English in a quiet way encourage these *linobambakoi*, and seem by protecting them to try to get a handle for an extended influence. Another interesting case is just now waiting decision. Seventeen years ago, while the Greek war was still afoot, a Greek woman of Limasol was torn by force from her husband and compelled to marry a Turk. Some years later her Greek husband died, and as the Turk treated her badly, five years ago she was separated from him, and since that time she went to the Greek church without any hindrance on the part of the Turks. But now that this new Helen wants to marry another Greek, the Turks object. She is now a Muslim, and cannot according to the law marry a Christian. Again it is the English consulate that takes her part, has addressed itself to the Pasha on her behalf, and will know how to make its view prevail.

According to the official list kept by the consulates of the yearly movement of shipping at Larnaca, taken as the commercial capital of the island, we have the following result (40 Turkish kiles go to a ship's ton)

| 4 | vessels under the English flag | tons | 1050 |
| 40 | (Including steamers) Austrian | | 7500 |
| 90 | Greek | | 8500 |

| | | |
|---|---|---|
| 10 | Jerusalem* | 750 |
| 10 | Russian | 1250 |
| 16 | Sardinian | 2550 |
| 40 | French | 6500 |
| 6 | Tuscan | 900 |
| 450 (including coasting vessels and a few steamers) | | |
| | Turkish | 18000 |
| 666 vessels | | 47000 tons |

[*The (Latin) Patriarch of Jerusalem has the right to grant a flag, which is sometimes preferred to that of the Turks.]

The most important articles of export are silk, wool, cotton, wheat, barley, madder, wine, oil and carobs: of secondary consideration are a few kinds of earths containing colouring matter. Of manufactures there are only coarse silk stuffs for shirts, a few cotton divan-covers, and a good many boots from Nicosia. Nearly all Syria, and the south coast of Asia Minor, are supplied from Cyprus. Imports consist chiefly of so called American linen (i.e. undyed cotton stuffs of English make, with which Greece too is flooded) woollen cloth, red fesses from Tunis and Leghorn, paper from Genoa, iron from Sweden and Russia, sugar and coffee, German hardware (knives, axes, glass &c.) and ordinary earthenware. The export is reckoned at about 8 million piastres, the imports at five millions (5 piastres to the Prussian thaler). Most business is done with Marseille, Triest, Leghorn and Genoa.

## IX
**Excursion to Olympos. M. Santa Croce. Ano Levkara. Graves. Notices of Olympos. Hasty return, and departure on the French brig l'Agile.**

*March 25–April 24, 1845.*

Easter was passed, and spring was upon us: I wanted to make my last big excursion in the mountainous heart of the island to Aoos and Olympos, and the Sardinian Consul Signor Cerutti, a keen dilettante in archaeology, was willing to accompany me. At 8 a. m. on Marsh 25 we left Larnaca. For an hour our road ran westwards across the bare plain: Then the country gets cut up by low ridges and river beds mostly dry. In the small tracts of cultivated land between are many olive and carob trees, the hills themselves are inclined to put on a vesture of pines, but very few of these reach the height of trees, because animals great and small mutilate them. We reached the foot of the M. Sta Croce (*Stavros Theokremmastos*), on which stands a monastery built probably on ancient foundations. Following its southern side we pass the villages of Klavdia, Aletrico, Upper and Lower Anglisides. The soil is chiefly a whitish clay. Between the hills on our left we saw now and then the sea at a distance of two to three hours from us. In four hours we reached the small Turkish village Upper-Kofinou, in a plain under olive trees, where we rested for breakfast, and a large part of the population collected curiously around us.

Immediately beyond the village we descend into the steep and deep bed of a river, the same which falls into the sea on the road to Amathus, near Mazoto, and rode up stream for about an hour under olive and carob trees. Then we turned left and west up the sleep slopes, and mounting always over well cultivated hill sides we go through Lower Levkara to the higher village where we meant to stay. It is a large village with a good trade in oil and wine. In 1570, during the siege of Levcosia the Levkarites sided with the Turks against the Venetians, and up to a few years ago were on that account exempted from the poll-tax. In the oil-trade they are reckoned very fraudulent, for they mix their produce with mallow-water.

It was yet early afternoon, and we had time to see the village and its surroundings. Between Upper and Lower Levkara lies the ruined chapel of H. Timotheos, with the sarcophagus of the Saint broken to bits. From this point you get a fine view to M. Sta Croce directly west, and through an opening in the hills to the S. E. Cape Kition. To the south of the village on vineclad slopes, are old tombs with Egyptian-Phoenician pedestals, and here too have been found Egyptian scarabaei. Immediately behind the church of H. Timotheos are other tombs of Roman date, put together out of rough stone slabs, in which lamps are found, other larger tomb-chambers have been discovered in Upper Levkara itself, and behind it near the chapel of H. Marina.

The next morning we meant to wander W. and N. W. among the higher mountains. Two hours N. of Levkara there should be on a peak the ruins of a Frankish castle called Syrjatis near a ruined and deserted village Pyena. But we were aiming mainly at Olympos or Troodos. On its highest point the ruins of an ancient building, without columns, are reported. They are described as resembling the remains of the Atabyrian Zeus at Atabyron in Rhodes. In Omodos on Troodos, ancient tombs have been found containing precious gold ornaments, and on the way thither by Xylouri are ruins.

But all our plans of travel were defeated in an unexpected way. Late in the evening arrived from Larnaca a messenger from the French Consul, M. de Fourcade, with the news that a French man of war was there, bound for Athens direct, and an invitation to avail myself of this chance . . . I decided with some reluctance to return. After a short nap we left Levcara at 3 a. m. and by the same road reached Larnaca at 9.

My things were packed in all haste, a store of sheep, fowls, etc. purchased: I took leave of my acquaintances, and on the evening of March 26 went on board the French '1'Agile,' of ten guns and about 90 men, under the command of Captain Clement Martin.

The next morning we weighed anchor, and light winds brought us off Limasol . . . On April 8 we entered the harbour of Peiraeus, where I had to undergo a quarantine of seventeen days. With the exception of a few excursions in the interior of Greece, this was my last extended tour in the East.

# Petermann—1852

## [Plate 7]

H. [Julius Heinrich] Petermann, *Reisen im Orient* (Leipzig, 1860) I 41–43 and 358–74. Julius Heinrich Petermann (1801–1876) traveled widely in the Near East in 1852–1853. His collection of Near Eastern manuscripts is housed in the Staatsbibliothek in Berlin. See further *Neue deutsche Biographie* 20 (2000) 238.

Next morning at nine o'clock [in the summer of 1852] we finally got sight of Cyprus; we then passed along its southern coast all day long and could see Mt. Olympus at all times. This is the highest mountain of the range which stretches through the middle of the island from east to west. On its summit there was once a famous temple to Venus, and later a Greek church was built there. We also passed impoverished Baffo, the former Paphos. Only in the late evening, at half past nine, did we reach Larnaca, but were granted a view of it only the next morning, just as had happened at Rhodes. That view was not at all an attractive one; apart from a few tamarisk plants, plane trees, and date palms there were no trees to be seen along the coast, only a complete wasteland, it seemed. Since we were anchored here until evening, we traveled that morning by boat to the harbor, the Skela of Larnaca. This is a place marked by poverty; its houses are all built of clay and sun-dried clay tiles, with flat roofs. From the outside these houses show nothing but the plain walls with the door and here and there a barred window, but on the inside one sees occasionally arcades and vine arbors. The bazaars, i.e. the alleys, mostly covered, vine-clad, and lined with shops on both sides, offered few things worth mentioning. To my surprise I saw there many potatoes, also love apples [tomatoes], which unfortunately are very popular, solanum melongena, watermelons, etc.; in other bazaars European and Oriental fabrics, tobacco, *etc.* were offered.

A letter from our ambassador, Herr von Wildenbruch, required of me to visit Larnaca, half an hour away, to call on the royal Prussian consul, Giovanni Matthei. On the way there I noticed the remnants of a mosaic floor and individual blocks of marble. A Greek who was accompanying me assured me that this was the site of a church razed by the Turks; also the rumbling of the floor indicated that we were standing on a subterranean vault, probably a burial vault. I found the consul to be a charming old gentleman, who had inherited the post of consul from his father and had administered it for no less than 42 years. He received us—Rose had gone with me—very kindly and at once, as is the custom in the Orient, had coffee and pipe brought to us. He readily offered me his services, but left me no hope to find among the Armenians in Cyprus old manuscripts or any other antiquities; he offered, however, to write in this matter to an Armenian in Nicosia, a friend of his, and then give me further news. We soon took our leave and still had time to sit down in the Skela in a coffee house where people played billiard, to enjoy a nargile [water-pipe] and drink a glass of lemonade. In a shop next door I found a variety of things: ancient figurines, but mostly in a poor state of preservation, urns, and Greek, Roman, and Byzantine coins, but all unreasonably expensive.

At half past five in the evening we set sail. For a long time we still could see Mt. Olympus and Cape Greco [at the southeastern tip of the island], until darkness made it impossible. A French merchant from the Skela of Larnaca, the same one who had the antiquities and who with his family had emigrated at the onset of the Revolution of 1789, introduced me on board to an Armenian from Nicosia, by name of Markosean. The latter assured me that indeed Armenian manuscripts were to be found on Cyprus, and thus I found a reason to visit the island again . . .

On Saturday, October 22 [1852], we reached the port of Larnaca in Cyprus, where I parted from my travel companions. Of the other passengers, two Armenian Protestants from Kaisarije (Caesarea in Cappadocia), several Jews, many Turks, and also some Greek merchants, I have nothing further to report, since I had had little contact with them . . .

On Saturday and Sunday I remained in the Skela of Larnaca,[73] and I had all of Saturday to walk about, since my two servants had forgotten the chest with all the kitchen dishes and other utensils . . .

On Sunday, October 23, I called upon the Prussian consul in Larnaca, and he at once invited me to lunch. Since it was still early, I first took a walk about the town, visited the new, beautiful, and large Catholic church of the Franciscans, and saw the funeral procession of a young woman . . .

After this I went to the consul. Here I ate, among other things, an unusual kind of white-feathered birds, called "Beccafichi" or "Feigenschnepfen" [a kind of snipe]. These are found, supposedly, only in Cyprus and only in the months of September and October, i.e. are migratory birds. At the same time I received instruction about the different kinds of wine which are available in Cyprus. There are three: The common wine is called "vino nero" or "black wine," of dark-red color. The dessert wine is called "vino della Commanderia" after the Commandery of the Templars and is produced only from over-ripe, half-dry grapes. The third kind is the "vino muscato" or "muscat wine." I have not drunk any of the latter. A bottle of the second sort costs four piasters (ca. eight Sgr.[74]), but when it is old one pays one guilder for it. I informed the consul of my intention to undertake some excursions on the island, in order to make good use of the time until the arrival of the next steamer to Beirut and, where possible, to buy some old coins and manuscripts. As for the latter he gave me no hope at all, but the former, he thought, I might find perhaps in one place or another.

I would have loved to go to Baffo, the old Paphos, where Venus was born from the foam of the sea and came ashore. But since I wanted to be back in Larnaca the following Saturday, I could not manage this and had to abandon it, as well as Mt. Olympus [the highest peak of the Troodos Mountains]. Instead the consul suggested to me to travel this week to Famagusta, called Mausa by the Turks, and next week to Nikosia and Tzerina [Kyrenia; also Kerynia or Kirne].[75] He promised to send me two letters of recommendation through his dragoman and to find a good mucker for me;[76] and he kept his word. Since the muckers do not live at the port but several hours away and get there only on Monday mornings, I could depart only on the afternoon of that day. I left my tent, suitcase, and travel bag with my host at the port and took only my bed and the most essential kitchen utensils, so as to need only three pack animals. There are few horses on Cyprus; the muckers have only mules, and I got a fairly good one. In Larnaca one also finds two-wheeled rackwagons; but here they are drawn by oxen, rather than by buffalo. Additionally one finds here many camels, which are smaller than those on the continent; their price varies, depending on their strength, from 300 to 1500 piaster. The horses are less good than the Arabian ones and are sold at 600-700 piaster. There are no buffalo, but many cattle, pigs, and herds of sheep and goats. I had lodged in the Skela not in the locanda [inn], but, to economize, with the Greek owner of a restaurant. I had been referred

---

[73] An earlier name of Larnaca was "La Scala," the present name not being in general use before ca. 1600.

[74] Sgr. = Silbergroschen; 30 Silbergroschen made one Thaler.

[75] See Hill, *History*, II 19.

[76] "Mucker" seems to be a corruption of Turkish "mucir" i.e. one who hires himself out. Professor Kemal Çiçek of the Turkish Historical Society, Ankara, kindly confirmed that on Cyprus there were people called "mucir" who guided travelers for pay.

there by a German painter whom I just happened to meet at my arrival. And there I paid only two piaster a day for a large room.

We rode off at about two o'clock in the afternoon, always in a northeasterly direction, sometimes close to the sea and sometimes in some distance from it across the plain. This plain was largely uncultivated and overgrown only with reed-like grass and scrub pine. After half an hour we passed two ruined buildings, which date perhaps from the Middle Ages, but perhaps from more recent times. After three hours of hard riding we reached the village of Ormylia [Ormidhia], which is four hours distant from the port. Here we had to stay overnight, because the mucker told me that the next village was four hours away. The local church is dedicated to St. Constantine.[77] I had much difficulty communicating with my mucker, who spoke such a gibberish of Turkish and equally bad Greek, that I almost could not converse with him at all. I would have loved to note down the names of the neighboring villages, but he pronounced them so unintelligibly that I could learn nothing at all. We stayed with a Greek peasant. But I did not want to sleep in his hut, and so I had my bed made up in the open hall on a table brought up for this purpose. And here, after we had eaten up the roast and bread which we had brought from Larnaca, I laid down without undressing. My servants slept before me on the ground and had stones for pillows.

On the morning of the 25th, before sunrise, we were on our way again and continued in the same northeasterly direction across a broad but not very high plateau, which for miles on end was not cultivated. In general, I was assured, the larger part of this beautiful island is quite uncultivated because of a lack of inhabitants. Perhaps this would be the best land for emigrants, since the soil is extremely fertile and generally few Muslims live here. And wherever people dig they strike fine, good-tasting water at minimal depth. Also hunting is excellent here. In addition to the "Feigenschnepfen" already mentioned there are lots of larks, partridge, and hare; the latter sell at 2 to 2½ piaster or 4 to 5 Sgr. Of wild animals, apart from fearsome wolves in the highest mountains which cross the island, one finds here many and poisonous snakes. One kind of them, a kind of boa, is supposed to have the thickness of a human thigh. The consul told me this story: One of his friends, while hunting, once came to a swampy place and used a block lying there to leap across, but his hunting dog, following him, refused to come across. Upon closer examination he saw that what he had mistaken for a block was a snake!

I had observed that in the course of all my excursions on the island I had found no evidence of viticulture; this is found only in the western part, particularly in the environs of Limassol. I was also told that this year a blight had affected the grape crop in Cyprus,[78] as it had in some parts of Lebanon. On the other hand there is an abundance everywhere of pomegranates, which are extremely cheap here; one can obtain 5 or 6 of them for one Sgr. Also people here grow a plant from which a red dye is extracted; as well as barley, wheat, sesame, and cotton. The latter had not yet been fully harvested, but had not been very plentiful this year and thus was more expensive than it otherwise would have been. A pound of cotton, cleaned of core and shell, sold for almost 4 Sgr., whereas in good years it would cost only half that much.

That this island must have been more densely populated in earlier times is indicated by the numerous churches and chapels which stand by themselves and of which

---

[77] Constantine Alamos, a 12th century saint.
[78] On this blight see Hill, *History,* IV 228.

some are totally ruined and others partly so. We saw several of them, both nearby and far-off, and one situated on the point of the promontory [Cape Pyla?]. After one hour we passed the village of Avgoro, [Avgorou] and after four hours we reached a village of Greek gardeners and potters; it is called Marasch by the Turks and Varosi [Varosha] by the Greeks and lies just outside [south] of Famagusta. Here we lodged with a Greek man who makes it his business to house strangers. I had not had any coffee in Ormylia; so here at last I enjoyed a cup of coffee in a vine arbor and had breakfast from what was left of our supplies. Then I went to call upon the commandant of Famagusta, Reschid Efendi, who lives in Marasch. He just happened to be in the fortress; so I immediately went there.

Famagusta is a strong fortress with its fortifications well preserved. Just before the gate there is a drawbridge across the moat, which in parts is still filled with water. There we dismounted—my host and I had been riding because of the deep sand and the heat—and found the commandant in a kind of guard house with his cawass [aides]. After the customary greetings and after I had received a nargile and some coffee, I handed him the consul's letter of introduction, whereupon he at once assigned one of his aides to guide me.

The city with its defensive works is of considerable extent, but, like everything else that has fallen into Turkish hands, ruined and desolate. The city itself is, with few exceptions, inhabited only by Turks. These live in the strong houses which have withstood destruction; but a large part of these is not occupied. Only about 200 Muslim families live in these houses, which are built of ashlar blocks of stone; the Turkish garrison numbers 210 men. We went first to the former palace, a large building built in a longish rectangle, of which only the outer walls are still standing. Two granite columns are built into the wall at the northern gate, and two other columns stand on both sides. Above the gate the coat of arms with six alternating black and white fields is fully preserved. Right behind the palace is the church of Ayia Sophia,[79] all in Gothic style with pointed arches and beautiful rose windows. The Muslims converted the church into a mosque and placed a minaret at the southwest corner; even that is now half-collapsed. The interior still stands in its entirety, but in the aisles the Turks have wiped out and covered with whitewash all that was Christian. The broad nave, which used to lead to the high altar, is separated from the aisles on each side by six columns more than eight ells[80] thick. The floor is adorned with many slabs of stone carrying coats of arms and inscriptions, which, unfortunately, are illegible; knights are buried beneath these slabs of stone.

We then passed behind the church and through the Sea Gate, on the outer face of which there is a stone relief of a lion holding an open book with his right forepaw. The city has only two gates on opposite sides; the one through which I had entered leads into the city from the land side; the other is this one, the Sea Gate. The broad and deep moat surrounds the city on only three sides, since the fourth side lies close to the sea. This, too, offers a good defense, inasmuch as the small harbor is, now at least, quite unsuitable for larger ships.

From there we crossed a desolate place densely overgrown with long, thick, pointed, and red-leafed aloe onto the walls of fortification, which offer a magnificent view of the sea and of the beautiful genuinely Oriental city. The city boasts numerous churches and chapels, from the ruins of which a multitude of palm trees rise up. Next to

---

[79] Also known as the Cathedral of St. Nicholas, now the Lala Mustafa Pasha Mosque.
[80] The length of an ell differs from country to country; an English ell measures 45 inches.

the cathedral is another beautiful church, nearly just as large;[81] along the fortifications one can see another ruined church or chapel almost every fifty paces, and in some of these fresco paintings have survived. My guide assured me that the city used to hold 366 churches, and that is a round number. Space on the beautiful, well-preserved works of fortification is densely occupied with cannons. Most of these carry as an escutcheon a winged lion with an open book and next to that Latin letters, such as B. R. V. F.; one has a wreath and within that the phrase *obsidionalis corona*.[82] A water conduit, now unusable, leads from Marasch to the drawbridge. Only reluctantly did I leave this magnificent view, which, however, also filled my mind with sadness over the destructive fury of the fanatical Turks, and returned to Marasch.

My host had next to his house a large garden, densely planted with mulberry, lemon, orange, and pomegranate trees, with irrigation ditches between them. Water is channeled into these ditches from a deep, lined well by means of a water wheel, which is run by a mule. These gardens could be very pleasant, if people were at all concerned about pleasantness. As it is, the trees stand so close one to another that one can pass between them only with difficulty. These gardens are laid out very much like those of Jaffa.

My host was, as a sideline, also a potter; at least he had a kiln in which to fire earthenware. This kiln was built of clay, half-round, in the form of a beehive; at the bottom it had an opening in which the fire was lit; in the middle it had a clay shelf which did not reach quite to the back and on which the objects to be fired were placed. Next to the opening through which the pots were placed in the kiln there was a seat. All of the houses in Marasch were built of broad, thin, apparently sun-dried clay tiles; the church is dedicated to St. Nicholas. The area around there is very sandy; only heather and *Basal fara*, "mouse onions," grow here.[83] The latter I had first seen south of Damascus, near the Antilebanon Mountains.

Before sundown I ate both lunch and supper . . . I did not see any grapes anywhere on my tour, as I already remarked. My host had a vine arbor, but no wine. Several frogs played around in the room in which I slept with my servants. This upset my servants, who were sleeping on the floor, but fortunately the frogs could not reach my bedstead. In the evening, at around eight o'clock, I saw for the first time a meteor, which was traveling from southeast to northwest, like a rocket, with a fiery tail, and then disappeared in the middle of the sky.

On Wednesday, October 26, we rode to the village of St. Sergis (Sergius), two hours north of Famagusta, bypassing two villages which are also called Marasch and are inhabited by Greek Christians. After one hour we came upon an old road. There we stayed in the house of the vice consul, who was a brother of the Prussian consul in Larnaca but was away on a trip. I had with me a letter from the consul to a fellow-countryman, who consequently offered himself to me as a guide. At the same time he canvassed the various houses and asked about old coins; manuscripts were not to be found. From time to time he brought me coins, of which I bought a few which seemed rare to me. Then, on the way, he showed me a stone with a Greek inscription, of which I unfortunately could make not much sense. Another stone with an inscription was built into the wall of a house.

---

[81] The writer is probably referring to the Greek Orthodox Cathedral of St. George.

[82] A crown bestowed on a general for raising a siege.

[83] A bulbous plant, called "Mäusezwiebel" or "Meerzwiebel," Latin *scilla*.

In the evening I visited the ruins of an aqueduct, of which only three single piers still stand, and then, near the village, two arches. Built into the latter is a black sandstone with a cross, and above that an illegible inscription. According to the information supplied by my guide it is supposed, like the earlier one, to contain the name of Archbishop Plutarch.[84] The aqueduct led from here to the former port city of Salamis.[85] Next to the house of the vice consul, where I had lodged, were the traces of an old building. Here, supposedly, stood the palace of the brother of the ruler of Salamis, and people think that all the utensils of the church lie buried in a cellar which has not yet been found. St. Sergis, which counts 112 tax-paying Greeks and 20 to 25 Muslims (Turks), has two churches. Outside the village lies the church of Ayios Sozomenos,[86] and within the village lies the church dedicated to St. Sergis (Sergius).[87] The latter church has two domes, and legend has it that it was built by Constantine the Great;[88] in later times it was enlarged on one side and in front and called a second Paraskeve.[89]

Here too there are gardens with lemon and especially pomegranate trees, the fruit of which is also very cheap. The inhabitants also grow much cotton, which, however, did not yield a good crop this year and was very expensive. One okka of 400 dirhem, i.e. ca. three pound,[90] was sold in the shell at 1 piaster (2 Sgr.); cleaned, it sold for 5½ piaster (11 Sgr). In better years the latter sells for 4 or even 3½ piaster (7 to 8 Sgr.)

I was told here that an old history of Cyprus, written in Greek, was printed in Venice or Rome in the 17th century.[91]

My bed was made up in the bedroom of the master of the house. After I had eaten I made some entries in my diary and did not yet want to go to sleep, since I had had a siesta. I heard something rattling in the closet, but paid little attention, because I thought it was rats or mice, to which I had already become accustomed, since they are to be found everywhere in the Orient. Soon it was rattling in the room, and lo and behold, a snake came crawling out of the closet. I could hear several more in this closet, also in the other closet, in my host's bed, and along the windows, by one of which my bed had been made up. Finally I saw a snake hole next to me in the floor. This kind of domestic animal was new to me, and even if I could with great probability assume that they were harmless, I shuddered at the thought that they might crawl across my face while I was asleep, and I

---

[84] For Archbishop Plutarch see Hackett, *Orthodox Church,* 310 and 687.

[85] The starting point of the aqueduct was at Kythrea, ca. 25 miles to the WNW. See now also Walter E. Kaegi, *Heraclius: Emperor of Byzantium* (Cambridge/New York, 2003) 208 with nn. 61 and 62.

[86] There are two Cypriot saints by the name of Sozomenos; one was a bishop of Karpasia, the other a hermit at Potamia. A village of Ayios Sozomenos is located ca. ten miles southeast of Nicosia, and close to the village is a cave reputed to be the tomb of a St. Sozomenos.

[87] St. Sergius was archbishop of Salamis/Constantia in the middle of the seventh century.

[88] There is no record of Constantine ever having visited Cyprus.

[89] This is possibly an allusion to the five-domed Byzantine church of St. Paraskeve at Yeroskipos near Paphos. Paraskeve is a legendary virgin saint, supposedly martyred under the emperor Antoninus Pius (138–161). She is a personification of Good Friday and depicted frequently in the wall paintings of Cypriot churches and in Byzantine and Russian icons, commonly with the instruments of Christ's Passion.

[90] More accurately, one okka = 400 dirhem = 1.282 kg. A good table of Turkish weights and measures is found in Halil Inalcik and Donald Quataert, *An Economic and Social History of the Ottoman Empire* (Cambridge, 1994) 987–94. I am indebted to Professor Virginia Aksan of McMaster University for the reference.

[91] This is conceivably a partly erroneous reference to the history of Cyprus by the archimandrite Kyprianos, published in Venice in 1788.

decided to stay awake all night. But at one o'clock in the night sleep overcame me so strongly that I had to lie down on the bed, without undressing, and soon I fell asleep. Next morning I related my adventure to the servants, who smiled and assured me that there were snakes in all the houses in the villages, and far more than in this one, and besides, they were quite harmless. I resolved to be less fearful.

On the morning of October 27 we left only at about half past seven, since I had slept little and had arisen somewhat later. Our first stop was the ruins of the old port city of Salamis, only half an hour from St. Sergis, which supposedly once was called Pyrgos.[92] Unfortunately hardly a trace is left; only a few stones and a few weathered fragments of columns can still be seen near the sea; further inland—the ruins are widely spread—they are better preserved and perhaps date from later times. There one can still see the foundation walls of two or three buildings; one of these, forming a longish rectangle, is the largest and lies on a small rise. Nearby there are still a few well-preserved, but toppled columns of granite. Also one can find the remains of another old building, which I had passed already the day before. It lies half under the ground and resembles a large cellar with two side doors; it is built of large rather roughly cut stones, one of which was almost eight ells long. But originally it was not a cellar, but a chapel, now half-buried, as one can tell from the entrance way, now also partly buried. Here St. Catherine is supposed to have lived, and the chapel to this day is dedicated to her and called Ayia Katharina.[93] Facing the entrance way is a small, dark chamber, in which we saw a kind of lizard, which, my people assured me, are poisonous. Nearby stand some ambara trees with thorns.[94] A quarter hour further west we came to an old domed church to which a small monastery is attached. Of the few monks who live there we saw none. The monastery and the church bear the name of St. Barnabas. A few steps away is an old chapel in which St. Barnabas himself is supposed to have lived.[95]

From there we took a southwesterly direction and after one hour reached the village of Stylos. Here the consul owned a house and had already announced us to his grandson, who was there. My mucker wanted to stop overnight already here, but I preferred to go on; for it was still early in the day and I wanted to be in Larnaca the next day on time . . . Therefore we kept riding for another four hours and stayed in the village of Pyla, in the house of a young Turk, where we settled in in his absence. When he arrived he introduced himself as the owner of the house and invited me to take a little walk with him through the village and to smoke a nargile with him in a coffee house, which, of course, I gladly accepted. We talked almost exclusively about hunting, which is limited for the most part to hare; here, too, one pays 2 to 2½ piaster = 4 to 5 Sgr. for one.

From here we had only a short ride to the Skela of Larnaca, where we arrived next morning in good time. In order still to become acquainted with the capital of the island and with Lapithos prior to my departure, I decided to resume my travels on Sunday the 30th, making an exception. I had intended to leave at noon, but the mucker arrived only after two o'clock, so that we did not get under way until three o'clock. It was a distance of four hours to the village of the mucker, where we intended to stay overnight, and so we rode hard. The way took us in a northerly direction first through Larnaca and then,

---

[92] This is not the village of Pyrgos near Amathus.
[93] Now tomb 50 of the Royal Tombs of Salamis.
[94] The ambara tree is native to India, grows tall and thick, and bears edible fruit.
[95] What Petermann saw is probably the chamber now called the Tomb of St. Barnabas.

after one hour, through Aridippo [Aridhippou]. It happened to be the feast day of the Evangelist Luke, and there is in this village a church dedicated to him.[96] Hundreds of people came to this church on a pilgrimage, from near and far, from north and south, by horse, mule, or donkey; the ladies even came in handsome carriages, that is to say in two-wheeled carriages, drawn by two oxen and equipped with a white awning and, most of them, even with a carpet. We, too, mingled with the crowd and found many still assembled, although most were already on their way back. We dismounted and saw the walled churchyard full of people. A coffee maker known to us from the port had set up shop and prepared coffee and nargiles. Others were selling hazel-nuts, roast corn, etc. The church was new and offered nothing noteworthy; the wooden partition in front of the high altar [the iconostasis] was covered with tasteless pictures. After a short stay we rode on and crossed a low range of hills, where there was a lightly flowing spring by the side. Then we crossed an extended, completely uncultivated plain and a second range of hills. One hour after sunset, in the darkness, we arrived at the mucker's village, which is called Afkjom by the Turks and Afiene [Athienou] by the Greeks and reportedly holds 305 families. The mucker put us up in his house and provided a clean bed as well as coffee and nargile.

On Monday, 31 October, we got underway one half hour before sunrise and rode in a westerly direction to the village of Tyroi, one hour away, crossing a stream which is called Yialias and flows from southwest to northeast right past Tyroi.[97] Then we turned more towards northwest, crossing unimportant rocky heights and extended, mostly uncultivated plains, and after two-and-a-half hours came upon a village, the name of which I could not find out. There we feasted on the beautiful view of the island's main fortress and capital, called Nikosia or Lefkosia. The many palm trees and twelve mosques with their thirteen minarets give to it a genuinely oriental character. It is the seat of the Pasha and supposedly has 19,000 inhabitants. Here, too, the works of fortification are still in good condition, as they are in Famagusta. We had to pass through many alleys before we came to the Monastery of Terra Santa [Franciscan], for whose superior I had a letter of introduction from the consul in Larnaca and who received me very kindly. During the night and still in the morning before sunrise we had had much sheet lightning, and now clouds gathered and it began to thunder. Hardly had we gotten our things secured, when the storm grew more intense, it began to rain, and the rain soon grew stronger. But after one hour the sky cleared, and after noon the superior took a walk with me through the city; we were accompanied by the dragoman of the Sardinian consul in Larnaca, who had once been Lord Byron's interpreter. We went first to the former palace of the Lusignans; there is nothing to be seen there other than the old entrance way with the winged lion above the portal.[98] Opposite this, on the other side of an open plaza before the palace, now next to a mosque and muslim graves, stands a tall column of granite; on its base, half-covered by earth, there are some single letters with abbreviations.

---

[96] The feastday of St. Luke is 18 October. Petermann is reckoning time by the Gregorian calendar; the Orthodox Cypriots followed the Julian calendar, which then ran twelve days behind and now runs thirteen days behind the Gregorian calendar.

[97] The Yialias joins the Pedieos a little west of Salamis.

[98] That, of course, would have been placed there by the Venetians. The entrance way was demolished in 1904; only the Gothic window was saved and is now displayed in the Lapidary or Jeffery's Museum.

The Church of Ayia Sophia, which we visited next, is built in the Gothic style, like the one in Famagusta, but is larger and has eight thick columns on each side, but is not as beautiful and not quite finished. It is said to date from the days of the emperor Justinian. Of the four towers which it once had the two in front have been made into minarets and the two in back simply covered over. Both within the church itself and in the narthex there are numerous inscriptions in stone. Nearby, on the left, was the episcopal residence, where one can still see the escutcheon with the bishop's miter. Also nearby, on the right, is the former Church of St. Nicholas with a beautiful portal and an escutcheon above it, now a magazine. Further on was the Church of St. Catherine; before its portal is a grave with a French inscription, of which I could read no more than the two initial words: "Ici git." From there we went to the Armenian monastery, where, unfortunately, we did not meet anyone; but at the entrance to the church we saw the year 1202 [in Armenian characters] of the Armenian era, i.e. A.D. 1753.[99] There is a single Greek Catholic family here, also a few Maronites, who live mostly in the neighboring villages, and even fewer Latin Christians, but all the more Greek and Armenian Christians. From there we went to the Café delle mille Colonne, which was quite attractively furnished and offers not only coffee and nargile but also canned fruit. We drank a sherbet of violet, which tastes like raspberries, and returned to the Latin monastery. This was built in 1733 and expanded in 1783. It is inhabited by one "Präses," one "Curato," two Fathers, and one lay brother.

I was unable to hand the consul's letter of introduction to the Pasha, since he was not present. On Tuesday, 1 November, we left Nikosia at eight o'clock in the morning. Only then did the mucker tell me that we would find nothing [to eat] on the way, but it was too late to prepare something. We rode off in a northwesterly direction and saw outside of the city a well-preserved aqueduct. Then, riding across insignificant, rolling hills, we came in the plain, after two hours, to the village of Dikomo [Dhikomo]. Here, for four piasters or eight Sgr., we bought two chickens; these we roasted and consumed. This held us up for a long time, so that we got underway again only at one o'clock in the afternoon.

Now we rode at first in a northeasterly direction, and then in a northerly direction across two very difficult and dangerous rocky ridges [of Mt. Pentadaktylos], where we were often obliged to dismount and found several long snakes lying by the way. From the height of the second ridge we saw the sea again on the north side of the island. On the way up, my saddle, which the mucker had not secured, gave way, and I fell off to the left side, hitting my chest on a stone, and this caused me very severe pain for a long time. The way down was no less difficult, so that I often had to dismount. Finally, after two hours of getting on and off, we reached the village of belli paesi [Bellapais]. This offers a charming view of the sea, across the floor of a valley which is one hour wide and covered with carob [St. John's bread] and olive trees. At the end of the village, on a rocky cliff, one finds the splendid ruin of a monastery of the knights of St. John;[100] its fully preserved refectory, 15 paces wide and 45 paces long, stands on the furthest slope. In this refectory there is also a kind of pulpit, which is reached by stairs within a wall two ells thick. From the windows one has a splendid view over the plain and the sea; the ceiling is constructed

---

[99] The first year of the so-called great Armenian era is the year 552 of the Christian era.

[100] Petermann is mistaken; Bellapais Abbey, sometimes called the White Abbey, was held by the Premonstratensian Order, whose members wore white robes.

of pointed arches. There are three escutcheons on the door:[101] in the first one on the right a rampant lion;[102] in the second a large cross with four small ones;[103] in the third one in the upper right quarter a rampant lion, next to that the same kind of cross, and below that the two designs combined.[104] Next to the refectory is the well-preserved cloister. In front of that, on the other side, is the church; in the back is a large room, once vaulted, and next to that a second, similar one, the ceiling of which has collapsed . . . Two open marble sarcophagi stand next to the entrance to the refectory. One of these is quite plain; the other is decorated at the top of the sides with heads and Arabesques. At the opposite end of the cloister a winding stair, now bricked-in, leads to the roof; next to that a door with four steps, also now bricked-in, leads into the church. The latter, now used for Greek services, is 20 paces wide and 30 paces long to the high altar; it is built with a cupola and has two thick columns on each side. Next to the former sacristy on the left a stairway of 27 steps leads to the roof, where there still is the wall of a bell tower with four openings for bells. In the neighborhood there are also a few remnants of the walls of other buildings, and also many houses built with stones from the monastery.

After a stay of about one hour we rode on at four o'clock, all the way down the mountain to the village of Tzerinia, which lies one hour away in a northeasterly direction on the sea. We arrived there at five o'clock and stayed overnight in the house of a Greek. This village, also called Kirinia [Kyrenia], has only Greek and Turkish inhabitants; the former constitute two thirds of the population. There was no food to be had here other than ship biscuits, olives, and bad cheese.

Next morning I first looked around in the village. In the small harbor two frigates, probably Turkish, were docked. The harbor was once enclosed by a wall, and at the entrance on both sides by towers, one of which perhaps was a lighthouse. The fortress is still well preserved; only the outer earthen walls are destroyed, and the moat is in part half filled in. An aqueduct, evidently no longer in good condition, leads to the small fortress, before the gate of which there is a drawbridge. There are two mosques in the village. Of the 200 houses about 60 are inhabited by Turks, the rest by Greeks. There also is a coffee house. On the west side there still is a strong tower, surrounded by a wall, and several ruins. On the same side outside the village some rock tombs can still be seen. Not until about eight o'clock did we continue our journey in a westerly direction through a forest of olive, St. John's bread, and mastic trees. There is significant export here of St. John's bread to Genoa; annually several ships coming from there are loaded with it. Also much cotton is cultivated here, and the best tobacco on the whole island. On our way we saw close to the sea a church and several ruins; on our right, against the mountains, several villages, at last Karawa [Karavas] and Lapitho[s].

Facing the latter lies the old monastery called Aschirowiito [Achiropietos], really *to panagion acheiropoieton (soudarion)*, i.e. dedicated to the holy *sudarium* [napkin], of which Bishop Eulalios[105] brought a piece to Lambousa. This is the site of the old town of Lambousa, of which only a few ruins can still be seen. The monastery is beautiful, built well of squared-off stones close to the sea and offering a beautiful view of the sea and the

---

[101] More correctly on the lintel.
[102] The escutcheon of the Lusignans.
[103] The Jerusalem Cross of the Crusaders.
[104] The royal quarterings of Cyprus.
[105] See Hackett, *Orthodox Church,* 319 and 688.

opposite coast of Karamania.[106] The old monastery church with two cupolas in the center still preserves a part of Jesus's *sudarium*, entirely framed in silver. About 90 years ago Turkish robbers came from Karamania, looted the monastery, and burned everything. The library went up in smoke; the *sudarium* was preserved.[107]

In the church one still finds a tombstone with the figure of the cleric who is buried beneath it carved in bas-relief and with an inscription. To the east, behind the monastery, one can still see a chapel and next to it remains of a mosaic floor. Right behind the small monastery garden there is a peculiar vault, cut into the living rock, which is free-standing. The vault has, on its three sides, three niches, which probably accommodated sarcophagi; so it is a kind of tomb chamber. Further on yet there are remains of the walls of the old city.

Here we ate and then rode on to Lapithos, which is built in terraces on the cliff; nearby there are the ruins of several churches, of which I visited only one, Ayia Mama.[108] In a village two hours further to the west there is supposed to be a stone with an inscription, and one-and-a-half to two hours away, higher up in the mountains, a destroyed monastery, Ayios Elias [Elijah], of which a hundred columns reportedly still stand. All this, unfortunately, I had to leave unseen. In Lapithos I still bought an interesting silver coin with an inscription, apparently Phoenician. Then, long after sunset, I returned to Kyrenia.

The monastery just mentioned follows the Rule of St. Chrysostom. There is a Greek archbishop in Cyprus, who resides in Nicosia; there also are three bishops who have their sees in Kyrenia, Larnaca, and Paphos, respectively.

On 3 November I rode back to Nicosia, where I stayed overnight again in the Latin monastery. On Friday the 4th I awoke at three o'clock in the morning, suffering from chest pain, which was still caused by the fall from the mule. I could not move and suffered severe pains in any position of the body. I tried to get up, but had to lie down again. Therefore I decided to stay down this day, but finally allowed my servants to talk me into moving on, because otherwise I would have had to remain on the island for another fortnight. With much difficulty they lifted me onto the mule, and it was eight o'clock before we got underway.

The ride became most difficult for me, but gradually I became used to the pains. Near Nicosia we passed the settlement of the lepers, who live here, far from the city, in a kind of village. After one half hour we came upon Achlankia, and after one-and-a-half hour we reached Tyroi, and then, after about three hours, Athienou, where we rested for an hour in the house of the mucker. On the way my pains became so severe again that I often despaired of my ability to go on. We made another stop at a lonely khan to drink coffee and at three o'clock we happily reached Larnaca. Here I called upon the consul, had him stamp my passport, thanked him cordially for his letter of introduction, which had proved so useful, and took my leave from him. Half an hour later I arrived at the Skela, also known as the Iskele or marina.

On Saturday, 5 November, before noon, I boarded [a steamer for Beirut].

---

[106] The southern coastal region of Asia Minor, facing Cyprus and comprising Caria, Lycia, Pamphylia, and Cilicia.

[107] Petermann, in a footnote, offers a lengthy digression on this *sudarium*. This is the *sudarium* or Mandylion of King Abgar of Armenia; it is not to be identified with the *sudarium* of St. Veronica, which was venerated in the West.

[108] But there is no Ayia Mama; there are four different saints by name of Ayios Mamas.

# Kotschy—1859

## [Plates 8, 9]

Theodor Kotschy, "Reise nach Cypern und Klein-Asien, 1859," *Petermann's geographische Mittheilungen* 8 (1862) 289–304. Theodor Kotschy (1813–1866) visited Cyprus in 1862 with Franz Unger, with whom he co-authored *Die Insel Cypern, ihrer physischen und organischen Natur nach, mit Rücksicht auf ihre frühere Geschichte* (Vienna, 1865). A species of plants, Kotschya, was named after him. His botanical observations have been largely omitted from the present text. See further Hunt Botanical Library, Carnegie-Mellon University, Pittsburgh, *Biographical Dictionary of Botanists Represented in the Hunt Institute Portrait Collection* (Boston, 1972) 218.

## Plan of the Journey

It was indeed a bold decision, given the clouded political horizon which prevailed in January of 1859, to undertake a journey to the Levant. For years it had been my dream to touch first upon Cyprus, then to reach, through eastern Cilicia, the famous mountain of herbs of the ancient Arab physician Lokman,[109] and finally to advance into the mountains of the middle Sarus River[110] and to conduct botanical research in the mountains of Kassan Oglu[111] . . .

## Journey from Trieste via Constantinople to Cyprus

. . . The next morning at nine o'clock we left Rhodes, at three o'clock the last mountains of Asia Minor disappeared, and in the morning of 29 March the outlines of the Troodos Mountains of Cyprus appeared. Soon the forested parts could be distinguished. We sailed around the promontory of Paphos and had an opportunity all day long, telescope in hand, to observe the mountain and the coast line. Passing by Limassol at some distance, we reached the wharf of Larnaca at 4:30 in the afternoon, and I gave instructions to find accommodations for us.

## Larnaca and Environs [Plate 9]

A calm spring morning allowed us to debark at eight o'clock in the morning of 30 March, and we gladly left the comfort of the Lloyd steamer behind us, in order to enjoy land air and greenery again. There are no accommodations for travelers at all, and thus it is advisable to obtain a letter of recommendation to the consul or to one of the commercial houses already in Smyrna. No one here builds more facilities than he needs for his family and his business. The German pilgrims bound for Jerusalem took advantage of the stop-over of the steamer to make an excursion into the environs of Larnaca and provided

---

[109] Lokman or Lukman, in Turkish folklore an Arab physician. See the *Encyclopedia of Islam*, new ed., vol. V (1986) 813b.

[110] The Sarus or Seyhan River rises in the Anti-Taurus Mountains of south-central Turkey, flows southwest, and empties into the Mediterranean Sea near Adana.

[111] A search on the Internet for Kassan Oglu yielded a webpage of the Botanisches Institut of the University of Munich with this entry: "in Ciliciae montibus Kassan-oglu prope pagum Gorumse, Th. Kotschy."

themselves with a supply of the noble Cyprus wine, in order to compare it, once back in German lands, with the wines from the Rhine. Everywhere the ground wore the dress of spring, for the temperature rose from 18° Réaumur in the morning to 20° Réaumur at noon.[112] The city at the sea [the Scala] has two-storied houses, among them many storehouses along the shore. A large proportion of the population consists of Muslims, especially so at the west end of the city, where Phoenix palms tower high above the houses. The city proper lies about twenty minutes inland. Here, in this port city, resides our consul, Herr von Dervent, who kindly offered us his hospitality, since we had no other choice. The clear light, the refreshing Zephyr, and a stay on the terrace with its distant view of land and sea are apt to make a newcomer fall in love with the Levant; but, really, there is nothing new to be seen here, for conical Mt. Santa Croce [Stravovouni] is too far away to affect the landscape, and the other heights, stretching towards east, are without any distinct forms.

The first morning on land was fully occupied with readying our collection and travel equipment for fourteen days—until the arrival of the next steamer. First we found some muleteers and settled on a wage of fifteen piasters daily for five animals. It was more difficult to find a servant for the kitchen, one who could also understand Italian and Greek; but we succeeded, still before noon, to engage the father of Branco, the consulate's "Diurnist."[113] Near Larnaca, to the southwest, there are long stretches covered with banks of half-petrified *conchylia*, of which I had made a collection already in 1840. But in order to complete this collection I led Branco, the "Diurnist," there so that during our absence he might collect undamaged *conchylia*. Immediately behind the last houses of the city, where drainage canals had to be dug through the low-lying land in order to make it available for cultivation, the eye is greeted by a laughing spring flora, especially by the tamarisks (*tamarix Meyeri Boiss.*) [Edmont Boissier], which grow to half the size of trees and are richly laden with blossoms. Ruderal plants grow abundantly on the ground in the area immediately around the city, while the salt-laden soil of the plain at the lower elevations is almost completely barren, offering only groups of salsocea far distant one from another. The ground of the area as far as the salt lake, only partly under cultivation, offers a lovely green carpet, which is decorated everywhere with many kinds of yellow, red, white, and blue flowers. The spring vegetation is so luxuriant here that one can compare it with that of our summer . . .

Just outside the city, towards Stavros, there is an interesting chapel, called Phaneromene. It consists of an excavated chamber, measuring four paces wide and six paces long and covered with some long, vault-like large stones; it is very old, probably dating from Egyptian times. An irregularly excavated pit forms the atrium. The vaulted chamber is kept very clean, and on the back wall there are some lamps, which visitors make it a practice to fill with oil. Furthermore this tomb chamber of Phaneromene is visited by those suffering from a fever; having said their prayers, these people leave in the firm belief that the fever will not return. The Greeks say: Φανερομένη κόφγη τὴ πίρεριν [κόπτει τὴν πύρεξιν], "Phanoromene cuts the fever," and this belief supposedly has healed many women. The air is cool and moist, that is, very pleasant during the hot season.

---

[112] On the Réaumur thermometer the freezing point of water is 0° and the boiling point is 80°.
[113] Perhaps a laborer or servant paid on a daily basis.

Turning south from this ancient structure towards the sea one crosses sterile ground . . . Just as at Alexandria and Damietta a large salt lake is separated from the sea only by a narrow strip of coast, so here, too, one sees a lake with many bays separated from the sea only by a narrow strip of sand dunes. Here, too, the lake evaporates in the summer, since it is fed by rain only in the winter. It is then that the salt is gathered, and the gain seems to be not inconsiderable, since large heaps of the purest sea salt are piled up along the beach. The northeastern edge of the sea is sandy and light, as is also the lake on all sides. The slightest wind ruffles the surface of the water and the small waves break on the flat sand, producing an uncommonly light foam which dissolves only with difficulty in the air. This phenomenon reminds one of the myth which tells that Aphrodite rose from the foam of the sea waves at the shores of Paphos . . .

On the other side of the lake, quite idyllically on a low sandy hill, there is a small Turkish mosque, called Hala Sultan Tekke [or Tekke of Umm Haram], with two slim minarets. Next to it is a small house, quite by itself and lonely, but from here one can overlook the otherwise quite level area. The banks of conchylia in the process of petrification lie a little further away on the promontory-like extension of land which stretches further towards the south between the lake and the seashore. The shell fragments are here piled up in large amounts, and these shells were still alive in the sea only a few hundred years ago. The seashore is surrounded by a broad strip of scree which a few steps further inland, where the waves do not reach even in the fiercest storms, is covered with vegetation . . .

The houses of the poorer sort of people, especially at the southwestern end of the city, are all built of loam. The yards between them and even the paths and terraces are covered with luxuriant growth, and *chrysanthemum coronarium L.* with its deep-yellow flowers graces all the terraces. Above the doors of the muslims' houses one sees *aloe socotrina* freely suspended in the air, where it flourishes very well. People bring this plant with them when they return from their pilgrimage to the tomb of the prophet at Mecca, in the superstitious belief that no evil persons can enter their home. Every house has a little porch with a few columns and a garden with nice orange, lemon, pomegranate, and St. John's bread trees. The farmers are anxious to speed up the harvest in the interior areas. In early May they have to be ready, whether the fruit is fully ripe or not, because the season of the locusts, which in a short time devastate everything, is threatening. As fortunate as Cyprus is in other regards, it must suffer much from this plague, especially in the eastern, more level part of the island.

In Larnaca a newly arrived visitor has to put up with a lack of beef, but mutton is very good, and there is nothing wrong with the milk, especially in the spring. Oil is, in spite of the many olive groves, bitter, because the good, sweet oil, which is gained from the first, light press, is exported. Only the oil of the second, heavy press, in which even the pits are ground up, remains in the country for domestic use. Larnaca has more Greeks than Turks among its inhabitants, also Syrians, Europeans, and Negro servants. Among the buildings one should note the Catholic church, which was erected mostly with the assistance of the Austrian government and is an ornament for the whole island.

We advise every visitor to spend as little time as possible in Larnaca and rather to move on to Limassol, where they will anyhow be at the source of commerce and in a pleasant area. The fever of Larnaca is known through the whole Levant; however, not only the environs of this city, but also all those coastal areas which stretch inland in wide, mostly somewhat swampy plains are full of the miasmata which bring on the fever. The

Europeans of Larnaca are in the habit of spending part of their leisure time in hunting and find different prey in every season; hare, snipe, and other beach fowl, especially ducks, quail, and flocks of migratory birds which rest on the island, are a gain for an otherwise modestly provided kitchen.

## From Larnaca to Nicosia

As everywhere in the Levant, one has here, too, opportunity to learn patience. My draftsman [Herr Seeboth] was quite surprised when on the morning of 1 April, the date agreed upon for our departure, I did not at once make a fuss; but, as was to be expected, the mules arrived very late. The new servant had purchased all his supplies and brought me three batches of paper for collecting plants; one of these he stashed away in his own saddle. All future travelers should carry as little baggage as possible, since it is sufficient to equip oneself with tea or coffee, sugar, rum, and rice. Everywhere on Cyprus one finds bread, eggs, a chicken, milk, and cheese; also the women are quite happy to fix the traveler a hot meal. There is no shortage of water in the mountainous parts, and it is good everywhere; also one finds wine in almost every place. To bring along a quantity of insect repellent is good advice. For all travels in the Levant people should provide themselves already in Smyrna with iron bedsteads, which, to be sure, are heavy, but a real necessity and of great benefit. I regretted almost daily not to have equipped myself with such bedsteads in Smyrna, for in Beirut I could not get them. In order to travel comfortably in the Levant at this early time of the year one has to have raincoats and protect all one's belongings well against rain. Only by the middle of June do the rains cease, and then a tent against the sun is necessary. One also must bring along one's own springy saddle, one which allows a horse to roll, and even strong, simple reins which can be used on a donkey, a mule, and even a noble Arab mare. Leather bags with a lock, two for each mule, are much to be recommended, for they hold much and nothing is lost. The most necessary item for any journey in the Levant is sturdy shoes and a warm, but not too heavy throw, which at the same time can serve as bedspread over the traveling-rug.

The mules arrived at noon, instead of in the morning, and after repeated loading and unloading we left Larnaca at one o'clock in the afternnon. The clouds which had been hanging over the mountains for days eased up and dissolved, and a pleasant spring air blew from the southeast across the plain on our backs. The barometer at the coast had stood at 259½ to 260 Paris lines [58.5 cm.] at 17° Réaumur.[114] Upon leaving Larnaca one enters at once a rather desolate area. On one's right, at a slightly lower elevation, there is a cultivated plain which is provided with a water line. The farms belong to the more prosperous people in Larnaca, which is three-fourths of an hour away. The value of the land depends, especially in the plain, upon the amount of the available water; therefore considerable amounts of money are spent on conduits from far-away sources. The appearance of the plain is an extremely depressing one, since there are no trees at all and the greater part of the area is not under cultivation. One hour from Larnaca there is the village of Radispu [Aradhippou], inhabited by Greeks only, who are experts at raising pigs. On the left side of the road, one-and-a-half hour from Larnaca, there is the village of Cilia [Kellia], inhabited only by Turks. In the middle of this village there stands a church of St.

---

[114] In n. 1, p. 303, Kotschy explains how to read the barometer which he was using, the so-called Heber barometer. 443.296 "Pariser Linien" equal 1 m. at 0° Réaumur.

Anthony, highly esteemed by the Christians; this shows that the village was once inhabited by Christians.

Below the first hills travelers reach Furni [Phourni], a small village, where, at a spring with a pasture and a small garden, on the right side of the road, a coffee house is operated by a native Russian. Furni lies at h2 5" from Larnaca.[115] A quarter of an hour away to the West lies Avdhellero, and half an hour to the East the somewhat larger village of Trullus [Troulli]. As far as Furni the road is always level, while the soil is chalky and therefore whitish, sometimes of firm and sometimes of loose consistency, depending on how much loam there is. Although this was the season of the richest vegetation, we found only meager plant growth on the entire south side of the heights of Furni down to the coastal area, where the flora is much richer.

Over gentle grades we advanced from Furni into the hill country, where, by way of narrow paths and deep cuts made by seasonal streams, a narrow pass leads to a plateau. The chalky walls were covered with myriads of small locusts, which measured hardly more than one quarter of an inch, and in places the ground, too, teemed with these animals. On the high plateau, steadily maintaining a course of h12, we reached one hour before Athiena [Athienou], the village of Archangelo. Here we turned towards northeast and arrived after a ride of five-and-a-half hours from the coast inland at the village of Athiena, which is inhabited by the muleteers. In a flat valley a long row of houses, surrounded by small gardens, stretches from east to west and ends at a well-built white-washed church. There is much activity in the village just before evening, when the domestic animals are returning from the pasture and several groups of travelers and beasts of burden are seeking their quarters for the night. The owner of our mules led us to his house, situated at the far end, and there his wife and children gave him a jubilant welcome. The house consisted of three rooms, of which we occupied the largest. The floor was firm, level, and kept clean. A few chairs and benches, a large table, and a wide bedstead made up the furniture, together with two large chests. Quite a few dishes were hanging from nails, decorating the walls. The housewife herself attended to the mules and also to an evening meal for us new arrivals. The village is inhabited mostly by muleteers, who provide communication between Larnaca and Nicosia and from there to other parts of the island and, for the most part, make their living from this. The flat plateau in the environs of the village is far and wide under cultivation. To the northwest, at h15, lies the village of Petrophani, and on the top of a hill the church of Limbia [Lymbia], and next to that the village of Lerudshima [Louroujina]. Turning towards Pentadaktylos we find the Turkish village of Meludscha Aja [Melousha], one-and-a-half hour away.

On the morning of 2 April the sky had cleared and all indications promised good weather. The Castello della Regina [Buffavento Castle] is located at h23¾ from Athiena, and the peak of the Troodos Mountains, at h18, straight to the west, was seen covered with fresh snow quite a way down . . .

As soon as we had left Athiena on our way to Nicosia we passed along cultivated land; the villages of Pyroi, where we crossed a bridge, Margo, and Timla were on our right, while Heistosimenos and Jeri [Yeri] were on our left.[116] The sight of the rocky chain of mountains which limits the wide plain to the northeast was made most beautiful

---

[115] In the directional system employed by Kotschy h3 equals northeast, h12 south, and h18 west. But not all of his readings appear to be accurate.

[116] For Timla, Heistosimenos, and Jeri see Stylianou, *Cartography*, 415, fig. 199.

by the sharply rising massifs with their jagged ridge and by the aroma of the mild spring light. Soon the villages, small as they were, became fewer, and to the same degree cultivated land disappeared . . . The villages of Athalassa and Aglandscha [Eylenja] are very near Nicosia; the latter has exceedingly beautiful plantations of Opuntia or Indian cactus-figs. However pleasant the view which is afforded by the palm trees suspended in the air above the city and by the minarets of the mosques between them, there was a sad feeling which seized our breasts when, in view of the attractive landscape, our ears were hit by painful sounds and our eyes met horribly disfigured and mutilated human figures sitting by the side of the road, begging for alms. These are people of the most pitiable kind, suffering the worst ill known in the Levant. These are lepers, banished and lining both sides of the road. They do not dare to approach those whom they ask for alms, have been excluded from all human company, must set up their huts in an out-of-the-way place outside of the city walls, and are suffering horribly in other ways from this dreadful disease.
. .

## Nicosia

The city is situated on level ground. Coming from Larnaca, the traveler finds himself on higher ground and can overlook the entire expanse of the city, which is enclosed by a strong wall of fortification. All around, outside the wall, one sees only cultivated fields without any trees. Towards east and north there is level land, while towards west and south there are rolling, low hills. At first look the appearance of the city, perfectly round, leaves an imposing impression. The public buildings are distinguished by their size, compared to other Turkish cities, for they are the remnants of an earlier, higher cultural niveau. But the majority even of important buildings are in a state of neglect, and those which are inhabited are, for the most part, in Turkish fashion, poorly built houses. Furthermore the streets are mostly narrow and dirty, as in all cities in the Levant. After a long search we found the house of Dr. Carletti, who represents the European interests, and we had to wait until the doctor appeared to receive his unwelcome guests.

In order to take care of our business still this day, so as to continue our journey the next day, we called on the Pasha,[117] who was to issue the necessary letter of recommendation. With much ceremony we reached his room . . . Dr. Carletti and several Armenians accompanied us and observed the ceremony to an extreme. But we were hardly outside when we heard derogatory comments on how unjust the Pasha was and how his recall was necessary. Our request for permission to visit the mosques and other buildings was granted by the Pasha with great kindness. By coincidence I told him of my travels in Cilicia and mentioned his friend Menem-Bey, prince of Adana. Then I learned that the latter's brother, Nafie-Effendi, was here in Nicosia, and I at once called upon him to ask him for a few lines to his brother. This little note later procured for me the good will of the prince of Cilicia and was especially valuable for me because of the recommendation to Omar-Bey in Kassan Oglu. After we had dined with Herr Carletti a kavas of the Pasha appeared and we entered the yard of the Sophia mosque, a large and splendid cathedral from the vaults of which the chanted prayers of the Muslims echoed back. In all parts one recognizes in this building, which adheres to pure Gothic style, the Christian cathedral of the former emporium. But the Muslims had too much light and bricked in several win-

---

[117] Ishak Haki Hafiz, who was governor in 1858–1859.

dows. There are other mosques from the time of the Crusaders, as well as many remnants of their other buildings, which were meant to last through the centuries and are worth a visit. The Greek church is laden with treasures; entire altars [icons?] are covered with silver and gold and were created for enormous amounts of money. At the church in the court of the Patriarch, by force of the new law under the Treaty of Paris [1855], a tower is being built, in order to let a peal of several bells sound above the city; but after many difficulties and petitions to Constantinople a decision came from there that only one bell may be rung in Nicosia.

After a walk on the walls of the fortification, which are currently being restored, Herr Carletti led us into his garden. The date palms grow here as luxuriously as in Egypt, and the dates are even ripening annually. The lemon and orange trees are laden with fruit, the apricot trees are blossoming in all their beauty, and the fig trees are sprouting their new leaves. If the gardens of Nicosia had sufficient irrigation and were given some care, all the fruits of Egypt, Syria, and Asia Minor could flourish there. The figs and peaches cannot be more perfect anywhere. Cotton plantations also are kept in the gardens and deliver such an excellent product that in the island's trade it has become the leading export article. Especially the southern coastal areas, the plains of Famagusta, and even the slopes around the mountain villages are suitable for raising cotton. Among vegetables, besides the others which are common in the Levant, artichokes do especially well.

## Excursion to Buffavento

Early in the morning of 3 April we rode out through the eastern gate of the city to reach the environs of the village of Mesamiglia. The day before a cleric had promised us, on his own initiative, to accompany us from this village to [the monastery of St.] Chrysostomos, a rich monastery located one-third of the way up the mountain of Buffavento. After one hour we stopped at the bridge across the Pedieos River and sent the servant after the cleric who was to accompany us but could not be found. In the meantime I took a barometer reading at the bridge and got a reading of 256 Paris lines [57.8 cm.] at 14° Réaumur, which corresponds to 297 Vienna feet[118] . . . The Pedieos River, which our guide simply called Potamos, has between its loamy, deep banks a narrow but deep channel. It takes in all the waters which collect on the northeast side of the Troodos Mountains and rises above its banks almost every winter. The arches of the bridge are very high and almost too flat; the roof of the vault is not surfaced, so that the animals step with their hoofs on the coping stones, and therefore riding across it is not comfortable. Most bridges in the Levant are better crossed on foot, because they are commonly built very narrow, often even so narrow that two riders cannot pass each other, which, however, was not the case here.

Having crossed the bridge, travelers cross an uncultivated plain and after one quarter of an hour reach the foot of the mountains in a most unusual hilly terrain which stretches along the chain of mountains at a width of one half hour . . .

After a steep climb the path, more level now, leads on a ridge flanked by precipitous gorges to the farm buildings of the Monastery of St. Chrysostomos. At this point one leaves the hilly terrain and reaches the mountains themselves, where the soil provides the

---

[118] A Vienna foot is 31.6 cm., while an English foot is 30.48 cm. Accordingly 297 Vienna feet equal 308 English feet or 94 m.

best acreage of the monastery. The environment suggests that there is no lack of water in this valley, for tall walnut trees rise along the way against the even higher monastery. I was most surprised by the presence of many half-grown and several old cypress trees, which do very well on a slope to the southwest of the monastery. The only care given to this charming forest landscape is not to allow goats to graze there. This is clear: If the herds of goats were done away with in the Levant and instead only herds of sheep were kept, within a single human life span the beneficial effect, upon the forests, upon the entire vegetation, and thus upon the poor climatic conditions which are caused by the barrenness of the surface, could be observed. There would not even be much need for planting trees, and where it is necessary it would not be much trouble.

The monastery is built on a rocky projection in an oblong shape. There is another steep climb, just before reaching the gate. Our arrival was expected, and a breakfast of eggs, which "hit the right spot," had been prepared for us. Several monks live here, but they do not show themselves to strangers . . . A path led us again to the south side, and here we stood right away before the entrance to the Castello della Regina [Buffavento Castle], which is said once to have had one hundred rooms . . . This castle had, in front of the main building, several terrace-like structures with built-in cisterns; also there are small channels carved into the rock, to catch rain water flowing off and to guide it into the cisterns. We climbed three of these structures, but then our way was totally blocked by a collapsed wall. We would have had to climb along a rock wall over three blocks lying one above another to get to the main building, and, since the heavy storm made climbing over the rocks dangerous and I had seen the main building already in 1841, I did not insist on exposing people to such danger. According to the barometer reading the altitude of the second structure is 3000 feet,[119] so that the ridge of the mountain, about 250 feet higher, rises to c. 3250 Vienna feet[120] . . . In the monastery a good meal had been prepared for us, namely chicken with rice, which can be obtained almost everywhere on the island and is tastefully prepared by the Greek housewives. The wine served us came from the gardens of the monastery and belonged to the better kinds. The supervisor told us of the taxes recently imposed by the Turkish government on the monasteries in Cyprus and complained about the pressure.

After some rest we visited the church, a well-known place of pilgrimage. It is named after the preacher Chrysostomos, who lived in Byzantium at the time of Constantine, and so is the entire monastery.[121] It is supposed to be a foundation of this famous man, or rather a mission founded by him. Queen Maria Antonia Molena[122] from Venice supposedly built the church as well as the castle on the mountain; thus these buildings might be dated to the years 1486–1570, when Venice was at its height and had unrestricted control of the Mediterranean Sea and the trade in the Levant. She had 14,000 elite troops under her command. Her tomb is behind the altar in the church; on the tombstone she is depicted in high relief, lying down and with folded hands.

---

[119] 3110 English feet or 948 m.

[120] 3369 English feet or 1027 m. Kotschy's editor, August Heinrich Petermann, adds a note saying that, according to the map of Captain Graves, the altitude of Buffavento is 3240 English feet; that equals 3125 Vienna feet or 987 m.

[121] The author is in error. St. John Chrysostom lived *ca.* 347–407; he was Patriarch in 398–404.

[122] Maria di Molino, a Bavarian lady married to a Venetian.

There is also an icon on the wall, showing her in robes of state with her daughter kneeling at the altar, her face radiating dignity and great beauty. We regretted not to have discovered this picture already in the morning, because it would be worth the effort to make a copy and to search the archives of the monastery for more information on the activity of this high lady. I therefore recommend this object to future visitors of St. Chrysostomos.[123] After the storm and a drizzle the weather had turned very pleasant, so that the area of Citrea [Kythrea] lay before us in a lovely light when we had reached the curiously irregular hill country. In a fast ride we reached the bridge still before sundown and hastened to the city. When we arrived we found the gate of the fort already closed, but the guard had been notified and obtained the key from the Pasha . . . When we reached Herr Carletti's house we took care not to trouble our host too much and ordered our animals for a departure as early as possible.

## Climbing Mount Olympus

When, on 4 April, we went to breakfast, the mules were supposed to be loaded and ready for departure. But it turned out that one of the muleteers, in the course of our excursion the day before, had seen fit to return with his two animals to his village, six hours away, and it took six hours before he showed up, after we had waited for him anxiously every moment.

Through narrow alleys and between high garden walls the path took us in a quarter of an hour to the Paphos Gate, where several water tanks stand in an open square. Here a kind of weekly market was held. The wares offered consisted of food items and wooden things, large and small, which obviously did not come from the plain but had been brought down from the mountains.

The next two villages before the Paphos Gate are Eudemedios [?] and Archangelo [?], the cultivated fields of which give evidence of prosperity and stretch far across the plain towards the softly rolling but barren hills. After a ride of two hours snow and rain forced us to stop in the village of Trimithia. The Castello della Regina lies to the northeast at h3 and the peak of the Troodos Mountains (Mt. Olympus) to the southwest at h15½. The inhabitants of this village belong to the poorer Greek population, since their fields are often broken up by stony ground and they, furthermore, have to turn over to their Turkish landlords all that they produce. It is an evil that, when there are years of crop failure, caused by the locust plague or drought, small villages fall into arrears with their taxes and almost become slaves to the landlords.

After a rest of two hours we reached, towards evening, the larger village of Peristerona, which already lies on the northern slope of the island. The soil of the area has many stony plains, so that only smaller areas, far away one from another, can be cultivated. After one more hour we reached the village of Alifotes [Aliphotes, Eliophotes], which has the ruins of an old monastery. At dusk we passed a little mountain stream next to a collapsed bridge which had several large arches. On the far side there is the somewhat larger village of Potami. From there the eastern cape behind Lefka at h19 drops

---

[123] The icon actually shows the lady and her son Antonio being presented to the Virgin and Child by St. John Chrysostom. See Hackett, *Orthodox Church,* 357. The icons of the monastery were looted by the Turkish army in 1974.

down to sea level. The highest peak of the eastern chain of Buffavento lies to the north-east at h1.

Our guide wanted to ride on one village further in order to be sure to reach the village of Prodhromos on Mt. Olympus the next day. We had hardly reached the cultivated fields when we were overcome by darkness and rain, and after half an hour it was clear that we were completely lost, having followed a field path. It took a whole hour until we discovered a group of impoverished houses, where we were willingly received. The family where we had stopped lived in a dark, long and narrow room, which looked fairly clean. An Italian fireplace served as a hearth; a few benches and even a table made up the furniture, weapons and items of clothing hang from the walls, and some chests in the back suggested a measure of prosperity.

A very pleasant sunny morning allowed us to get on our way already at six o'clock on 5 April, through a pretty valley, passing a lonely church, and towards a height of the mountain spurs. The distant view to the north, towards the cities of Morphou and Lefka, ranged over gently descending cultivated fields to the blue-grey sea. The mountains of Olympus were entirely obscured by fog, but soon the sun dispersed the fog at least in part. The whole northern slope from the high mountain down to our path is covered with dense forests of deciduous trees and green spruces. Many small valleys and gorges with murmuring brooks cut up this mountain side. Bushes of olive, myrtle and others common in Mediterranean flora lined the sides of our uneven and partly rocky path. On a narrow path through a ridge of slate, which was covered with *thymus hirsutus MB.* in full bloom, we arrived at 10:30 in the picturesque valley of Evrico [Evrýkhou] and were hospitably received in the house of the Hadji Petri Georgi . . .

The location of Evrico, 1550 feet above sea level, is one of the most pleasant on the island of Cyprus and especially suitable as a summer residence during the hot season of the year. The floor of the valley, only one quarter of an hour wide, with the lower part of the adjoining slopes is carefully cultivated and well irrigated. The other heights, which are not reached by water conduits, are planted with mulberry trees and grape vines. In addition to the cotton plantations viticulture and silkworm culture are the most profitable. The many farmsteads show considerable prosperity, such as is found only in the valleys with Christian population.

On the very floor of this charming valley, near the steep slope of the high mountain, on the west side, we find the village of Galata with attractively built houses, surrounded by luscious gardens. The view over the whole valley towards north offers a picturesque landscape with the city of Lefka and the sea in the distance . . .

At the height of the saddle, 4590 feet above sea level, the ground and the trees were covered with snow, which had fallen the previous night in granular form, and the thermometer registered only 3° Réaumur. After a short rest and refreshed by a sip of rum, descending 500 feet, we arrived thoroughly frozen in the small village of Prodhromos, which is situated on the southern slope. The surprised inhabitants allowed a fair amount of time to go by before quarters in a heatable room were allocated to us. There was not too much comfort; the best that the people had was wide benches, on which we could make our beds. Only under the blanket could we find some warmth, since the large fire which had been lit in the pitch-blackened chamber had to be extinguished because of the thick smoke. This house, half built into the slope of the mountain, its interior with the piled-up heaps of wood, the utensils, and the wooden benches, and the tiny windows, reminded me vividly of the houses of the Goralen at the headwaters of the Vistula.[124]

When I took a barometer reading early in the morning on 6 April I could see the peak of Mt. Olympus quite clearly; the heights above the island and the southern shores were also clear, and only down at the sea, at some distance from the shore, there was a heavy layer of clouds. I therefore decided to find a guide in the village and to begin the ascent right after breakfast. A vigorous man, twenty years old and familiar with the whole mountain, was found, and I also took along another man as carrier. As soon as we began to ascend we occupied ourselves with collecting plants, since we could not know if the weather would be favorable on the way down . . .

To our delight we were able to reach the highest point at 11:30. The peak of Mt. Olympus is broad, but one height is higher by a few feet than the uneven rest and forms the highest point. When the Lusignans were in control of the island it was their practice to take their summer vacations here, and many traces of numerous houses roughly built of stones are supposed to date back to that time . . . At 5° Réaumur we were at a height of 5970 Vienna feet [6190 English feet], that is a little lower than the average tree line at Bulghar Dagh on the opposite shore.[125] At noon the fog from the southwest quickly rose to the peak, so that only the eastern horizon and the entire eastern landscape up to the shore remained free. When we first arrived we could clearly see the ships and the area of Cape Gata near Limassol. The valley of Prodhromos also was clear, and the guide showed me to the west of Prodhromos the villages of Demicho [Lemithou] and Trisulies [Tris Elies]. He also showed me Cicio [Kýkko] Monastery on a mountain peak; here there is an icon of the Virgin painted by St. Mark, who is said to have painted four such icons.[126] The light on the plain was very favorable; while we sat under a cloud, the sun was shining there everywhere . . .

[Having returned from my excursion] I spent the rest of the day properly storing my unexpectedly rich booty . . . While I was thus engaged the people, especially the women, became so importunate, without any embarrassment, that I had to ask them to leave my things alone; and when that did not help I showed them all the door.

## From Olympus to Limassol

On 7 April I sent two local people to the north side of the mountain to quickly obtain some moss so that I might pack my rich booty of living plants of the previous day for shipment to Vienna. The village of Prodhromos lies at an altitude of 4028 feet above sea level on a wide, halfmoon-shaped terrace carved into the slope of the mountain. The south side of the cultivated ground is covered with extensive vineyards, the grapes of which furnish an excellent wine. The fields, lying next to the irrigation ditches, are so extensive that they can provide for fifty families, who live in twenty-eight houses. The houses on the southeast side of the slope stand in several rows, as if on a terrace, one

[124] The Goralen are the people who live in the Beskids, a mountain range which is part of the Carpathians and located in southeastern Poland.
[125] The Taurus Mountains of Anatolia.
[126] Kotschy is in error; the icon, probably the most famous on the island, is said to be the work of St. Luke, and the number of such icons is three, not four. See Hackett, *Orthodox Church*, 339–44, and Athanasios Papageorgiou, *Icons of Cyprus* (New York, 1970) 42–43.

above the other, in such a manner that their back part is built right into the mountain and the flat roof at the same time forms the yard for the neighboring house above.

In addition to the usual grains potatoes are grown here in large quantities and have provided the village's main income for several years; they are bought up by dealers from the port cities. Even now in the spring the inhabitants live largely on potatoes, and we found them to be of excellent quality. There was no blight yet, neither in the potato fields nor in the vineyards[127]...

After the living plants had been carefully stored we began our journey, while it threatened to rain, to the monastery of Prodhromos. From the pleasant village landscape we moved into the forest, which is crossed by a path cut into the side of the mountain. At various places there are clearings with little meadows which offer a charming view across the mountainous island down to the sea. After two hours we reached the famous monastery of Troodiza [Troodhitissa] just before a heavy downpour. The monastery consists of a group of buildings which, at the same altitude as Prodhromos, lie in a narrow forested gorge so hidden away that one does not have a view from there, neither over the sea nor over the island. The main building, one story high, is laid out as a quadrangle in which the church and the archimandrite's apartment take up the front, the monks' cells the left wing, and the reception room and the refectory the right wing. The rear of the quadrangle houses the lay brothers, who provide services within the monastery and tend the vineyards and wide-spread fields. In more recent times the Dutch consul in Larnaca has donated three fairly large bells to the monastery; these bells have been placed on a scaffold in the courtyard and from there announce the hours of prayer throughout the day. In front of the monastery, on the left, there is a one-story building for accommodating visitors; here I had found quarters already in 1841. Other small structures serve the domestic economy; all are covered with high and steep roofs of wooden boards. The reception given us by the monks was very kind. Two of them remembered my three black servants who had given them trouble enough during my earlier fourteen-day stay.

It rained heavily while a common meal was being prepared. The head monk apologized for not being able to take a seat in our midst or to serve fresh meat, because of a fast. About fifteen monks gathered and, after a short prayer, sat down with us. The dishes which we were served consisted of boiled rice with fat, a cereal with milk, dried meat of moufflon, the wild sheep of these mountains, excellent cheese, and fresh bread. Large earthen pitchers with aged wine filled our glasses, and there was no end to the toasts. The monks' food consisted of beans preserved in vinegar, dry bread, and a salad of the green stems of the caper bush, which are gathered in the spring and preserved in salt water. Apart from coffee it was not allowed this week to partake of anything hot, because the venerable patriarch in Nicosia had, unfortunately, died recently.[128]

Although the rain partly ceased it now began to snow, and the monks wanted to provide a pleasant evening for us if I should decide to stay overnight. We were forced, however, because of the [expected] arrival of the steamer to hurry and to leave at once, lest we might be snowed-in here overnight.

---

[127] The famous potato blight, which devastated Ireland in the years 1845–1849, also struck continental Europe in 1845 and 1846.

[128] Kotschy is not very clear here. The head of the Orthodox Church on Cyprus holds the rank of archbishop, not patriarch. The archbishop at the time was Makarios I, who was in office in 1854–1865. Does he mean, perhaps, that the *hegoumenos* of the monastery had died while on a visit to Nicosia?

At three o'clock in the afternoon, after a friendly good-bye, we began our way through the valley, in the direction of h12½, that is nearly south. At the well below the monastery, after the strong wine, we refreshed ourselves with cold water. Apart from a few mulberry and fig trees, which are cultivated in gardens, there are no fruit trees here . . . In a drizzle, riding through abundant vegetation, we reached the small village of Tino [?] and [?] at an altitude of 3000 feet above sea level . . . At dusk we reached the village of Omodhos. Here our guides took us to the large monastery, where we were hospitably received, although the monks could not offer us proper comfort, because a large church was being built of cut stone in the yard. The evening was noticeably cool; the temperature dropped to 4° Réaumur at an altitude of 2800 feet above sea level. Thus we were pleased to be served unexpected hot dishes and excellent wine.

In the morning of 8 April we were quite astonished to see by the light of the rising sun that the whole mountain, down to the village of Tino, was covered with snow. The village of Omodhos boasts about one-hundred houses, which, almost all of them being built of cut stone, are topped by flat terraces. The location of the village on the south side of a hill offers a pleasant view across the chalk-land as it gently descends towards the coast. The hills of the area are all planted in vineyards, while the lower elevations provide beautiful fields. After a short breakfast we were in a hurry to reach the shady environs of the coast before the heat [of mid-day] . . .

A decision was made to look for accommodations in Civides [Kividhes] and then to continue the journey during the next night; but since the place was quite deserted and not even water could be found, thirst forced us to continue our journey to the coast . . . During a brief rest we turned our eyes towards the mountain and saw that all the heights almost down to Omodhos were still under a cover of snow at nine o'clock in the morning. Even the lower, forested ridge which stretches eastward towards Santa Croce presented its trees at the upper limit covered with powdery snow. Whereas at our departure from Omodhos in the morning we had had a temperature of 4° Réaumur, the thermometer registered 17.5° Réaumur at ten o'clock and a light, pleasant west wind blew from the sea to our south—a sharp contrast to the near-by winter landscape. On rocky, sometimes very difficult paths and in a heat to which we were not used we reached the village of Eremi [Erimi] in the coastal plain at two o'clock. During a short rest I took a walk along the road which leads from Limassol to Paphos, in order to inspect the ruins which lie towards the village of Episkopi. The short walk would not have been worth the effort if I had not collected a number of plants, for of antiquities nothing of consequence was to be seen other than a few column fragments. After a ride of three hours across the rich plain of Cape Gata we arrived in the small town of Limassol, which is different from most towns of Cyprus by its pleasant location, its neat houses, and its notable cleanliness.

Although the town is not lucky enough to have a harbor and ships are forced to lie at anchor a nautical mile[129] out, Limassol nevertheless engages in the most lively trade on the island. Along the shore there is a long row of houses with storage space and coffee shops, and behind these there are three or four rows of dwellings, and between them there runs a street paved with cobble stones. Limassol has the appearance of a narrow but long complex of houses. One should mention also the gardens, which, thanks to plentiful irrigation, produce so many vegetables that they are shipped even to Beirut. I noticed several sycamore fig trees, which protruded above the wall of a garden at the western end of the

---

[129] 1853 m. or 6080 feet.

town. This must be their northern-most occurrence. Among commercial products the excellent Cypriot Commanderia wine takes first place. Also the other, less noble, red varieties do well enough in the district of Limassol, the true wine district of the island. Another profitable article is St. John's bread, the trees of which grow in those places which do not lend themselves to cultivation because of their stony substrata. I was told that more than one-hundred shiploads of St. John's bread were exported from the area [annually]. Apart from cotton and red dyestuff animal skins from all the mountains are brought to market in Limassol. Through the kindness of the Lloyd agent we received quarters for this night in a garden house.

## From Limassol to Larnaca

Because of the negligence of the muleteers, who had allowed one of their animals to wander away, we were unable to use the freshness of the morning for our departure. As soon as we had left the gardens the route took us along the elevated coast past Juniperus Phoenicea bushes. The land-side of the path is bordered by vineyards and fertile fields, on which trees of St. John's bread, the size of our oaks, stand scattered about, so that the shade of their dense foliage does no harm to the seeds. We took a mid-day rest at a mountain stream, next to the village of Moni, which lies one-half hour inland from the coast. A quarter of an hour north from there one comes upon the village of Manavreli [?], which is far larger than Moni, and after the first high ridge to the east upon the village of Patma.[130] The flora of the area was rather poor and already wilting.

At two o'clock in the afternoon the path led us, along a height, over loose stone to the sea. The coast at this point is very steep and high, formed of reddish loam and mixed with loose stones. It is easily eroded by the waves, especially in the winter and during storms, so that entire sections, the size of a house, collapse into the sea . . . After we had followed the tiring and sandy path for one half hour we turned inland again and reached the small village of Pentaaonos [?]. It lies on a small height and offers a wide view over the sea. Since leaving Limassol we had already passed nine promontories, and at the village of Maroni we crossed the fourth, very weak river. Half an hour after that we came to a fifth river, at which the village of Laria is located.[131] The entire area, gently rising towards the mountains, is almost completely cultivated. Here, too, there are trees of St. John's bread, the fruits of which were piled up in large heaps along the coast. Some small boats were lying at anchor, waiting to be loaded with these fruits.

At seven o'clock we reached the large village of Massoto [Mazotos], which is distinguished by the good construction of its houses from the others that we had seen along the coast. While this village is located on the loamy, infertile soil of a height, the fields all around, in contrast, on deeper, black, humus-like ground, are very well tended; also numerous herds of oxen, cows, and horses were returning from pasture and gave proof of the prosperity of the inhabitants. The population is made up entirely of Greeks, who have built themselves a large, beautiful church at the west end of the village.

On 10 April, in an effort to reach Larnaca before the worst heat, we rode quickly across a sterile area . . . Having arrived next to the Turkish village of Dschebelsini [?] we were facing the cone-shaped, steep mountain of Santa Croce or Stavros [Stavrovouni],

---

[130] Not far from Amathus. See Stylianou, *Cartography.*
[131] See Stylianou, *Cartography.*

the peak of which is crowned by a monastery. Cape Kiti reaches far out into the sea. At its base rise the minarets of the market hamlet of Aja Barbara [Ayia Varvara], a place which has always been of strategic importance, as is shown by the ruins of a fort from the time of the Lusignans . . .

Passing the villa of the Greek consul, which is surrounded by a luxuriant garden, we hurried to an aqueduct at Alpera [Arpera], which is borne by high arches and provides the city of Larnaca with excellent drinking water. There is so much water here that not only is the aqueduct always filled, but also a mill can be operated and a large garden laid out by a Pasha about one-hundred years ago can be adequately watered . . .

The steamer which had been expected this day had not yet arrived in port; happy to have accomplished our travels with such good fortune, we reached the house of our consul at ten o'clock [in the morning]. Our excursion had proved for the first time that in the time until the arrival of the next steamer a visit to the most important places on the island, including the ascent of Mt. Olympus can comfortably be managed.

### Voyage along the Syrian coast to Mersina

The steamer, which we had expected two days ago, approached the coast only in the morning of 12 April. The day before the steamer coming from Syria had picked up our plants bound for Europe. So much time was taken up by sorting and unloading the cargo that we could begin our voyage to Beirut only at five o'clock. Since the establishment of the Lloyd service the connection with the coast of Cilicia has been discontinued; travelers must join the line along the Syrian coast, by way of Beirut, in order to reach the port of Mersina [Mersin] by way of Tripoli, Latakia [Laodicea], and Alexandrette [Iskanderun]. During the pleasant voyage the captain brought several maps of Cyprus. A special hydrographical map of Cyprus was prepared by the English captain Thomas Graves with great care.[132] This superior and accurate map served Gaudry and Amadé d'Amour as the basis of their *Charte agricole de Chypre*.[133]25 M. d'Amour has lived for many years in Larnaca as a businessman and has traveled over all parts of the island; thus he was able to produce, with Gaudry, such a specialized work.

# Unger—1866

### [Plate 10]

Franz Unger, *Die Insel Cypern einst und jetzt*, a lecture delivered in Graz, winter of 1866 (Vienna, 1866) 3–21. Franz Joseph Andreas Nicolas Unger (1800–1870) traveled widely in the 1860s in Greece and the Levant. He was co-author with Theodor Kotschy of *Die Insel Cypern, ihrer physischen und organischen Natur nach, mit Rücksicht auf ihre frühere Geschichte* (Vienna, 1865). See further Hunt Botanical Library, Carnegie-Mellon University, Pittsburgh, *Biographical Dictionary of Botanists Represented in the Hunt Institute Portrait Collection* (Boston, 1972), p. 411; Online AEIOU* Österreich Lexikon in either English or German.

---

[132] Stylianou, *Cartography,* 150, 408–10, figs. 194, 194a, 194b, and 194c.
[133] Stylianou, *Cartography,* 151–52. This map in turn was used by Unger and Kotschy in their *Cypern.*

If art, science, and civilization advanced in the main from East to West on the open, broad, and level route of the Mediterranean, and if this passage could take place only gradually and by fits and starts, then the islands along this route and the outlying stretches of the coast of the mainland must have been the most important stations through which this movement of culture was promoted and maintained. Of these islands three, Rhodes, Cyprus, and Crete, are closest to the East and are large, spacious, and blessed by nature. In all likelihood they must have been the first halting places, received the first immigrants from the Asian and African mainland, and with them continued the imported elements of culture. Indeed this was the case. Rhodes on the one hand, smaller and situated close to the mainland, and Crete on the other hand, cast out far into the sea, participated in this process less energetically. But Cyprus, by its location and nature, was the island most qualified to become the emporium of culture on the move. Historians and natural scientists have long cast an eye on this island, which is privileged in every regard. And if historians and archaeologists were the first to gain treasures, they made the natural scientists all the more eager for the spoils which they might rightly expect from the exploration of organic as well as inorganic nature.

It was these considerations, and no others, which prompted me four years ago to acquaint myself with this island, which measures 173 [German] square miles,[134] and to do so more intensely than in the careless manner of a tourist. My like-minded companion Dr. Theodor Kotschy and I pursued our objectives on many far-flung paths. And if I at the same time cast side glances on the island's present as well as past cultural conditions, I merely followed the press of an urge to obtain information on some of the most important questions of our society.

Allow me now, in a few but comprehensive lines, to draw a picture of the island, not only of its present condition but also of its past development. I am accustomed to consider nature not as something which simply exists but as something which developed and to approach the riddle of the present by uncovering the past. Thus it was not hard for me to familiarize myself with the facts and peculiarities which have given to life on this island its present characteristics.

One may say very well that the waves of history, in the course of several millennia, as long as the island lay in their surge, have come across it so mightily that they have washed away nearly everything but its rocky foundation. Nothing of the original condition of the island can still be recognized. All political and ecclesiastical institutions, all societal relations have little by little yielded to changing fortunes. Peoples of various descent and language followed one upon another and have disappeared again. Nature herself has taken off her original dress to such an extent and has brought about such changes in the condition of the land that, apart from the firm mountains, one no longer perceives anything that has not become different, outlived its usefulness, run its course, and fallen into decay. If this marks in general the heavy footsteps of history, it is all the more remarkable here, because these footsteps, confined to a small space, have left open a view of past, happier times.

But if we will, for a moment, go back further into prehistory, we shall see what excellent land, what natural wealth was available to the human race when it took possession of this island. I may, I think, consider it a firm result of my geological research that Cyprus once was connected to the mainland. Only after the Aegean Sea spread across the

---

[134] Correct: 273 German square miles = 3572 statute square miles.

Sporades and the Cyclades, did this connection to the Syrian mainland come about and thereby change the natural character of the island. But, while Europe moaned under the burden of the glaciers, this fragile bridge again submerged; only the Karpas Peninsula has survived as a remnant.

When the first inhabitants came here from the mainland they found the island still fully in its original dress. An unlimited forest covered mountains and valleys. Streams and rivers were richly provided with that source of life which the sun could use to bring about luscious vegetation. Showers of rain alternating with sunshine and fertile thunderstorms occurring even in the summertime must have blessed the hilly country with an exuberant flora. No wonder then that the first settlers felt very comfortable and, as now in the hinterland of North America, made an excellent business of providing an entrance to the gifts of Ceres by clearing the forests. Eratosthenes, one of the oldest geographers, provides us with this prehistorical picture of the island, according to Strabo [14.682].

A broad valley between two mighty mountain ranges,[135] with two rivers of considerable size flowing through it in opposite directions, was especially suited to give a firm foundation to agriculture.[136] And if one of these, the Pedieos, competes even now with the Nile of Egypt for the first place in fertilizing power, this has a real, physical reason, as a comparative chemical analysis of the silt has shown. Furthermore all the banks of the small rivers and streams descending from the mountains are in an excellent position to allow agriculture and the growing of useful fruit trees.

The forests of evergreens and oaks are unlimited, the soil at the lower elevations is fertile, and the climate is happy, allowing roses and violets to bloom all year. But it was not only these factors which invited the immigrants to stay, but also the gifts of Pluto. Surface veins of ore, perhaps accidentally brought to melting, brought to an astonished people for the first time a knowledge of metal. To this day we maintain in the word "Kupfer" or *cyprum* a memory of the land of *Cypros*, where this metal was discovered or at least extensively introduced into world trade.[137] The copper and silver mines, once so energetically operated, have, all of them, ceased to function; but even if history had in this regard left us no record of the wealth which once was present, the numerous slag heaps, scattered throughout the land, would do so.

The national hero of grey antiquity, Kinyras, a contemporary of Agamemnon, priest and king at once, is lauded as the discoverer of the veins of ore and the inventor of hammer, tongs, anvil, and crowbar. What a happy land in which kings do not squander and destroy but discover and found the nation's wealth! It is no wonder then that a land like Cyprus not only was self-sufficient but received a stream of immigrants from all sides and that neighboring countries looked upon this blessed island with jealous eyes and allowed it to become an apple of discord, the subject of dispute, both open and secret, to this day.

Allow me now to consider the earliest immigrations to which this island owes its original national character, a character which—it is hard to believe—is clearly demonstrated even now by more than a few monuments.

In this regard, too, the shape of the coasts and the availability of a stone most useful for building purposes, the quaternary sea sandstone, have shown themselves to be es-

---

[135] The Mesaoria, with the Pentadaktylos Mountains to the north and the Troodos Mountains to the south.

[136] The Pedieos, flowing north before turning east, and the Yerasoyia, flowing south.

[137] Unger points out in an endnote that the Phoenicians called the island Kittim.

pecially significant. In the strata of this sandstone, wide-spread and even reaching inland, it was an easy thing to expand the natural grottoes and thus gain suitable habitats for humans and domestic animals, temples for the gods, and tomb chambers for the dead. Lapithos on the northwest side of the island, a completely ruined city, allows us even now to recognize strange walls of rock and vaulted grottoes, which reach up from the rubble and to which stone and wooden structures were once joined in a primitive way. Just as puzzling rock formations, both larger and smaller, are found near Larnaca, on the southernmost tip of Akrotiri, at Amathus, Kyrenia, etc. Special mention, however, must be given to the tomb grottoes of Kouklia and Paphos, since they are provided with well-preserved inscriptions. Our famous fellow-countryman von Hammer [Joseph Baron von Hammer-Purgstall, 1774–1856] visited one of these places as a young man and has left us a facsimile of the inscription of the stone which closed a tomb chamber. This stone has since been removed by French archaeologists who visited the island at the same time as I; at the same time a second, similar inscription was found. The inscription above the entrance to a similar burial grotto at Paphos is even better preserved, in spite of the rough surface of the stone and the corrosion which occurred in the course of millennia.

The characters of all of these inscriptions, which we find again also on the earliest coins of the island and which appear also on the now famous bronze tablet of the Egyptian king Amasis, have, with few exceptions, not yet been deciphered with certainty and point us back to a time on which all historical sources are silent. Monuments with archaic Phoenician inscriptions are also scattered across the whole island, are more easily accessible, and have in part been already deciphered. This proves that the Phoenicians, nearby and fond of traveling and of trading, founded their colonies here too. Their being governed by their own kings might be dated much before Alexander, to the fifth and sixth century B.C.

But also around this time and even earlier the first settlements were established by the Greeks, who, like the Phoenicians, built cities, cultivated the land, built aqueducts, exploited the deposits of ore, and thus attained a level of civilization which perhaps was not much inferior to that of the mother country. Especially we must mention here the Attic colonists who founded Salamis, the Argive colonists who founded Nea Paphos, and the Lacedaemonian colonists who founded Lapithos.

But already the Phoenicians brought with their religion a new and powerful cultural element to the island. This element gave to the island an almost supernatural aura and lasted far into the future, when the Apostle Paul and Barnabas preached the Gospel here and the latter, a disciple of Matthew, suffered a martyr's death here for the Christian faith. Kings and emperors undertook pilgrimages to this Mecca of the faith and deposited their votive gifts here on the altar of the almighty goddess. This is the introduction of the cult of Astarte, to whom temples were erected at Kition [Citium] as well as at Dali [Idalion], Paphos, and Amathus.

There is still a question on the religious meaning of this nature deity, on her relationship to the Greek Aphrodite, and on how these concepts developed one from another and finally determined her formal worship. That even Greek and Roman authors were not well informed on this point can be seen from their comments, which refer much more to her cult than to her essential nature.

This much, however, is certain: the idol which was worshiped at Paphos as *konon kyprion* was without question a meteoric stone; such also was the *baitylos* [meteoric stone], which was worshiped as a symbol of Cybele at Pessinus in Galatia, at Delphi, in the temple of Jupiter Amon in the Libyan desert, and in many other places. We do not know where these stones came from and whether an epiphany, by name, of the Phoenician Astarte, who appeared with fire and lightning in the sky, was accompanied by the fall of that stone which was later worshiped as the Cyprian cone, just as we do not know the origin of the meteorite which is enclosed by the Kaaba of Mecca.

How deep the worship of this sacred place and the name of Aphrodite associated with it entered into the psyche of the people is shown by the worship of our black Mother of God and the epithet Aphroditissa,[138] which in Cyprus to this day naively refers to the mother of our Savior.

As is well known, the Greeks let their goddess of beauty and love rise from the foam of the sea and land at Paphos when she had not been received at Cythera, today's Cerigo.[139] What lies at the bottom of this myth is not entirely clear; but we know for certain that the formation of foam on the reefy coast of Paphos is a rare phenomenon not to be found elsewhere to the same degree. This happens only in the early spring, but is so significant that the snow-white foam builds up several feet high along the beach and frequently is carried inland by the wind.

Although I have not observed this phenomenon at Paphos, I have encountered something quite similar at the salt lake of Larnaca, a body of water which is separated from the sea only by a narrow strip of land. Here the foam is due to an accumulation of slimy sea-weed and to just as plentiful crustacea beginning to rot. At a later time I approached Mr. Smith, the obliging consul in Paphos, for a portion of Aphrodite-foam and even sent him some containers suitable for this purpose; but I did not succeed in obtaining any of it and therefore must leave it open to question whether it is formed in the same manner as that of the salt lake.

You will ask me: What is the appearance today of these old cult places, of the sacred groves in which love was practiced, and of the dove cotes in which the birds sacred to the goddess were kept? One can readily understand that of this sanctuary, once known in the whole civilized world, nothing has survived, apart from a few traces, and even that one hardly knows where exactly it stood.

In Amathus, too, where perhaps the oldest temple of Astarte stood and which still existed at the time of the Crusades, nothing is left of the whole city but a pile of stones. On the acropolis, the likely location of the temple, I still saw under some bushes two colossal sandstone vessels, which, as a shepherd boy on the scene thought, might have been used for purposes of purification. One of them is broken into fragments; the other is still in one piece, but weakened by a fissure of such kind, that it cannot be moved from its location without falling apart. And yet, as I hear, this has already happened when the French brought this monolith [weighing 14 tons] to Paris [in 1865].[140]

---

[138] See Hill, *History,* I 81.

[139] Cythera was called Cerigo in Venetian sources, being in Venetian hands from 1238 to 1797.

[140] The intact one of the two vases was removed to the Louvre in 1865/1866; it weighs 13 tons, and its diameter is 3.91 m. See the following: Vassos Karageorghis, *Cyprus: From the Stone Age to the Romans* (London, 1982) 151. Antoine Hermary, *Catalogue des antiquités de Chypre: Sculptures* (Paris: Musée du Louvre, Département des antiquités orientales, 1989), no. 918. Antoine Hermary and Olivier Masson, "Deux vases inscrits du sanctuaire d'Aphrodite à Amathus," *BCH* 114 (1990) 187–214 at 211–14. Pierre Aupert, *Guide d'Amathonte* (Paris, 1996) 34–35 with fig. 9.

Paphos, once an extensive city with splendid buildings, temples, aqueduct, etc., but repeatedly the victim of devastating earthquakes, now has only the appearance of a village resting on the rubble of its palaces. Of the temple of Aphrodite, which was built here later, there is no trace. Equally so the sacred gardens nearby and the fresh spring, which once watered the pomegranate trees and myrtle bushes, have sunk to the level of a communal laundry for the village. The whispering winds no longer carry Cypris' laments for the wounded Adonis through dark arbors, although the soil would still be fertile enough, judging by the age-old terebinth trees which still stand.

Only in Palea Paphos, where the dirty village of Kouklia now spreads out, there is still a piece of the Cyclopean wall which once enclosed the temple, but of the temple itself not a single stone is left.

Where once incense and the scent of amber rose in clouds, where the stone idol, washed, anointed, and wrapped in cloth, was hidden from the view of the people, where the doves were cooing in the pleasure groves, where love was celebrating its orgies, it is only rubble and ruins of columns which cover the naked rock, and no living creature disturbs the wanderer lost in the contemplation of now and then.

Finally there is Dali [Idalion], the sacred place of pilgrimage, the oracle in the interior of the island, in the midst of fertile fields which are watered by a pleasant mountain stream. What is it more than a collection of miserable huts, interspersed with house-high piles of rubbish? Only tentatively, on the slope of a hill where now fields of grain spread out, can one identify the place where once stood the temple to which thousands of pilgrims came every year, filling the sanctuary with their gifts. This is also one of the richest sources of such votive gifts, of which I brought home a whole chest full, although their artistic value is small.[141] Wherever there is an excavation one finds smashed statues, implements, etc. which the zealous adherents of the new faith destroyed in blind fury, filling wells and cisterns with them.

I will pass over the fate which the island experienced over a period of more than a millennium. It developed more or less comfortably, sometimes under its own princes, sometimes under foreign rule; it was exposed to wars, conquests, and devastations, but always recovered from the misfortunes which had befallen it, until the beginning of the Crusades brought to it a new turning point.

Kition, Paphos, and Salamis were already destroyed. From the Ptolemies the island passed into the possession of Rome and then, after the partition of the world empire, into the possession of the Greek [Byzantine] empire. Byzantium was still ruling when, enthused with the idea of retaking the Holy Land from the hands of the Muslims, King Richard I [Lionheart] and Philip II [Philip Augustus] of France established a firm foothold in Cyprus (1191). Cyprus, as the strategically most important base against the advancing crescent, became from now on a halting place for all crusading knights and orders. It became a Germanic feudal state under independent rulers from the House of Lusignan. French became the official language, French etiquette the etiquette of the court.

---

[141] Unger reports in a footnote that he brought home two heads of Aphrodite and deposited them in the Joanneum in Graz. The other objects, too, were acquired by the Joanneum. See Anton Mell, *Das steiermärkische Landesmuseum Joanneum und seine Sammlungen* (Graz, 1911) 284. All the objects currently are kept at Eggenberg Castle, a branch of the Joanneum. Information kindly provided by Dr. Gunda Pfunder.

In spite of the continuing battles which the ruling house had to endure in the constantly rebuilt might of the arch enemy and in its own family disputes the prosperity of the land increased. Cities were founded, fortresses built, monasteries established, and under the care of the secular orders of the Templars and the Hospitalers the country prospered all around and grew in fame abroad. To this period belong: the fortification of Famagusta and Nicosia, the older and the later city of coronation; the splendid building of the cathedrals, in Gothic style, in both of these cities; the Premonstratensian abbey de la pais, now called Bellapais, laid out on a generous scale and located in one of the most charming parts of the island; and also the numerous monasteries of the Greek rite, which rather resemble small fortresses. Viticulture, farming, and silk production flourished in the country, all the land along the rivers was turned into a garden of olive, karob, and mulberry trees, and trade rose to a level never achieved previously.

Although several of these Cypriot kings also put the crown of Jerusalem on their head, there were, nevertheless, constant fights with the Genoese and others to endure, until finally the island passed by marriage into the hands of the Republic of Venice, which, however, was able to maintain its hold for only 85 years.

During this time the Turks had hard-pressed the island on numerous occasions and had captured the capital after a siege of seven weeks. But the most gruesome barbarism ever accompanied the final strike against the fortress of Famagusta. It was not only that thousands of the courageous fighters were led to slaughter and that blood flowed in streams, but that the courageous defender [Marcantonio] Bragadino was, in a genuinely cannibalistic manner, flayed alive and that his skin was stuffed to make a doll (1571). A numbness of death followed the catastrophe.

No matter how significant the time that has passed since those unhappy days, the country did never again rise to its previous greatness, prosperity, and moral strength; it felt the weight of the iron chains and little by little became used to it. Not only did the population, primarily consisting of Greeks, diminish by a factor of almost twenty, but all commercial activity had suffered a paralysis which led to the utmost impoverishment.

One can see how here the fields, the vineyards, and the olive trees, the major sources of sustenance, are managed in the most primitive manner, while in the West agriculture has risen to a level of sophistication; one realizes how many of our cultivated plants here grow wild, while the population, instead of growing them in gardens, prefers to live with the animals on whatever grows wild; one can observe what lethargy prevails in all branches of industry and commerce. And thus one surely cannot say that the condition of the island has returned from that numbness of death to life.

And then one must consider that one of the greatest enemies of agriculture, the locust, used to be a rare phenomenon, but now has established itself on the island and annually makes a tour of the whole island right up to the mountains. And billions of these small creatures in places leave no blade and no leaf untouched, but deprive the farmer of all that he has not already harvested. And, one can observe also, that the same farmer, in a child-like way, seeks protection in the recitation of prayers and in [religious] processions, while the government acts completely helpless. Thus one should not be surprised by the depressed conditions which prevail everywhere.

I remarked at the beginning that Cyprus distinguished itself by its wealth of forests, which, it seems, still existed when Lebanon had long been robbed of this ornament. In spite of the considerable consumption for the land and the numerous fleets, which were built from the earliest times to the present, the forest has not been completely destroyed, although it has been pushed back to the remotest corners of the mountains.

The shortage of wood is, however, already felt in the country, since all fuel must be taken from brushwood and timber must be largely imported from abroad. And one cannot help but see with astonishment with what lack of concern and how nonchalantly the last remnants of this precious national treasure are consigned to destruction, and with what childish naiveté the government stands by while pitch-pickers and tar-burners, for the sake of negligible gain, ruin entire stretches of forest. It is a good thing that people generally have no axe and no saw. Otherwise, surely, it would be impossible to find a single tree on the island.

Thus Cyprus has, apart from insignificant stretches, already lost its forests, and, since the ground cannot to the same extent be converted into arable fields, a wild and uninviting terrain has, little by little, taken their place. No longer do forest-clad heights, as they once did, gather the clouds which might provide mild rains during the hot season. No fructifying dew refreshes the seeds when the sun aims its vertical rays, like injuring arrows, at the thirsty ground. Everything at that time is burned, the springs have dried out. The climate at the lower elevations, already ill-reputed in antiquity, has only become less tolerable and more murderous.

While diligent hands and an intelligent government would be able successfully to counteract the impoverishment which has taken place, the people numbly stare and conscientiously observe formal religious rituals, waiting for a better future from heaven. No impetus, no intellectual life seeks the means to put an end to the conditions of rot and dissolution.

Is this perhaps no longer possible? Have the prerequisites of a physical and moral rebirth been lost forever? This is a question which is very closely connected with the question of a revitalization of all the countries of the Orient. This question has always been answered in two ways. Some believe that the material prerequisites for a revitalization are lacking and that countries whose natural resources have been exhausted, neglected, and destroyed, never regain their earlier importance. Others are of the opinion that such a destruction of productivity is not possible, and that every land, however badly it may have been exploited, still harbors within itself the buds of new life, and that just this is the task of revitalization, to arouse, protect, and develop these buds. After a careful examination of the natural conditions I have always decided for the latter view, maintaining my conviction that an aging of nature and a lasting change of climate have not occurred in historical times.

Another question, far more difficult to answer, is by what means the changes which have occurred can be arrested and nature be persuaded to reverse course and rehabilitate itself. It goes without saying that such change must be initiated by human intelligence and energy. Only new vitality and energy can affect substantial change, and there is, in my opinion, only one way in which these can be infused into a generation which is run down like a silted-up harbor. Neither a change of minister nor a change of the system of government can help here. What has been ruined in a moral way does not return to a different track. Only a change of race can here bring help; only with uncorrupted powers and fresh drive can ruined countries be helped to rise again, in no other way. Yes, even the beautiful island of Cyprus, the most precious pearl in the shell of the Mediterranean, must abide by this law if it wants again to attain its prosperity and became a Western nation, as it once was.

Our neighbors to the west, thinking that they are called to a civilizing mission, have never lost this island or the whole Orient out of their view. Someone, traveling on government business, recently remarked: "One finds on Cyprus many footprints of the French, and there is a widely held opinion that this nation will some day regain the rule of this island." I can only, from a cosmopolitan perspective from this continent, extend my best wishes for success. On the other hand I must confess that I have neither perceived any traces of such prophecies nor observed any particular liking for this civilizing nation. I was reminded of a saying of the German emperor Maximilian I, who once said of the French: "They sing higher than the notes indicate, they read differently from what has been written, and they speak differently from what they feel in their hearts."

And now a heart-felt farewell to the native country of the goddess of beauty and love. I shall never forget the hours which I spent in intimate touch with the splendid nature and the good, pitiable people; and I shall never deny the sad emotions which your ruins evoked in me or the pleasure granted me by a look in the nursery of the human race. May the friendly spirit that keeps watch on the progress of mankind and drives it to deeds worthy of him also set foot on this island and may he reveal himself in the foam of the raging waves as a new divinity and show you and level for you the paths which you must walk. All human effort is perishable; when the big things are at stake we must now, as in the past, seek refuge with the gods.

## Unger and Kotschy

[Plates 11–13]

Franz Unger and Theodor Kotschy, *Die Insel Cypern, ihrer physischen und organischen Natur nach, mit Rücksicht auf ihre frühere Geschichte* (Vienna, 1865). This book is concerned primarily with matters of geology, climate, botany, zoology, and agriculture. Historians will be more interested in Chapter X, pp. 502–69, "Historisch-Topographisches," of which Franz Unger is the author. It is divided into three sections.

### I. Churches and Monasteries

Churches and monasteries are so numerous and spread across the entire island that one would have to deem the inhabitants to be especially pious, if one did not know that the number of religious buildings is no measure of the veneration of the deity to whom they were erected. I am referring, of course, to the Greek churches, although there is no shortage of mosques either. The largest and most beautiful of these mosques owe their existence to a conversion from their original Christian purpose.

As in all things, so also in these places which are dedicated to God, decay and neglect are expressed in such a manner that the observer is seized by sadness and disgust at the same time. One is saddened when one observes how valuable buildings, to which centuries dedicated their resources and their talent, are recklessly surrendered to irresistable decay. At the same time one is filled with anger against the incomprehensible carelessness which does not deem it worth the effort to repair minor damages and rather condemns the whole to destruction.

As there must be something incomplete and unbecoming in their dress, in their house, and their business, so the Cypriots carry this attitude over also to sacred places, even to the icons of the deity and of the saints in the church; these, it seems, they learn to love only when they look just as ragged as they themselves do. I have seen in the churches icons which could no longer be recognized because of dust and grime and damage, and which had been put into this condition solely by the endless osculation, the essence of adoration. On many an icon of the Mother of God (Panayia) and Christ, as well as St. George and other prominent saints, I have seen crusts, as thick as a knife blade, of saliva and dirt.

There is on the whole island not a single church, and even less a monastery, in which signs of decay could not be observed to a greater or lesser degree. Only in a single monastery, the most prosperous monastery of the island, in the monastery of St. Panteleimon,[142] I saw, to my surprise, new construction under way. On the time of foundation of the monasteries nothing is known locally, for nowhere are there libraries or archives, and the monks make it their business to remain in complete ignorance of the matter. In all probability most of the monasteries were founded during the crusades and were gifted with considerable lands by the generosity of Christian princes. The oldest, however, surely date from the very early days of Christianity, since we know that the Apostle Paul and the Cypriot Barnabas already preached Christianity here.[143]

I do not doubt that the original duty of the monks, apart from divine services, was to tend the land; this would be true especially of those monasteries which established themselves far from all villages in the wilderness of the mountains.

It is amazing to see in what dimensions and with what fortifications most of these monasteries were laid out. On the one hand they are like fortresses, while on the other hand they also provide for comfort. The monasteries of Makhaeras and Khrysoroyatissa may serve as examples of fortified monasteries, and the monastery of Ayia Napa as an example of a comfortable monastery built of cut blocks of stone. Everywhere the church, the real sanctuary, stands surrounded by the monks' quarters and the domestic buildings in the middle of a court yard formed by these buildings. The large number of cells, spacious and airy, and the size of the communal assembly and dining room suggest a once larger population of the monastery. At Khrysostomos, where only one monk lives today, Herr Kotschy still found several fifteen years ago. Ali Bey[144] fifty-six years ago counted three, and Mariti[145] a hundred years ago speaks of ten to twelve. Under the portico which encloses the court yard of Ayia Napa on two sides, there are eleven cells of substantial size, of which not a one is occupied now. Only a single Papa and his wife live in these extensive buildings. The same is true at St. Barbara, Akhiropiitos, Morphou, and several others, which could accommodate five to ten times as many conventuals as they do. Quite regularly one finds in even the greatest monasteries only five to eight monks. Only Khrysoroyatissa is an exception; there are currently twelve monks there.

---

[142] At Myrtou in the Kyrenia district.

[143] The monastery of Ayios Nikolaos on the Akrotiri peninsula lays claim to being the oldest on the island, reportedly having been founded in the days of the emperor Constantine. See Hackett, *Orthodox Church*, 358. It is also known as the monastery of St. Nicholas of the Cats.

[144] El Abassi Ali Bey (1766–1818, actually Domingo Badia y Leblich), *Travels in Morocco, Tripoli, Cyprus*, etc. (2 vols. London, 1816).

[145] Giovanni Mariti (1736–1806), *Travels through Cyprus, Syria, and Palestine* (London, 1791).

Also the appearance of this band of men dedicated to God is not inspiring. Their robes are mended, their boots are torn, and their hair gushes forth in long locks from under their black caps and joins the beard. Their eyes and their slinking-about tell their indifference and weariness, and thus, however good-natured they generally are, they do not make a favorable impression. If one adds to this the monks' total lack of familiarity with the world, their ignorance of things which daily touch their lives, and their indifference to everything that is outside of the walls of the monastery, then one can call their existence nothing other than vegetative.

At most of the monasteries there are gardens, larger or smaller, dating from the time of their foundation . . .

One will note the lavish use of gold, while everything that requires good order is visibly neglected. The altar paintings (above which regularly a Russian eagle is suspended)[146] frequently display much gold, not only in the rich ground on which they are painted, but also in the frame and in dress, while everything else in the church is veritable junk. The light shed by the wax candles and oil lamps increases the mystical impression made by the icons painted in the Greek style, but leaves the heart cold and contributes even less to an elevation of the spirit. Even with those who confess the faith such a purpose is not attained in any large measure. This is shown by the constant coming and going of the worshipers, who think to have done everything by kissing dozens of icons on the iconostasis one after another. It is remarkable also how much Christ the Savior is kept in the background compared with the Mother of God, the Panayia. And truly it is not from a sensitive appreciation of female beauty that the Virgin is placed on the right side of the altar and Christ on the left side.[147] Furthermore the Panayia is often shown under a canopy and wearing splendid robes, while all of this is absent in the case of Christ.

For all of the apostles and other saints as well a certain order of rank has been established, which, however, is modified according to circumstances. Thus there are, to give an example, two saints named George in two monasteries, not far from each other, near Larnaca. One is named Ayios Giorgios Makris, the other Ayios Giorgios tou Kontou.[148] The two of them are not at peace with each other, but are seriously making war upon each other. And as things go, sometimes long George and sometimes short George has more prestige and honor. Of course this is determined by the willingness of the public to contribute, as is the prosperity of one monastery or the other. Not infrequently a pious city dweller, a small oil lamp and some saved-up coins in his hand, will wander to one or the other George and quietly calculate the advantages of one patron over the other, not at all understanding that the long saint and the short saint are one and the same person . . .

An appendix to the two Georges is the dispute between the churches of St. Croce [Stravovouni] and Lefkara [Stavros], both of which claim to own a particle of the True

---

[146] "Altar paintings" is misleading. Unger means the icons on the iconostasis. The "Russian eagle" is also misleading. The double-headed eagle was the emblem of the Byzantine empire and is commonly found in Orthodox churches. Its use in Austria and Russia is a later development. The flag of the Orthodox Church features a black, crowned double-headed eagle on yellow ground.

[147] The icon of Christ Pantocrator is placed on the right side (from the viewer's perspective) of the "Royal Doors" of the iconostasis (not the altar) and the icon of the Theotokos, with the Child, on the left side. The two icons represent the "eschatological Christ" and the "historical Christ," respectively.

[148] The curious names refer only to the relative distance from Larnaca.

Cross.[149] St. Helena, wife of Constantine,[150] returning from Jerusalem, brought with her a piece of wood reportedly from the cross of Christ. Over this relic, on the peak of a high mountain in Cyprus, she ordered a church to be built, and next to it a monastery. Envying the prosperity of the monastery of St. Croce (ὁ σταῦρος ὁ Θεοκρέμαστος) [the cross on which God was hung up], the priests of Lefkara manufactured a similar little cross, wooden, but mounted in silver, and claimed that their gem was authentic. A dispute between the two churches and a confrontation of the particles developed, and it turned out that they were so similar that they could easily be confused and indeed were. Now no one could know any more which of the two relics was the one brought by St. Helena, and the one kept in the church of St. Croce and the one kept in the church of Lefkara are equally likely. In short, the clerics of Lefkara had attained their purpose, which was to bring more attention to their church. To this day the dispute over the location of the genuine relic has not been settled, and in the end, of course, the public took part in it. Of course I was shown the one at St. Croce as the only genuine one.

As already mentioned, all the lavishness in the Greek churches is concentrated on the altar (iconostasis).[151] This is a wall of boards which separates the altar area from the rest of the church and is broken up by a little gate which is covered by a curtain.[152] On this wall one finds a considerable collection of portraits, occasionally exceeding fifty. The Greeks like to know their saints by sight only and are less concerned with other aspects, and thus their art seems to limit itself to portraiture.[153] I was all the more surprised to find once also a historical scene. This was in the monastery of Makhaeras in the high mountains. This monastery probably derives its name—knife or sword—from some knightly deed; but none of the monks there know about it. Nevertheless they are capable of knightly deeds, not only in acquiring earthly, perishable wealth, but also in gaining heavenly, imperishable goods; this is demonstrated by a picture boldly done in crayon [?] across a good part of the wall before the entrance to the church; it probably owes its creation to the artistic impulse of one of the conventuals.[154] It depicts a ladder standing on earth and reaching into heaven. On the highest rung sits the Savior, while the other rungs are occupied mostly by monks, who try to cimb upward. A fair number of them still stand at the bottom, apparently only waiting until the others have managed the wall between earth and heaven. But making one's way up is not easy, for every rung is guarded by a winged, ram-like, two-footed beast with the head of a dragon, which fights everyone who attempts to advance, worse than bombs and grape-shot, death and perdition. And yet the boldest of the monks has already arrived on the highest rung and has been kindly taken by the hand by Christ. Such a picture before the door of the church cannot fail to have its effect, but seems to have been splashed down more for the edification of the people than

---

[149] The best account of the relics of the True Cross is that of Anatole Frolow, *La relique de la Vraie Croix: Recherches sur le développement d'un culte. Archives de l'Orient chrétien 7* (Paris, 1961).

[150] Unger is in error; Helena was Constantine's mother, not his wife.

[151] Unger fails to distinguish properly between the two.

[152] Far from being a mere "wall of boards," the iconostasis of Greek churches tends to be rather elaborate.

[153] Unger is not well informed. Icons are more than portraits. A narrative element is by no means absent from Byzantine ecclesiastical art, and certainly not from the painted churches of Cyprus.

[154] The picture no longer exists, as the monastery was devastated by fire in 1892.

for emulation by the monks themselves. Historical depictions of similar type are not, however, limited to Cyprus.[155]

It is generally known that in the entire Near East, excepting sea ports and other large cities, there are no inns where travelers might find accommodations. This applies also to Cyprus, where even in Larnaca, the island's greatest port city, there is at this time no guest house.

This makes it necessary for every traveler to bring his own house, food, as well as kitchen and utensils, with him. In Greece, Syria, and other countries one finds in some places public places, so-called khans, where one finds at least shelter against the elements. In Cyprus hospices of that kind do not exist,[156] and a traveler is therefore required to put up his own tent or to seek hospitality, which is generally willingly given, in whatever wretched hut he finds along the way.

Given the lack of specific accommodations, it is customary for the numerous monasteries of the island to assume the function of hotels, where strangers, without asking, simply ride up and dismount. Usually they are at once greeted by one of the monks or lay brothers with the words καλῶς ἤλθατε (welcome!) and assigned lodgings; of these there never seems to be a shortage even when quite a few travelers arrive at the same time. Here travelers make themselves as comfortable as possible and usually do not have to wait long before they are served with a small cup of coffee or a drink of sweetened water, depending on the prosperity of the monastery. In unusual cases they might also be served some special dishes to supplement the self-prepared meal.

The noble archbishop of Nicosia, who carries the traditional title of μακαριώτατος (most blessed), was kind enough to give us a letter of recommendation, signed by himself in red ink[157] and addressed to all the monasteries in the country, which was to give us admission everywhere. But in most cases we did not have to make use of it, because no one had refused our simple request. On these occasions we also had an opportunity to become acquainted with the better and more educated class of the population and to learn about the customs and practices of the country.

On the whole I can comment positively only on a single point, while I found everything else well below my expectations, and this point is the temperance which is practiced here. It is amazing to what degree this Christian virtue, which cannot be overrated, is practiced here. But it loses much, if not all, of its value, when one observes at the same time that it is practiced at the expense of activity, which equally enobles mankind.

I do not have to mention that Greek religion enjoins upon all of its adherents, without distinction, strict moderation in the enjoyment of food and drink at certain times, and especially upon those who are expected to serve as a model of moderation for all others. I was astonished to see how sparingly the table was set in all of the monasteries even outside of the times of fasting and how all the conventuals ate food of limited variety and little nutritional value. At times I had the impression that they abstained from all food for days on end. To prove my point I shall name a few dishes which are everywhere consid-

---

[155] Unger is again in error. The scene which he describes is not at all historical but allegorical. St. Catherine's Monastery at Mt. Sinai has a famous twelfth century icon, inspired by a treatise of St. John Climacus, which depicts the same scene.

[156] This not entirely correct. Nicosia had two khans, the Beuyuk [Büyük] Khan and the Koumardjilar [Kumarcilar] Khan.

[157] The use of red ink is a special privilege granted to the archbishop of Cyprus; it is a sign of the autocephalous status of the church of Cyprus.

ered delicacies and were occasionally served to us as dessert. To this category belong, for example, cheese, or rather "Topfen" [?] with grape juice poured over it and also a kind of cake made of sesame, flour, and honey, which has exactly the same effect as *electuarium lenitivum* [a laxative] sold in our apothecaries, and other foods of that kind . . .

At a supper given in our honor by a bishop in one of the most prosperous monasteries . . . our food had been served on fayence plates, and knifes, forks, and spoons were not lacking either . . . But with all of that His Grace the Bishop could not resist the inborn and customary drive to pick the salad from the bowl with his own hands; I shall be sure to mention, however, to exonerate him, that before the supper he had washed his hands where all could see it.

Unfortunately I have not attended a Turkish meal, where all Occidental utensils are quite superfluous, and so I cannot judge, but I have heard that it is even less civilized.

This will suffice to show that the fast is observed here in a manner that destroys both body and soul and that the stomach is not an idol to whom any offering is made.

I shall conclude this section by remarking that anyone who might harbor doubts about the reliability and correctness of my observations should visit the refectory of the monasteries of Khrysoroiatissa or Troodhitissa and convince himself that these locales are no better, except for size, than those inhabited in our country by the dirtiest of animals . . .

I shall now offer some special remarks for the purpose of describing some of the most famous monasteries.

## 1. The Monastery of [Ayios] Khrysostomos

Khrysostomos has a splendid location on the southern slope of the northern chain of mountains [Pentadaktylos] and overlooks the larger part of the fertile plain in the middle of which the country's capital is located. It lies 1250 feet at par above sea level and about 1750 feet below the peak of the mountain, which rises steeply behind it and is crowned by the ruins of the Castello della regina [Buffavento Castle]. The monastery buildings are extensive and surround a double church which consists of two chapels joined together. One of these is directly connected also with a crypt in which rest, below a stone already destroyed, the mortal remains of Maria Molino, who, if she did not build the monastery, at least laid the foundations for its prosperity. From the western chapel a doorway with polished marble and mosaic decorations leads into the tomb chamber, which apparently was built at the same time as the chapel itself; the opposite door opens into the monastery garden. An inscription above the cornice I could not read. The tomb chamber is a rectangle with corbels that reach the floor. Behind the altar of the adjoining chapel there is a painting on wood, unfortunately disfigured by a split which runs right through the middle. In this painting, as the inscription tells us, John Eleemon[158] is depicted, and on the left side the Mother of the Savior with her child. A beautiful woman in a black dress is kneeling below her, with her small son and these words:

$$\text{῾Η δέησις τῆς δού-}$$
$$\text{λης τοῦ θεοῦ Μαρίας}$$

---

[158] Or John the Almoner, a Cypriot by birth and archbishop of Alexandria in 610–619; his feast day is 12 November. But Kotschy (elsewhere in this volume) identifies the saint as St. John Chrysostom; given the name of the monastery, this would be more meaningful.

τοῦ (Φιλίππου) Μολίνο
καὶ Ἀντωνίνου τοῦ
Φιλίππου Μολίνο

The prayer of Maria,
servant of God,
wife of Philipp Molino,
and Antoninos, son
of Philipp Molino

In the adjoining garden there are orange and apricot trees more than three hundred years old, as tall as our oaks, also vines as thick as a man and winding to the crown of a cypress tree just as old. And these create a cool, dark place, spreading its shade peacefully also over the spot where the bones of this high Cypriot lady and her son are resting. Whatever her fate may have been, of which only uncertain legends have come down to us, she surely is to be envied for such a lonely and quiet resting place, where even in the daytime the little screech owls are not prevented from singing their mournful dirges.

## 2. Bellapais Monastery [Plate 11]

Another monastery entirely in ruins is Bellapais Monastery, almost across from Ayios Khrysostomos, on the northern side of the same mountains and at approximately the same altitude. It is, however, located in an incomparably more fertile area, which extends to this point from Kyrenia. Here rich fields of grain alternate in a most charming way with olive groves and carob plantations. From this monastery one's view can take in the larger part of Cyprus' northern coast and even reach across the sea to the mountains of the highland of Karamania. A visitor will be astonished at the extensive, solid, excellent Gothic-style structure, of which, unfortunately, only separate parts are still standing.

King Hugh III [1267–1284], with whom the new Lusignan line in Cyprus began, erected this monastery in the middle of the 13th century[159] and provided it with all splendor and riches. He called it the abbey of peace (de la paix), of which popular parlance made Dellapais and then Bellapaise; this happened all the more naturally as the monastery, majestically located on a rocky promontory, really dominates a magical, peaceful area. It was assigned to the order of the Premonstratensians,[160] and also the mitred abbot, like secular knights, was allowed to bear a sword and golden spurs.

Of the various buildings, all constructed of blocks of sandstone, the refectory, sixteen fathoms [90 feet] long and five-and-a-half fathoms [32 feet] wide, with its very nice pulpit, still stands; so does a part of the cloister, which on the inside on all sides adjoins the quarters of the clerics. Of the three stories even the lowest vaults have collapsed, and the knights' hall [chapter house?], recognizable only in its lay-out, before too long will also fall victim to desolation. The monastery church outside the rectangle[161] has now

---

[159] Hugh was the monastery's principal benefactor, but not its founder.
[160] The monastery was sometimes called the "white abbey," from the white habit of the Premonstratensian order.
[161] It is actually adjoining the south wing of the cloister. Having the main entrance on its west side and a side entrance in the north aisle, it could serve both the local people and the monastic community.

been converted into a Greek church and is the best preserved of all the buildings. Here also rest the remains of the founder, without any epitaph to praise him, although this prince was a friend of the arts and sciences[162] and had earned for his small kingdom the title of "the Great."[163]

Directly above the door of the great refectory, in which cattle are now roaming about, there is, besides the arches of the cloister, a well preserved ancient sarcophagus of white Parian marble and with wonderful relief decorations, such as garlands carried by a genius. Probably found in the country, it served the abbey as a water trough, as is clearly shown by the openings cut into the bottom. Now, having lost even that function, it stands deserted, serving only the cattle and the bats as a shelter.

As far as is known, the destruction of the abbey was not accomplished over time, but by ruinous human hands. In fact it was granted only a relatively short period of existence; for already with the surrender of the fortress of Kyrenia to James II (1464) this structure, which would have served for a thousand years, was made uninhabitable. Le Brun,[164] still in 1700, gives a picture of the abbey, which by no means shows a ruin; he even describes several rooms and chambers which now are no longer accessible.

What a strange fate! While this royal house is close to total ruin, all-around, in almost undiminished vigor of life, there are still growing, gray with age, those old olive trees, which probably had been tended already by the careful hands of the first residents.

## 2. Akhiropiitos Monastery

This monastery is one of the largest and best-preserved on the island. It is situated directly on the sea on a sandstone promontory; below this promontory there is a grotto with excellent water bubbling forth abundantly. Only a few monks inhabit the monastery, and the church of St. Pantaleon[165] in the middle of the courtyard is without any distinction. We took quarters in the great refectory on the first [second] floor, but did not dare to open the shutters because of a continuing storm.

Before these and before the corridor one of the island's most charming landscapes lies spread out. The high mountains extending to the west were to our left, the raging sea to our right, and between them the plain richly planted in fruit trees. The effect on one's mood is so powerful that this place has rightly been called ἱμερόεσσα (exciting desire, lovely).[166] Immediately adjoining the monastery one finds the ruins of Old Lapithos, here called Lampusa (Λάμπουσα), while the new village Lapithos, built with ancient stones, lies half an hour distant at the foot of the mountains.

---

[162] [Author's note: Thomas Aquinas dedicated to him his book *On the Reign of Princes [De Regno Principum.]*]

[163] For the judgment of a more recent historian see Hill, *History,* II 178.

[164] [Author's note: *Voyage au Levant,* tab.128.] Unger means Cornelis van Bruyn, whose *Voyage au Levant* was published in French in 1714, having first been published in Dutch in 1698 and in English in 1702. See Cobham, *Excerpta,* 236–44, esp. 238–39.

[165] In the West St. Pantaleon is one of the Fourteen Holy Helpers and one of the patron saints of Cologne. In the East he is known as St. Panteleimon. The monastery's church, however, is dedicated to the holy mandylion of Edessa. Did Unger inquire orally and misunderstand?

[166] [Author's note, expanded: βήλου δ' αὖ Κίτιον] Alex. Ephesus [sic] apud Stephanum. Belus, legendary king of Tyre and founder of Lapithos. Alexander Ephesius, 1st c. B.C. epic poet. Stephen of Byzantium (floruit c. 528–535), *Ethnica,* s.v. Λάπηθος (ed. August Meineke, p. 412). See Hadjiioannou,, *Kypros,* vol. II, no. 155.2, s.v. Lapethos. See also *SHC* VII (1999), no. 33.2.

I was not able to learn anything about the foundation of the monastery. Ludwig Ross[167] says that it is of fairly recent date and received its name from the sudarium of our Lord (τοῦ ἱεροῦ ἀχεροποιήτου μαντιλίου), a piece of which is kept in the likeness of the Panayia.

## 4. The monastery of St. Mama[168]

Morphou is really more like a large village than like a town. In contrast the large monastery building with the church, right in the center of the town, looks strange. This church was built in Byzantine style of sandstone blocks, but it is remarkable that every column capital is different from all others, that some of them are painted, and that the arcade on one side counts sixteen columns, but that on the other side, although equally long, only eleven, and these are not even placed in equal distances one from another.

On the north side of the wall, under a vault, the sarcophagus of the miracle-working (θαυματοῦργος) St. Mama is so placed that it can be seen both from the inside and the outside of the church. And above the sarcophagus which contains the remains of the saint a likeness which shows her [sic] riding on a lion has been placed.[169]

This large monastery consists of many buildings and is endowed with large holdings of land. On its foundation the few monks had nothing to say. They knew just as little about the origin of the column fragments which lie about in the courtyard and among which there are columns of Egyptian granite. Most likely they had been used at one time in a smaller building on this site. I found it amusing that the capital of a Corinthian column, turned upside-down, now must serve as a mortar for various culinary purposes. Do these ruins stem from the ancient city of Limenia, which stood on the site of modern Morphou?

Of the wondrous water which became famous in this monastery I saw nothing. The deep well offers good drinking water, in spite of being so close to the sea. And here, wonder of wonders, I saw the monks occupied with keeping silk worms.

## 5. Kykko Monastery

This monastery was built in the high, lonely mountains on a rock almost inaccessible. I only saw it from the distance, and thus can say about it only that it is one of the island's most famous places of pilgrimage.

It is proud to own an icon of the Madonna painted by St. Luke himself and brought here from Constantinople by King Isak [sic].[170] The miracle-working power of this icon is so famous that even Russians come here to take advantage of it. Given these

---

[167] Ross, *Reisen,* 147.

[168] Unger is mistakenly assuming a female saint Mama (Das Kloster der heil. Mama). The reference correctly should be to a male saint Mamas or Mammas, who has given his name to numerous locations in Cyprus.

[169] One end of the sarcophagus has been built into the thickness of the wall, just east of the north door; it is this end of the sarcophagus only which can be seen from the outside. The likeness above it is a stone relief. Depictions of St. Mamas, the male saint, riding a lion are found elsewhere in Cyprus, both in wall paintings and in icons. See the following: W. G. Constable and D. Talbot Rice, *The Icons of Cyprus* (London, 1937); Stylianou, *Painted Churches*; Sophocles Sophocleous, *Icons of Cyprus, 7th–20th Century* (Nicosia, 1994).

[170] Correctly, the emperor Alexios Komnenos (1081–1118). The "Madonna" is of the Panayia Eleousa type.

circumstances one can understand how 170 monks of the order of St. Basil could find their support in this eagles' nest. I very much doubt that conditions are still so as they were in the days of Mariti, to whom I owe this reference.

## II. Fortresses and Castles

### 1. Buffavento

There is no lack in Cyprus of strong fortresses and castles which might serve as hide-outs for unruly vassals, strong points for pretenders, and places of refuge for unfortunate rulers. There are the walls which ring some of the cities and fortified places of the island and have since early historical times been a bone of contention among quarreling parties and the goal of neighboring peoples seeking to expand their dominion. Apart from these, there are those castles on the mountain tops which were built in the times before, during, and after the crusades, on which I now wish to focus. Already their location on the tops of nearly inaccessible rocks and even more their type of construction and equipment place them in the same category as the medieval fortresses of the Occident.

Three of these belong to the same northern chain of limestone mountains, are almost equidistant one from another, and strategically dominate not only the northern slope of this chain to the nearby sea but also the wide plain which opens up to the interior of the island on the southern side. These castles are Buffavento, St. Hilarion, and Kantara. The first of these is the most stately, the highest, and the most famous; the other two protect its flanks from certain distances. But all three are nearly unintelligible ruins, and only with difficulty can a visitor find individual parts which belong together.

We climbed only Buffavento, with much effort, and left the other two castles out of consideration as being less important. Buffavento can be climbed only from the south side; on all other sides the rock is almost vertically precipitous and absolutely inaccessible.

Travelers usually undertake to climb up to Buffavento Castle from the monastery of Ayios Khrysostomos, with the help of a local guide. We followed a footpath recognizable only from one place to another, between rough stones and thorny shrubs of the *Ulex europaeus species* [furze]. After some time we reached a ruined chapel and next to it a cistern. At last we faced the vertical walls of a terribly broken limestone breach, and this we had to cross, anxiously seeking a footbreadth of ground for every step.

After a few moments of rest to gather our strength, we gained on a higher level, winding our way through walls of rock, the lowest gate of the castle and then advanced from one tower to another until we reached a stately two-story residential building on a dizzying height. Only a few circuit walls give an indication of the extent of this complex, and broken tiles and pieces of mortar, which I took with me, let an expert recognize how strongly these walls had been built. Under the second defensive tower, still intact, the ground drops down to a mighty cistern. And, in addition to this, numerous channels cut into the rock indicate the presence of other collection basins within the area enclosed by the circuit walls; these, however, are filled with rubble and difficult to identify. Without the collection of water in such basins even the construction of such an extensive complex would have been absolutely impossible.

The walls continuing toward the peak of the rock may have been connected one with another, but at the moment one is no longer able to reach the peak by any other way than by a neck-breaking climb on the vertical walls. I intended to reach the peak, if for no other reason, to measure its altitude. Our guide had brought a rope along for this purpose, which I willingly let him fasten around my middle, and with this leading-string I began the dangerous climb up. Notwithstanding all my efforts I could manage only a few fathoms and had to be content with getting stuck in a tight crevice in which I could not even turn around. Kotschy, on the other hand, clever and strong, safely reached the peak with our guide and then returned to my station. In the meantime I had here taken a reading with my altimeter and measured the altitude of this point at 2892 feet at par above sea level. Assuming that this point is about 100 feet below the peak, one obtains for the highest point of the castle of Buffavento, which is crowned by a tower, nearly 3000 feet; this agrees fairly well with Gaudry's measurement of 3041 feet for this peak.[171]

This mighty rock is also known as "Castello della regina," not because it was built by a queen of the country, but rather because it is in some regards an unusual and regal structure. Sakellarios remarks that this epithet is applied also to similar magnificent structures.[172] According to a legend there were, supposedly, 101 chambers here; this is, however, impossible when one surveys the ruins and has its explanation in the Turkish practice of calling every medieval ruin by the expression "yüz-bir-oda" (hundred-and-one rooms). Just so Maria Molino, a Cypriot woman of noble descent—the same one who built her crypt at Ayios Khrysostomos—is said to have founded this eagles' nest. Some add that she did so to protect herself against the persecutions of the order of the Templars or, what is less likely, to isolate herself from the world because she was suffering from incurable leprosy. The legend further tells that she bathed in a spring, either on the advice of John Chrysostom, or prompted by her lap dog, which was suffering from the same malady. In gratitude she built the monastery of Ayios Khrysostomos over this spring. Le Brun [van Bruyn] assures us that still in his days (1700) the sick came to visit this spring.[173]

Since I did not see a mineral spring in the vicinity of the monastery and heard nothing about it, it must be that the meagre monastery well, which provides drinking water and irrigates the surrounding gardens and fields, once served as healing spring but has lost much of its reputation.

Ali Bey in the course of his travels paid much attention to this structure on the rock and—this is hard to believe—declared it to be very ancient, although neither he nor others could learn anything definite about its origins. He even goes so far as to conclude from the style and elegance of the construction that the builder was a female and, following the legend, Maria Molino. On pl. XXI of his work he provides a plan of the castle, which, however, in my estimation, can lay little claim to accuracy. Ali Bey is of the opinion that the castle was built in four levels one above another and that the lowest parts of the fortress were designed for the guards, the next higher for the armory and magazines, the third for the attendants, and the fourth for the residence of the reigning lady, and that a chapel was attached to that.[174]

But all these parts bear the mark of a medieval structure and hardly differ from any of our European castles.

From the history of the Lusignans we know this much, that William de Rivet, one of the five regents appointed by the emperor Frederick [II, 1215–1250] during the minor-

---

[171] On Albert Gaudry's cartographic work see Stylianou, *Cartography,* 150–54.
[172] Sakellarios, *Kypriaka,* I 148, gives a brief description of Buffavento.
[173] Cornelis van Bruyn, *Voyage au Levant* (1714) 377.
[174] On his description of the castle, see Cobham, *Excerpta,* 399–402.

ity of Henry I [1218–1253], had taken refuge in this mountain fortress when he was pursued by [John] d'Ibelin after the unfortunate battle of Nicosia [1229].

Later the same castle received the supporters of Henry I and was defended valiantly when Frederick's army, crossing from Beyrut to Cyprus, invaded the country (1231).

It is known that, on 10 October 1373, Famagusta fell by treason into the hands of the Genoese. Young King Peter II [1369–1382] fled to Buffavento, which was besieged by the Genoese in vain.

Finally, at the beginning of the Venetian rule (1486), this mountain fortress met the same fate as all other fortified castles. It was razed, and for no better reason than that it should not in the future serve as a place of refuge for malcontents and open enemies of the government.

## 2. Hilarion

The ruins of St. Hilarion stand on a mountain top a little lower than Buffavento, a few miles above Kyrenia, on the same chain of mountains which extends to the west. This castle had once, in pagan days, received its name from [Cupid,] the god of love, who had an altar here.[175] It is told that St. Hilarion exorcised the devils living here, whereupon the place was named after him. He died at a ripe old age in the year 371 and was buried in a garden, where the church dedicated to him now stands.[176]

When this fortress was built is not recorded, nor do we know who built it. John d'Ibelin, regent during the minority of Henry I, fled here with his supporters when he was pursued by the emperor Frederick II and undoubtedly would have resisted his enemies successfully if a siege had taken place. But since the emperor had to return to Europe, d'Ibelin's situation changed, and it is now he who laid siege to this fortress, in which Barlais, Bessan, and Gilbert, the regents appointed by Frederick II, had ensconced themselves. He did, however, take this fortress (1231), after the famine there reached its peak.

Just so, as fortunes changed, the royal family again chose this castle as a place of refuge when the troops of the emperor Frederick II came from Syria to the island, stripped of its defenses, and committed atrocities of every kind.

Finally yet, St. Hilarion was also besieged by the Genoese in the year 1373, but in vain.

The fate of destruction which the "Castello della regina" has suffered also befell this castle, at the same time and for the same reason.

## 3. Kantara

As far as Kantara is concerned its ruins, too, are in the eastern continuation of the same limestone mountains, and it, too, served fugitives as a temporary place of refuge. Rossi, another of the five regents appointed by the emperor Frederick II, fled here when pursued by d'Ibelin. But the castle surrendered to the emperor's army when the emperor, coming from Syria, landed in Cyprus. Soon, however, it fell again into the hands of King Henry I, when the Cypriots, after the successful landing of d'Ibelin at Famagusta, took courage and slew the emperor's men. Here, too, we find again the name ἕκατον σπίτια (one-hundred rooms). The other fortified castles, such as Sygouris,

---

[175] Hence another name of the castle was Dieu d'Amour.
[176] Hilarion's disciple Hesychios reportedly removed the body to Majoma near Gaza.

Cava, and Potamia, of which even the smallest traces have disappeared, also owe their destruction to the Venetians.[177]

Also on Cape Kormakiti, the former Κρόμμυον (promontory of onions) [κρομμύδι = onion], there must once have been a fortified castle, but, as far as I was able to see, nothing of it remains other than a ruined watch tower.

One of the five sons of Hugh III [1267–1284], the Constable Guy, occupied this castle after the murder of his brother Aimery and heavily fortified it. After some time, when his brother Henry II [1285–1324] had returned to his kingdom a free man, he was thrown into prison and, because he was suspected of a conspiracy, was starved to death.

Not far from there sandstone caves and pieces of building stone indicate the place where the ancient city of Kormion was located.

The best-preserved of all these fortified places is Kolossi. It is situated one hour distant from Limassol in one of the most fertile areas and is a large square fortified tower built of sandstone blocks and provided with a crenelated top and a balcony-like projection [machicolation] for the defense of the gate. Under Henry II, it is known, the Knights of St. John and the Templars received permission to settle in the recently founded city of Limassol and to cultivate and fortify the area. The castle, first built by the Templars, was later reinforced by the Knights of St. John and forms to this day a stately strong point, which dominates not only the immediate area but even Cape Gata. It is four stories high and currently serves Mr. Fancudi, the owner of a large estate, as a granary. A marble escutcheon of the Lusignans has been built into the east side of the tower.

Next to it stands an old commandery of the Knights of St. John; its condition is in no way better than that of the castle. But an excellent aqueduct passing by, no doubt also the work of the knights, irrigates to this day the entire area as far as the Cape.

It is supposed that the ancient city of Kourion was located here.

## III. Ancient Buildings

### 1. The Chapel of Phaneromene

Not far from Larnaca, i.e. from the Marina toward the west, among fields and at the intersection of some paths, there is an old chapel, cut into the rock, which now is called Phaneromene. Since it hardly rises above the level of the ground one could easily overlook it if one is not specifically alerted to it.

Whatever once was its purpose, we may be sure that even in earlier times it did not rise much above ground level and thus was from the beginning built into the ground from above. For this purpose conglomerate, a kind of stone widely distributed in the Larnaca area and easily worked, is the most suitable material. One notices at first glance that the natural rock has been excavated here by almost vertically cut walls to a certain measurement and the space dressed with massive blocks of sandstone. But while elsewhere such a primitive structure is simply covered with a slab of the appropriate size, here this heavy slab has been carved out on its under side in the form of a vault.

As far as the structure is still recognizable at the present time, it consists of two chambers or compartments and an antechamber which is now quite filled with rubble. The outer compartment, actually the middle section, is open toward the northeast and

---

[177] Sygouris lies ca. 12 miles west of Famagusta; Cava, also known as Athalassa, lies ca. 4 miles southeast of Nicosia; and Potamia, also known as the "Royal Manor," lies a short distance northeast of Dhali.

adjoins the ruined antechamber; it is covered by a huge monolith like a vault; this latter measures 6 x 3.1 m. and is 1.4 m thick at its thickest point. A door opening, as L[udwig] Ross thinks formerly closed by a slab of stone lowered from above like a portcullis, leads into the innermost chamber. This also is covered by a stone almost as large and massive; it receives its only light through that pocket-like opening into which the slab serving as a shutter was inserted from above. This pocket is placed exactly where the two ceiling slabs meet.[178] The middle chamber, here seen as the first one, measures 5 m. long and 3.5 m. wide, while the innermost chamber is slightly smaller. On the antechamber, completely filled with rubble, nothing can be said, but it must have been of the same dimensions.

There is not a trace of inscriptions to be found anywhere in this Cyclopean building, but a comparison with similar rock structures on the island suggests that it dates back to the earliest historical times and probably served as a burial place. L[udwig] Ross, to illustrate these tomb chambers, provides a plan and an elevation.[179]

When this tomb of pre-rational times was dedicated as a temple of Panayia Phaneromene is uncertain, but it must have happened in a not very enlightened time, and the same spirit allows it to remain even today in the honored memory of the people. Many a matron comes here, a burning lamp in her hand, to get rid of a fever or to ask that she might be blessed with posterity. If the soot-blackened walls and the collection of lamps left as an offering in the innermost chamber are any indication, this chapel certainly had many visitors.

L[udwig] Ross also mentions two other burial chambers, also located to the west of the Marina but less well preserved;[180] I searched for them in vain, however.

Six years ago in the garden of Madame Bargigli in Larnaca, when the soil was turned over, an old tomb was found, which came to light only at a depth of one and a half to two fathoms. It consisted of an antechamber two and a half fathoms wide and more than three fathoms long. It was built of blocks and well preserved. From this antechamber a doorway led into the tomb chamber proper; it was of the same dimensions, but differed in having a pointed vault built of blocks and a nicely carved frieze. Opening the same I found nothing other than a lamp and a hollow cylinder of stone. An inscription on the inside of the door is evidently of rather recent date, and its letters are cut in a notably careless way.

The letters are, in sequence, MDIII PET PISANI, which seems to indicate that the tomb was used during Venetian days (1503) for the burial of Pietro Pisani. According to L[udwig] Ross there are several other, similar chamber tombs in and around Larnaka in addition to the ones already mentioned.

In general the environs of this city, which stands in part on the site of the ancient Kition, offer a rich field for researchers in the field of antiquity. It is a shame that the tombs have long since been robbed of their contents and the historically important objects perhaps still in place are too scattered and too deeply covered with rubble to allow retrieval at reasonable cost. When the ground is randomly ransacked in the search for squared stones to use for building purposes it may happen that urns, pithoi, lamps,

---

[178] [Author's note: L. Ross records the monolith as measuring 6 x 5.1 m., with an average thickness of 1.5 m. This tells us that he considered the two monoliths as one.] Ross, *Reisen,* 199–201.

[179] [Author's note, modified: *Archäologische Zeitung* 9 (1851), p. 327 and pl. 28.]

[180] Ross, *Reisen,* 201.

glasses, and the like are excavated; but only on rare occasions do more interesting and valuable antiquities, such as inscriptions, art objects, etc. come to light.

A pair of Phoenician inscriptions in the possession of the merchant Pierides[181] has recently been deciphered by Professor Ewald.[182]

[A lengthy description of these inscriptions, pp. 530–32, is here omitted.]

Here I still must consider one very important find which also was made on this soil eighteen years ago and was mentioned by L[udwig] Ross in a brief description and depiction.[183] This is a stele 6.2 feet high and 2.5 ft. wide, of a blackish basalt-like stone, which carries a bas relief with an inscription. The relief depicts the figure of a priest or king in a tightly fitting ankle-length skirt. A pair of tongs above the head, which bears a conical cap, seems to point to the inventor of tongs, the national hero Kinyras;[184] but the Assyrian cuneiform inscription, which fills the entire ground of the relief and the margins as well, argues against this.

According to the latest investigations this figure represents King Sargon of Nineveh [721–705 B.C.], who in the course of his campaigns conquered in addition to the Phoenician coast also the island of Cyprus. At this time this rare monument of the earliest history of the island is in Berlin.[185]

Kition was founded by Phoenician colonists and, judging by the extent of its ruins and its necropolis, must once have reached considerable size and have flourished in the arts and sciences.

Zeno, the founder of the Eleatic school, called Kition his native city, where he once was a merchant.[186] Apollonius [1st century B.C.], a disciple of Hippocrates, was also born here. Cimon, son of Miltiades, was wounded while laying siege to Kition and died there.[187] This city was destroyed already by Ptolemy Lagos.[188]

2. The Fountain Temple at Salamis

This building, too, belongs to the massive Cyclopean buildings, inasmuch as colossal blocks of stone were used instead of the usual smaller stones. Nevertheless it is different from the Phaneromene building both in plan and in method of construction and shows an advance in art.

---

[181] On Demetrios and Zeno Pierides see the Schröder text in this volume.

[182] [Author's note (edited): "Entzifferung der neu entdeckten phönikisch-kyprischen Inschriften," *Nachrichten von der G. A. Universität und der königl. Gesellschaft der Wissenschaften zu Göttingen*, Nov. 1862, No. 23.] Georg Heinrich August Ewald was a distinguished Orientalist and theologian. For further biographical data see the article by Friedrich Wilhelm Bautz in *BBKL* I (1990) 1577–78.

[183] [Author's note: *Hellenika* 1846, p. 69, t.1.] *Hellenika: Archiv archaeologischer, philologischer, historischer und epigraphischer Abhandlungen und Aufsätze von Ludwig Ross.* Halle, 1846.

[184] According to Pliny *H. N.* 7.195 Kinyras invented the tongs, the hammer, the lever, and the anvil.

[185] The stele was discovered in 1845; in 1846 it was acquired by the Prussian consul and shipped to Berlin. See Hill, *History* I 104 with n. 2 and the photograph facing p. 106. It is part of the collection of the Pergamon Museum, inv. VA 968.

[186] Unger is in error. Zeno of Kition, 335–263 B.C., is in no way to be identified with Zeno of Elea, 5th century B.C.

[187] Thuc. 1.112 reports the death of Cimon, but does not say whether he died of a wound or of disease. Plut. *Vit. Cim.* 19 mentions both possibilities. The date is 450 B.C.

[188] This appears to be an erroneous statement.

If one travels from the hill on which the old city of Salamis stood across the plain to the west one crosses the ruined aqueduct of Justinian. This aqueduct supplied this Attic colony, now completely in ruins, with water from the distant [c. 25 miles] Kythrea. A few stone pillars, which once carried the arches, still reach boldly into the air and fade into the distance like ghosts. Like unconquered giants they stand there, witnesses of mightier times.

But soon the serious observer's attention is drawn to another, no less remarkable object, the vaulting of a strange, temple-like structure protruding from the flat field. It forms a rectangle, whose longer side, running from northwest to southeast, measures 11 m., and the other a little more than $5^{1/2}$ m. Above it is a barrel vault of wedge-shaped, massive stones fitted one into another.[189]

The back wall, turned toward the northwest, is partially destroyed and shown in the drawing here provided as a facade which delimits the vault. From here one can look down into the interior of the temple and also climb down into it on the stones which have fallen down. Only down there does the visitor notice a portal opening toward the northeast, which from the outside is entirely covered by rubble, and on the opposite side a small, niche-like depression in the wall.

One cannot fail to notice in the middle of the temple a well, which provides good, cold, and very refreshing water of 10.8° Réaumur; this is all the more remarkable here, hardly more than fifty feet above sea level, since at this elevation one would rather expect a temperature of six degrees or less. This strange anomaly can be explained only by assuming that this spring found its way here from a great distance and considerable height in lower strata of rock.

There can be no doubt that this structure, like that of Phaneromene was originally at least partially under ground and was purposely built above this excellent, though modest spring, which probably once had much greater significance than today. For this reason I cannot agree with L[udwig] Ross, who declares this building to be a tomb chamber.[190]

Kugler[191] already points out that treasuries, of which a visitor is first reminded, may be built as a protective enclosure of springs and as such meet the first requirements of a permanent settlement with which religious veneration was generally associated. A similar fountain house (*castellum*) with a barrel vault, only smaller than this one, has also been discovered in the ruins of Pompeii. That one stands at an intersection (*bivium*), and nearby is a small altar, which is dedicated to the patron goddesses of roads (*lares compitales*).[192]

Now this building is called the "Prison of St. Catherine." Catherine was a daughter of King Costa, the founder of Famagusta.[193]

---

[189] [Author's note: Vaults of wedge-shaped stones are found already in ancient Egyptian buildings; the temple of Amenophis III at Medinet Habu is notable for its barrel vault.] Amenophis or Amenhotep III, 1417–1379 or 1405–1370 B.C., 18th dynasty. But the great temple at Medinet Habu was erected by Rameses III.

[190] [Author's note, modified: Ross, *Reisen,* 119.]

[191] [Author's note, corrected: Franz Theodor Kugler, *Geschichte der Baukunst* (5 vols. Stuttgart, 1856–1873) I 142.]

[192] Unger is wrong in equating the Lares with goddesses.

[193] The "Prison of St. Catherine" is tomb no. 50 in modern accounts. Max Hermann Ohnefalsch-Richter, "A Prehistoric Building at Salamis," *JHS* 4 (1883) 111–16. See also Vassos Karageorghis, *Salamis* (New York, 1969) 54–63. While St. Catherine is more often said to have been a native of Alexandria, a variant of the legend tells that she was a native of Cyprus and, further, that her father was a certain king named Costa or Costus or even the emperor Constantius. "Costa" and "Costus" obviously, then, are corruptions of "Constantius." See Cobham, *Excerpta,* 24–25, 35, 53, 57, and 256.

Not far from this monument of gray antiquity, at a slightly higher location, there is the monastery of St. Barnabas and, a few steps further, belonging to this monastery, a half-ruined chapel. This chapel is famous for its healing waters (ἀγίασμα [holy place]) and also because, in a small side cavern which leads to the subterranean spring, the Gospel of St. Matthew was found, the one which Barnabas, a disciple of this apostle and native Cypriot, had used to transplant Christianity to this island.[194]

This find seemed so important to the emperor Zeno [474–491] that on this account he granted special privileges to the archbishops of Cyprus: the title of μακαριώτατος (most blessed), the right to wear purple robes, and the right to sign all of his documents in red ink made of cinnabar, but now of madder.

As for the mineral water to which special healing powers are ascribed, it is nothing other than ordinary tasteless drinking water; its temperature (10.8° Réaumur) agrees exactly with that of the spring at the ancient temple and it should be considered merely a branch of that spring.

Pococke[195] tells that the body of St. Barnabas, who died a martyr's death here in the days of Nero [A.D. 54–68], was not put to rest in the monastery church but in a natural cave of conglomerate half an hour east from there. For this purpose the cave was fitted with its own niches which, of course, suits this ruined chapel.

3. Dhali

The village of Dhali (τὸ Δάλιν) lies in a very fertile valley which is watered by the stream of Setrakhos, which comes from the mountains of Makhaeras.[196] All the water is channeled through canals, some of them artfully laid out, and distributed across the plain in such a way that the river bed thereby is completely drained in the summer time.

It is easy to see from this area that an ancient civilization was spread across this soil, and even later barbarian incursions could not deprive it of all of its advantages.

The name Dhali is derived from the ancient τὸ Ἰδάλιον and probably of Phoenician origin.[197] Dhali is known for the sanctuary which was erected here by Phoenician settlers to Astarte (Aphrodite), but the exact location of which is no longer known. Judging by the numerous ancient objects which have been excavated, one should look for the temple of Aphrodite on the northern slope of the hill which rises in the southern part of the village.

Here one can find, close together, mutilated statues with mural crowns, just like Paphian Aphrodite on ancient coins, and numerous votive gifts; some of these are of terra cotta but most, like the statues, are of the soft limestone which breaks in the vicinity of Dhali in large masses and forms even the hill on which the temple once stood. Of these larger and smaller statuettes I brought with me a collection of one hundred pieces which, by chance, was offered to me for sale in Larnaca. These seem to bear the mark of Phoenician art only in part, while several forms indicate only too clearly an Egyptian or Assy-

---

[194] For more complete accounts see *SHC* VII (1999) nos. 31.6, 53.1, 74.3, 82.1, 84.10, 85.10, 88.4, 101.1, 118.9, 127.1, 135.11, and 137.5, 8.

[195] See Cobham, *Excerpta,* 256-57. Also *SHC* V (1998) 42.

[196] Correction: The Setrakhos River flows from the northern slopes of the Troodos Mountains and empties into the Bay of Morphou. It is the Yialias River which flows past Dhali.

[197] [Author's note, modified: According to Bochart from "Jad" and "ela," i.e. *locus Deae or locus Veneri sacer*.] Samuel Bochart, 1599–1667, French theologian and Orientalist. For further biographical information see the article by Friedrich Wilhem Bautz in *BBKL* I (1990) 637.

rian type. The prevailing objects are bas reliefs of a seated woman in a long robe and with a child in swaddling-clothes in her lap. Of most of the figures only the heads are extant, but these, as far as coiffure and adornment are concerned, conform on the one hand to Greek and Roman patterns and on the other hand to Assyrian and Egyptian patterns. Of animal sculptures there are some looking like monkeys, some oxheads, etc. Of obscene male figures those sitting with their feet crossed are especially notable.[198]

In the picture here provided the reader can easily recognize those two peaks of the hill, with their steep decline on the southwest side, at whose near end L[udwig] Ross thought he had to place the temple of Aphrodite.[199] Indeed a few prominent sandstone blocks and the earthen wall, where it has not been flattened, give us grounds to seek here a piece of the ancient city wall; this extends from the height to the plain, but disappears here. Even now the pleasant valley at the foot of that precipice is called τὸ Παραδεῖσον, calling to mind the sacred grove which once surrounded the temple. But how far this grove extended and whether it reached as far as Amochostos, as some people believe, can no longer be determined. Now, in contrast to the former *Idalium frondosum* [leafy Idalion],[200] there are no more woods on the wide plain. Only the fragrant *Crataegus orientalis* [a kind of hawthorn], like a loyal, steadfast soldier, has not given up its post in the midst of golden fields of grain. But where the ruins of the ancient city of Idalion itself should be looked for is hardly subject to question, as the eastern end of the modern village could be spotted as a mine for antiquities, and there, too, a hill outstanding above the valley can easily be identified as the acropolis.

## 4. Yeroskipos and Paphos

From Kouklia, where ages ago the first temple of Aphrodite stood, we rode by way of Yeroskipos to Paphos, probably on the same route once followed by the festive processions from Paphos. The area can almost be called flat, for it is interrupted only by insignificant hills and advances with many projections, like the fingers of a hand, to the nearby sea.

The soil, which in places can well be irrigated, is for the most part under cultivation, and thus there are villages round-about. But undoubtedly, with diligence, the yield could be doubled or tripled, and the area must have looked more prosperous in times past when sugar cane was grown here.

In Yeroskipos we stopped for a short while to visit the sacred spring and the gardens watered by it (ἱερὸς κῆπος). But as everywhere, so here, too, we found a *tabula rasa* on which only poverty, dirt, and misery can be read in broad strokes. The layer of conglomerate which here covers the white, soft limestone has below it significant caves and crevices, so that the ground under one's steps at times sounds hollow and rumbling. Next to the Greek church a fairly large subterranean opening, by a break in this layer, has become accessible and available for use.

The sacred spring, offering beautiful, clear water of 16.6° Réaumur, flows abundantly from such a subterranean crevice in the soft limestone and is a blessing for the

---

[198] On these votive offerings see the Unger text in this volume.

[199] Ross, *Reisen,* 163.

[200] [Author's note, modified: *Quae regis Golgos, quaeque Idalium frondosum. Catull. 64.96.*]

area.[201] Modern industry has not yet made use of this inexhaustible source of power, and the spring gushes forth as freely and unimpeded as three thousand years ago across the rocks to its near grave—the sea. But what the spring once created and caused to flower, the beautiful trees, shrubs, and flowers, even the pomegranates dedicated to Aphrodite, have long since withered, and their poor descendants are too weak to maintain themselves on this sacred terrain against the ravishes of time. Here and there one sees lonely ancient terebinth trees, perhaps six or seven hundred years old, eloquent witnesses of the nourishing strength of the spring, extending their powerful roots through all layers of rock down to it.

The friendly consul Smith, a native Cypriot and well familiar with his area, accompanied us from here to the nearby Paphos and did not fail to instruct us on all important objects and local conditions.[202]

Paphos is now only a village, but one spread far out; its impoverished houses and huts almost disappear between the ruined churches and palaces, in the ruins of its own former temples and splendid buildings.

We put up our tent under a picturesque sandstone rock on which a small Greek chapel stood in the shade of a terebinth tree. The stubble of the field was the carpet on which we rested.

Anyone seeing the many granite columns, some standing upright, some lying on the ground, will be astonished at the prosperity and luxury which once existed here and allowed these beautifully cut and polished monoliths to be brought here from far-away Upper Egypt.[203] And anyone further considering the marble monuments, column shafts, capitals, inscriptions, and the many sandstone blocks lying about, will obtain at the same time an idea of the size and population of the city. And this city, although destroyed in the days of Augustus by an earthquake, soon rose even more splendid from its ruins and thus later was called Augusta.[204]

A height right by the sea, not far from the fort built by the Genoese, is believed, perhaps rightly, to be the place where the most important building of the city, the temple of Aphrodite, stood. Broken columns and mosaic fragments lie about like meaningless wood shavings. On the north side of this height numerous entrances to underground spaces can be seen. There even are steps leading down, but these have been made completely inaccessible by accumulated rubble. Special attention should be given to some cistern-like pits from which spring water was drawn.

Another building in the middle of the former city, called the bath of Aphrodite and built of blocks of Cyclopean size, was later turned into a Christian church and then, getting closer to its original purpose, into a Turkish bath. Now it serves as a stable for cows.

At the northern end, where mighty sandstone rocks tower above the ground, man-made enlargements of the natural caves were used as dwelling places. This was at a time when the island was still a continuous forest and no stone was brought here for the sanctuary of the goddess of love. One of these caves, reached by stairs leading down, was converted into a simple, apparently primitive chapel of St. Solomone; perhaps this happened

---

[201] [Author's note, modified: An estimated 1½ buckets per second.] Ross, *Reisen,* 184, erroneously calls this spring a conduit cut into the rock.

[202] This refers to Haji Smith, a native Cypriot, born Andreas Zimboulaki, who had, as a young man, been appointed British vice consul by Sir William Sydney Smith; hence the peculiar name. See also Ross, *Reisen,* 184.

[203] [Author's note: I have seen ancient granite columns also at Famagusta, Salamis, and Episkopi.]

[204] Cass. Dio 54.23.7. Hill, *History,* I 232.

already at a time when the apostle Paul preached the Gospel here and converted the pro-consul at the time, [Sergius] Paulus, into a firm believer and follower of Christianity.[205]

Next to it, a few fathoms higher, there is in the same cave a spring of sweet water. This spring and the one already mentioned indicate that the city, although right by the sea, was not lacking water. Nevertheless it is conceivable that these springs no longer suf-ficed as the city grew and that the additional demand was met by the aqueduct which brought water from the valley of Tala.[206] In places and following a straight line there still are piles of rubble testifying to the existence and course of this aqueduct.

As is generally known, the temple of Aphrodite at Nea Paphos is of a later date than the one at Palaipaphos (Kouklia); the latter was built by one of the earliest Phoeni-cian colonies which transplanted the cult of Astarte to this island.

[Pp. 542–48: Unger next examines the etymology of "Aphrodite" and then, at great length, the qualities of the foam formed on the shore of the salt lake of Larnaca.]

I add to these observations another one of interest to natural historians and closely related to the cult of Aphrodite in Cyprus.

It is well known that Aphrodite was worshiped in her temple at Paphos not in hu-man form, but as a cone of stone (κῶνος Κυπρίων). Gems and coins into the age of Tra-jan, Vespasian, Severus, Antoninus, and Domitian[207] provide not only the picture of the cone, but also its incidental decorations, such as rings, etc., as well as the essential parts of the temple itself, in the adyton of which the cone was put up.

There are other witnesses as well: Tacitus,[208] Maximus of Tyre,[209] and Servius.[210]

[Pp. 549–52: Unger discusses at length the practice, among various ancient peoples, of venerating sacred stones.]

After this digression let us return to the ruins of Paphos!

Not only is Paphos rich in monumental remains within its ancient parameters, but also the area surrounding it allows a significant collection. Here we must include especially the chamber tombs in the sandstone hill which rises toward Ktima and Yeroskipos to a plateau. In several places in this sandstone hill, as everywhere on the island, tombs were once cut out and provided with special courtyards. Most of these are now fully ruined.

---

[205] Acts 13: 6–12. A.D. 47–48.

[206] A location about four miles directly north of Ktima.

[207] These are in no chronological order at all.

[208] [Author's note, corrected: *Simulacrum deae, non effigie humana, continuus orbis, latiore initio, tenuem in ambitum metae modo exsurgens, set ratio in obscuro.*] "The goddess is not portrayed in the likeness of a human. Her image resembles a truncated cone, tapering from a broad circular base to a top of slender cir-cumference. The reason for this is obscure." Tac. *Hist.* 2.3 (Transl. Kenneth Wellesey).

[209] [Author's note, corrected: Παφίοις ἡ μὲν Ἀφροδίτη τὰς τιμὰς ἔχει, τὸ δὲ ἄγαλμα οὐκ ἄν εἰκάσαις ἄλλῳ τῳ ἤ πυραμίδι λευκῇ Max. Tyr. *dissert.* 2.8.] "Among the people of Paphos Aphrodite is honored, but her statue cannot be compared to anything other than a shiny pyramid." Maximus of Tyre, 2nd c. A.D. Platonic philosopher, author of 41 extant *dissertationes*.

[210] [Author's note, corrected: *Apud Cyprios Venus in modum umbilici vel, ut quidam volunt, metae colitur.* Serv. *Ad Aen.* 1.720.] "Among the Cypriots Aphrodite is worshiped in the form of a navel or, as some will have it, a cone."

L[udwig] Ross describes such chamber tombs in the so-called Paleocastron, northwest of Paphos, and provides illustrations.[211] According to his descriptions the entrance into the subterranean grottoes is protected by a once open court yard, surrounded by Doric columns. A small entrance to this courtyard has been cut through the rock in the southwest corner.

It is likely that this courtyard, measuring c. 30 m. square, being quite square, was covered with massive stone plates. The chamber tombs themselves, accessible on all sides behind the peristyle, are so filled with rubble and animal dung that one cannot advance further. From the Doric order of the columns and some other circumstances Ross concludes that these tombs were of Phoenician origins. Even if the form of these chamber tombs conforms entirely with the Egyptian tombs, I still perceive, as far as the form of the columns goes, a significant difference from those which are found, for instance, in the rock tombs at Beni-Hasan in Egypt.[212] Ali Bey, too, mentions chamber tombs west of New Paphos, but mistook them for dwellings. They belong, however, to a later period of art history.

I very much regret not to have seen these tombs with their courtyards in Paphos and suspect that they are no longer accessible.

But Consul Smith took us to another chamber tomb in the eastern part of the same district. This one did not have such a courtyard but had a fairly wide entrance way cut into the rock. Access to the grotto itself was by a wide opening. Above this, on the vertically straightened rock wall, there was an inscription in Cypriot characters.

Although the sandstone, by no means uniform and finely grained, has been exposed for millennia to the effect of the atmosphere and in places shows unevenness and depressions, still the carved characters had suffered so little damage that especially by good light they could well be distinguished and their forms be recognized. Not content with making a copy, as accurate as possible, of this inscription, given below, I went to the trouble of making a fairly successful squeeze.[213] [Plate 11]

The interior of this grotto consists of two fairly roomy chambers, one behind the other, the second of which has a vaulted ceiling. The sidewalls of both chambers bore Old-Cypriot inscriptions. The inscription in the first chamber had some characters purposely destroyed, so that only a part of it could be read.[214] That in the second chamber had become quite illegible through use, erosion, and a deposit of soot.

New Paphos is an Arcadian colony founded by Agapenor[215] and perhaps younger than the Sikyonian settlement at Golgi. With the immigration of the Arcadians the Dodonaean cult of Aphrodite[216] came to Cyprus, but it soon grew into one with the kindred

---

[211] [Author's note, modified: *Archäologische Zeitung* 9 (1851), pl. 28.]

[212] An important Old and Middle Kingdom site 155 miles south of Cairo, on the right bank of the Nile.

[213] This inscription is a dedication to Apollo Hylates. It had already been published by Honoré Duc de Luynes, *Numismatique et inscriptions cypriotes* (Paris, 1852), p. 50 and pl. XI. See Olivier Masson, *Les inscriptions chypriotes syllabiques* (Paris, 1961), pp. 96–97 with fig. 7 and pl. VI.2.

[214] This is a second dedication to Apollo Hylates. See Olivier Masson, *Les inscriptions chypriotes syllabiques* (Paris, 1961) 96–98 with fig. 8 and pl. VI.3.

[215] [Author' note, corrected: εἶθ' ἡ Πάφος, κτίσμα Ἀγαπήνορος, λιμένα ἔχουσα καὶ ἱερὰ εὖ κατεσκευασμένα. Strab. 14.683.] "Then there is Paphos, a foundation of Agapenor and having well-built temples." Agapenor, mythical king of Tegea, on his way home from the Trojan War was diverted by a storm to Cyprus. Paus. 8.5.2.

[216] Unger does not say in what sense the cult of Aphrodite may be called "Dodonaean." There were at Dodona, in addition to the temple of Zeus, small temples of Heracles and Aphrodite.

cult of Astarte; just as under Amasis the Egyptian deities of Isis, Osiris, and Serapis were received into the cult of the local gods [6th c. B.C.].

## 5. Palaipaphos (Kouklia) [Plates 12, 13]

Palaipaphos is only two miles distant from today's Paphos.[217] One can see it from the hill of Aphrodite's temple here, and so the two major sites of the cult of Aphrodite were in sight of each other. Every year at the celebration of the Aphrodisia, just as from Athens to Eleusis, a festive procession moved from the daughter-sanctuary to the mother-sanctuary, and here, too, the road on which the procession moved became sacred (ἱερὰ ὁδός). Although Palaipaphos probably was at the sea and a port city, yet the temple was undoubtedly on the height, there where, in the midst of scattered rubble and a few still notable foundation walls, the gigantic colossi of a Cyclopean structure still are standing as the last remains.

Two of these, especially prominent, are more than 2 m. high, almost 5 m. long, and more than 3/4 m. thick. On the construction of this simple structure the holes in the sides of these stones provide some information. These did not, as von Hammer will have it, serve to dispense oracles, but to accommodate wooden planks and thus to connect or link adjoining stones.[218] Similar openings occurring also in other locations suffice to disprove the earlier opinion about their purpose.

This rough sandstone structure can only have been a part of the sanctuary, only within which the artfully constructed temple stood. This is evident both from the plan and from the many blocks of marble and inscriptions which, as their dedication tells us, obviously formed part of the temple. Here is one of these inscriptions:

ΑΦΡΟΔΙΤΗ ΠΑΦΙΑΙ
ΔΗΜΟΚΡΑΤΗΣ ΠΤΟΛΕΜΑΙΟΥ
Ο ΑΡΧΟΣ ΤΩΝ ΚΙΝΥΡΑΔΩΝ
ΚΑΙ Η ΓΥΝΗ ΕΥΝΙΚΗ
ΤΗΝ ΕΑΥΤΩΝ ΘΥΓΑΤΕΡΑ
ΑΡΙΣΤΗΝ

To Aphrodite of Paphos
Demokrates son of Ptolemy
chief of the Cinyradae
and his wife Eunike
[have dedicated] their daughter
Ariste.

This inscription was lying in the shade of a terebinth tree and served us as a table for our humble meal.[219] Numerous other inscriptions, also parts of the former sanctuary, were still lying about or had been built into the fabric of the small, half-ruined Greek church. I made squeezes of all of which I could get a hold.

---

[217] Two German miles equal ca. nine English miles.

[218] Hammer-Purgstall, *Ansichten.*

[219] It was published by Philippe Le Bas and William Henry Waddington, *Voyage archéologique en Grèce et en Asie Mineure* (Paris, 1853–1870) III 2798.

Herr von Hammer[220] still was able to draw the ground plan of the temple, or rather of its court yard; this would no longer be possible at the present time without clearing away the rubble. Based on this plan and on the depictions found on coins, especially those of Antoninus, Herr G. Hetsch has made an architectural drawing of this temple. The picture here provided is largely based on that drawing.

The temple stood in the far part of the rectangle, which is formed by the Cyclopean walls and measures 100 paces long and 150 paces deep. The outer part of the temple was separated by a thin wall from the inner part and seems to have been surrounded by a colonnade. Next to the temple a cistern-like pit suggests a water tank, which would be required for the cult of Aphrodite.

The temple proper consists of a taller building in the middle and of wings adjoining it on both sides. The former had in its upper story narrow windows which probably were openings for the doves which are sacred to the goddess. The latter contained the votive gifts of the temple; some of these, however, may also have found a place in the niches of the Cyclopean wall. The far part of the center building was the adyton, where the stone cone (meteorite) was set up, flanked by two candelabras.

The gate was flanked by two obelisks, split at the top; these were joined with each other by a garland of metal disks, which served the same purpose as our bells. In front of the temple there was a half-round area, enclosed by a delicate fence (of iron?). Within this area stood the sacrificial altar, spreading the aroma of incense and, according to the legend, never touched by a drop of rain, although standing in the open.[221]

The decorations depicted the priest's sacrificial service, in the course of which, in keeping with the practice of the times, the initiates were handed the facsimile of a phallus and a handful of salt. It is likely that Asian sacrificial practices were transplanted to this island and that the small groves, the clusters of bushes, and the arbors which surrounded the temple of Aphrodite were meant to enhance these practices.

[Here omitted is an excerpt from Wilhelm Heinrich Engel, *Kypros: Eine Monographie* (2 vols. Berlin, 1841) II 150.]

Where once the temple stood now the unattractive and ill-famed village of Kouklia spreads out. Not far from that point, in the same chain of hills, there is a cave which is called the cave of the queen (ἡ σπήλαιος τῆς ῥηγίνας); it, again, bears the royal title only in order to indicate a splendid building. It is of the same sandstone which is found around almost the entire coast of the island and everywhere forms caves, which already in earliest antiquity were used as tombs.

The entrance even to this cave, which is the largest of them, is narrowed and made difficult by the accumulated rubble. In the interior this cave expands into neatly cut-out chambers. There are three of these, which, one following upon another, seem to form a burial suite. But the first two of these chambers each have on the sides four small closets. Narrow doorways connect the chambers, each about 4 m. wide and 6 1/2 m. long. The innermost one, slightly smaller than the first two, must have been meant to receive

---

[220] Hammer-Purgstall, *Ansichten*.

[221] [Author's note, corrected: *Sanguinem arae obfundere vetitum; precibus et igno puro altaria adolentur nec ullis imbribus, quamquam in aperto, madescunt.*] "It is forbidden to pour blood on the altar. The altar is sanctified by prayers and pure fire and never becomes wet, although it is out in the open." Tac. *Hist.* 2.3.

the body. It was closed by a massive stone, which still was lying before the opening at the time of my visit. It bore an inscription in old Cypriot characters which was copied already by von Hammer, but of which I made a better drawing, I think.[222]

A few weeks after my visit this inscription was removed by French archaeologists, and on this occasion a second, similar inscription was found under the rubble; both were considered a good prize.[223] The expansion of this cave may not have been difficult, since the coarse conglomerate-like sandstone here alternates with a layer of marl. I found the compact ceiling of this cave declining by 10° toward west.

A second burial cave, further to the east, is smaller, but at the moment no longer accessible.

Old Paphos was built by Phoenician settlers soon after Kition for the service of Astarte, on the model of the temple of Ascalon or of one of the sanctuaries of this goddess in the mountains of Lebanon. Of the original temple complex only the wall of the courtyard would have survived into later times. In the word "Paphos" one can recognize the Semitic root "aphi." The Hebrew cities of Japhia, Mephaath, etc. derive their names from the same root.[224] Homer already mentions the ancient sanctity of the temple at Paphos,[225] with which an oracle was associated.

## 6. Amathus

Amathus, today also called Old Limassol (παλαιὰ Λιμησσός), is about as far from Limassol, a foundation of Hugh I [1205–1218], as Old Paphos is from New Paphos. Of the former existence of this city only a few remains of the walls give any indication. According to Gesenius[226] the name "Amathus" can seemingly be traced back to the word "hamath," i.e. *arx*, and thus is unmistakably of Phoenician origin. There was a fortified city named Amathus on the Jordan.[227] There was a city named Hamat also on the Orontes,[228] and it is likely that the Canaanite tribe living there later settled here. As Movers remarks,[229] according to an inscription found in Kition, the Phoenician way of spelling the Cypriot name agrees fully with the biblical name of the Hamaites on the Orontes. Scylax, Tacitus, and Stephanus [of Byzantium] are all in agreement on the age of the city. Stephanus calls it ἀρχαιοτάτη, Tacitus *vetustissima*, and Scylax even believes the inhabitants to be autochthonous.[230] Many coins of the oldest times bear the name of Amathus in Cypriot script.[231]

---

[222] Hammer-Purgstall, *Ansichten,* erroneously believed the inscription to be Phoenician. Unger does not provide a copy of the drawing which he made.

[223] Both inscriptions are now in the Louvre. For a more detailed account see Olivier Masson, *Les inscriptions chypriotes syllabiques* (Paris, 1961) 101, 112–15 with figs. 15–17.

[224] Japhia or Japha in Galilee, near Nazareth. Mephaath in trans-Jordan Ammon.

[225] *Od.* 8.362–63.

[226] Wilhem Gesenius, 1786–842, renowned German Orientalist and biblical scholar; author of both a Hebrew grammar and a lexicon of the Old Testament.

[227] Actually ca. 2 miles east of the river, ca. 30 miles north of the Dead Sea.

[228] The modern Hamah.

[229] [Author's note, expanded: Franz Karl Movers, *Die Phönizier* (2 vols. Bonn, 1841–1856) II.2, p. 221.]

[230] [Author's note, modified and expanded: Stephen of Byzantium, *Ethnica*, s.v. Ἀμαθοῦς (ed. August Meineke, p. 82); Tac. *Ann.* 3.62; Pseudo-Scylax, *Periplus* (Müller, *Geogr. Gr. Min.* I 78); Ἀμαθοῦς αὐτόχθονές εἰσι. Sakellarios, *Kypriaka,* I 51–52.]

[231] [Author's note, modified and expended: Honoré Duc de Luynes, *Numismatique et inscriptions cypriotes* (Paris, 1852). Olivier Masson, *Les inscriptions chypriotes syllabiques* (Paris, 1961) 209–12.]

As in Paphos, so here the Cinyradae ruled, and with the same privileges and the same religious influences as in Paphos.

The city of Amathus was built on a height steeply rising from the sea, and on the right and left delimited by valleys. Only piles of stone, alternating with cultivated fields, currently mark the location of the rather extended city. Pococke[232] found at Amathus still the remains of old walls which were 15 feet thick and downward built with blocks of stone. On the west side, near the sea, presumably where the ancient city had stood, one still sees the remnants of a building, which is the destroyed church of Ayios Tykhonas. Pococke believed that this church may have extended eastward to the point where there are great masses of ruins. Under these is a beautiful ruined church, which perhaps stood in the place where the temple of Aphrodite and Adonis stood; the festival of Adonis [the Adonia] was celebrated here annually (Strab. 14.682).[233] Pococke suspects that toward the east also a suburb extended as far as the River Antigonia [?].[234] Of stones, the inscriptions of which Ali Bey depicts on pl. 35 of his work,[235] nothing is to be seen any more.

At the top of the height, the Acropolis, the most important monuments are to be seen, especially the gigantic sandstone vases described in greater detail below. One of these, located toward north, is entirely broken into pieces, while the other, larger one is still complete. Both are large sandstone monoliths. On the four handle-like protrusions walking bulls were depicted beautifully in high relief, but are now partly ruined and eroded.

The dimensions of the vessel are as follows: The diameter from one handle to the other measured 3.22 m., the interior diameter 2.5 m., the opening 1.2 m., and the interior height exactly 1.58 m. Thus, a tall man, standing upright in the vessel, can just touch the rim with his chin. The vessel is so situated that the north-south line passes right between two of the handles. Approximately in the same direction the vessel has a hairline fracture. This does not go through the entire thickness of the wall; nevertheless a removal from the place where it is slightly lowered into the ground can hardly be undertaken without incurring the risk of breakage.

And yet, I hear, the vessel is supposed to be removed to Paris shortly.[236] On the purpose of this most remarkable, and in its kind unique, vessel nothing can be said with certainty, since no ancient author has made mention of it.

A shepherd boy who guided us to the vase expressed his idea, which seems to be widely held by the people, that it once was used to implement a regulation of the sanitary police.

Between the village and the middle of the ridge on which the ancient city was located L[udwig] Ross observed a row of foundations of pillars which probably belonged to an aqueduct which once brought the necessary drinking water to the people of Amathus.[237]

When we had spent several hours here we were glad to be able to quench our thirst with a few mouthfuls of rainwater which had collected in a depression in the rock.

---

[232] On Pococke see the Hammer-Purgstall, *Ansichten;* Cobham, *Excerpta,* 253; and *SHC* V (1998) 35.

[233] The reference in Strabo is actually 14.683.

[234] Cobham, *Excerpta,* 253. There is no river by that name. Was Antigonia perhaps the name of the suburb? Is Pococke in error here?

[235] See the beginning of this text.

[236] The vase was removed and shipped to the Louvre in 1867 by Comte Melchior de Vogüé and Edmund Duthoit. The broken twin was still in situ as of 1995.

[237] Ross, *Reisen,* 172.

One also encounters burial grottoes along the valley which runs toward the mountains. These consist, according to Ali Bey,[238] of a rectangular main chamber which on all sides leads into small side chambers. Now these grottoes are no longer accessible, because the entrances are filled with rubble.

## 7. Lapithos and Kyrenia

The ruins of the once extensive city of Lapithos (Λάπηθος) are among the most peculiar remains of gray antiquity and distinguished by the simplicity and uniqueness of the buildings. These ruins begin immediately to the east of the monastery buildings of Akhiropiitos, continue for a distance directly along the sea, and then through the fields before they are lost under the cultivated land.

There is a ruined tower-like structure, built of squared stones, which perhaps was built in Frankish or Venetian times as a watch tower. The rest of the city is no more than an uneven field of rubble, in which broken columns, pieces of mosaic, and sherds of glass and terra cotta lie about in wild disorder. In the search for usable building stones, which are dug out of the rubble, the ground has been plowed up in all directions; that is why it has such a wild appearance. The worked-over rocks protruding from the ground and the subterranean chambers within them contribute no little to that impression. Fantasy here has free rein to imagine the most curious abodes for gods and men in the walls of rock facing each other and in the colossal towers with their niches, stairs, door and window openings, and the recesses cut into the rock to accommodate beams.

When a building which was erected in irregular forms because of local conditions has burned, the surviving bare walls allow the most curious configuration of their former connections. And this is the case here as well. After a careful inspection, from all sides, of these masses of rock, which have been worked on and cut, on the outside as well as on the inside, one can only rarely come to any conclusions about the former connections and purpose of the structure.

No doubt the peculiar combination of the natural with the man-made was considerably favored by the conditions of the terrain and by the fact that the massive rocks easily yield to the chisel.

We find ourselves once again standing on fine-grained, slow-to-erode, younger sandstone, of which, as already mentioned repeatedly, all large buildings on the island are built. The unusual feature is only that individual tower-like and wall-like structures rise in isolation above the horizontal layers and, furthermore, frequently have expansions and excavations on the inside. It was therefore a quite natural challenge posed to the first inhabitants of these areas to expand and complete what nature had provided half-ready for their shelter. Therefore, as one can readily understand, on the one hand the natural caves were enlarged and converted into regular shapes, and on the other hand the wall-like rocks standing close one to another were connected by wooden constructions, and thus living quarters for people and stables for domestic animals were created.

As far as is known it was colonists from Lacedaemonia under Praxander[239] who must be regarded as the builders of these rock-structures. Strabo (14.682) mentions them, and specifically the anchorage and the dockyards which existed in this place.

---

[238] On Ali Bey see Cobham, *Excerpta,* 409.

[239] See also Vassos Karageorghis, *Cyprus: From the Stone Age to the Romans* (London, 1982) 117. But according to Hill, *History,* I 87 and 99, n. 6, his name was Proxanor.

As I have already emphasized in my description of the nearby monastery of Akhiropiitos, this area belongs to the most fertile and most picturesque areas of the whole island. The low-lying areas along the sea, with their gentle hills, offer a rich variety of fertile fields and rich gardens of olive trees or St. John's bread trees, while in the south the craggy peaks of the limestone mountains rise up and thus alleviate the scorching heat of the summer.

On the far-spread field of the ruins of Lapithos antiquities of various sorts are constantly being excavated. Inscriptions, of course, are not lacking. An inscription found only recently and set up in the courtyard of the monastery of Akhiropiitos deserves special attention. It contains a decree of the emperor Tiberius [A.D. 14–37].[240] Here I made my first attempt to make a squeeze, which turned out accordingly.[241]

To Tiberius Caesar Augustus the deified, son of the deified Augustus, emperor and pontifex maximus,

in the 31st year of his tribunician power [A.D. 29], when Lucius Axius Naso was proconsul, Marcus Etrilius Lupercus was legatus pro praetore, and Gaius Flavius Figulus was quaestor,[242]

Adrastos, son of Adrastos, loyal servant of the emperor, hereditary priest of the shrine and the statue of the same Tiberius Caesar Augustus erected by him in the gymnasium,

Lover of his Country, Man of Excellence,[243] at his own expense and by his own choice gymnasiarch and priest of the gods who are worshiped in the gymnasium [Hermes and Heracles],

has at his own expense erected a shrine and a statue to its god,

while Dionysios, son of Dionysios, and Apollodotos, loyal servant of the emperor, were supervisors of the ephebes.

Adrastos, son of Adrostos, loyal servant of the emperor has dedicated it, together with his son Adrastos, loyal servant of the emperor, at his own expense and by his own choice gymnasiarch of the boys,

on the birthday of Tiberius, the 16th year of his reign [A.D. 29], on the 24th of Apogonikos [16th of November].

As Ludwig Ross already observed, people erroneously call this field of ruins by the name of Lambousa, while a village removed from it, on the slope of the mountains, goes by the name of Lapithos.[244] This village and the nearby village of Karavas bear, as only few other villages of the island do, the marks of prosperity, which is bestowed on them by an abundant spring which comes from the mountains. But even with this inexhaustible silver spring the village cannot rise to that size and prosperity which it still had in the Middle Ages, when sugar cane instead of wheat grew in the fields and the number of fortunate inhabitants amounted to 10,000.

---

[240] Not a decree of Tiberius, but a dedication to Tiberius.

[241] The translation here given is based on the Greek text as given in *IGRom.* III, p. 354, no. 933, rather than on the text given by Unger. See also Sakellarios, *Kypriaka,* I 144, and *OGI* II, no. 583.

[242] On L. Axius Naso, proconsul, see *PIR*[2] I, p. 343, no. 1691; on M. Etrilius Lupercus, legatus pro praetore, ibid. III, p. 89, no. 103; on C. Flavius Figulus, quaestor, ibid. III, p. 152, no. 268.

[243] These appear to be honorary titles rather than mere adjectives.

[244] Ross, *Reisen,* 147.

Most of the houses of Lapithos are built of stones from the ancient, lost city, as is evidenced by the column capitals, the ancient reliefs, and damaged inscriptions which are there immured. But what gives to this mountain village the greatest charm in the view of the people is the numerous churches and chapels which crowd into the mass of houses. Even to retain their names was impossible for me in the course of my hurried passing-through.

I can describe more briefly the rock tombs of Kyrenia, not too distant from Lapithos. These, too, are subterranean caves in the sandstone and lie on the west side of the city, so to speak before the gate, in an uneven terrain next to the sea. The graves are not arranged in rows but scattered in irregular fashion, next to and above one another, as conditions permitted.

The small door openings lead either into a small rectangular room adjoining a second and third similar room, or else a few steps down. These obviously served for the deposition of the dead and in this regard are quite similar to Syrian or Egyptian rock tombs. But nothing has remained of the contents of these tombs, nor has any inscription survived. All this suggests that they were opened and plundered already long ago.

Next to these rock grottoes there are the great quarries, the material of which must have been used in building and fortifying the city. Now the former well-fortified city Keryneia [Kyrenia] (pronounced "Tscherinia" — ἡ Κερύνεια) can hardly be called more than a dirty village, which is inhabited almost exclusively by Turks. Only the works of fortification are still imposing, although the rusty iron pieces and bronze canons without mounts could hardly be defended against a company of European soldiers.

## 8. Lamnias

Among the subterranean structures cut into the sandstone we count also that on the peninsula of Akrotiri near Cape Gata. This flat spit of land, rising only a little at the cape, seems to have been selected already in earliest times but also later for settlement. Near the salt lake there was the lavishly built monastery of Ayios Nikolaos, which, judging by the marble columns scattered about, could even be considered rich.[245] Starting from the southeastern end of the salt lake and going south on the rising plateau toward the cape mentioned, we came to a stony, totally desolate area of brush. A few prominent rocks attract attention by the manner in which they have been cut. And soon one notices steps cut into the same sandstone, which lead to a subterranean chamber. The same consists of an oblong, vault-like hall flanked on both sides by narrow galleries. The main room in the middle measures 15 m. long, 4 m. wide, and almost 5 m. high; it was in direct connection with the 2 m. wide galleries by the openings in the side walls, which are like wide pillars. The whole inner room, which in the back had a few niches probably for the placing of divine images, is blackened by soot. Another, similar grotto, located nearby to the west, has been made more or less inaccessible by the collapse of the ceiling.

In the foreground of this temple there is a cistern, which can be reached by a well-preserved stairway.

Whatever else may have existed here is difficult to ascertain, since the pits are uneven and the steps cut into the rock run in different directions. The entrance was in the

---

[245] [Author's note, expanded: The monks of this monastery are reported to have kept cats to get rid of the snakes frequently found here; hence the name "Cape Gata."] On the tradition of the snake-fighting cats see further Cobham, *Excerpta,* 48 and 172, and Gunnis, *Cyprus,* 156–59.

north. Our guide, the local judge from Akrotiri and a knowledgeable farmer, as it seemed, called this place Lamnias; but I do not find this name in the older writers.

A little to the west from there he also led us to an extensive field of ruins, which contained, like the cape itself, many potsherds. Whether this was a settlement destroyed only in later days or whether it dated from antiquity he was unable to say.


# Friederichs—1869

[Plate 28]

Carl Friederichs, *Kunst und Leben: Reisebriefe aus Griechenland, dem Orient und Italien* (Düsseldorf, 1872) 30–50. Carl (also Karl) Friederichs (1831–1871) visited various Mediterranean and Near Eastern countries in 1869 for the purpose of acquiring antiquities. The letters were sent home to his wife, and the private matters are here omitted.

Early Wednesday morning we cast anchor at Cyprus, in the Bay of Larnaca, and when I stepped out of my cabin the boatman of my friendly host, the consul, was already waiting to meet me[246] . . .

Larnaca, 11 October 1869

How happy I was to receive the letter with good news from home! My friend D. was able to forward it from Constantinople to me here. You cannot imagine how isolated one is here and how seldom one hears anything at all about the German homeland. Mail arrives once every two weeks. At that time American newspapers are received, and also an English newspaper which is published in Constantinople, the *Levant Herald*; but it is a rare occasion when anything about Germany is reported.

Thank God that this first station, Cyprus, will soon be behind me. But I must not forget that I have spent here an incredibly rich and interesting time. Together with the consul I traveled through three-fourths of the island in a fourteen-day journey. This journey was rich in hardships, deprivations, and adventures of every sort, but it was even richer in natural beauty and in the most remarkable and in part most splendid antiquities. I shall describe it in detail to you and to all who are interested in my well-being; for it was equally interesting for the past and the present of the people, for nature, and for history.

But first I must tell you of the surprise which came to me by the invitation of the Viceroy of Egypt to the opening of the Suez Canal.[247] How I was chosen for that honor is a complete enigma to me, but I thought that an opportunity to see Egypt must not be passed up. In any event I shall go there, and, of course, from here. But what is even more remarkable and has deeply moved me, if I may say so, is that this invitation of the Viceroy fulfills another wish of mine, the realization of which I never believed possible, namely to see Jerusalem and Golgotha. The way from here to Alexandria passes Jerusalem by a distance of eight hours; Jaffa, a station of the steamer, is eight hours away from Jerusalem. This being so, how could I fail to enter the Holy Land? This is for me the

---

[246] Friederichs means Luigi Palma di Cesnola, American consul in Cyprus 1865–1876.

[247] The Suez Canal was officially opened on 17 November 1869 under the Khedive Ismail (1863–1879).

dearest and most remarkable thing about this whole invitation, although I will not deny that Cairo, the pyramids, and also the festivities will certainly be of great interest.

As far as my stay on Cyprus is concerned, the first half of it is told easily enough; for I spent fourteen days here in the house of the consul with an inspection of the collection, which daily gains in importance in my view.

Larnaca is probably the most dreadful city of the whole island. Thus I was happy to leave it when the consul invited me to accompany him on a journey into the interior of the island for the purpose of scouting locations for future excavations. The city lies in a desert of sand, a treeless, waterless, and sad desert, which is twice as sad at this time of the year, when all herbs and flowers have wilted long ago. Here for the first time I have felt the awful quality of the sun and understood the myths of the ancients about the deadly power of the sun. The temperature was 24° [Celsius] day and night when I arrived. I could not even think of going out before sunset, because already one hour after sunrise the sun has a really burning effect. Add to that the total lack of rain during the summer and this desolate and sad environment.

When we took our first walk to the ancient tombs, of which there are quite a few here on the soil of ancient Kition, we passed the carcass of a camel, and indeed decomposing animal carcasses complete the picture of this utterly sad desert. You see, all over Cyprus, when an animal falls and cannot get up again, it is the practice to let the poor creature die a miserable death and rot away wherever it may lie, and thus the view of camel carcasses is quite common here. And yet, there is also much beauty. When we turned around for the way back the last evening sun was just shining above the city, and I must admit never to have seen such a strangely interesting and quite specifically Oriental sight. Before us was the desert with the ancient tombs, the dead camels, and the living ones, which move by in long trains, then the gray city with its flat roofs, especially the Turkish quarter with its palm trees, which everywhere at once indicate a Turkish quarter, and finally behind that the blue sea.

Larnaca actually consists of two cities, the marina immediately at the shore, where the European consuls live, one next to the other, and Larnaca proper, which is a quarter hour away. But the marina is the larger and more important part, and it is quite a hike from one end of the city to the other. Each one owns his own home, which in the case of ordinary people is of one story only, and therefore the city is quite spread out in relation to its population. The houses are built on foundations of ancient stones, which are found everywhere, and above that of sun-dried clay tiles. That was the practice here also in antiquity, and just so in Nineveh and Babylon. On the ground floor there are usually no windows, and for this reason a walk through the streets is incredibly desolate. The door leads right into the courtyard, in which the inhabitants spend the better part of the day.

The bazaar is really in all Oriental cities the place where life is centered, and then there are the coffee houses, which are filled all day long. The houses of the consuls are, of course, set up in the European fashion, as far as possible. And I had here the best accommodations in the world, designed for coolness, with a high ceiling and thick walls. My bed was quite wide, as is the fashion in Italy, and provided with curtains against the mosquitoes, which, however, did not bother me here.

But now we leave Larnaca and begin the journey into the interior of the island; to help you orient yourself let me begin with the following preliminary remarks: Larnaca is situated in the southeastern bay of Cyprus. From here draw a line northward, not quite straight, but slightly leaning toward the west, so that on the right side a good one-third of the island is cut off, and that part I have not seen. As soon as this line approaches the sea in the north turn left towards west and stay close to the sea until you have followed along the whole northwestern, western, and southern side of the island and again have reached Larnaca. This was our route, which I shall now describe in detail.

First we traveled from Larnaca to Dhali, the ancient Idalion, a distance of about five hours by camel (the camel is here the unit of measurement). The two mules of the consul were saddled up, and then there was a two-wheeled, ox-drawn cart, on which a soft bed with pillows and blankets was spread out and which was equipped with a white awning against the sun. A uniformed kawas (military policeman) rode at the head. (Each consul has four of these, since the consuls have legal authority.) We started out one hour before sunset. I preferred to walk, much to the astonishment of the others, since even the lowest people have a donkey and no one walks. After a few hours I lay down on the soft bed of the oxcart and was shaken to and fro on the rough road and through deep river beds. Without the soft bed I surely would have broken all ribs. And this road is one of the best in all of Cyprus and is at least passable for an oxcart.

But the pleasure of the cart was not to last long; for suddenly one of the oxen collapsed and could not be made to rise again. The ox-driver had made the trip to Dhali already once on the same day and furthermore had given the animals nothing to eat. No wonder then that the animal went down. What to do? We could have mounted the mules, but unfortunately the kawas had allowed one of them to run away and it had not yet been captured again. So we decided to walk and to take turns riding the one mule left to us, while the kawas rode into the next village to requisition a fresh ox. This beginning of the journey was incredibly funny. We continued our travel through the night by the bright and beautiful light of the moon, crossing a vast, desolate, and silent area.

Only once we passed a vineyard, where some boys were still picking grapes. The kawas, who was still with us, ran across a field to obtain some grapes for us. But then the boys were gripped by fear when they saw the kawas with his saber running toward them, and they all fled. We had a hard time to get them to stop and to obtain the most delicious grapes from them. Then we continued, and I was deeply touched to hear, after a while, in this desolation and quiet, the shepherd's pipe of a small boy. He was sitting in a vineyard and played the strangely mournful and long-drawn-out sounds which are peculiar to this instrument, along with the most amazing trills and flourishes.

At about eleven o'clock we arrived in Dhali, at the country house of the consul, whither some of the servants, the cook and a second kawas had already preceded us.

Here everything was, by Oriental standards, splendidly appointed. I even had two glass windows in my room, especially sent ahead for me from Larnaca. The other windows could be closed only by wooden shutters, like the door. This stay in Dhali, which lasted four days, was in every regard wonderful.

This is the ancient Idalion, and this was a major site of the cult of Venus, and one truly can understand how a cult of Venus could be founded here, and also the enthusiasm of the ancient poets who speak of the shady groves of the Venus of Idalion. It is a lovely, wonderfully lovely place, doubly so when one comes from the desolation of Larnaca. There is abundant and good water, not from the river, which is completely dried up in the summertime, but from good wells, which are, however, most primitive; and there is luxurious vegetation, vast numbers of olive and lemon trees, and a lovely location in the midst of the mountains. Like a green oasis Dhali lies in the midst of a triple row of mountains, of which the furthest one is always rising above the closer one. Also for antiquities Dhali is thus far the most important place on the island, because nowhere have excavations been as rewarding as here. The collection of the consul comes almost entirely from the tombs of Dhali, of which he has discovered about 3000. Here then there was enough to study. We would ride out at six o'clock to see tombs, one part after the other, because the distance of the individual tombs is often several hours. By nine o'clock we had returned and then sat until four o'clock in the dense shade of the garden under pomegranate and lemon trees, reading, taking notes, etc.; then it was off again to other sites, until after sunset.

I will not tell too much here of the antiquities themselves, since I intend to write a detailed report on the antiquities found on Cyprus and the sites, especially, since a selection of the antiquities will soon reach Berlin.

In general the tombs of Dhali are extraordinarily poor in architectural form, almost no more than holes in the ground, such as the people still use to bury their dead. The most interesting site is a recently excavated Phoenician temple with most remarkable monuments. At this point the journey as such really was to begin, and we departed from Dhali. There were a total of seven people and seven mules: two kawas, the cook, and two muleteers, who also helped out as servants. We were well provided with everything needed for eating and drinking: the cook had all of his utensils with him on his mule; there were wine, all manner of fruit, and delicacies; also we had bedding and blankets. Thus we really needed only water, eggs, chickens, and bread, which can be obtained at least in the larger places. So the whole caravan departed two hours before sunset, guided by the homeowner from Dhali; it is the custom here for the host to accompany his departing guest for hours. We were headed for Nicosia or Levkosia, the country's capital, fairly in the center of the island. Here we arrived after dark, and, since of the two gates of the city the one may never be opened at night—I no longer remember for what ill omen or other reason—we were turned away and had to continue for another half hour around the city until we reached the correct gate.[248] This was now opened to us, and the first dragoman of the consulate was waiting for us there, because the consul had announced our visit to the Pasha. A young boy with a lantern went ahead of our caravan, which now moved noisily through the deserted streets of the city.

Nicosia is an impressive fortress from the times of the Venetians or Genoese. It has been the capital of the island since Richard the Lionheart, who was followed by the time of the Genoese and Venetians.[249] At that time Cyprus flourished almost as it had in antiquity, so that Nicosia was a city of 50,000 inhabitants, until the rule of the Venetians was followed in the second half of the 16th century by the Turkish rule, which to this day kills everything. The whole population of Cyprus amounts to 200,000 people, and these must annually raise 3,000,000 Taler, which are sent to Constantinople; additionally they must maintain a whole army of officials, who draw colossal salaries. Nothing is done for the island. There are in all of Cyprus only a few bridges from the time of the Genoese; otherwise everyone sees for himself how he gets along on the roads. And if something is

---

[248] There were three gates in the Venetian walls; they are now called the Paphos Gate, the Kyrenia Gate, and the Famagusta Gate.
[249] Nicosia was at no time in the hands of the Genoese. Richard the Lionheart took possession of Cyprus in 1191, followed briefly by the Templars. The Lusignan dynasty held the island from 1192 to 1489; the Venetians from 1489 to 1571.

done, as at the moment a small effort against the locusts, the poor people have to pay extra, like three Taler a head for the locusts. In short, it is a pity to see this land, one of the richest in antiquity.

Here in Nicosia there was also a kind of inn, probably the only one that exists in all of Cyprus, and it even is passable, if one is not bothered too much by the fleas. I must remark, however, that here already was the beginning of the trouble with our nightly accommodations, which increased tremendously now during the following days. So we turned in at this Greek hotel, and the beginning of the ceremonies, such as the passing around of sweets, was quite acceptable. This is the first, either coffee or jelly, or both. But already the supper was, for some reason which I do not remember, inedible, and so was lunch the next day. Here I tried ordinary Cypriot wine for the first time, but it tasted dreadfully of pitch, and although that is supposed to have been the case also in antiquity, I was not enough of an antiquary to drink that stuff. In short, I was glad when the consul's foreign wine was brought out. We utilized the day in Nicosia first to see the beautiful Gothic churches dating back to the Genoese, but now converted into mosques. After that we paid a visit to the Pasha, everything in solemn ceremony, led by two kawasses with their staffs. The watch was lined up in the courtyard of the palace to pay us honor, and on the way to the room of the Pasha an army of servants was visible.

The Pasha is a very elegant, fine man, whose Turkish barbarism is thinly covered by French refinement, but comes to the fore now and then.[250] The reception hall was, like all Turkish rooms, quite different from our style. There are in it no tables, which generally find little or no use at all, and little other furniture, but only a wide divan (wide so that one can pull up one's feet), and the rest of the room is filled with lots of chairs. The walls are empty, without mirrors or pictures. Coffee and cigarettes were offered, and the conversation revolved at first around the antiquities of the island and our journey. He was kind enough to offer us military escort, and the consul accepted one sagtieh [zaptieh], as they are called, and he was a great help to us.

Then the Pasha cleverly turned the conversation to the subject of the horrible plague of this island, the locusts, which here every year completely gobble up a certain area of the island. He seemed to be intensely interested in the subject and explained to me, plan in hand, how one kills these animals. Along the roads and at certain distances pits are dug, and then, when a swarm approaches, a cloth is put up in such a manner that a slope leads from the cloth into the pits. This arrangement is really a large trap which is put up in the path of an approaching swarm. The animals attempt to climb up on the cloth, are unable to do so, march along the cloth, fall into the pits when they get to them, and are then trampled underfoot. The Pasha related that within ten minutes such pits, about four feet long, three feet wide, and two feet deep are completely filled with locusts; that is how incredible their mass is. After high politics had also come up and the conversation had lasted more than an hour, we withdrew, with much mutual courtesy, in the same way that we had come.

In the afternoon many visitors came to the hotel to see the consul and Milordos Bey—that is my official title. Antiquities of the poorest sort were offered to me at exorbitant prices. Even the doctor in Nicosia, if you can believe that, held me for a treasure hunter who had come to show hidden treasures to the consul, and he thought that their location was given in my book (I had a decription of Cyprus by [Ludwig] Ross with me)!

---

[250] Mehmed Said Pasha.

It is generally believed here that we are hunting for treasures, and how many adventurers and loafers are trying here to find treasures! In general, no one can conceive of the level of stupidity which prevails on this secluded island.

The next morning our journey began in earnest, and we traveled long distances. The Pasha had told us that we would need six days to reach Paphos, but we hoped to manage the distance in three days. Twelve hours by camel were planned for the first day, according to the calculations of Mr. Besbus, the dragoman, who accompanied us from now on to facilitate communication with both Greeks and Turks. He was able to tell us many interesting things about their religion and their customs; he himself exhibited Oriental apathy and lethargy to a high degree. Since none of us knew the route, Mr. Besbus was the one on whom we had to rely, i.e. on the information which he obtained from local people. But there is no one on Cyprus who knows his whole homeland; there is no occasion to travel, there is no commerce and no traffic, and so people know only the area immediately around their village. Mr. Besbus assured us that, if we traveled for twelve hours, we would find excellent accommodations for the night.

So, press on! Our caravan started out at sunrise and traveled on until 9:30 a.m., part of the time at a gallop, part of the time in the so-called Bismarck-step (there is here on Cyprus really a quickstep called Bismarck-step, and I can prove it black on white!). We passed through a desolate and barren area, directly toward west, through the plain which stretches through the whole of Cyprus between two mountain ranges. This was, it seems to me, a respectable beginning for a stay-at-home like myself, who had not been on a horse since his student days. On the whole I managed without great difficulty; only I found it difficult to ride in the hot sun between ten and two or three o'clock. And that is when we took a break. On the first day we found a resting place in a small olive grove with running water. Running water in the Orient, where nearly everything dries up in the summer! And now running water, after we had for hours passed through a treeless desert with burned bushes! One cannot imagine what a delight that is for one's eyes. And even shade! When one has himself experienced a little of the languishing in the desert, then one learns to understand the care of the ancients for their springs. Here, in the shade of the olive trees, our cook prepared for us a wonderful breakfast of eggs, coffee, and delicious fruit.

So we did things every day, always having breakfast in the open, in the nicest, shadiest places. Then, since I could not handle the whole distance by mule, I was placed on an oxcart, which could still manage at this point, and was driven for three hours by a very jovial Turk. Then I had to mount the mule again and ride for another four hours; for that was the distance to our quarters for the night, just as the dragoman Mr. Besbus had promised.

This place, which we reached in the middle of the night, was directly on the northern coast and consisted of a few houses, which contained nothing but grain storage bins and a few sleeping rooms. This is a place for loading grain aboard ships and is inhabited only during a certain time. We moved into the largest of these houses, and the owner soon appeared in his night-cap and offered us accomodations for the night. We stepped into the large dormitory, where some eight to ten people were sleeping, each one on his table or wooden rack; for there are no beds. People take a pair of sawhorses, put some boards across them, and the bed is ready. Everything else each person must provide for himself, but most require nothing more. The air in this room was so bad that it repelled us as if we were stunned, whereupon the owner offered us his own room. But the air was no better, and we asked for permission to stay in one of the grain storage bins. One of the rooms was not quite full of grain, and so two wooden racks were set up for us and on those we spread out our blankets. I shall not easily forget this room; that is how much fun I had with it. It also was a stable, at the entrance of which two old tombstones had been placed. It was half full of grain, on which large scarabs were crawling about; unfortunately not ancient ones, but live ones, larger than the Egyptian scarab-shaped stones. There was no lack of smaller pests either, and, so that the nose might receive its share, there was an unbearable smell as if of petroleum. There was no thought of sleep; we turned on our tables, like the sausage in the pan, to use the Homeric comparison.

At sunrise we continued our journey in good spirits. For this day the sagtieh of the Pasha, who knew the road well, was supposed to provide our nightly accommodations, for we had lost confidence in Mr. Besbus. The sagtieh, a Turk, promised to put us up in a beautiful Turkish house in the evening. The day's travel was demanding and we were in the saddle for more than eight hours, for now we came into the mountains where the mule or the Arabian horse is the only means of transportation. Always up-hill and down-hill toward the sea, through a series of gorges which were initially beautiful but in the long run tiring. So we arrived soon after sunset at the Turkish house of the sagtieh and found a wretched little hut of clay with one room for everything. The floor was of clay and had mountains and valleys, and in the corner the hearthfire was burning. Here the Turkish woman sat with a bunch of dirty little children and prepared their supper. All the while she took care to turn her back toward us as we stepped in or rather looked in: for they [Turkish women] are not allowed to show themselves to any man, especially not to a giaur. But the man was willing to move with his family into an earthen hut, partly under-ground, which was also his. So the fire was extinguished, and the woman moved out, shy and fully covered up like a ghost, together with her children. Now we [the consul and the author] had at least a covered space to sleep; the rest of our company always slept under the open sky and I would have been happy if I could have dared to do likewise. This night's lodging was a good deal worse than the grain bin. Here there was a great variety of animal inhabitants, large and small; of the former especially the crickets, which re-freshed themselves at the warm hearthfire, and a cat, which all night long was noisily eating I do not know what. Then, when we had lain down, defying death, in this awful, dirty, and smelly room, every few minutes something fell down from the ceiling into our faces. In short, here we had even more reason to toss and turn sleeplessly. Through a fortunate misunderstanding we all got up at one o'clock in the morning, believing that it was close to morning; the cook first, and he had built a fire to cook the coffee. This fire shone through the shutters of our windows and woke us up. So we all sat around the fire, comfortably, like a troop of soldiers on bivouac, telling stories and making jokes.

Now comes the most beautiful part of the journey, the tour right across the west-ern side of the island, through the valleys and over the mountains. If thus far in the whole landscape the character of a desolate, burned, and treeless desert had prevailed, the pic-ture now changed completely. We rode for about four hours through the most lovely val-leys with an abundance of running water, luxurious trees, and even flowers! Tall oleander bushes, in full bloom, stood wherever one looked. I have seen here the most picturesque and most lovely places, sometimes of truly surprising beauty, such as villages, tucked away in a green forest, individual houses in the valley of a river, etc.

An amusing intermezzo was provided by the kaimakam (governor) of a Turkish village through which we passed. This man had offered offense to a member of the consul's staff and now, since the consul demanded his deposition, had come on the advice of the Pasha to ask for pardon. The consul, however, was not willing to grant him audience and had him so informed through the dragoman. But the poor knave could not be deterred and always stood before the consul with the words "addio, signore," in the mistaken belief that "addio" meant "pardon," until he finally understood the true meaning of the word and went away.

This day we rode into the noon-day heat and at twelve o'clock were at a level of several thousand feet, when we took a rest in a village at this height. The Greek priest, who was more peasant than priest, invited us into his house, where we found what we had been looking for more than anything else, namely an inviting shady place, where our noon meal was prepared. Here I had an opportunity, with the help of the dragoman, and through that which I observed with my own eyes, to gain some information about the Greek priests in Cyprus. I believe that they rank intellectually below the Turkish [imams]; with few exceptions they cannot read or write—this particular one I examined myself—the few texts which they must recite in church they have memorized in a mechanical way, and otherwise they live just like the peasants. Mr. and Mrs. pastor were just occupied with baking bread and heating the baking oven, and next to that was the pig pen, where there was also at all times something to be done. The only pastoral function was that the priest, when we took our leave, came with a vessel of incense and blessed us and our journey. My companion said that this was against the evil eye—this superstition is far-spread even now, just as it was in the Middle Ages. He had a low opinion of the priests, although this surely was an act of kindness.

From this village at its high elevation, Stroumbi, we climbed even higher, up and down on paths most dangerous and littered with rocks and stones, often right at the edge of deep ravines. I must admit, I would not have been able to do this on foot, nor would I have wanted to, but, given the mule's incredibly sure footing, I could remain mounted in spite of all seeming danger, while our sagtieh, who was riding a horse, had dismounted and was leading his horse by the reins. We reached an elevation of at least 3000 to 4000 feet and as the sun set could see the whole island from this height. Now it was downhill, and for safety's sake we dismounted and climbed down the rocky path with our animals. Here we got a good idea of what Turkish roads are like!

After a journey of two hours in the dark through the plain we finally reached Paphos, which is equally famous for its pagan and Christian associations and which in every regard made the deepest impression on me. A larger village, Ktima, lies next to and on the ruins of Nea Paphos, and here clean and decent accommodations, even with beds, were waiting for us! Mr. Besbus had arranged these accommodations for us with a Greek friend, a young couple which vacated their best room for us! Here we spent two days, which were more enjoyable for me than any of the others, in part because of the natural properties, and in part because here there are really highly significant remains of antiquity, tombs of the greatest interest. But I never have felt the piercing heat of the sun as much as here, where once, not taking enough care, we crawled around at noon among the ancient tombs, often on hands and knees. Here I saw, among many others, one tomb so splendid as no other that I am aware of and which until now has been quite unknown and would have remained unknown to us also if we had not had an excellent guide. This is an impressive hall cut into the rock, about 80 feet wide, just as long, and 50 feet high. Three mighty pillars support the ceiling, and on the walls one can still see the places where the sarcophagi stood. What people built these magnificent tombs? That is here, as elsewhere, the question to which so often we do not have the answer.

We spent much time with archaeological explorations and examinations, and the consul at once leased the ground on which in all likelihood the temple of Nea Paphos stood. The rest of the time was taken up in part by visits from owners of antiquities who wanted to have their things evaluated or wanted to sell them, but at ludicrous prices, and in part by official visits to and by the Turkish authorities.

On the third day we continued on, always along the southern coast, to Palea Paphos. This lies about four hours further east [16 km. southeast] and is the real, oldest foundation. A sacred way leads hither from Nea Paphos for the many processions which undertook the pilgrimage to Palea Paphos and the famous temple of Venus. In antiquity the famous temple of Venus, the most famous in all antiquity, was in Palea Paphos. A few sad remnants are still about and still make a powerful impression. One corner of the wall, whether of the temple or of the enclosure, is still well-preserved, and here we measured one of the stones: 15 feet long, 6 feet high, and 3 feet thick! Who today still builds with such stones! Only in the distant past, only in the rough greatness of those times, were such blocks of rock piled one on top another.

Here our lodging was again more than modest, in a Turkish clay hut on two tables, but without the small population of our earlier lodging. But our meal was that much better, for our host had accompanied us and had shot for us some birds which can be found only in Palea Paphos and which in the judgment of competent people are the best for eating anywhere. In the evening we observed from the distance the festivities of a Turkish wedding, white figures dancing around a large fire. The music, provided by a large Turkish drum, such as is used also by our military, and, if I am not mistaken, by a shepherd's pipe, was very strange to my ears.

From there it was a good day's travel to Limassol, the second trade center of the island, in the center of the southern coast. Here was the only place where we crossed bridges; but these had not been built by the Turks, but rather date from the time of the Genoese. In Limassol golden lodging was waiting for us with the American consular agent, a Greek and the richest man on the island, who owns the largest wine business in Cyprus. I at least was dead-tired when we arrived at nine o'clock in the evening, but unfortunately we had to wait another two hours for our opulent supper. This, in the opinion of the consul, was served only out of vanity, to display the host's wealth. Then, for the first time in a week or more, I slept in my own room with a measure of European comfort. I took advantage of this so thoroughly that I did not rise until ten o'clock. The consul, a former cavalry officer,[251] for whom it is no hardship to ride a horse, wanted to leave at five o'clock in the morning, but I protested strongly, because I needed some rest.

At one o'clock, after we had visited our host's winery and tasted the strangest wines, in which I found no pleasure, we were served another sumptuous meal, together with the ladies of the house, who, however, for the most part spoke only Greek. The whole large table was twice completely set, literally, first with meat and fish dishes, then with cake and fruit. Most of these delicacies I could not eat, and the consul was so mean

---

[251] In the American Civil War di Cesnola commanded the Fourth New York Cavalry Regiment. There is a monument to this regiment at Gettysburg.

as to praise only the bread, which, however, was as white as snow. Some things were served only for decoration, such as a large turkey or similar creature, which was cleared untouched, just as it had been served. Yet, our host was well-intentioned.

Then, in the afternoon, together with his son-in-law, he accompanied us as far as Amathus, the second place in the south famous for its associations with Venus. He showed us what little there is to see there, the tomb and the large stone vases which probably stood at the entrance to the temple as lustral basins. Then, taking his leave, he assigned a kawas to us as a guide; this man was to introduce us to a Turkish lady, who, so he said, had ample lodging in a place between Limassol and Larnaca, and there we would be able to stay overnight. And indeed, this lady's hospitality left nothing to be desired, and her room was clean, too. Her husband, a Turkish clergyman, welcomed us, and her brother sat with us the whole time, fascinated by us and everything that we did. All the good things which had disappeared at noon untouched from the table of our host in Limassol now emerged from the basket of our kawas to make our supper, including an almond cake, which I would have loved to send to my Carli.

In the morning I opened my door to the terrace or balcony, since our lodging was on the first floor [European reckoning], to walk about on the flat roof. There were two sleeping figures, whom I believed to be men, part of our company, and so, without concern, I continued my walk next to them. But suddenly one of the figures got up and fetched from my room a veil, to provide a tight cover for both of them. This was the genteel Turkish lady and her serving woman, who had given us their room and slept on the balcony. This is what I call hospitality! The serving woman later engaged in a conversation with the dragoman and told of her husband, who supposedly was very learned, and why? Because he had been to Larnaca, to Limassol, and even to Nicosia, i.e. because he knew the area for eight to ten hours distance around his home village. You can see how rarely a person leaves the narrow confines of his village. But the earnestness and admiration with which the woman spoke of her "learned" husband were touching.

When we rode off, the Turkish clergyman, our host, held our stirrups, an unheard-of honor, the consul thought, for a giaur. From this village it was only a short day's journey to Larnaca. But on this short stretch we got a good demonstration of what desert sand is; for a strong wind in this most depressing of all areas gathered dense clouds of dust, and then there came a brief cloudburst. So we arrived in Larnaca not exactly in clean condition but in excellent spirits.

Until my departure I now had about a week, which was fully occupied with my official business. Today, one day before my departure, nearly everything that I purchased from the consul's collection for our museum in Berlin has been packed up, and tomorrow the boxes will be on their way. How pleased I am to leave! This morning the steamer came which is bound for the north, for Constantinople. You cannot imagine what a happy feeling this is, after fourteen days again to see a ship, a possible way home! Tomorrow, 12 October, the steamer will come which will take me to Syria; first to Beirut, where I shall have a stop of one day, and then to Kaifa [Haifa] and Jaffa [Tel Aviv], where I shall arrive Saturday morning; then, on Sunday, I shall be in Jerusalem.

I now shall leave you, but my yearning grows with the distance.
Jerusalem, 22 October

On 13 October in the afternnoon I boarded the ship. The consul and his family conducted me aboard, with all possible honors, kawasses and flag; a number of acquaintances were there as well, to bid me farewell. I boarded the ship most happily, together with my antiquities, which were carefully packed in fifteen boxes and soon will arrive in Berlin.[252]

# Archduke Ludwig Salvator—1872, 1873

[Plates 14–27]

Ludwig Salvator [Plate 14], Archduke of Austria, *Levkosia, die Hauptstadt von Cypern* (Prague, 1873). English translation by Ferdinand Krapf Ritter von Liverhoff: *Levkosia: The Capital of Cyprus.* London: Kegan Paul & Co., 1881. Re-issued London: Trigraph Ltd., 1983. With an epilogue by Sir David Hunt. Reprinted here by kind permission of Lady Iris Hunt, Trigraph Ltd.

## PREFACE
[Plate 15]

When, after passing a pleasant range of hills, Levkosia first bursts upon the sight, with her slender palms and minarets, seated in a desert plain, a chain of picturesque mountains as the background, it is like a dream of the Arabian Nights realised—a bouquet of orange gardens and palm trees in a country without verdure, an oasis encircled with walls framed by human hands.

Great is the contrast between the town and its surroundings, and greater still between the objects within the city. There are Venetian fortifications by the side of Gothic edifices surmounted by the Crescent, on antique Classic soil. Turks, Greeks, and Armenians, dwell intermingled, bitter enemies at heart, and united solely by their love for the land of their birth.

These contrasts form the principal charm of Levkosia; and my object in publishing the following pages of my journal, is to record my impressions during the months of January and December a few years ago. I hope that my descriptions will be aided by the accompanying sketches in conveying a faint picture of the brilliant panorama still dazzling my eyes.

## CHAPTER I
## GENERAL REMARKS UPON THE CITY

The city of Levkosia (Nicosia) is situated on a slight elevation in the plain of Messaria, 147 English feet above the level of the sea, and only about 10 feet higher than

---

[252] On the acquisition of these antiquities see the following: Elizabeth McFadden, *The Glitter and the Gold: A Spirited Account of the Metropolitan Museum of Art's First Director, the Audacious and High-handed Luigi Palma di Cesnola* (New York, 1971) 92; Anna G. Marangou, *The Consul Luigi Palma di Cesnola, 1832–1904: Life & Deeds* (Nicosia: The Cultural Centre of the Popular Bank Group, 2000) 118, 171, and 176–77.

the surrounding country. The immediate neighbourhood of the town is perfectly flat; to the south only some terrace-shaped heights make their appearance.

The soil is marly; in some places gravel and clay.

The climate is healthy, but the inhabitants frequently suffer from ophthalmia, which is the case in most parts of the East.

The summer at Levkosia is exceedingly hot; especially so with the north wind, which is stopped by the range of mountains extending on that side of the town; but the nights are cool, even with the Hampsi blowing over from the burning coasts of Africa, though it is cooled by the waves of the broad Mediterranean.

The winters are mild, with little snow, which falls almost exclusively in January; it seldom if ever freezes. January and February are considered the coldest months. By February 15 the almond-trees are bursting into leaf, in March everything is blooming; and if it is considered that in the middle of December all the trees are still standing in their full natural beauty, the period during which the trees are bare is a very short one.

The south-easterly wind (ostro a Scirocco) is the strongest, then come the northerly (Tramontana) and south-easterly, principally during the months of January and February.

The town and, in fact, the whole of the island, is subject to earthquakes, but not in the same degree as Limasol. Smaller shocks occur almost every year. The last considerable earthquake occurred in the year 1852, which, however, did no great damage. These disturbances occur mostly in summer; usually in the month of June.

On October 26, 1859, Levkosia also suffered from an inundation of the Pidias, a small river which enters the town under the gate of Paphos, and flows out through the gate of Famagosta. Since that time the gate of Paphos is closed at high water. This rivulet usually is half dry, and more like a brook than a river. Besides this stream the town is provided with fresh water by means of two aqueducts, one of which, called Arabahmet Su, reaches Levkosia by the gate of Paphos, and gives the best water; the other follows the boundaries of the city as far as the gate of Cerinja, past the gate of Famagosta, both distributing their water to all parts of the town.

## CHAPTER II
## THE CITY WALLS
[Plate 15]

Before entering on a description of the town itself, a few words may be said about the boundary wall.

This wall (Muraglia), which was built by the Venetians in the year 1567, is bordered by a trench, and a pathway runs the whole length of it. It is constructed entirely of solid square stones, and is three miles in length. Here and there it is crowned by battlements, which are evidently of a later date. There is a small scarp at the bottom of the wall, and a much more abrupt one on the top of it; the angles are of such a shape as to facilitate climbing, which, besides, is made easy by a great many rotten squares, whole parts of the wall being decayed. Eleven ramparts spring from the Muraglia, all similarly built, but not of the same size. They have each a bastion with receding flanks, an oblique edge, and two prominent rounded shoulders. At the bottom most of these ramparts are provided with small escarpments under the plinth; some, however, are without these. The edge of the wall is truncated on the top, and extends to the receding flank of the bastion.

The Muraglia is pierced by three gates, situated nearly due east, west, and north; there is no gate on the south side. They are closed at sunset and opened at sunrise, nobody being allowed to pass in or out after that time without special permission of the Governor. There are some cannons of ancient date posted near these gates; all the better ones have been transported to Constantinople.

We may begin our detailed observations on the Muraglia with the Gate of Famagosta, looking to the east. This gate, at which the road to Larnaka begins, is so far the most important of the three that it leads to the so-called Scala. It derives its name from the place of the same denomination, which was once situated in that direction, but is now in ruins. From the outside this gate is quite plain, and protected by the rounded shoulders of the ramparts immediately adjoining on the north. The entrance to the town leads up a small incline. In the middle of this is a large round cupola, which has a latticed lunette on the top and a small niche on each side. The interior of the gateway shows a round gable with a Turkish inscription, and on the left, under a Gothic canopy, a running spring with a marble tank, fed from the aqueduct imbedded in the wall itself. There is also a small guard-house on the gate, with a flagstaff and two lightning-conductors to protect the powder magazine underneath, which is said to be very large. On the rampart, by the side of the gate, there remain five Venetian guns behind the walled-up portholes. An arch of the aqueduct leans against the gateway, another spans the cavity of the adjacent rampart, and follows for some distance the level of the ramparts. From the top of the gate the view extends over the road to Larnaka, with camels wending their silent way to the Scala, some of them stepping slowly and painfully along, suffering from the mange, which has made great ravages amonst these animals in Cyprus.

And what horrors on the roadside! Human beings dragging themselves along, covered with leprosy, extending their emaciated arms towards the passers by, trying to attract their attention with frightful yells, and begging for alms. They pray to God for relief in their agonies, and not being allowed to enter the town they make the open fields their dwelling-place. A fitting frame to these scenes full of horror and misery are the desolate Turkish graveyards bordering the road on both sides. A little higher up, near the village of Pallurgotissa, is the Greek cemetery, where also stands a small church. Continuing our walk along the first rampart to the north of the Gate of Famagosta, we reach a second road running in a contrary direction; from here are seen the picturesque houses of Upper and Lower Kaimakli, built of clay and surmounted by palm-trees, and behind them the mountains in the distance. Turning our eyes to the interior of the town, we observe the Ayia Sophia and St. Catharine's Church amongst the flat roofs covered with clay, orange-gardens and groups of palms, and here and there a majestic cypress-tree. The wall is crowned at distances by ragged loopholes, and the aqueduct runs along the narrow ramparts. From here the wall leads in a straight line to an extensive rampart, which forms the corner of another turning to the north, straight up to the mountain range. These mountains are brilliant at sunset with the loveliest hues of purple and azure, forming a strange contrast to the greyish-yellow desolate plain opposite. Looking into the town again from here, our view extends over rich plantations of palms, raising their heads from the deep green of the mulberry, olive, and carob trees which surround them on all sides. The whole length of the Ayia Sophia is visible from here. But let us go on. We pass a rough spring by the side of a small resting-place, and come to another rampart surmounted by telegraph-poles; there are still visible here the stone platforms of the guns on the edge of the bastion. and on the receding flanks. In the wall between this and the next rampart is the Gate of Cerinja, near which the aqueduct branches off.

This gate, leading to Cerinja, situated on the northern coast, and on the opposite side of the range of mountains before us, has the shape of a vaulted passage, with Turkish inscriptions. It forms a turret, which seems to be of Turkish origin, and ends in a cupola-shaped room for the officer on duty. Immediately adjoining there is a small guard-room, which is only accessible by two narrow staircases leading up from the interior. Here there are three Turkish and four small Venetian cannons; on the left a spring. On the right side of the gate there is a decayed lion of rough workmanship inserted in the wall.

Opposite the gate and outside the town is the large Turkish burial-ground, surrounded by a clay wall. The graves are mostly in a wretchedly dilapidated state, the greater number marked by a wooden block only, although a few are surmounted by a marble turban. In the middle of the cemetery is a Koubba with two tombs; one of them is that of Geng Abtal, which is said to be very old, with a green cover and a flag under a small cupola; by the side of it stand water-jugs for the ablutions of the devout believer, which have to be performed before beginning his prayers. The other tomb is situated under one of the arches of the Koubba.

Returning to the wall we continue our way on the rampart, which here widens out again, and pass by an abandoned windmill and a platform for guns; then by a rampart with only one loophole, after which the rampart becomes considerably narrower, so that the clay houses of the town almost touch the principal wall. From here is seen on one side the Seray in the town, on the outside the village of Aurela, and further on, in the middle of a wide dazzling plain, Chioneli, inhabited exclusively by negroes. Further on there is another rampart, which is partly used as a burial-place, and is provided with a gun on the top and two platforms on the sides. Here the wall turns to the west. In front extends a range of hills rising terrace-like in the distance on the west of Levkosia; looking down into the trenches below there is bustling life, Caramanian goats and fat-tailed Arabian sheep, the rams with long horns, grazing amidst queer-looking little lambs, which skip about in spite of their enormous tails. After another rampart, in the battlements of which there are some old guns left, the Gate of Paphos is reached, which forms a simple arch-way through the narrower wall; over this gate we find again a Kisla or barrack of the same name, with two narrow staircases leading up to it through the body of the wall. This edifice has a small yard with the residence of the Kajmakham Bey, which consists of a little eastern pavilion with low divans round the walls, from which extends a magnificent panorama over the town, the walls with the far-extending plain and the mountains behind them. There are three to four hundred soldiers in the Kisla, who inhabit a fairly large building situated on both sides of the courtyard; they sleep in the Turkish fashion, on boards slightly raised from the floor, and fitted up with blankets and cushions; their arms are piled up at one end of the room. Although the whole structure seems very comfortable and airy, I hear that they intend to build a new Kisla. By the side of the barracks are nine guns, two of which are of a new system, and are used for the drilling of the troops.

Near the Gate of Paphos, as has been mentioned before, the two aqueducts of Arabahmet Su enter the town. In front of the gate is the timber market, and a little farther Tahahane, shaded by old olive and other trees, where clay jugs are principally made.

Directing our eyes from the straight almost perpendicular wall, which looks due west, downwards, we see the Yikko Monastery of Arkanyelos and Ayi Omoloyitathes; near this last place is the still, shady Greek cemetery, and right under our eyes the fresh green vegetable plantations in the trenches. Further on we again come upon a deserted windmill, an old abandoned burial-ground, and another rampart, which forms the turning-point to the south. The view from here in the direction of the mountains, with the lofty Troodos, the usual gathering-place of the storms, is magnificent; and equally charming is the other side, which commands the town, with its innumerable palms and the mountain ranges behind it. Behind this rampart a small aqueduct, now neglected, penetrates the city. The rampart is broader here, and overlooks Tchiflik Kei, belonging to a Turk. Two more bastions follow now, on one of which there is an angular turret, half in ruins, and quite close to it is the other, a smaller one, and far projecting, through which the Turks broke into Levkosia on September 9, 1570. In commemoration of this victory, and in gratitude to God who helped them to it, they built a mosque, and called it Pairaktar Djami si (the temple of the flag-bearer). We shall return to this building in a following chapter. This rampart, once the scene of a stubborn, bloody strife, is now covered with verdure and gay, peaceful flowers. The part of the town nearest to us contains most beautiful palms, raising their slender stems and graceful heads over all the other trees. The wall continues from here to the east, giving an extensive view over the neighbouring cliffs, and turns behind the last bastion, bordered by houses, to the Gate of Famagosta, our starting place.

## CHAPTER III
## THE DIVISIONS OF THE TOWN,
## ARCHITECTURE AND INTERIOR OF THE HOUSES,
## GARDENS
[Plates 16–19]

Levkosia is not divided into districts in the usual sense of the word; the only divisions that could be drawn would be by the different populations of the town. The Turks, for instance, occupy the parts about the Gate of Famagosta, near the mosque of Tahta Cala, and especially those between the gates of Cerinja and Paphos. In these last-named districts there are quantities of wretched little houses which are too bad for the Greeks, and of very little value. The Greeks have chosen principally the district between the episcopal residence and the Ayia Sophia for their dwelling-place, but are also sprinkled amongst the Turkish population between the gates of Cerinja and Famagosta. The Armenians are mixed up everywhere with the Turks.

The narrow, winding streets bear sometimes various names within a short distance, and usually the name of the street is not given, but the various places are designated after the neighbourhood in which they are situated. The names of the localities appear in white characters on blue tin tablets in Turkish and Greek; the houses are numbered in the same manner. The pavement consists of rough shingle, and in many cases there is none at all. The principal street of Levkosia, which is naturally the broadest and longest one, is called Tripiotis (in Turkish, Pasch ma hallè); the next in importance is the Tahta Calà, which leads from the Gate of Famagosta to the bazaars, thus forming the main entrance to the city. By the side of it runs the dry bed of the Pidias, with several bridges.

There are very few houses built of stone at Levkosia; some of these are adorned with Gothic arched windows and flowing tracery, but nobody seems to pay much attention to them. Most of the houses are made of big clay bricks, as they say, for fear of the earthquakes. The price of 1,000 of these bricks is 100 piastres, or about a pound sterling. Building is done with great rapidity; some mortar, composed of earth and straw, is poured from a mason's tray with two handles over the brick, another one, half crumbled and dusty, is put on the top of it, some more of the pap follows, another brick, and so on and a house is finished in less than no time, and has the advantage, moreover, of being dry soon after it is finished.

These houses are exceedingly cheap, a fine building costing hardly more than about 200 *l.*, and the finest stone house in Levkosia was sold a short time ago for 400 *l.* Clay houses will last a hundred years, but they must be frequently repaired, as the straw with which the bricks are plastered up will get rotten and leave holes in the wall.

The foundations of these buildings are in most cases of stone, and usually of ancient origin. Remains of old walls are frequently found under modern houses, some of them leaning half over, as also old arcades with rough arches.

Most of the Turkish houses have prominent pavilions, with lattice-work windows: others, to the number of about 150, mostly in the Turkish and Greek districts, are surmounted by wooden gables; the roof projects far out, and has a sort of wooden casement under the prominent part of it, made in the Turkish fashion; the water is allowed to run down from it into a wooden gutter running all round the eaves. The great majority of the houses, especially in the mixed districts, are simply covered with clay, mixed up with some chopped straw; this kind of mortar is poured over the cross-board and rushes, which are usually supported by marble cornices. Sometimes the beams are left sticking out under the roof instead of cornices, or else some simple boards. With clay roofs of this kind the gutter consists of a clay or wooden pipe running along the edge of it, and the level of the roof is gently sloped down at the sides. An opening covered with two marble slabs, leaning at a sharp angle one against the other, forms the chimney of these houses.

In the old parts of the wall we often meet with Gothic arches, hood-mouldings, and projecting turrets; the doors of the houses have usually only a wooden frame, which is sometimes inserted in a Gothic arch.

Over the entrance-door of the Turkish houses we often found a wooden frame in the shape of the crescent and star, or of the star only, with little wire hoops to hold the oil cups for the illumination on the anniversary of the Sultan's accession and other festivals.

The entrance-doors usually exhibit three rows of nails, one in the middle, one on the top, and one below; narrow strips of wood run down closely from the top, each of them fastened by a nail in three places. Some of the doors are formed in lozenge-shaped squares made in a similar manner. The cross-bars of the doors are most elaborate in some Turkish houses. With the Greeks they are usually in the shape of a cross; they have knockers also, which are either arabesque-shaped or simple rings.

These rings, if provided with a chain and lock, will serve also to fasten the door. As a rule a plain bolt on the outside is the only protection against intruders. A bit of wood stuck through the bolt from inside prevents it from being opened from the street. Some of the bolts will slide in by themselves. In some houses a key and a solid iron bolt complete the arrangement. Here and there horse-blocks with steps at the side of the door are to be seen.

The windows of both Turks and Greeks have lattices on the sides, and often blinds besides. Many of these windows are also protected by wooden projecting shades, which are carved on the sides.

Now let us step in. The doors of the Turkish houses are in most cases carefully locked, and a screen stands immediately behind, so that when the door is opened no one can see in; having passed the screen the visitor enters the paved hall, usually facing a garden or a courtyard. The roof of the hall frequently rests on Gothic arches with round pillars and Byzantine square capitals.

In the absence of arches the roof is supported by round columns, and the beam is then adorned with carved consoles. All the windows opening into the hall are provided with Moorish lattice-work. From the entrance the stairs lead to the upper floor either by a regular staircase, or steps on the outside of the wall. Pretty little doors with carved Moorish arches form the entrance to the interior. The floors and ceilings are inlaid with large, dirty-grey marble slabs, which come from the village of Aglanjá. They cost a piastre, or about twopence-halfpenny a-piece. The roof is generally unceiled; in many cases it is pointed; for the most part, however, flat. Generally the round beams are ornamented by pretty basketwork, or else they are simply overlaid by boards. Rich people have their floors inlaid. The doors are made of wood, often with fine fretwork.

In the Turkish houses we usually found a small divan-room, which is also frequently found in Greek houses. The ceilings of these rooms are usually supported by arches resting on brackets, or simple beams. The floor is covered with mats from Egypt, and in the middle of the room stands the copper fire-pan with the glowing charcoal. In the houses of the poorer the rooms on the ground-floor are also inhabited, and the light comes in through handsome-looking little windows made by apertures in the thick stone walls, and having glass panes on the inside, like those usually found in the mosques.

Ornamented shelves are carried all round the rooms. The furniture consists of a rude bed, with curtains hanging down from the ceiling, which can be drawn up or let down by strings. By the side of this bed pictures of saints and little Greek crosses, with a chain to be put round the neck, are seen hanging by nails. We also find chairs with carved backs and low seats, and other more or less common pieces of furniture. Often a basket is suspended from the ceiling to keep the bread in, called Tabayia, or there is a piece of board in a corner with the water-jug standing on it.

The Turkish inhabitants of the richer class have a reception-room on the upper floor, richly furnished with divans along the walls, and shelves garnished with various objects of glass and china. This opens into other rooms with broad divans and pillows; sometimes in the corners there are small shelves containing all sorts of bric-à-brac and slender scent-bottles. Most of the Greeks have modernised dwellings, and all their houses contain an airy pavilion with a large divan running all round the room, upon which persons are seated with their backs to the windows. Rich Turks have large latticed pavilions, which are delightfully cool in summer if there is the slightest breeze. They also like, as a cool resting-place, the flat roofs of the houses. The kitchen is situated on the ground-floor, with the fireplace in the corner, or in the middle of the wall, after the Turkish fashion. Many houses have a perfectly round baking-oven with a marble floor and stone sides, covered on the top with clay and straw. Most of the houses have their own wells; otherwise the water is brought in by donkeys, which have two pitchers hanging on either side.

There are very few houses worth seeing at Levkosia. However, an old stone house in the Yegni Djami Street, called Kaloiro al Effendi Konak, is worth mentioning, which is inhabited now by two Turkish families. It has a Gothic arched gate, the outer cornice of which is crowned by finials and a shield of arms over them; there are also arms on both sides. Some traces of Byzantine windows and gargoyles at the corners of the cornice are still visible. The Turkish inhabitants have erected a wooden pavilion in front. The interior of the edifice was once richly decorated in Oriental fashion; now, we are sorry to say, the whole of it is sadly neglected and half in ruins. The balcony shows elegantly-shaped stone ornaments, different grotesque figures, and tiny carved windows. Entering the house itself we find in the first place a large divan-room, with soft, inviting seats all round; the fine ceiling, elaborate shutters on the latticed windows, and a neat inlaid cupboard by the side of the door, remind us of the best Moorish works: there are also little hanging stairs or shelves, on which the thousand little nothings of a harem are neatly arranged. On one side we enter a smaller room with a wooden ceiling, divided into squares, and a low balustrade in front of the latticed windows. Some steps lead up to a higher platform with divans, separated by another balustrade from the rest of the room. Neat shelves are visible everywhere. The doors are partly of a square design with Turkish fretwork, partly carved in the elaborate style of the Renaissance, or else arched. There are rooms with groined arched ceilings, others simply covered with flat beams, which are supported by small consoles. On the second floor there is an exceedingly fine room, the ceiling of which is composed of Turkish wood-work. Over the door-posts is a small latticed balcony which rests on the slender columns of the balustrade separating the upper divan from the best of the room. Ornamental shelves with turrets in the middle give the room a lively aspect, which seems to have been open in olden times for family feasts and dances.

Amongst the houses belonging to Greeks we may mention one called Celebi-janko, which is situated in the Ayios Andonis Street, on the right-hand side, in the direction of the church at the bottom of this street. It is a plain house, built in two storeys of solid square blocks: over the gate stands the lion of St. Mark, behind it a hill crowned by a castle. It has a large courtyard with four arches on each of the sides, and three on the side of the entrance hall, that is to say, a broad one in the middle and two smaller ones on each side. The corner pillars support four arches. A wooden balcony over the entrance gate, approached by steps of the same material, lately added, is a good illustration of the bad taste of the present day.

Almost every house has an orange garden, with gigantic palms towering over the fruit-trees; and besides these private inclosures there are extensive public gardens within the boundaries of the city, occupying more than one half of the whole extent of it. All these gardens are bounded by clay walls on the side of the street; the side adjoining the open hall of the house is fenced only by a low wooden balustrade; and they are watered either from cisterns or directly from the aqueducts. All sorts of fruits are cultivated there; some are very sweet, orange-shaped lemons (Lemonia gligia), which are very cheap on the island, and can be bought therefore by the poorest classes; citrons of an extraordinary size, with very few stones, and a sort of white paste inside: as these rot very quickly, they are often preserved by putting a coat of wax over them. This last fruit is eaten either fresh or as a preserve, cut in slices, with sugar. Apricots and other kinds of fruit are equally famous; St. John's bread, pomegranates, and dates, which are rather dark-coloured, but very good. The bunches of dates are wrapped up in soft straw mats to protect them from the millions of ravens, rooks, and jackdaws, which sometimes cover the palm-trees in such numbers that they appear quite black. Vines and mulberries are also frequent: these latter are reared for the sake of the silkworms. The ground by the side of the fruit-trees is occupied by fine vegetable gardens, watered with the help of a sort of shovel, which takes up the water like a spoon, and throws it over a considerable area. Carrots, onions, cabbage; these are eaten raw. Prickly pears and various flowers are plentiful.

Gardens pay a tax of ten per cent on their produce. Offers for the purchase of this tithe are received during the whole of March, and on the last day of the month the highest bidder is accepted. The locusts, which have made great ravages in former times, are now completely exterminated, thanks to the energetic efforts of Richard Matei, one of the richest land-owners of the island, and by those of the local Government. Grapes are still suffering very much from the vine-mildew.

## CHAPTER IV
## MOSQUES—TEKE—TOMBS OF THE SAINTS
[Plates 20–23]

The piety of the Mussulmans has, since the occupation of the island, erected several mosques, some of which have been newly built, others transformed from existing churches. Among the latter of these, the principal mosque, Ayia Sophia, occupies the first place.

It is a massive Gothic structure, built with a nave and two aisles and with an almost flat roof, which originally consisted of a stratum of siliceous lime. Now the right aisle and the nave are covered with lime only; in fact, part of the aisle is unroofed. The nave receives its light through three large Gothic windows and two double windows of the same style, over which the cornices of the roof project in the shape of gables. The fourth Gothic window has disappeared. The choir has five windows, one of which occupies the centre. From both sides of the principal gable of the porch portions of unfinished towers are visible, with crockets on the gable-doors, and large Gothic windows. Only the left side of the upper part is in a tolerably good condition, and contains one room, inhabited by a few pigeons: the ceiling is vaulted, and has some pendants with crockets in the corners.

The front of these towers is square, the back round, and contains a winding staircase, leading to the top of the minaret which now crowns the structure.

The view from the top of these structures over the twelve minarets of the city (including the two of the Ayia Sophia), and its various other buildings, the magnificent mountain range reflecting the various hues of the setting sun, is perfectly enchanting. Whilst we gaze, the melodious voice of the muezzin calls the faithful to prayer. There are five of these muezzins in the service of the Mosque, two of whom are constantly on duty, being relieved every week by two new ones. They have free lodgings and a hundred piastres (about 1l. sterling) a month for salary, which is paid out of the rich revenues of the Mosque.

Following the outer wall of the church, we are struck by the beauty of the buttresses: there are six on each side, supporting the principal nave, and connected by an open frieze. The third buttress on the right side is higher than the other ones, and joins the roof by a flying buttress with steps on the top of it.

These steps are accessible through an octangular turret with a winding staircase, which turret is joined to the left corner of the facade. A similar turret stands on the opposite or right side. There are in the two sides of the church two transepts, which form the two arms of the cross, of which the left has three, the right only two buttresses. The left transept has a plain Gothic porch, over which there is a Catherine-wheel window, the outline of which is still to be distinguished although it is walled up: the back part of it forms a semi-circular apse at its termination, where the altar was placed and the clergy sat. The interior now contains two separate spaces, one of which is used as an oil store-room, and the upper one is quite empty.

The lower room has a simple groined arch for the ceiling, pillars with helices in the corners, and a half-decayed holy-water stoup. An arch spans the entrance to this room, which has a small window in the middle. The upper room, lighted by a Gothic window, is a simple vault, the four arches of which form also an apse, and rest on a capital. This capital crowns a column, the base of which probably once rested against an altar.

The entrance to these rooms is from the interior of the Mosque. The transept on the right side of the church has a round apse, and a moulded, projecting cornice. As in the choir of the church, in the middle, and on each side of this transept, there is a Gothic window. The side entrance, now closed, is much finer on this side. It is in marble, carved with crockets on the edges, and a hood-moulding in three divisions. By its side is a small desolate burial-ground. Between the first and second buttresses there is a small building, very much like a chapel, with a cinque-foil, two shields of arms, and a Gothic window. It contains a plain vault with broken brackets and pendants. On the second buttress on the right there is a mutilated sun-dial, and against the last one, the sixth on this side, has been built an additional buttress to support it. After this follows the choir, supported by four buttresses.

Entering the Mosque, we find ourselves in a magnificent building, having a large Gothic nave in the middle and two smaller ones on the sides, dividing the body of the church into three parts: the two side-aisles are, as in all mosques, slightly raised over the floor. The interior of the Mosque is most striking. Five Gothic arches separate the nave from the two aisles; from the fifth arch the transepts branch off on the right and left. The presbytery is formed first by two lower arches, parallel with those separating the side-aisles, two on either side, and one somewhat narrower in the middle. The pillars are very massive and round, having octagonal capitals and circular bases. Of late years these capitals have been painted abominably—green and blue, with yellow and red borders, contrasting strangely with the white ground of the rest of the wall. The pillars of the presbytery are slighter, especially so the four outer ones of granite with Byzantine capitals. The clerestory is most magnificent, rising by three steps at each arch and carried on by low flat arches. We get to this gallery by the staircase of the minaret. At the time the church was transformed into a mosque, all the additions had to be built in such a way that the faces of the devout should be turned towards Mecca, according to the Mussulman rite. The right wing contains the Mihrab, the left wing the Mèm Ber, the Mahfil occupies the middle. All these are new, ugly Turkish constructions. Part of the marble floor near the Mihrab is raised, so that the bases of the columns even in the presbytery are partly covered. Lifting up the carpets and mats, we discovered many old tombstones. Other tombstones had been taken up and used for the pavement of the platforms. The windows of the Mosque contain tracery, creating an agreeable twilight in the vast building.

Although the Baptistery lying on the right of the Ayia Sophia cannot be counted amongst the mosques, I will here say a few words about that building.

It is an old edifice, now divided in the interior and used as a granary and a store-room for oil. It bears traces of many an alteration made in the course of time. The nave ends in an octagonal apse, and has in the centre a circular cupola with four plain Gothic windows and an arched cornice, which is supported by two engaged columns at the end of the nave. The part with the portal, as shown in the engraving, which forms the outside of the nave, has four buttresses, is flat on the top, and is of a later date. The aisle on the right has vanished. The nave has a Gothic window in front, and a Catherine-wheel window at the back. A porch composed of four rude arches is of later construction. With regard to the interior, the nave is composed of four low Gothic arches resting on round corbels, with plain crossed ribs and similar arch-stones. The last of these arches separates the cupola from the presbytery. The cupola passes over from the circular into the square shape in corbels. In the presbytery we see a plain crossed vault ending in a Gothic arch borne by a clustered column. From the keystone of the apse six ribs run out, and rest on three coupled, slender columns. A Gothic window occupies the centre. The aisle has a similar vault, and an apse shaped like a niche.

After the Ayia Sophia we must just mention the Haidar Pascha Djami si, which is close by. It was once a church sacred to St. Catharine. On the right-hand side of the building the spot where the tomb of the saint is said to have been is still shown, and the Greeks often come and light their lamps there. The front portal is in a fine Gothic style, the arched cornice of which ends in a poppy-head; there is also a Catharine-wheel over it. On the right side a clumsy minaret shoots up, the highest one of the town after Ayia Sophia's; on the left a half-ruined building, of which only a few Gothic arches are left, joins the Mosque. There is also a portal with ornaments and finials on the right. Three Gothic windows, two of which are divided by slender columns, occupy the space between the buttresses, which have gargoyles on the top. On the left of the Mosque there are similar buttresses, and a sort of square turret. The interior is whitewashed and much damaged. Two Gothic arches support the vault, consisting of simply crossed ribs. In the apse six ribs, resting on a clustered column, spring forth from the keystone. Both the Mihrab and Mèm Ber are on the right in this Mosque. In a house opposite the Mosque, belonging to one of the Imams (Turkish priests), they showed us a cup cut out of nephrite (a dark-green stone), which the owner had dug out from a garden near St. Catharine's tomb, and which in all probability was formerly used for ablutions. Going to the south from the Ayia Sophia, we come first to the Emerghé Djami si. This also was a church in ancient times, dedicated to St. Nicholas: it stands in the middle of a cemetery. Opposite the entrance we see a fountain with marble columns, and in front of the porch a couple of tombstones, out of which a palm-tree is growing. On the left there is an addition of a later date, with two windows of the Renaissance style, the gables of which are formed by the cornice of the roof, and supported by two shouldering pieces: in front of it stands an oblique minaret. All that remained of the entrance-hall is the right side, with an old Gothic arch. A simple Gothic portal leads us into the inner room, consisting of six plain arches. On the last arch, and the four making the apse, the decayed pilasters of the old vault are still visible. Near the entrance-gate, and in the pavement, we observed fragments of old Christian tombstones.

The other mosques of Levkosia are without exception Turkish buildings, and although built of masonry are of no artistic significance; we shall therefore only give a cursory description of them.

The Pairaktar Djami, with a Persian wheel and a water trough in front of it, has a Gothic vaulted hall with side arches, a latticed wing, and a minaret. Over the door we read a Turkish inscription; three arches carry the flat roof. The stone Mihrab and Mèm Ber decorated with gold, but somewhat heavy and obsolete, are standing on the left: there is a balcony over the entrance. On the left of it the grave of the first Turk coming to Levkosia: it has a green cover and a flag of the same colour; by the side of it an alms-box. The floor is covered with roe-skin rugs.

The Tahta Calà Djami si is on the end of the same street, with a desolate graveyard and an arched spring. This Mosque is very small, and has a round vault behind Turkish wooden lattice-windows, having three round arches in front and two on the sides. On the left side stands the minaret. Three Gothic arches support the roof, which is a rough new Turkish structure.

The Jegni Djami is also built in the middle of a cemetery, where are to be seen the finest tombs of Levkosia. There formerly stood in the same place an old mosque, previously a church, and part of the Gothic vault and minaret are still visible. This Mosque was destroyed by a rapacious Pasha, who dreamt that a hidden treasure was to be found underneath it. The Turkish residents complained about this at Constantinople, and the Pasha was consequently ordered to be executed. The Koubba by the side of the new Mosque (Jegni means new) is his tomb.

Jegni Djami has a rude entrance-hall formed of four Gothic arches, which also runs along the right side of the building as an open corridor; in front of it is a covered spring.

Laleli Djami si is near a group of high palms, and has a slender minaret. Over the entrance-door, with a Turkish inscription, is a latticed vine-screen; in the small courtyard, facing the school, are some orange and olive trees. The entrance-court of this Mosque is formed of four Gothic arches, and the ceiling of the interior is made of simple beams resting on similar arches.

The Mèm Ber and Mihrab are rudely gilded. On the left side we see the apse of the old church, which formerly stood here, Serai, or Seraimus Djami si, opposite the Serai or palace. The telegraph office stands in the dreary-looking courtyard of the Mosque, built of clay bricks. Near a high plum-tree, which is the favourite meeting-place of the crows, is the so-called Venetian column. This column is round, has a sexangular pedestal with four escutcheons, one of which is crowned by the cap of the Doges and is made of granite; the capital, architrave, and arms of marble. On the other side, the right, is an antique sarcophagus with a Greek inscription, which is said to have been standing once close to the column; it is used now as a water-trough to a spring. The Mosque, in front of which we see a Turkish grave, is built of large square stones, with a porch consisting of three low Gothic arches, the side walls of which are made of old tombstones with half-effaced inscriptions. On the right stands a plain minaret. The interior of this Mosque is a melancholy example of the national Turkish style; it is supported by two pointed arches and receives light from the side. The candles by the side of the Mihrab are ridiculously small.

Not far from it is the Iplik Bazar Djami si, with an arched hall and a small minaret; it is of an oblong shape and the roof stands on a rough arch.

About the middle of the Turkish quarter stands the Arabahmet Djami, one of the prettiest mosques of Levkosia. A door, barred by a chain to prevent horses and cattle from entering, leads us past a spring into the courtyard, where fine orange-trees and magnificent palmachristis overshade the numerous graves. The Mosque has a cupola and a minaret on the right; over the entrance hall are three small cupolas. The interior is very plain, with a number of pointed arches which support the cupolas. It has a fine Mèm Ber and Mihrab, in front of which hangs an ostrich egg.

Turuslu Djami, with magnificent trellised vines over the passage leading to the small yard, on the right an octangular fountain, on the left a gigantic palm-tree. It has two entrance-courts, the one in front with six, on the right with four pointed arches; a minaret on the left. The interior is formed by four very flat arches; has windows on the top, and rough Turkish ornaments.

Tukiannar Djami, with one flat Gothic arch in front, two on the sides; there is also a minaret and a fountain on the right.

Stavros Misir Djami si, or Mehemmed Seid Djami, was formerly the Greek Church of the Holy Cross, which has in front a court composed of three arches and three side arches and a minaret, all joining the court. It has an octangular cupola, lighted by four windows, and supported on the inside by pointed arches. The Mihrab stands half to the left.

In the broad street, starting from the gate of Cerinja, we come to a Take, or Turkish monastery, with thirty-six dervishes. Near the entrance stands a water-tank, protected from the sun by a latticed vine-shade adjoining a pavilion, by the side of it a deep well. There is also here a dancing-room, supported by three arches, with a floor of pinewood, and an arched balustrade for the spectators. The dervishes dance here every Sunday. Along the street we see six balloon cupolas (Koubbas) all in a row, and connected with one another, containing fifteen tombs. These tombs have frequently rough stone blocks on each end, with a common dervish cap on the top. The Scieh, two in number, have a green turban and dervish caps of stone. One of them belongs to Ahmet Pascha, who died here. The outside of the windows is covered with wooden lattice-work, which allows the passers-by to look in.

There are several holy tombs at Levkosia, one of them behind St. Catharine's Church, in Asim-Effendi Street, with a green cover and a flag with rough inscriptions, and an adjoining dry spring, also with a Turkish inscription. Another one, not far from Turuslu Djami, with seven roughly-made tombs. A few steps further up from Jegni Djami on the left side of the street there are three more of them; one on the ground-floor of a house, the two other ones with a Koubba. At each of these tombs there are a number of little ribbons and rags hung on the outside of the lattices by the believers, as a sort of offering.

# CHAPTER V
# CHURCHES AND MONASTERIES

Levkosia is said to have possessed during the Christian era two hundred and fifty churches, of which the number has been greatly diminished in later times. With the exception of a Catholic and Armenian church, all now belong to the Greek religion. They are mostly small stone buildings with uncovered vaults; some of them have no steeples, the erection of which has only been allowed since 1856. Wooden seats, not unlike choir-stalls, are placed all round the interior for men; over the entrance there is a raised latticed room for women. The court round the churches is often adorned by olive-trees, which are a very favourite symbol of peace. The church-service is conducted by Greek clergymen (Popas), often by monks. Every church has rooms to let to strangers, who stay either for devotional or business purposes.

The oldest church of Levkosia was the Phaneromeni, but as it was said to be near falling down they pulled it down, and are now building in its place a new church with three aisles in a partly Greek, partly Renaissance, and partly Byzantine style. Near the church is an open passage, partly vaulted and partly covered by a flat corniced roof supported by round columns.

Amongst the churches now existing the Tripiotis church is the oldest. It is a uniform, massive fabric, not without some elegance, having a triple vault and a large ante-chapel composed of three large and two small pointed arches, into which the principal rudely-carved gate opens; on the right is the newly-built steeple. Over the second column of the dark inner room rises a plain cupola with four windows. The fifth round arch belongs to the apse. Behind the Ikonostasis, glittering with gold, in front of the niche-shaped apse, stands a richly ornamented wooden altar with a baldachin, with windows on the sides and at the back. A handsome canopy, inlaid with mother-of-pearl and tortoise-shell, leans against the second column on the right, under which the images of the saints, painted on panels with a golden ground, are exposed on their respective feasts. Between the first pair of columns a large gallery for women is suspended. By the side of the entrance court old olive-trees stand, near a small orange garden and a spacious yard, surrounded by a covered colonnade with ten and four arches on two opposite sides, the whole planted with orange-trees. Behind the church of Tripiotis stands the monastery of Macerà, with a very small chapel but a very large inn, much patronised by the neighbourhood. Near Tripiotis we find the new Ayios Savas church, covered with tubular tiles, and a small steeple on the right; the courtyard, with four and nine columns on the sides is planted with orange and olive trees. The vestibule rests on columns behind, and joins the church by a couple of pointed arches. The interior is divided into two aisles by two pillars, and has two altars; the one on the right has large crosses inlaid with wood and fretwork. The altar on the left stands on a Roman capital turned upside down. Over the entrance and on the right side is placed the painted gallery for women.

The church of the archiepiscopal palace, called Ayios Joannis, situated within the courtyard, is a plain and substantial fabric, the vault of which is borne by four pointed arches and closely painted over; the Ikonostasis is overlaid with gold.

Ayios Andonis, with straight buttresses, which are flat on the top, and a new steeple in front, finer than all the rest of them. The arched porch has a pointed vault. A similar vault with imposts is the principal feature of the interior. There are windows at the sides and a gallery over the entrance. We see also a fine canopy, similar to the one in the Tripiotis church. The front bears the date 1736. This church has also an irregular courtyard, surrounded by a colonnade, and planted with olive and orange trees.

Ayios Jakovos is a small building with four barrel vaults; upon these stands a square wall, carrying the cupola with eight little windows. The interior shows four pointed arches; the one on the back is lengthened out. The Ikonostasis, carved of wood, bears the Russian eagle. The apse is a niche with pointed arches.

Hrisalinniotissa, with two round cupolas, an open vault, and a new bell-gable, has a court formed of eight arches and a portal with a Gothic arch ornamented with some finials, and two side entrances. The interior is very peculiar; strong, massive, flat arches surround the principal cupola, another strong arch carries the roof, and the side-wings or arms have irregular-shaped vaults. Of the three niches, only one has an altar with a baldachin. On the right there is an additional vault. Handsomely carved galleries for the women, which remind one a little of the Turkish style, are crowded all around. The church has a large courtyard of six, nine, and ten arches, as also an extensive inn kept by the monks.

Ayios Kassianos is a new church without a steeple, with three crossed vaults and two doors. It has two naves, and therefore a double apse formed by three arches and a large gallery.

Ayios Yeoryios is small, with two pointed arches on the right, a wooden ceiling on the left. It has only one altar, and is joined by a large garden.

Ayios Lukàs has a three-arched vestibule and a bell-gable on the right, on the left plain buttresses with flat tops. This church has two aisles, the right one ending in an octangular projecting apse. A small Gothic portal opens upon the street. The interior, divided by two columns, has some pointed arches and a plain vault; the arches rest on corbels on both sides, and on the right there is an altar. A large latticed gallery occupies the back and part of the sides of the church. On the right stands the throne of the bishop. Two rows of arched galleries run round the inner yard, which is full of olive-trees.

The Armenian church, called Panayia, has a vestibule with four pointed arches, resting on pilasters. The interior is a plain crossed vault, separated from the apse by a pointed arch; six ribs, starting from a keystone which rests on an impost, form the apse. The altar, standing under a baldachin with an eagle, is elevated. Quite at the bottom of the church is the women's gallery. The floor is covered with mats and carpets. By the side of the church is a garden with olive-trees.

The Roman Catholic monastery of the Holy Cross, inhabited by five Spanish and Italian monks, must here be described. The church is small, has a vault carried by two pointed arches on chaptrels, and an apse in the shape of a niche, and two side-altars. At the back we find a deep vaulted room for women, and a gallery over it. The Spanish arms are visible in several places, and the church is painted in very bad taste, and is, besides, draped at great feasts with red and yellow draperies. The numerous lamps made of ostrich eggs look rather pretty. In the monastery, which was built in 1733 and extended in 1863, there is a small cross-passage; below a small divan-room, used for receptions, and by the side of it the dining-room with marble tables: On the upper floor there is a passage built at right angles with twelve cells, and a side-passage with three. The side facing the extensive garden is adorned with two wooden balconies, below which are orange trees, reaching up with their branches covered with balsamic jessamine. The view extends from this to the gate of Paphos, and in the distance a range of mountains overtopped by the Troodos; a splendid panorama for the contemplative ascetics, with mountains melting into each other like a dream of olden Cyprus, its classic ground, magnificent temples, and luxurious cities, now inhabited by poor Greek peasants and shepherds. On the top of the monastery near the church roof is an open commanding balcony, looking over the new Kislà. Opposite the monastery, on the other side of the street, lies the orange garden of the monks, with delicious oranges, of which many a basket is sent to the Pasha. We also got a rich share of them from the good fathers. The garden is bordered by several houses to be let belonging to the convent, but all empty at the time.

## CHAPTER VI
## PUBLIC BUILDINGS—BATHS—INNS—BAZAARS
[Plates 24–26]

Amongst the public buildings we must first mention the Serai or Palace. It is an extensive building of rough aspect, one front of it looking into a square with three plane-trees and several large coffee-houses. A gate crowned by an ugly lion of St. Mark, with a tomb and a palm-tree on the left, leads through an arched passage into a broad courtyard, which forms an irregular square. Over the inner side of the gateway there is a Gothic window with mullions and tracery; underneath a saint with a damaged cloak, and two lions supporting an oblique shield of arms. Only two lions are perceptible now in the escutcheon, the other parts being quite indistinct. The Christ, raising his arms in blessing, which stands by the side of the gate, was excavated near the Venetian column. The yard is surrounded by arcades, resting partly on arches, partly on round columns with wooden corridors over them. At the bottom of the yard an arched well is situated. On the left we go up a staircase to a platform and the debtors' prison. On the right another staircase brings us to the upper corridors and the Governor's residence. When paying our visit to the Governor, we stepped from the corridor through a door covered by a cloth curtain into an ante-room, in which some soldiers were lying about, or sitting in the Turkish fashion with crossed legs. The dragoman, an elderly man with a long beard, who is a Roman Catholic of Tripoli de Soria, speaking Italian fluently, showed us into the reception-room. This room, a Turkish structure projecting from the old Venetian building, looks over the neglected garden of the serai. The ceiling is painted green, in the modern Turkish style, the ornaments being without teeth. The floor is covered with fine mats, and two leather arm-chairs were placed in the window. The dragoman would insist upon my sitting down on one of them. I preferred, however, to have a good look over the different objects in the room, and enjoy the view from the window over the numberless sweet citron-trees which are cultivated in the gardens here, and the mountain range glowing with purple tints.

After a while the Pasha entered, a middle-aged man, wrapped up in a fur caftan or long coat. Mehemed Veiss is a native of Constantinople, a thorough Turk of the old breed, with mild friendly manners, and speaking nothing but Turkish. He made me sit down on one of the leather armchairs, occupying the other one himself. The conversation was carried on with the help of the dragoman in Italian, and turned principally on matters connected with the island. When I asked for permission to visit the prisons and other public institutions, he answered, smiling: 'You will find nothing but bad things here, but I know it is the duty of travelers to see bad things as well as good.' He then talked about his Governorships at Beyruth, Bagdad, and other places. After coffee we took hearty leave of each other. The same evening he sent me his carte de visite photograph, and also the citrons and fresh dates I admired so much in his room. He came to see me one evening before my departure, escorted by soldiers with lamps, to offer me his services, and to make me all sorts of various declarations required by the rules of Turkish courtesy. Mehemed Veiss is a man who has acquired the esteem and love even of the Greeks, although he had been only in office four months at that time. His predecessor also, Said Pasha, enjoyed a good reputation amongst the inhabitants.

Adjoining the Serai, or, properly speaking, forming part of it, are the gaols, serving as a central prison for all Turkish possessions in Asia. The prisoners, 300 in number, are mostly from other provinces. The prisoners extend over two courtyards, and although they occupy the basement, have plenty of air. A wooden railing and a door close the entrance; they are vaulted with pointed arches, and have raised seats all round for the prisoners, as also a square one in the middle.

The Christians, who are rather numerous, are separated from the rest; on my entering the prison they addressed me in Italian, bringing forward all their complaints. By the side of the captain or gaoler was a stout negro. There is a small infirmary, with a little curtain over the door. The prisoners have a chain on the right leg, hanging down from a hook at their belt. Prisoners condemned for a smaller crime have only a ring on the ankle. As an extra punishment for bad behaviour, they have chains placed on both legs and one round the waist. The prisoners receive 300 drams of bread, always the same, also clothes and soap. All prisoners have an hour's recreation, during which they are allowed to walk in the yard. They make tobacco-pouches, and are also employed on the public works in town.

Not far from the Serai is the telegraph office. The existing cable was laid about a year ago by an English company on account of the Government, and goes from Pallura on the Cape of Karpathi to Ladakie on the Asiatic mainland. By the side of it stands the house of the Kadi (magistrate), with a large lemon garden, with lamp-posts on each side of the door. A small military hospital is in the neighbourhood.

The archiepiscopal palace, in the courtyard, flanked by clay houses and colonnades, the church of which we have spoken before, is an irregular building with lofty halls, surrounded by wooden and stone balustrades. The interior is plain, but spacious, the Archbishop having a suite of fifty persons, of whom twenty are priests. On my visit to the Mavkaristatos I find the following notes in my journal:—Approaching the church of the archiepiscopal palace, I heard loud prayers inside. I entered; some devouts were sitting on the chairs round the walls, and a couple of Popes (Greek clergymen) and a lad were singing prayers from a pulpit inlaid with mother-of-pearl on the left-hand side. On the right sat some more Popes, one with a carpet under his feet by the side of the bishop's throne. Coming out, my attendant told me that was the Archbishop. I entered again, to have a good look at him. On leaving the church again, a Pope followed and informed us that the Archbishop had ordered him to show us over the palace. We accepted this friendly invitation, and inspected the outer corridors first. But the whole thing appeared to have been arranged beforehand, because, when approaching the apartments, the Archbishop, followed by a numerous suite, came up the stairs. As I told our Pope that I should not like to disturb his excellency, he replied, 'Not at all, on the contrary;' and some other Popes insisted on my entering. After passing through a bare looking ante-room we came into a hall, where we found the Archbishop: he was sitting on a divan covered with Turkish carpets, on which he also offered me a seat after a friendly greeting. He is a middle-aged man with a rather long black beard, and has studied at Athens. The conversation proceeded with the help of a dragoman. There were also present a Greek, an official in the Governor's office, and the Bishop of Larnaka. We spoke about ecclesiastical affairs until the inevitable jam and Turkish coffee came. As he hinted that it would take months to visit the most important spots of the island, I replied that I intended to do that on some future occasion. He said he wished that I might return happily to my home, and that I might enjoy such good health as to enable me to come back to Cyprus soon, and remain a long time with them. He added that he intended to come and see me, which offer I declined with many thanks, calling to my help all my Oriental eloquence. We shook hands most cordially, and I left the Archbishop; my Greek attendant kissed his hands most reverently. Several Popes conducted me now through the other apartments. First we went across to a new wing of the building, in which there is a modern Turkish reception-room, with a fine view over the garden. We entered now the very modest bedroom of the Archbishop, with a few pointed arches supporting the ceiling, and a very small alcove. From the balcony you look over both the gardens belonging to the palace and the azure mountains at the back. A small apartment over the arcades and the stable of the mules contains a small library and the insignia of the bishop. The new orb with a cross on it is studded with diamonds, rubies, and emeralds; the old one, much finer, is of handsome chiselled work, also inlaid with emeralds and garnets. Each of these orbs is borne as a knob on a big stick at solemn church ceremonies. There is also a clumsy crown, adorned with pearls, emeralds, and rubies, and a throne, both used by the Archbishop at grand festivals.

The Archbishop told me there were at that time three hundred boys at Levkosia preparing for the priesthood, and fifty seminarists. There are classical schools besides, where Homer is studied for a year. The young Greeks who wish for further education have to go to Athens, and the same with all candidates for professorships. The principal school is opposite the Archbishop's palace. By the side of a Greek cotton-mill there is a girls' school (Partenagoyo), in which one hundred and thirty-five little girls receive elementary instruction before they can enter a higher class. (Plutarchus etc.) The school is a large, well-lighted room, with a gable-shaped wooden roof and a small ante-room formed by four pointed arches; on the right there is another hall.

Behind Ayia Sophia, the Turks have a Medressé, with a little orange and fruit garden. A corner house, with a cupola and a vaulted hall, with a large quantity of Koran verses all over the walls, is a Turkish school where boys study the Ilm. The small library contains many books given by the Sultan. There are besides several other Medressés and Mektébs at Levkosia.

There are eight hot-air baths altogether at Levkosia: they are got up in the usual Turkish fashion, and have small bathing cells with the well-known glass light-holes on the top of the vault, in each of them a marble floor and an octangular water-tank in the middle of the principal hall (Djéamekeann). The hours before noon are appropriated to the men; in the afternoon the women are admitted, on Mondays and Thursdays Turkish women, on Tuesdays and Saturdays those of Greek nationality. The same arrangement prevails in all baths, except a very small one, which is exclusively for men. Anyone wishing to have the whole bath for himself alone, or a family, must give notice the day before to the manager. Two baths belong to the Government, the rest are private property. Amongst the former we may mention Bejuk Hamam (the large bath) in the first place. It stands by the side of Iplik Bazar Djamisi, built of stone, with an old arched gate, to which a few steps lead down, and rests on two mighty pillars. It seems certain that this building was formerly devoted to some other use. The principal room has a latticed roof carried by two pointed arches, an octangular tank, and divans along the walls. There are two smaller rooms adjoining, and also a larger room with a cupola and four niches with fresh water, a marble seat in the middle, and two side-chambers. Glass bells with bell-shaped glasses are used for lighting. People pay here two Turkish pounds a month. The other bath belonging to the Government, called Emerghé Hamam, has been closed for many months.

Emir Hamam is one of the few private baths worth speaking of, by the side of Laleli Djami si and a house with very slender arches belonging to a rich Turk, which also has two pointed arches supporting the roof and four small bath-cells. Another bath, named Yegni Hamam, is situated near Jegni Djami si. It is of considerable size, and belongs to a native of Candia, who has been fifteen years in the gaol of Levkosia for a murder committed by him. There is a large bath-room in it, the ceiling of which rests on four low Gothic arches, with an octangular water-tank, and a divan all round. At the back there is a latticed room for distinguished personages, and brides preparing for their wedding; also a bathroom with side chambers.

The Greeks have a meeting-room, a sort of club (Circolo) in Tripiotis Street, where a few newspapers may be found, but none of them are published in Cyprus. The Turks and Greeks generally use the Bazaars, of which we shall speak by-and-by, and coffee-houses, for the purpose of obtaining news. In these last the visitors are seated on low benches covered with carpets, the backs of which are sometimes very nicely carved. The doors also are sometimes covered with handsome carvings.

There is only one inn or hotel at Levkosia, the Locanda della Speranza. This idyllic refuge for pilgrims and painters stands in the middle of a small garden, and is kept by a good-natured simple Greek of the name of Yorgios Christodulo.

There are five Turkish inns (khans), namely Bejuk Khan, Kumarigillar Khan (gambling inn), Tuchar bashi Khan, Pasmagilar Khan, and Alì Effendi Khan. The three first are the largest, amongst which Bejuk Khan occupies the first rank, with a colonnade of eleven pointed arches in front, the middle one higher than the others, a courtyard with seven arches on each side, and two flights of steps on the outside, leading to the upper rooms. In the middle a spring affords cooling drink to the thirsty.

At Levkosia, as in all Turkish towns, the Bazaars are the centres of social life: they extend between the gates of Famagosta and Paphos, and in this manner cut the town fairly in half. The shops have shutters made in the Turkish fashion, which can be pushed up and down. Here and there in the Bazaars we found small wells, with wooden windlasses and a trough for the cattle, often overshadowed by a gigantic vine; or big earthenware jugs, from which everyone can take water for his own use by means of small cups, thus making them useful for the public in general.

The Bazaars of Levkosia are generally open, simply covered with mats and linen rugs; only four and a half of them have a regular roof.

There are twenty-three Bazaars in all.

1. Manufactures.
2. Tailors.
3. Calico, rugs, hides.
4. European shoemakers.
5. Shoemakers.
6. Turkish shoes.
7. Yarns.
8. Cabinet-makers.
9. Carriages.
10. Copper articles.

11. Silversmiths.
12. Ironware.
13. Earthenware.
14. Haberdashery.
15. Taverns.
16. Vegetables and meat.
17. Fish.
18. Halava (sweets).
19. Women.
20. Cotton.
21. Flour.
22. Wheat and barley.
23. Mules.

There are some of them in which the articles are sold on Fridays only, the usual market day. The last-named five Bazaars are standing in other localities, of which we shall speak later on: all the rest form such a crosswork of little streets that it is only with the greatest difficulty one can find the right way. Let us try to describe our wanderings in search of them.

The broadest and largest one is the Bazaar for Manufactures, covered with a gable-roof, having holes to admit the light. With the exception of some silk stuffs made on the island, all other articles sold there come from abroad. By the side of it is a small one covered with a vine trellis, in which peasant boots are made. In front of it stands the small Bazaar of the Cabinet-makers, and after that the house of the President of Yikko. Opposite this last-named place is the Yikko Bazaar, with a cross and the date 1866. This large new Bazaar has a roof with pointed arches resting on keystones, with light-holes, and is mostly occupied by merchants and street letter-writers. On the other side stands the Ducks Basi Bazaar, with the city magistrate's office. It is followed by other, half-covered Bazaars, until we come to the tailors, some of whom are even working with sewing machines. The Bazaar for European Shoes is adjoining, with a gable roof and light-holes. Following the Manufacture Bazaar in the direction of the Paphos Gate, we come into the Makri Bazaar (Long Bazaar), in which we find first some shops with Rumelian fishers' cloaks, some Greek tailors, and further on tin-plate and copper-ware makers. Projecting roofs, sometimes cane-mats, are the only protection from the sun. Then we come into the Calico Bazaar, where men, mostly Turks, manufacture this article on the right and left. The Jai Bazaar joins it, also that for calico and rugs. A little further on we find leather merchants, who also prepare hides. On the right stands a coffee-house with handsomely carved doorposts, the best of their kind at Levkosia. This Street of the Bazaars contains near the end some shops for provisions, wood, marble slabs, and white stone jugs made of Asieno, and ends near some dyers' shops at the little Mosque of Mehemmed Seid Djami. Close to the entrance of the Calico Bazaar is another one, where boots and leather are sold, and which branches off in two wings, one for drugs, and the other, on the right, for victuals. Following up this lane we come to little places were Turkish wadded blankets with various designs formed by the seams are made: further on Turkish slippers may be procured in shops reaching nearly up to the Ayia Sophia. Continuing our way in the same direction, we come to the silversmiths' department, opposite the Bapistery, and further on to shops with arms.

If we turn straight back now at the point we started from, we are led to the great Provision Bazaar. Here we see citrons, bread, kolokasias, Jerusalem artichokes, carrots, long radishes, turnips, raisins, dates, chesnuts, filbert nuts, big almonds, confections, poppy-seed for soothing children to sleep, linseed, pulse, vegetables of all kinds, Larnaka and foreign soap, pinetree gum for barrels, which the Turks like to chew also, all this sheltered only by rags, tattered mats, and projecting roofs. By the side of these are tobacconists, sitting with their legs crossed under them, and cutting fine tobacco with sharp knives on horseshoe-shaped iron. At the Tahta-Cala end of the Bazaar we find children's stools, yokes, carriages, saddlers, and inns; and also little shops with 'Turkish delight,' Halava, and unusually small fox and hare skins. It is very interesting to watch them preparing the favourite Halava at distances of a few yards apart. They use for this purpose large copper cauldrons, mixing up the Halava paste with an enormous wooden ladle stuck into a ring hanging down from the ceiling on a rope. The paste consists of dried syrup made of grapes, Halava, which is a special kind of seed, and sesame oil. All this is kneaded up first in the cauldron for about an hour, then left standing in a flat tin dish, and after another hour the whole thing is ready. The operation lasts about five to seven hours. A small Meat Bazaar connects the large Provision Bazaar with the Inns Bazaar, which starts from a tomb shaded by an olive-tree. Turkish wooden or horn spoons for Pilaff (rice and mutton), table services, and a little further the wax candle-makers bring a little change into the scene.

In all these places the most motley crowd in the world is hurrying up and down, especially before noon; peasants in showy dresses, veiled Turkish women, boys with widely opened eyes. Here we knock against an ambulant Salep shop (a kind of tea which people drink on winter mornings); there against roaming oil, salt, or water vendors, bakers, carrying brown bread on wooden trays, pedlars with cakes, fellows offering dainty little bits of meat to the knowing purchaser. The most varied scene is everywhere before our eyes; the shopkeepers alone are like statues, motionless, smoking in deep silence. Here and there you see a towel hanging from a stick, which is the characteristic signboard of all barbers, most of them Greeks; all coffee-house keepers (kafedjis) are Turks, lying about lazily on their benches waiting for guests. From one or the other shop round cages with turtle-doves or red-legged partridges are hanging over the pavement. Turkish mongrel street dogs are slinking about, especially in the evenings, when they choose the deserted Bazaars for their playground, holding their disgusting orgies on the heaps of dirt and dust simply thrown over the threshold by the inhabitants of the houses around. Then nothing is heard but these wretched curs snarling at one another if one of them has snatched a dirty bone, or every now and then the hoarse croaking of the crows on the top of a high tree or a minaret. Except these uncouth noises, the deepest silence reigns everywhere, and only from time to time a woman or a man clad in white, with a lantern, will slip along the wall: then again the dark, lonely night rests uninterrupted. A poor-looking lamp hanging on a rope from some corner or a mosque throws a dim light over the scene.

Of the Bazaars standing apart we must first mention the Women's Bazaar, open on Fridays, where all sorts of needlework and everything belonging to it are sold. The vendors, the Greek women especially, are singularly loquacious whilst displaying their merchandise at their feet in the neighbourhood of the principal Bazaars. We see here heaps of cotton and yarns wound in various shapes; silk-yarns spun at Levkosia, Alatjia, Burundjik, white calicoes, foreign prints, and whole shirts made of curled silk, for Turks and women; raw silk stuffs, such as the Greek women wear round the waist (Zostra), some of them half cotton, handerkerchiefs of fine linen, Chervé for Turkish women, sometimes with ugly, rudely-embroidered golden flowers in the corners, as they are used at Turkish weddings; Skufomata (bands to fasten the fez, or red cap, to the forehead), cotton and silk lace, some black and white for ornaments for women's head-dresses, silver spangle-lace, also used as pocket-handkerchiefs, artificial gauze flowers, little babies' hoods and bonnets made of foreign stuffs, strangely shaped caps with extraordinary designs, hand-knit cotton stockings, knit purses, one piastre (about twopence-halfpenny) apiece, knitted tobacco pouches, some of them coloured, others made of foreign silk embroidered with gold thread, foreign glass bracelets, and necklets composed of beads. You will also find pottery clay pitchers with pointed spouts, others of a slender shape with two handles; sugared almonds, Turkish delight (Rahatlukum), fantastic birds and other creatues formed of coloured sugar-stuff, tartlets, a yellowish sweetmeat made with honey, Mersinokoka, berries called Tremiskia, which people eat with bread, fruit, chick peas, chestnuts, oranges, dates, and soap.

On a small square by the side of Iplik Bazar Djami si, Turkish women sell cotton articles; a little further up there is a street, Sokkagi to Klymatu, with a vine as thick as a man's leg sending its branches all over the street.

In front of the Kumarigillar Khan there is a building to which barley and other grain is brought for sale. The barley is in sacks. By the side of it are several cook's shops extending to the Bejuk Khan.

In the arched hall in front of the Bapistery is the flour market, which article is principally furnished by the mills near Kytrea; mostly wheat-flour, with small quantities of barley-flour. They weigh the flour in small hand-scales and sell it by the oka (about two pounds), pouring the quantity purchased into the small provision-bags of the peasant. Larger quantities stand under the supervision of a Government officer, who, after weighing the sacks, shoulders his scale, and stalks majestically up and down the market-place.

On the square facing Serai Djami the cattle-market is held on Fridays, with horses, donkeys, and small Paphos mules. We saw only the commonest cattle, with long legs, and often hump-backed.


## CHAPTER VII
## POPULATION—HABITS—AMUSEMENTS—AUTHORITIES
[Plate 27]


The population of Levkosia numbers about 20,000, but the exact number of inhabitants cannot be ascertained, the women not being included in the census. The majority of the inhabitants are Turks, although they are nearly equalled in number by the Greeks. There are besides a few Armenians, about eighty to ninety Roman Catholics, and no Jews at all.

The Turks of Levkosia often have strangely-shaped eyebrows, growing upwards about the middle of the forehead, a broadly cut mouth, large dark-brown eyes with long lashes, and the hair shorn in the Turkish fashion. Most of them have sea-green shirts, which suit them very well, and are distinguished by their wide white trousers and many-coloured garments. The women wear in the streets upper garments of a snowy whiteness, and underneath frequently rich silk dresses. The Armenian women dress in the same style, the men 'alla franca', that is, in the European fashion.

The Greeks are a fine race, but are often disfigured by too big noses. They wear long bag-shaped trousers, which are often fastened to the belt behind, to prevent them from swinging about at everystep they make: stockings and boots in winter only. Nearly all women have a fez, or red cap, which is fastened to the forehead by a band, called Skufomata, and a handkerchief over it, sometimes the latter only. If their hair is getting grey, they dye it red with sheuna, as the Turkish women do their nails. The dye is applied in the evening and the next morning the hair is perfectly red. The lashes and brows of children's eyes are painted black, with what is called Holla mavri, by the Turks as well as Greeks, more frequently by the former.

The language of the Turks in Cyprus is very pure; they say it is the best after that spoken at Constantinople. The Cyprian Greek, however, is more of a dialect, and contains many Italian words, such as *petra, porta, tavola, bunazza*, etc., as also a number of Turkish expressions. The Turkish language is that most generally used at Levkosia; we found very few men who could not speak that language, and a great many who knew Turkish only; even most of the Greek women are perfectly acquainted with it. A very widely-spread usage may be mentioned here, according to which Greeks or Turks will never say 'no', but simply lift up their heads, without uttering a word, as a sign of negation.

The inhabitants of Levkosia do not possess, as a rule, great riches; a Turk who has 40,000 piastres (about 400*l*) is considered here a very wealthy man. The Turks and Turkish women are often servants in the houses of the Greeks: on the other hand, Greek women will sometimes becomes Mahomedans and marry Turks. The Turks here keep no eunuchs, only two or three boys as servants, and one or two negresses as slaves, which are brought by way of Cerinja, for fear of the Consuls who reside at Larnaka: they are therefore also kept constantly at home. There are no man-slaves here. Most of the negroes, who are rather numerous at Levkosia, are Mussulmans, but some of them belong to the Greek Church. We met also some mulattoes, a cross-breed of Turks, who are fine tall men. The young Turks who have completed their eighteenth year have to become soldiers; formerly they were left on the island, but since last year they are taken away. The Christians pay, from the day they are born, 27½ piastres (about one guinea) a year, and are free from military service. There are also Greeks who pretend to be Mussulmans, and they are called Linopambagi, which means half linen, half cotton. When they attain the age to enter the army they would often like to pass to Christians again, but the Government enrols them nevertheless, saying that it is illegal to give up Mahomedanism: for that reason they do not follow that proceeding as they would otherwise like to do. The majority of the Greeks are hostile to the Government, the chief reason for this being the heavy taxes. As a sort of protection, the Greeks often employ the Russian eagle, although they will not listen to Russia, since the latter look favourably on the Slavonian subjects of Turkey. Such Greeks as have been at Jerusalem are called 'Hadji', the same as pilgrims to Mecca, and this denomination is, according to Mussulman usage, constantly put before the name whenever the person is addressed.

The superstition is equally prevalent among Turks and Greeks that, after a house has been finished, an aloe-plant must be suspended, or a blue-stone affixed on the roof, to protect the building from the evil eye. Another curious custom of the Greeks, to which they cling tenaciously, is to bake a loaf of bread about new year with a gold coin inside, and to divide it into as many pieces as there are members of the family. The one who finds the coin is supposed to be happy all through the next year. This bread is called Vasilobita, or St. Basil's bread.

Visitors always receive jam made of melons, cherries, quince, apricots, the juice of the crataegus plant, or rose-leaves. With this sweet-stuff, called Tatli in Turkish, Glikon in Greek, the servants bring little baskets of silver-wire with small ornamental spoons: these are divided into two compartments, one for the clean spoons, the other for those which have been used. After that comes the coffee, as a sort of invitation to leave, especially with the Turks. If the visitor bores his host, a second cup of coffee will soon follow: if he is liked, he is on the contrary kept waiting a long while for his coffee. After the coffee, cigarettes are usually offered, and a servant brings small brass plates for the ashes. It is a peculiar custom with the Greeks, and is considered a sign of exceptional politeness, to put a chair before the feet of the visitor, who places them on the lower bar, and he is not obliged then to keep his feet on the cold marble floor. The Turks keep their Sabbath in Cyprus not on Friday, but with the Greeks on Sunday, on which day the streets are most quiet, and the Bazaars, which are open in the morning only, look as still and solitary as graveyards. All the offices are closed on Sundays.

From three o'clock, according to Turkish time (three hours after sunset), when the tattoo is sounded, nobody is allowed to go out without a lantern. Any stranger infringing this regulation is shown home; if an inhabitant of the town, he is brought into the Serai, where he has to pass the night.

The most favourite games of the boys are marbles (Pirilli) and raffle (Siccia), which are much played on the old walls; but the grown-up people prefer music and dancing.

The Turkish music is very primitive indeed; a tambourine and a banjo accompany some tipsy men singing Turkish melodies, of which as a rule the air only is Turkish, the words Greek. Their heads are crowned with orange-flowers and fruit. During the intervals they warm up the Tambulek again, to keep it tight. The Tambulek is a sort of drum, consisting of a clay pot, the top of which is covered with a goat's skin; the player holds it in the left hand, playing on the drum with the fingers of the right hand. Liquor soon brings fresh enthusiasm and musical feeling into the assembly, till the whole entertainment ends in confused barbarous shouts and boisterous uproar.

The Greeks are better musicians. Usually the band consists of a mandoline, which is sometimes very handsomely made of dark and light wood, and two violins. A lute often takes the place of the tambourine, being smaller, but of a similar shape. Sometimes the players are youths of antique beauty, their feet crossed with coquettish elegance, and the violin resting on the left knee. One of them soon begins a lively strain, running a little stick over the strings of the mandoline, which is placed over the right leg, the notes of Turkish and Greek songs sounding far beyond the walls of the simple hall, decorated with orange-flowers, into the balsamic night with its millions of stars. The musicians are frequently treated with Mastica (fir-gum brandy) or sparkling Comandaria. There are several kinds of dances known at Levkosia. One the Turks like particularly is executed by hired dancers. The Tambulek-player begins his song with a nasal voice, and accompanied by the lute and violin (the musicians are often Greeks), another lad sounding his bronze castanets. The air soon swells into livelier notes, all the instruments falling in with increasing force. The dancer, dressed only in a light kaftan or gown, tied round the waist, and stockings, now stepping forward, bows, turning all round with open arms, leaps into the air, shaking his feet and beating his castanets: then he turns round again, and begins to move his stomach about. Now the well-known movements of the body begin, not unlike those of a screw, with the convulsive movements of the muscles, all this going on with the castanets beating time. From time to time the dancer joins the chorus. Sometimes there are two dancers; they bow to each other, swing their arms, play the castanets, move their stomachs, bending right back and hopping with their feet.

Another dance, rougher still, is the Zeibekrikos. It is danced by one person only, in the common Turkish dress, a Handjar (long dagger) sticking in the belt, and without shoes. The dancer spins round and round, leaps about as if lame, then on one foot, falls on his knees, stretching his arms now upwards, now sideways. He acts as if he meant to smash everything, beats the floor, then his own soles with two sticks, hops and jumps, points finally to a corner, and begins to roar with all his might.

The Greeks have different dances. A violin and lute are played, but there is no singing. The Palo is the customary dance at weddings, the man and wife facing one another. They jump from one leg on to the other, holding each other by the belts and dresses; then they lift up one foot, play the castanets, one of them turns round, looks back on his partner, then turns towards him again.

The Sirtosch is danced by men only, two of whom always hold together by a handkerchief. One couple only dances at a time; the others stand in a row. When one has finished he walks behind the last pair, and the next one follows, until all of them have had their turn. All this maybe more properly called jumping and hopping, than real dancing. Many of our readers will remember having seen this kind of amusement at night in the coffee-houses of Stamboul.

The first, named Tschenky, is executed at Turkish weddings and circumcisions, both of which are celebrated with great festivities, by men and women. The men occupy the first rank. In the bride's room a blind man plays the violin. The wedding ceremonies begin invariably on Mondays and terminate on Thursday night. The woman first goes to the bath. An Imam (priest) enters a dark room in which the bride and bridegroom are, says a prayer, and leaves them alone then. The marriage contract is made in presence of witnesses, the woman appearing veiled. The man has to deposit a certain sum of money, which becomes the property of his wife in case he deserts her. After this, the woman and her dresses and other things belonging to her outfit are promenaded through the streets with great pomp.

The Greeks christen their children forty or sixty days after they are born, and after the mother has been present at the thanksgiving service. The godfather makes a present to the mother, which invariably consists of a dress, the value of which varies according to the means of the giver.

At Greek weddings (Greeks cannot marry any nearer relatives than their third cousins) the priest walks three times round a table, and then throws cotton-seeds and coins into the air, which are given by the male witnesses: the two female witnesses have to pay for the bride's wreath. The next day all of them pay a visit to the newly-married couple, bringing presents to the bride, who also receives many presents from the parents and relations.

At Turkish funerals the body is first washed in a bath, and then dressed. They put a stone and a penny in his hand, and then cover it up with a cloth; after this the men carry the dead into the mosque, where some prayers are said, and from there to the cemetery;

the body is not put in a coffin, but simply wrapped up in a sheet. The next day all the relations put on their holiday dresses. On similar occasions Halava (which we have described before) is prepared in great quantities, which, three days afterwards, is offered in front of the gates of the mosque to all passers-by.

The Greeks' dead are carried about openly with a torchlight procession, then put into a coffin and buried: poor people sometimes cannot afford a coffin. All proprietors of houses pour a glass of water into the street before the body passes. After three, nine, and forty days, as also after three, six and nine months, after a year and on November 2 of every year (the Feast of the Dead), a cake of wheat, saffron, almonds, raisins and other spices is baked, as also a bread seasoned with sesame-seed, into which they stick a yellow wax candle. The body is first carried into the church, where mass is said, and then carried to the tomb. The Pope recites a prayer and distributes the cake amongst those present, after having taken a piece for himself. He keeps also the whole bread. Rich people light a candle on the grave every Sunday. The mothers wear mourning three years for a son; older women never leave it off; the mourning for a father, brother, or sister last ten months; for cousins, forty days.

Levkosia is the seat of the Pasha or Governor of the island, who receives a salary of 3,500 piastres (about 35*l*) a month. There is also a Kairnakham Bey (commander of the troops) and a Greek archbishop, who dresses in purple, signs his name with red ink, and is called Mavkaristatos, the holiest. He is the chief of the independent church of Cyprus. There are besides, residing here, the president of the monastery of Yikko, which is the richest convent of the island: he is entirely independent of the archbishop. There is also an Armenian Archimandrite. Only Greece, Austria and France are represented by consular officers.

## CHAPTER VIII
## INDUSTRY AND TRADE

Cotton-cleaning is a very important branch of industry at Levkosia. A factory belonging to an Englishman, Mr. Samuel Perks, with seventeen working-tables, and an engine of seventeen horse-power, stands by the side of Ayios Jakovos. This gentleman on one occasion told me that he is not doing a good business. A second factory is near Phaneromeni, and has six tables, made by Platt Brothers and Co. in 1871, and a twelve horse-power engine. There are besides for the same purpose a steam-mill and several mills driven by animal power. The construction of the latter is about as follows. The wheel on the table is connected by a strap with a vertical wheel, which is put in motion again by another horizontal one with cogs and driven by a mule. The cotton is simply stamped into bales by the feet, then carried to Larnaka on camels, where they press it and put iron hoops on.

Weaving is done in the following simple way. The thread, which can be purchased spun at Levkosia, spun on a rough heavy reel, or ready-made, is wound on a cane spool from a cane reel, which they stick into clay or a stone. The pipe of the spool is inserted during this process into an iron spindle, which is turned by a reel-drum with a wooden handle by means of a string running round bath of them. For calicoes, the many-coloured threads are mixed by a machine with thirty cane bobbins, from which the single threads run over a reed of fifteen little sticks, and wind on palm-sticks fixed in the ground. If only a little of such mixed yarn is wanted, a woman simply mixes the single threads with her hand and winds them on little pegs stuck on a zig-zag into the wall. By this process weaving on the loom is much simplified, the yarn being already mixed. It enters the frame as a sort of plait, the two parts of which are kept asunder by little cane sticks; from here it comes into the reed, the shuttle running up and down with the usually dark cotton-weft, and the stuff comes out ready-made. Linen-stuffs for shirts are also made; sheets and napkins with designs like bees' cells; white calico and striped Alatjia. A very pretty light fabric, half silk and half cotton, called Burundjik, is also manufactured here, and has usually white cotton stripes running down the whole length on a yellow silk ground.

The silk industry is extensively cultivated in the island, the women and girls collecting and spinning the material. It is a great pity that the silkworm disease has made great ravages on the island in the last ten years, especially in rainy weather of a long duration. Silk is woven in the same manner as cotton. The yarn-reed is different according to the colour wanted. The four treddles are simply stuck on an iron bar resting on two nails in the ground. For two-coloured textures only two treddles are used, but four reeds, two and two tied up and moving together. In this manner various stuffs are made: raw-silk fabrics for Zostras, some of them of a bright yellow colour with red and blue cross-stripes; a fine stuff for dresses, called Metaxodo; a very thin fabric, Amusia, with golden thread, for women, but also used for mosquito-nets; also checked tissues and Spinato handkerchiefs, some of which are really beautifully woven.

Sacks are also made of cotton on common looms, with two reeds and a big wooden comb. The man driving the pedal often stands in a recess, to have more room. Then camel sacks made of goats' hair; woollen riding bags (Lisaki), some of them of very handsome brown shades; Taari, long bags carried in front of the saddle on mules with straps on the top, and woollen socks.

Woollen blankets, used for the lining of saddles and other purposes, are made in the following manner. The rudely-picked wool is put over a square mat and sprinkled over with water from a clay cup by means of a small broom; an equally wetted, ready-made blanket is now rolled over a wooden cylinder and put on the top of the mat covered with wool. The whole mass is now wound up inside the elastic cane mat, covered with a thick linen sheet, and then rolled about on the floor. Two men push the whole bale on the rough ground to one end of the room with their left foot, then turn round and push it to the opposite wall again with the right foot. The rolling is continued for an hour, and the parcel opened after that. The new blanket is now hung on a vertical pole, and bits of black wool are tied into the loose fabric, forming various designs and dots. Such a blanket costs 25 piastres (about 5s).

The women make pretty silk-lace, all of little knots, with the needle; also strings on a small cushion with little sticks, which are very cleverly handled by the girls. The knitting of purses and tobacco-pouches is very generally done.

A very considerable industry of Levkosia is the dyeing of white English calico, imported *via* Beyruth, being dyed and printed here. This is done in the following manner. The dyed stuff is wetted and laid on thick woollen felt. The workman has a colour-box covered with cloth, to prevent the pattern from taking in too much dye. The patterns, which are made here, are of hard, generally walnut, wood. This pattern is placed gently on the proper place; and the workman beats on the top of it with a small round cushion fitting into the palm of his hand. In this way the stuff is printed first on one side, then on the other. If the design is made in several colours, a piece of cardboard is laid over the first print. This kind of work is necessarily incorrect and rude. After washing the calico, it is hung up for drying, either in front of the shop in the Bazaar itself, or on the city walls, especially about the gate of Paphos, which is the nearest to the factories. A portion of these fabrics is consumed at Levkosia for wadded Turkish blankets with red lining turned over at the edges. There are besides dyers of yarns and different stuffs who principally use indigo, bought in small jars.

Shoemaking on an extensive scale is here carried on, and all kinds of shoes are made, from the Turkish slipper and peasant's boot up to the highlows of the Europeans. Raw leather is also prepared here, tanned outside the town, and afterwards cleaned and smoothed with wooden hammers in the city. The leather industry was introduced only two years ago; formerly such articles were imported from France and Syra. They make small bags of it, in which various things are kept; also coloured saddles, after the Egyptian fashion. The material, except the girths and the lining, which are home-made, comes from Anatolia.

The cabinet-makers are famous for their boxes made of pine wood on the front are ornaments of flower-pots and fantastic plants executed in high relief; they also make carriages and yokes. The wild teasel is prepared at Levkosia for cleaning silk. Chair manufacturers, especially those making children's stools, use very primitive turning-lathes for their work. The string of a large fiddle-stick is wound round the object itself, which spins first in one direction and then in another, as the workman pulls the string up and down. The piece to be carved is fastened between two iron spikes in the ends. The bow has a handle at the bottom, which can be pushed up and down if the string wants loosening or tightening. With a piece of wood dipped into some colour, red, green, black, or other rings are painted on the object while it is in the turning-lathe. Boring is done in the same way, an auger being screwed to one of the pikes, the handle turned with the fiddle-stick, and the piece kept steady with one foot.

Willow-baskets are made with great skill, very often near the place where the trees grow; the flexions are made of green brushwood. Another kind of smaller baskets made of green rushes is made for keeping fresh cheese; they will last for a year.

At Levkosia great quantities of raw wax are consumed by the workmen. This comes partly from the island, partly from abroad. Another article produced in this town is violet-syrup, and, in three rather primitive distilleries, brandy made of fresh and dried grapes, still wine, and dried figs. There are also turning-mills worked by hand, with vertical wheels, for tanners' bark brought from Caramania. The bark produced in Cyprus is not so good. We also saw a sesame-oil mill, consisting of a horizontal wheel, which turns upon a round stone with a wooden hoop forming a brim over it. There is a hole on one side of the hoop, through which the oil runs into a vase underneath. The oil is strained from this vase into salt water, left there twelve hours, and put into an oven for six hours more. The white paste is sold to make Halava; of the red residue more oil is gained by putting it into a cauldron with cold water and treading it, which makes the oil rise to the surface. Sesame-oil is consumed in great quantities by the Greeks during Lent.

The cutlers, who stand in front of the Baptistery, are not better provided with tools than other workmen. A lad moves the common bellows behind a stone, whilst the flames of the burning charcoal are blown over another stove on which the blade is placed. The knives are ground on a wooden wheel with an iron hoop, and it forms another part of the aforesaid boy's duty to turn this wheel with a string. These knives are of the well-known shape of Handjar, and have often dotted blades: some of them are ornamented near the handle, which makes them stronger at the same time. The handles of some of them are made of auburn, those of others of buffalo-horn, inlaid with coral; common knives usually have a handle of sheep's-horn. There are a good many smiths at Levkosia; they have double bellows, with two handles each, moved by their apprentices. The coppersmiths make small and large flat plates and dishes for the Turks, partly of tin, of very handsome workmanship and nicely ornamented. The bellows of silversmiths are very much like bagpipes made of goats' hides; a boy blows the bag up and then presses the sides of it. We found scent-bottles, belt-clasps in the shape of a heart, and hooks for women's dresses; Turkish cupholders, some of them of filigree work; Greek crosses, neat golden earrings, small necklaces in silver filigree and gilt and little gold aigulets; also heaps of very thin chains with tiny beads to be worn round the neck; other little chains for the breast, neat filigree-work bracelets with precious stones, and a thousand other such things. There were also a little further on large-bellied jugs, called Pithares, for oil and wine. The principal articles of export from this land are—calico, chiefly for Constantinople; silk, which is carried to Greece and Turkey; violet-syrup and leather bridles to Constantinople; and lambs'-skins to Trieste. The bulk of the imports consists of tissues and fancy and hard-wares.

Industry and trade are fairly prosperous in Cyprus. The different taxes are the income tax, which is levied in proportion to a person's wealth, and a small communal tax. The collecting of this tax is the only visible sign of the municipal council's activity; their offices are one of the Bazaars. The only class of shopkeepers who have to pay extra taxes are the spirit and tobacco merchants. This tax is measured according to the rental, and if the shopkeeper happens to be the owner of the house, an estimation of the probable rent is made by the council.

## Schröder—1870, 1873

[Plates 29–32]

Paul Schröder, "Meine zweite Reise auf Cypern im Frühjahr 1873," from letters to Prof. Heinrich Kiepert in Berlin, *Globus: Illustrierte Zeitschrift für Länder- und Völkerkunde* 33–34 (1878) 135–39, 152–56, 168–72, and 183–86. Paul Schröder (1844–1915) was dragoman of the German Consulate in Constantinople (1869–1882), German consul in Beirut (1882–1885), dragoman in the German Embassy in Constantinople (1885–1888), and consul general in Beirut (1888–1909).

I. 135–39
Constantinople, 30 May 1873

On 11 March I arrived in Larnaca on the Lloyd steamer coming from Egypt and Syria. Having spent that and the following day with various preparations I began my excursion into the interior of the island on 13 March. Apart from four or five rainy days this excursion was blessed with good weather at all times. This winter, too, there had been little rain on the island, and therefore the land offered a sorry sight, with the exception of the northern coastal strip, which differs much from the other parts of Cyprus as far as the climate is concerned. In the Mesaoria (the great plain in the east) the fields were unattended and consisted of ground dried-out, cracked, and hard as rock. Cyprus has been suffering from a lack of rain for six years already and declines further with every year. The peasants are emigrating in large numbers to Syria and the opposite coast of Asia Minor, although the government is making emigration as difficult as possible. If the drought will continue for several more years the island will finally be totally depopulated. This happened once already, in the fourth century, when reportedly there was no rain for thirty-six years in a row.[253] A few days ago I also read in a letter to the *Levant Herald* from Cyprus that, because of the drought, the locusts have reappeared; Cyprus had been free of them since 1869, thanks to the energetic measures of Said Pasha, the governor before the last.

In my excursions into the interior I have endeavored to follow the routes suggested by you wherever it was feasible. I have avoided as far as possible my old routes of 1870; only on the way fom Paphos to Limassol I followed my earlier route, along the coast. Since the mountains were fully passable I decided to turn first to the west of the island, since it offers more geographical lacunae than the east. Of instruments I carried with me besides a compass also a barometer and thermometer. Unfortunately I was lacking for my barometric observations readings taken at the same time at the sea, since no barometer could be obtained in Larnaca. But on the whole during my journey, given the prevailing clear and dry weather, the barometric pressure was subject to few variations.

I left Larnaca accompanied by a cavas of the Italian consulate and by my guide Perikles, whom I knew well from 1870, who was still very devoted to me, and whom I enthusiastically recommend to all travelers on Cyprus. I chose the shortest road to Nicosia, namely the highway which was begun in 1870 and only recently completed; leaving Aradippou on the right and Goshi, Petrophani, and Athienou on the left, this highway leads by way of Pyroi to Nikosia. Here it was my purpose to pay a visit to the Pasha, hand him my letter of recommendation from the Grand Vizier, and ask him for a Bujuruldu [Buyrultu] to his officials on the island. I decided to proceed from Nikosia to the northwestern corner of the island, which I did not know yet. After a stay of one day in the interesting capital I proceeded to Lapithos on the northern coast; since I already knew the Kyrenia pass I chose a more direct, western way, which was extra-ordinarily difficult and leads across the ridge at a much higher altitude than the Kyrenia pass. I touched upon the villages of Geunyeli, one hour from Nikosia, Photta, and Blessia and made my descent on the other side to the large village of Karavas, next to Lapithos. These two villages are only five minutes distant from each other and almost form one whole. They are two of the largest and most prosperous villages of Cyprus; they are inhabited by ca. one thousand families, four hundred in Karavas and six hundred in Lapithos. From Karavas a ride of a quarter of an hour leads to the Greek monastery of Ἀχειροποίητος [Akhiripiitos; "made without hands"], situated right by the sea, where I stayed overnight with the monks. I was surprised by the remarkable difference in vegetation between the southern and northern side of the northern chain of mountains [the Pentadaktylos Mountains]. The whole northern coast, but especially the immediate environs of the two villages mentioned, was like one large garden. There had been sufficient rain here during the winter, and even

---

[253] Leontios Machairas, *Chronikon Kyprou* 1.3 (ed. Dawkins I 2–5).

without rain this area would hardly lose its luxuriant vegetation, since the streams carry abundant water from the mountains all year long. I counted a large number of mills.

From Acheropiitos I took a path which leads along the foot of the mountains at a distance of half an hour from the shore to Vasilia, which is an hour and a half from Lapithos. From there I crossed again to the south side of the mountains and reached the fairly large village of Larnaca; this is situated on the southern slope of the mountains, about half-way up, and is called Larnaka [tis] Lapithou in order to distinguish it from the Scala Larnaca. Nearby is the monastery of Kathari [Panayia ton Katharon = Our Lady of Purity], a dependency of the monastery of [Ayios] Panteleimon [at Myrtou], where I stayed. From here one has a good view over the Maronite mountain villages lying below. The ground formations in this area are curiously riven and broken up.

At Larnaca I copied several Greek inscriptions, among them also the one previously published, but not accurately copied by Waddington (*Inscriptions grecques et latines recueillies en Grece et en Asie Mineure*, III, 7. partie "Ile de Chypre" Nro. 2779).[254] This inscription is a decree of the chief priest Praxidemos and the priests of Poseidon in honor of a citizen named Noumenios. In line 6 one can clearly read τοῦ Ποσειδῶνος τοῦ Ναναρκίου, and not, as Waddington wants us to read, Λαρνακίου. The latter reading is attractive, and Waddington deduces that "l'ancien nom de la localité devait aussi être Larnax." But in spite of repeated examination of the stone I could read only an N, and also my squeeze indicates an N. Accordingly the old settlement which was situated here (graves, too, were found) was named Narnax, and later, by analogy with the port city, that became "Larnax" or "Larnaka," unless one were to assume that in this inscription N instead of L is a stone-cutter's error, which is not impossible either. I also copied at Larnaca the curious bilingual Phoenician/Greek inscription which a certain Praxidemos dedicated in memory of and for the glorification of the victory of Ptolemy Soter over Antigonus.[255] The donor evidently was Phoenician; his name was Baalschillem, for the Phoenician text has this name instead of Praxidemos. Thus Phoenicians were probably settled in these parts also, pace Engel[256] (even the name of Lapithos seems to be Phoenician; cf. Leptis in North Africa). These Phoenicians, however, were with time fully displaced or absorbed by the Greek element. Our inscription shows how the Phoenicians adopted Greek names already at the time of the Ptolemies. This inscription, first published by Vogué,[257] is cut in very fine lettering into a rock which is conically shaped, apparently placed by human hands, but naturally tall and easily attracting attention; the people of Larnaca call it Laropetra.

From Kathari I traveled west, by way of Kambyli, where only a few Maronites still reside, and Margi[258] (only a dilapidated church there, not a village) to Myrtou. The Monastery of St. Panteleimon, now the see of the Bishop of Kyrenia, is in this village. The Maronite village of Karpasia lies about a quarter of an hour distant from there.[259] Leaving this village to our left, we continued in a westerly direction for twenty minutes to

---

[254] See also Hill, *History,* I 183.

[255] Le Bas and Waddington, *Inscriptions grecques et latines recueillies en Grece et en Asie Mineure,* III 2778. Max L. Strack, *Inscriptiones Graecae Ptolemaicae* (Berlin, 1897; repr. Chicago, 1976), no. 6. See also Hill, *History,* I, p. 99, n. 6.

[256] Engel, *Kypros,* I 78.

[257] Marquis Melchior de Vogué (1829–1916), *Journal asiatique* 1867, p. 120.

[258] There is a village by that name also near Dhali.

[259] It is named after the Karpasia peninsula, where the Maronites first had settled.

Dhiorios. All these villages lie on the same high plateau; specifically, Myrtou west of Margi, and the latter west of Kambyli. Here, to the west and north, the Akamas Forest begins, which consists of low pines, cypresses, and underbrush. For an hour and a half we rode through this wilderness, in which there was a stifling heat. Continuing south from there we came to the plain of Morphou, which is separated from the forest by a river bed, which now, of course, was completely dry. This plain is in its northern parts sandy and therefore only spottily settled. After a ride of three hours (from Dhiorios) we came to Morphou, whose bell tower had been visible to us from the distance, and took lodging in the splendid Monastery of Ayios Mamas. From the church tower I surveyed the various visible villages of the area with the compass. I had previously done the same from the highest minaret of Ayia Sophia in Nicosia. From Morphou we continued through Nikitas, Kokkina, Prastio, and Ghaziveran, past Pendayia and the nearby Monastery of Xeropotamo to Lefka. From there I intended to visit the virgin area of the Tillyria (on the northwest slope of the Troodos), which is nearly unknown even to the Cypriots.

In Lefka the people were earnestly shaking their heads over my peculiar idea of going into the area of the Tillyria. The inhabitants were described to me as half-savage, dressed only in rags, and living in holes in the ground; I would find nothing to eat there beside coarse barley bread. The people were so little civilized, I was told, that they did not even know if they were Muslims or Christians.[260] These reports aroused my curiosity all the more, and on the very day of my arrival in Lefka I departed again, in order still to reach Galini, which of the villages of the Tillyria is nearest to Lefka. A cavas of the Mudir[261] of Lefka served as my guide into this inhospitable area. We first headed north to the sea, almost as far as Karavostasi and then, about a quarter of an hour from the sea and leaving the ruins of Soli, Paleokhora, to our right, we turned west into the valley of the Kambos [Potamos tou Kambou], which still carried plenty of water. We followed this for about an hour upstream, but then left it and turned into the mountains to our right, towards the sea. After we had climbed upward on a terribly steep footpath we reached Galini, the first village of the Tillyria, which lies at a considerable altitude and yet in a crater-like hollow, so that one cannot see it until one is immediately upon it. The whole area partakes of an Alpine character; it was covered with fresh sod, and the houses cling singly to the slopes.

The reports which I had received about the inhabitants' state of civilization were not exaggerated. They went about in rags, dressed mostly in home-spun sackcloth, which by long usage had gradually turned black. Colored materials, otherwise so popular with the Cypriots, I saw hardly at all. Tables, chairs, beds, etc. are completely unknown; people sleep on the ground, like dogs. I stayed with the richest and prominent inhabitant, whom I had met on the way; his hut was available, since he lived in Kambos with his family. A bed, even one of straw, could not be found for me anywhere in the village; such a luxury item does not exist in the Tillyria. Thus I actually had to sleep on hard boards, so that in the morning all my limbs were stiff. Coffee, an article which otherwise can be found anywhere in the Levant, even in the poorest places, could not be had in Galini. Most inhabitants of the Tillyria never leave their mountains. Anyone who has visited Nicosia and the Scala is a far-traveled man. Nicosia, the "polis," is to them the essence of beauty and excellence. The people seemed to me to be very good-natured but in general not very intelligent. The women and children were in my presence extraordinarily fearful

---

[260] This must refer to the so-called Linobambaci. See Hackett, *Orthodox Church*, 535.

[261] The headman of a village is normally called a "muchtar."

and shy; they probably were seeing a European for the first time in their lives. By evening there had gathered around my hut a large crowd of villagers who in silent and respectful astonishment gazed at the strange foreigner. And if I spoke to someone and asked a question of him, he shyly backed away in most cases.

From Galini I proceeded by way of Loutros, which is situated to the West, to Pyrgos, the principal city of the Tillyria. The route there is exceedingly difficult, since it always goes uphill and downhill and constantly cuts across the valleys which run south to north, that is towards the sea. The most important of these valleys is that of the Limnitis River, which at the point at which we crossed it, about one half hour from the shore, is fairly wide and at its floor still offers sufficient room for olive and fig trees. Before one climbs the last ridge, on which Pyrgos lies at a considerable altitude, one crosses the valley of the Platys River, which rivals the Limnitis River in the amount of water it carries and in this area is well planted with olive, fig, and carob trees as well as with grain. After a most miserable ride over bumpy, stony, and often very steep footpaths, passable only to a donkey or mule, but not to a horse, we came to the village of Pyrgos or, as it is sometimes called, Lakkos [tou] Linardou. For the travel from Galini to Pyrgos, which in direct distance comes to one and a half hour at most, we had used exactly three and a half hours because of the difficult terrain and bad paths.

The Tillyria is settled only very sparsely, and all villages lie in the proximity of the sea, but half an hour to one hour inland, in the mountains. At the coast itself there is not a single village; the reason for this must be sought in the plundering expeditions of pirates in the Middle Ages. The interior of the mountainous area is totally uninhabited, covered with pine forests, and without any means of communication. The district contains the following villages, some of which consist only of a few huts: Galini, Amadhies, Pyrgos-Khaleri-Piyenia (these three are situated very close one to another), Loutros, Varisha, Ayios Theodoros, Ambelia, Xerovounos-Messili [?]; all these are in the Kaza [district] of Lefka. Kokkina, Pakhyammos, Pomos, Livadhi, Ayia Marina, Iaglia, Argaka, Magounda, and Kinousa; all these are in the Kaza of Khrysokhou. Lyso and Pelathusa do not belong to the Tillyria, which is bordered in the east by the valley of the Kambos, which leads from Lefka to the Monastery of Kykko; the latter belongs to the district of Marathasa.

Educated Cypriots confirmed my observation that the dialect of the people of the Tillyria has many peculiarities. To me it was almost entirely unintelligible; my two companions, on the other hand, although they had never been in this area, could readily converse with them. I noticed some expressions, for example:

σύμβαλλε τὰς ἀνθρακιᾶς (scrape the coals together), instead of the otherwise customary σύναξε;

ἀνασπῶ κριθάρι (I am pulling barley, i.e. I am mowing) for κόπτω κριθάρι;

dwarf pines are called πιτύδια (instead of πεῦκαι, from classical Greek πίτυς);

ewes are called τόκαδες (from τίκτω or τέκω, to give birth) instead of γενημέναι, which is commonly used elsewhere;

a hearth is called νιστιά instead of ἐστιά.

I would have loved to gather some folk songs, but, given the oddly shy nature of the inhabitants, I was unable, in spite of money and good words, to coax some τραγούδια out of them. Unfortunately I had no wine with me, which surely would have loosened their tongues after only one glass. Without wine, i.e. without the right mood and occasion to sing τραγούδια, they were ashamed. Furthermore they were baffled by my request not to sing the songs as loud as possible and with full voice, as they deemed proper, but to recite them slowly. (Of sung verses one can understand nothing, since the words are always drawn out in long, shrill tremolo.) So I succeeded in collecting only a few verses, which my host in Pyrgos recited for me on my insistence.

It had been my intention to travel further from Pyrgos in a westerly direction through the Tillyria and then in a southeasterly direction by way of Lyso, Sarama, and Asproyia to climb up to Kykko Monastery high in the Troodos Mountains. This monastery is the most famous place of pilgrimage on the island and visited even by Russians; it owns an icon supposedly painted by St. Luke himself. But a number of considerations made me decide to leave the Tillyria and to ascend to Kykko Monastery by a shorter route. These considerations were: the difficult travel conditions in the Tillyria, the lack of suitable roads, our mules being worn out by the constant up and down, the reluctance of our guide, who wanted to save his animals, and also the cheerless expectation to have nothing to eat for eight days other than bread and water and some eggs at most (I could not agree to snails and onions) and to sleep on the hard ground without a mattress; furthermore the limited approachability of the inhabitants did not promise rich linguistic results. My decision was made easy all the more by the inhabitants of Pyrgos telling me that the villages of the Tillyria not visited all lie not far from the shore, which I already knew from my first journey. Therefore, when the inhabitants of the Tillyria wish to go, for instance, from Pyrgos or Galini to Pomos or Polis, they always choose the convenient coastal road, and it occurs to no one to use the difficult mountain paths, which are crossed by a multitude of valleys and gorges. Since I knew the coastal route and, on the other hand, did not want to return to Lefka by the same route by which I had come, I decided to take a southeasterly direction right across the wooded wilderness of the Tillyria to Kambos, which is a good five hours distant from Pyrgos. Given the dreadful paths and the utter lack of inhabitants in these wooded mountains, this route could not be followed without a guide familiar with the area. We took such a guide along in the person of a peasant from Pyrgos.

As far as the Limnitis River we followed the same route as the previous day, and then we headed southeast up a narrow side valley, at the top of which Xerovounos is located. This we left on our left and traveled first to Varisha, which is only one half to one hour distant from Galini, and then south right across the pine forest, riding past deep gorges, often on a narrow ridge. The mountains drop off on both sides so steeply as to make one dizzy. After a ride of two and a half hours through the lonely forest of young pines we finally reached the valley of Kambos; this is narrow, romantic, and rich in luxuriant vegetation and contrasts curiously with the woods which we had just crossed. The slopes are covered with vineyards, the ground for which is gained only by clearing the low forest. From the point at which our wooded path enters into the valley we still had to ride another three quarters of an hour to Kambos. This village is fairly large, makes an impression of comfort, and lies at a high altitude. The fields all around and down the whole valley, as far as its floor offers room, are well cultivated. The wine of Kambos is not bad; it tastes like Commanderia, without being that sweet.

From Kambos, the valley of which closes half an hour further up, above the village of Chakistra, a good and very romantic path leads by way of the latter to the famous Monastery of Kykko, always on the ridge of the mountains, so that one looks down on both sides into precipices which are deep, steep, and covered with pines. In the monastery, which lies in a hollow in the middle of the forest, I was most kindly received by the monks—there are about one hundred of them—and treated to a rich breakfast. Also I received from some of the young monks very valuable information about the geography of the area. After the exertions of the last few days I appreciated the friendly reception at Kykko and I would have done well to accept the monks' offer of overnight hospitalty. But I was determined to reach Prodhromos still the same day and thus took my leave from the monastery at three o'clock in the afternoon, unfortunately a little too late and without the precaution of taking a guide with me. The result was that we lost our way several times and finally landed up not at Prodhromos but in the valley of the headwaters of the Dhiarhizos River, which empties into the sea at Kouklia. For an hour and a half, over loose stones and blocks of rock and in the pitch-black night, we followed the stream in the hope of coming upon a village. Finally we gave up and were forced at a considerable altitude to camp under the open sky. Fortunately the night was in spite of the season (21 March) not too cold (the thermometer registered 6° Réaumur at dawn); also we tried to protect ourselves against the cold by keeping a well-supplied fire going all night. In the morning we learned from a peasant that we were in the vicinity of the village of Tris Elies, which, he said, was only a quarter of an hour away.

From our camp we still had to ride for an hour and a half in a northeasterly direction by way of Lemithou to Prodhromos, the highest village on the island; the vegetation there was still quite delayed. Early, at half past eight, we arrived there. Our mules, who had nothing to eat the evening before and had had to ascend the steep and very difficult way to Prodhromos on an empty stomach, were dead-tired. I stopped at the best farmhouse, for whose owner, an intelligent young Greek, I had a recommendation from Kathara. Everyone who wishes to climb Mount Troodos, which can be reached in two to two and a half hours from the village, usually seeks quarters here and employs the owner as guide. My host still remembered Kotschy and Unger, who ten years ago had stayed in his father's house; he also told of a young French scholar who some years ago had lodged with him and had climbed the mountain.

In the afternoon I climbed Mt. Troodos in two and a half hours. It was a warm day; the thermometer still registered 17° Réaumur at the peak, and the barometer exactly 600. From there I took some compass readings. At the top there still was snow, but only in scattered fields, while, according to my guide, the mountain normally is completely snow-covered at this time of year and the route which we took hardly passable; this year's spring was abnormal, he said. The view from here is quite imposing and simply magnificent. It reminded me of the Brocken;[262] one can see almost the entire island. The highest peak is quite barren; only moss and a kind of crocus, the flowers of which were poking through the snow, were growing there. The lower parts of the summit, on the other hand, are covered with mighty pines, which begin about twenty minutes above Prodhromos at the spring Vrysi. Unfortunately this old pine forest, all that is left of the island's former riches of forests, comes closer and closer to extinction, since the government does nothing to halt the systematic deforestation by burning the trunks. (The peasants, not yet familiar with a saw, use fire instead.)

There are three routes that one can take from Prodhromos: one is through the valley of the Dhiarhizos, which empties into the sea at Kouklia; the second is the valley of

[262] The highest peak of the Harz Mountains in central Germany.

the Platres stream, which empties into the sea near Episkopi, not far from the ruins of Kourion; the third, most direct one is through the limestone mountains of Paphos to the town of Paphos. After much hesitation I chose the third of these routes, leading west-south-west, although its topography was the least interesting and least rewarding one; I did so primarily to bring some clarity to the location of the mountain villages, which had never been accurately established. So I traveled from Prodhromos down the narrow, romantic valley of Paleomylo. A mountain stream called Charki [?] flows through this valley but soon joins the Dhiarhizos as it comes down from Tris Elies. I followed this main stream for a good two hours downhill and finally crossed over to the left bank of the Dhiarhizos on a solid stone bridge.[263] Then, riding up the mountains on the other side, I took the path to Vrecha, which was still three hours away. The path did not lead past any village, only past a mill which is called Roudhias and is driven by the River Xeros [Xeros Potamos],[264] which has its source one hour upstream. (This river flows almost parallel to the Dhiarhizos and empties into the sea not too far to the west from the latter.) From there a direct path, in the direction of west-south-west, leads right across the broad ridge by way of Kilinia, Galataria, Ayios Photios, and Khoulou to the river of Kourtaka, which is crossed at that village.[265]

Past Kourtaka the path climbs up in a southwesterly direction towards Letimbou, Kallepia, and Tsadha; there one has reached the summit and has a good view of the plain of Paphos below. From Tsadha to Ktima (in the plain not far from Paphos) the traveler needs two hours; the route passes between the neighboring villages of Mesoyi on the left and Trimithousa on the right and leaves Konia and Anavargos on the left and Khlorakas, Petridia, Emba, and Lemba on the right. I made an effort to fix these mountain villages above Paphos with the compass, as far as they can be seen from the roof of the episcopal residence, where I was staying.

In Ktima I was held up for a day and a half by continuous rain and, with it, a storm from the south. I used my time to visit once again, in spite of the rain, the heap of ruins (west of Ktima, on the sea) which bears the name of Paphos and the rock-cut tombs of Palaeokastro. In Ktima I was offered for sale two well-preserved inscriptions in so-called Cypriot characters, found supposedly by a peasant in the village of Dhrymou. I lost no time to buy these valuable stones at once, but later, at Larnaca, I had to convince myself that the inscriptions were forged. Thus deception and fraud have found their way even into this area, which is cut off from all culture and tourism.

From Ktima I followed my old route along the sea eastward by way of Kouklia to Limassol; this is the only route, apart from the Athienou-Larnaca route, that I have taken twice, because it could not be avoided. Between Paphos and Kouklia three rivers empty into the sea:

1. just before Akhelia the Potamos tis Ezousas;
2. fifteen to twenty minutes before (that is west of) Kouklia the Xeros;
3. five minutes further east the greatest of them, the Dhiarhizos.

---

[263] Schröder must mean "right bank."

[264] [Author's note: In its lower course this river flows by the villages of Malounda, Sindi, Ayia Marina, Stavrokono, Nata, Kholetria, etc.]

[265] This is the Potamos tis Ezousas. [Author's note: This river comes from Kannaviou and Melamiou and flows by Khoulou, Lemona, Kourtaka, Letimbou, Kallepia, Pitargou, Moronero, Amargeti, Apilu, and Episkopi (not to be confused with the Episkopi near Limassol) and empties into the sea as Potamos tis Ezousas at Akhelia between Paphos and Kouklia.]

This latter river and also the first can be crossed by stone bridges. Past Kouklia there is a fourth river which empties into the sea, the Khapotami. It supposedly has its sources in the area of Platres, but I was unable to obtain reliable information about its course. This was so because even among the Cypriots of this area there is unbelievable confusion about its hydrography. At Episkopi there is the mouth of the Kouris River, or, as I heard people in Limassol call it, the Karis.

The Garyllis flows right through the middle of Limassol. An hour further to the east and parallel to it is the Yermasoyia, which has its source at the Adelphi Peak, or, as the Cypriots say, not knowing the name "Adelphi," at the Papoutsa.

These data I have gathered at Limassol.[266] I would have liked to visit the area on the southern slopes of the Troodos and the Paputsa myself, in order to gain a clear picture of the direction of the various river valleys and the location of numerous villages here, which are notable for their viticulture. But I had been on the road for more than two weeks, my horses were worn out from traveling in the mountains,[267] and fresh mules were not available in Limassol. So I decided to explore the mountains north of Limassol later in a separate expedition, after having visited the eastern part of the island—a plan which later for lack of time unfortunately could not be realized—and to take the route from Limassol to Dhali (south of Nicosia), which you had recommended and which offers few difficulties. This route leads in a northeasterly direction by way of Amathus, Pendakomo, Mari, and Tokhni, past Skarinou, into the valley of the Pendaskinos (which flows south) and then along the western foot of Mt. Stavrovouni to the Monastery of Ayia Thekla, and, passing Alambra on the left and Lymbia on the right, to Dhali. From there I turned west to Pera and down the valley of the Pedieos towards Nikosia, followed the road from there for two hours, and turned left by way of Margo to Athienou, where recently, near Gorgus (Golgoi), more interesting finds were made, and reached Larnaca by way of Kaki Skala.[268]

In my next letter I shall give you a report on my excursion to the east. My epigraphical results turned out less rich than my geographical ones. I have copied three fragments of unedited Phoenician inscriptions from Kition, a Cypriot inscription from [Ayia] Phyla, and a number of mostly brief Greek funerary inscriptions.

II.152–56
Böyükdere,[269] 30 July 1873

Akanthou[270] (i.e. "mountain of thorns") is after Kyrenia, Lapithos-Karavas, and Yialousa the most significant place of the north coast; it is four hours from Dhavlos and

---

[266] [Author's note: Also a number of other, purely topographical data, which have been omitted here but were used on Heinrich Kiepert's map of Cyprus (Berlin, 1878).]
[267] By "horses" Schröder must mean mules; some of the routes taken were, as he had mentioned, impassable for horses.
[268] Schröder gives no reason for such a circuitous route, nor does he say in how many stages he accomplished it. Finds made at ancient Gorgus by Cesnola, particularly some large statues, are now in the Metropolitan Museum. Other finds from Gorgus are at the Louvre.
[269] Or Buykdere, called *kalos agros* in Greek, a residential suburb of Istanbul, on the west side of the Bosporus.

ten hours from Kyrenia. Above it rises, dizzyingly steep, the granite mass of Lithari [?] with its many crags; it is bare except that its lower ranges are covered with pine trees. Further to the west it is joined by even higher Elympos [Olymbos]. The pass which leads from Lefkoniko across the northern chain to the north coast is the Boghazi [?]; the mountain to the west of it is called Gamni [?]. Further yet to the west there are Mt. Antiphonitis, which is the highest peak of the chain and accommodates a monastery [Apati] on its broad ridge, craggy Pentadaktylos, and Mt. Koutsovendis (Buffavento). To the east, on the other hand, Lithari is followed by a peak which is called Dyolicharka [?] (perhaps = δυολυκάρια, the two wolves), then by Mt. Rusupi [?] and Mt. Hekatospitia [?] with the ruins of medieval fortresses. These are joined by broad Ayios Photios, the peak of which is said to carry a chapel of this saint. As the last link in the chain appears Mt. Gudi [?], which at Kilanemos [now Ceyhanli] reaches toward the sea and forms a bar right across the coastal strip. Beyond Yialousa the mountains lose their height rapidly, the peaks disappear, and at Rizokarpaso the chain gradually dissolves into a system of high plateaus and individual hills.

On the morning of 7 April I left Akanthou for the east, in order to travel along the coast as far as Yialousa. I abandoned my original plan to visit the extensive ruins of Moulos (two hours west from Akanthou), since I would have had to return to Akanthou by the same route and would thus have lost an entire day. But I could not deny myself a visit to the location of Koroniaes,[271] northwest of Akanthou. Thus I did not choose the most direct way to Panayia Pergamitissa [Pergaminiotissa] (east-north-east), but descended from the mountains toward the mouth of the Boghazi pass, which connects the coast with the Mesaoria. The foothills, consisting of fertile loam, are grown over with shrubs and low wild carob bushes; at the slightly lower elevations one finds olive and carob trees. After crossing several ravines, travelers pass, after one half hour, a small stream called Stirakylia [Styrakoulla], only a short distance from the sea. From there it was another twenty-five minutes to some roughly built sheepfolds close to the shore, near the hill of Κορωνιαῖς. Among the stones scattered about the fields I saw also several large cut blocks, but no remains of architecture or sculpture. I shall leave open to question whether the settlement, which in any event once was here, can be traced back to classical antiquity or only belongs to the Middle Ages. (If the former be correct, then Κορώνεια, which Stephanos of Byzantium calls the "fourth city of Cyprus,"[272] would be the nearest.) On an island like Cyprus, which has passed through so many storms of war even in post-classical times, it is often hard to say, whether the many fields of ruins which the traveler encounters everywhere indicate a medieval or ancient Cypriot settlement. One can easily be deceived in this regard. Under Byzantine or Frankish rule many new settlements were founded which have now vanished from the surface; they have left their traces only in disorderly heaps of stones, from which one cannot always tell to what period they belong. But in general one may say that we are dealing with an ancient settlement where we find larger, squared-off blocks among the small stones, traces of thick

---

[270] [Note from the publisher of *Globus*: Dr. Schröder had reached this place on the north coast of Cyprus in early April from Larnaca by way of Pyla, Pergamos, Kondea, Prastio, and Lefkoniko.]
[271] Koroniaes is actually 2 miles northeast of Akanthou. It is not to be confused with Koronia near Kantara Castle.
[272] Stephen of Byzantium, *Ethnica*, s.v. Κορώνεια (ed. Meineke, p. 377). See also Hadjiioannou, *Kypros,* vol. II, no. 155.2, s.v. Κορώνεια, and *SHC* VII, (1999), no. 33.17.

walls, etc. On the other hand it cannot be denied that the existence of large blocks which by their workmanship or other external marks suggest antiquity does not yet provide a certain criterion for the existence of an ancient city where they are found. This is so because the stones could very well have been dragged here from another location and used for medieval structures.

One half hour east of Koroniaes lies a second field of ancient ruins, Liastrika [?]. Indeed, the whole northern shore from Kyrenia to Cape Andreas is exceedingly rich in ruins. Nothing, however, still stands upright, and everything is broken to small pieces. But the presence of old foundations of walls, fragments of columns, rock tombs, and wells frequently indicates an old age. This coast must have been well populated and cultivated in antiquity; anyone traveling along it will be convinced of it. Its fertility, the fresh climate, the abundance of springs, and finally the large number of small bays and ports as well as the proximity of the Cilician coast must have invited settlements quite early. The Phoenicians undoubtedly had numerous colonies here. Kyrenia and Karpasia were Phoenician foundations. Of the latter Hellanicus says in his History of Cyprus (as quoted by Stephanos of Byzantium) that it was founded by Pygmalion.[273] I shall next give a list of locations between Kyrenia and Cape Andreas where ruins are found (the more important ones in **bold**). I have visited all of them except for nos. 2 and 3.

1. rock tombs at Kyrenia.
2. supposed ruins between Kharcha and Ayios Ambrosios.
3. Moulos (see above).
4. Koroniaes and 5. Liastrika near Akanthou.
6. an extensive field of ruins at the church and monastery of **Panayia Pergamou** [Pergaminiotissa], one hour east of Akanthou.
7. Galounia and Stiti [?], two locations close to each other on the coast, one hour east-north-east from Dhavlos.
8. many rock tombs and fragments of columns and architecture in the coastal plain below Yialousa (Γιαλοῦσα = Ἅγια Ἐλεοῦσα).
9. Macherkonas [Machairiona] or Ayios Therizos [Thyrsos] (traces of human work on the rocks at the shore as well as rock tombs are reported to be nearby).
10. **Selenia**, half-way between Yialousa and Rizokarpaso.
11. **Ayios Philon**, one half hour north of Rizokarpaso on the sea.
12. **Aphendrika**.
13. **to Kastron** [Kastros] on the tip of Cape Andreas.

From Koroniaes one can reach, in one half or three-quarters of an hour, crossing two small rivers, the area which is named after Liastrika. At a chapel of the Archangel, close by the rocky and precipitous shore, there are numerous traces of a destroyed village. In addition to a large quantity of broken tiles, some of which show some decoration, and squared-off stones, I noticed a cistern cut into the rock, here and there the foundations of thick walls, a stone hollowed out like a mortar, with a hole on one side, probably for draining liquids, and many stones shaped like a trough. The chapel is evidently built en-

---

[273] Hellanicus (of Lesbos, c. 480–395 B.C.), *Kypriaka*, *FHG* I 65, fr. 147, or *FGrH* IA 4, fr. 57. Stephen of Byzantium, *Ethnica*, s.v. Καρπασία (ed. Meineke, p. 361). See also Hadjiioannou, *Kypros*, vol. I, no.11.5, and vol. II, no. 155.2, s.v. Καρπασία, and *SHC* VII (1999), no. 33.16. The ancient site of Karpasia is just north of the village of Rizokarpaso.

tirely of ancient material (sandstone blocks). The center of this place of ruins is a high, rocky point, which steeply drops off into the sea; on each side there is a small bay. The ruins continue toward the east, but are hard to track down, since the coastal strip, at this point broader again as the mountains recede, is planted in barley.

After a ride of three-quarters of an hour we reached the church of Ayios Mikhalos, where the ruins of Panayia Pergamitissa [Pergaminiotissa] begin. This latter church lies about ten minutes from the shore on a hill, southeast of Ayios Mikhalos. These ruins are among the most extensive ones of the whole north coast and stretch out to the chapel of Ayios Charalambos, which is situated on the sea, one half hour from the Panayia. They were visited also by Ludwig Ross, but I am surprised that he dealt with them so carelessly and without attaching much importance to them. In any event there must have been a significant city here in antiquity. Sakellarios[274] suspects Urania [Ourania], which is mentioned by Diodorus Siculus[275] in the context of the campaign of Demetrius [I. of Macedonia] Poliorcetes against Cyprus in 306 B.C. Demetrius landed, coming from Cilicia, with his fleet on the north coast at Karpasia, to move from there against the capital city of Salamis (north of Famagusta), the residence of Menelaos, the brother of Ptolemy [I], and to lay siege to it. To accomplish this he first had to conquer Karpasia and Urania. The former we have to seek in the area of the modern Rizokarpaso, commonly also called Karpaso (not far from Cape Andreas), near Ayios Philon or Aphendrika, while Urania seems to have been neighboring on Karpasia. Therefore I do not deem it very likely that Urania will be found near Panayia Pergamatissa [Pergaminiotissa], i.e. almost fifteen [?] German miles from Karpasia. Also it is hardly to be supposed that Demetrius and his army moved along the narrow north coast (between Yialousa and Dhavlos the mountains touch directly upon the sea), where the terrain makes the passage of large bodies of men difficult by the valleys which must be crossed one after another.[276] In Sakellarios' scheme Demetrius would have had to move on Salamis in a great detour through the gorge of Akanthou by way of Lefkoniko. Between Yialousa and Kyrenia there is no pass across the mountains other than the difficult and narrow path from Pentadaktylos. It is much more likely that Demetrius moved from Karpasia along the south coast of the peninsula or took the even more comfortable inland route, across the high plateau on which Ayios Andronikos and Leonarisso are situated, to Komi Kebir and from there through the defile of Gastria to Salamis.

Urania was, in my opinion, not located on the coast but inland; I believe to have found its location near Karpasia. At Rizokarpaso, about twenty minutes to the southeast, there is a high hill from which one can overlook the entire southeast coast of the peninsula from Cape Andreas to south of Galinoporni and also a strip of the northern sea. The people call it Rani (abbreviated, I suspect, from Οὐράνιον; the stream in the gorge by which the hill steeply descends towards west was called ποτάμι τοῦ Ῥανίου by my guide). This hill is ideally suited to be a mountain fortress; it rises steeply on all sides, but its top is leveled off—artificially, it seems to me—and offers sufficient space for a fortification. I climbed this hill in spite of its almost perpendicular grade and found traces of

---

[274] Sakellarios, *Kypriaka,* I 152–53.
[275] 20.47.1–2. Also Plut. *Vit. Demetr.* 16.
[276] [Author's note: Even for the individual traveler the route from Dhavlos to Yialousa along the coast is not practical. When the peasants of Dhavlos go to Yialousa they always choose the route by the inland villages of Ephtakomi and Platanisso.]

earlier habitation on its top. An artificial chamber, cut into the rock and measuring 2 m. high, 5 m. long, and 4 m. deep, is the most remarkable. The walls were in part still covered with plaster, and the ceiling, a large natural block of rock, was supported by four pillars; but these seem to have been added at a later time, judging by their material, i.e. broken stones joined by mortar. The room receives light from a large square hole, which takes up exactly the space between the four pillars. The whole leaves the impression of a very ancient installation; perhaps it was a hypaethral sanctuary. I crept into the interior through a hole in the northwest corner. On the platform there are several cisterns. If we assume that the fortress of Urania was located on this hill, Demetrius' route of march is easily explained. Urania, southwest of Karpasia, blocked his way to Salamis, as it controlled the southern coast as well as the high plateau of Rizokarpaso. He had to take it, if he did not want to see his further advance threatened by the occupiers of the fortress.

But let us return to the ruins of Panayia Pergaminiotissa. At Ayios Mikhalos already the rocky ground along the sea is strewn with squared-off blocks of stone, masonry, and broken lids of sarcophagi. All this lies in wild confusion amidst thorny shrubs, making movement difficult. Special mention must be made of a large number of rock tombs, very close one to another; I counted about thirty of them. Most of them are filled with rubble, and the entrance often can be spotted only by a cut into the rock that has been filled with dirt. I crept down into several of these tombs whose entrances still were open. These are rectangular, carefully cut-out chambers. Typically on three sides there are niches for the sarcophagi (missing, of course), while on the fourth side there is the door, usually reached by stairs cut into the rock. This then was the necropolis of the city, which was located a little further inland. From the outside one notices almost nothing of the existence of this necropolis, and only late and by coincidence did I become aware of it. The tombs all lie under the horizontal rocky ground, which is grown-over with bushes. When laying out these tombs people first excavated a rectangle to the depth of one meter and then dug under the rock in horizontal direction; through the hole they then descended on stone stairs into the chamber. Probably the adjacent cultivated fields, too, are full of graves. The ruins become denser as one gets closer to the church of the Panayia. In its immediate area the ground is covered with huge blocks of stone, column fragments, and sarcophagus lids. The whole complex is difficult to survey, since dense briers and nettles grow everywhere among the masses of stone; where there was a little more soil barley was growing. I could easily make out in the heap of ruins the foundation walls of a rectangular building which were constructed of large blocks and still clearly indicated the entrance. Behind the church there is a deep well cut into the rock. The center of the former city was obviously formed by the height which is situated a few minutes north-northeast from the hill of the Panayia, is covered with huge blocks of stone, and is called Epsilon by the people living in this area. Among other things I saw there two stone sarcophagi. The rocky ground was often cut in rectangular patterns, and in this manner man-made walls had been created. [Plate 29]

From here I moved on to the chapel of Ayios Charalambos. Scattered in the fields nearby are a few huts, which are called Trigateratscha, or Tria Teratsia, i.e. "three carob trees." (The carob tree, or St. John's bread tree, is called ἡ κερατέα in Greek, and the Cypriots pronounce it like "teratscha.") From there we still had to travel three and three quarters of an hour to Dhavlos. The coastal strip is planted everywhere in carob trees and barley, the mountains jut out right to the sea, and our route took us steadily across narrow and deep gorges with small streams and olive groves. The constant up and down makes travel in this area very difficult and badly tires the mules. On the other hand the coastal strip forms one of the most charming landscapes of Cyprus, given its fertility, its richness in carob and olive trees, and the splendid view. On the left there is the deep-blue sea, its surf loudly crashing against the rocky shore, and beyond that the blue mountains of Karamania, their highest parts gleaming with snow. And on the right there is the majestic chain of mountains with its sharp, angular lines and high peaks; among these Kantara, crowned with splendid ruins, the Hekatospitia, is particularly picturesque. This is the ἀκτὴ Ἀχαιῶν (coast of the Achaians)—not low land, but hilly land, Engel rightly observes[277]—where Teucer landed and, having crossed the mountains, founded the city of Salamis at the mouth of the Pedieos.

The further one advances east, the closer the mountains come to the coast, and the route sometimes leaves the sea and seeks the more comfortable valleys inland. After one hour and a quarter we passed Phlamoudhi, but left it to our right on the mountain. The stream coming from Phlamoudhi flows in a beautiful valley shaded by cypress trees. This we followed for a distance upstream, but then, having climbed the eastern wall of the valley, we turned toward the sea again. To reach Dhavlos from here took us another hour and a half, while the direct distance is hardly one hour. But it took much time constantly having to cross the deep gorges, which open toward the sea and so closely follow one upon another that even the cultivation of grain ceases.

Dhavlos (ὁ Δαυλός) is a small Greek village; it consists of thirty to forty poor clay huts in sharp contrast to the handsome and clean church. It lies at the foot of the mountain which rises sharply from the northern chain, is visible for miles around, and carries on its top a medieval fortress, the Frankish castle Kantara. In popular parlance the ruins are called Hekatospitia, or "spitia tis reginas," and "jüzbir oda" in Turkish. By Kantara, on the other hand, the local people mean not the ruins of the castle, but the monastery of the Panayia tis Kantaras; this is located about another three quarters of an hour further to the west (on the other side of the watershed and offering a view of the bay of Salamis and Famagusta). The peak with the ruins lies to the southeast of Dhavlos, while the monastery, not visible, of course, lies to the southwest, below the craggy peak of Koronia, which joins the mountain with the ruins in the west and lies directly to the south above Dhavlos.

On 8 April, starting out from Dhavlos at six o'clock in the morning, I climbed on foot to the top of Mt. Kantara, intending to visit the ruins of the castle.[278] The weather was at first clear and dry and later very hot. But I had told my guide that I wanted to see Kantara and was, of course, thinking that Kantara was identical with Hekatospitia. After an hour of climbing I observed that we were turning too far to the west from the mountain of the castle. But I calmed down when my guide, responding to my questions, repeatedly assured me that this was the right way to Kantara. At seven-thirty we were at the watershed, from which both seas can be seen. At the top there was fog. Now, instead of turning east at the watershed, where in my judgment the mountain with the ruins, invisible because of the fog, had to lie, my guide turned right, i.e. west. After we had marched for another twenty minutes along the ridge of the mountain, covered in the clouds and at a temperature of 13° [Réaumur], he finally led me down—to the monastery of Kantara. When I saw it at a distance of a quarter of an hour, below my feet and lying on the southern

[277] Engel, *Kypros* I 83.
[278] Schröder refers to the ruins of Kantara both as a "Schloss" and as a "Burg."

slope of the mountain, I realized the misunderstanding. When I confronted my guide and asked why he had not led me to the "old fortress," he was very surprised, saying that I had all along wanted to go to Kantara, not to Hekatospitia; the latter was one hour distant, he said.

Since we were so close to the monastery, which, surrounded by green gardens, looked very inviting, I did not turn around right away, but made my way down to it, although I was a little angry about the loss of time. The monastery is inhabited by only two monks and offers a fine view of the southern foothills. After a rest of half an hour we walked back in half an hour to the place where we had first reached the watershed, i.e. to the western crag of the Koronia. Then, in another half hour, proceeding in the same direction, we climbed to the top of the mountain with the ruins, often making our way only with difficulty through the dense underbrush. The extensive and beautiful ruins differ in nothing from our German medieval ruins and vividly reminded me of Giebichenstein, the Rudelsburg, the Schönburg at Naumburg, or Hohenurach in the Swabian Alb.[279] They are crowning a bare rock which stands isolated on the peak of the mountain, rises steeply on all sides, and seems wholly inaccessible. After a lengthy search I finally found on the south side a place where this rock could be climbed with the help of my hands and a sturdy stick. Having climbed up some forty to fifty feet, I found a hole in the wall, from where narrow and dilapidated stone stairs led up into the area of the fortress. My old guide Savas opted not to participate in this break-neck climbing and preferred to take a nap at the foot of the rock in the shade of a lilac bush, while I crept about above in the Hekatospitia.

The view from the top was inspiring: At my feet to the northwest there was the village of Dhavlos, sharply contrasting by the yellow color of its houses with the green coastal strip, and the far-stretching north coast with its many small bays and cliffs in front of them. Beyond the sea there was the coast of Karamania, clearly visible. To the south there were Famagusta and the bay of Salamis, as well as the villages around Trikomo. In the east there was the hilly interior of the Karpas peninsula with the large village of Komi Kebir in the middle. Further away I could see, at 35° west of south, Stavrovouni (the ancient Olympus, west of Larnaca), closer and in about the same direction the white monastery of Panayia tis Kantaras, and in immediate proximity, at 55° west of south, the peak of Mt. Koronia. On the north coast I discovered, apart from Dhavlos, the chapels of Panayia Pergamitissa [Pergaminiotissa], Ayios Mikhalos, and Ayios Charalambos, while the monastery of Ayios Nikolaos could be seen halfway up the mountain of Hekatospitia, a little to the east of Dhavlos. The ruins of the fortress itself are rather extensive and well preserved, include many vaults, galleries, loopholes, and towers, and would be worthy of a precise survey. The outer walls are very strong and built at a slight inclination. At the highest peak of the rock there are the remains of a small building with pointed arches, the chapel of the fortress, it seems to me.

The descent took another route, directly in the direction of Dhavlos, leaving the Church of Ayios Nikolaos at a short distance to our left. In no more than an hour, at twelve o'clock noon, we reached Dhavlos, where it was very hot, while at the castle of

---

[279] Burg Giebichenstein is located in the city of Halle. The Rudelsburg is located at Bad Kösen, and the Schönburg not far from Naumburg. All three locations are in the Saale valley, not far one from another. When Schröder was a student at the University of Halle, 1862–1865, he must have become quite familiar with them. Burg Hohenurach towers above the small town of Urach, not too far from Reutlingen, in the state of Baden-Württemberg. If or when Schröder visited it, is not known.

Kantara the thermometer registered only 14° [Réaumur]. The barometer reading was 706 at the highest peak and 753 at sea level.

Still on the same day I continued my travels to the east along the coast. I had planned to be back from Kantara at nine o'clock in the morning and then to continue right away, in order to reach Yialousa in the evening. This was now impossible. Besides, people in Dhavlos assured me that the way along the coast was very bad and difficult, because of the need continually to cross deep gorges. It was easier and faster, they said, to take the inland route to Yialousa by way of Komi Kebir, and that was the route chosen by anyone traveling there from Dhavlos or back. Furthermore I was told that there were no old ruins along the coast, except at Galounia, a place one hour distant. Thus, although I would rather have traveled along the coast, I finally yielded to the advice of my companions, in the interest of the mules. I decided, however, not to go by way of Komi Kebi and Leonarisso, which route I already knew, but to follow a more northern route by way of Ephtakomi, Platanisso, and Kilanemos, at the foot of the northern chain of mountains. This route leads first along the coast, crosses several deep gorges formed by mountain streams, and after an hour leads to an extensive and confused field of ruins. The local people call it Galounia, while Sakellarios identifies it with the ancient city of Aphrodision, which is mentioned by Strabo and Ptolemy.[280] The ruins lie directly on the sea, opposite Ayios Photios, the last high mountain of the northern chain. Further to the east it loses considerable altitude and rises only once more before Yialousa to a higher peak with the promontory of Goudhi [?], which sharply advances toward the sea.[281]

From here we turned more inland, toward the mountains, which we crossed east of Ayios Photios at a low elevation. But our guide missed the pass, so that we emerged too far to the west, above Komi Kebir (or simply Komi). We therefore rode down there and rode from it, on an even, but slightly rising path to Ephtakomi, our goal, situated three quarters of an hour away to the northeast and on higher ground. Both villages lie on the same high plateau, which is planted in barley. It is bordered on the left, to the north, by the chain of mountains, and on the right by a low and rocky row of hills (τραχῶνες) grown-over with bushes. The width of this cultivated land may only be one quarter to one half of an hour and narrows even further toward Ephtakomi. Beyond the row of hills in the south lies a hilly area richly covered with trees and fields; I had passed though this area in 1870 on my way from Komi Kebir to Leonarisso. We took quarters for the night in a large village situated on the slope of the mountains and inhabited by both Turks (in the lower part) and Christians.

Past the village the land again levels off somewhat, and after a ride of an hour and a half along the foot of the northern mountains, always through hilly land, we reached Platanisso, a small village inhabited exclusively by Turks. I had been told in Larnaca that the population of Platanisso was descended from Druzes and that the village was known by the Turkish name of Druskjöi. But this name was not known to anyone in the Karpasia (the eastern peninsula), nor did anyone know anything about the alleged descent from Druzes. The inhabitants speak both Turkish and Greek, but are generally Muslims. I was amazed by

---

[280] Sakellarios, *Kypriaka*, I 154–55. Strab. 14.682. Ptol. *Geog.* 5.11.1.
[281] Not to be confused with the village of Ghoudi on the Paphos-Polis road.

the many red-haired children. Of plane trees I saw none, just as at Tremetusha [Tremithus] near Atheniou I saw no terebinth trees.[282] The mountains above the village are all bare.

Behind the village the route climbs up the bare wall of the mountain and then drops down to a hilly area, which in many places opens up toward the sea and in which olives and barley are cultivated. One half hour after having climbed the steep height above Platanisso we reached Tschilanemo (Κοιλάνεμος, i.e. windy hole?) [Kilanemos]. This little village is located at the head of a valley which opens up to the northwest, toward the sea. The inhabitants of this village, particularly the women, attracted my attention by their colorful costumes and their long blond curls. Directly behind the village (i.e. to the east) the path climbs up to the high plateau, on which Leonarisso (not visible) lies to the south and Ayios Andronikos one quarter of an hour away in front of us to the east. The latter boasts many gardens and a handsome church. It stretches far, since every single house is surrounded by gardens and fields. The ground is rocky but covered with a thin layer of red earth, which is especially well suited for mulberry and fig orchards. Ayios Andronikos is, like Yialousa and Rizokarpaso, known for its considerable production of silk, which the peasants spin and weave themselves. There are 160 houses in the village; the population is half Greek and half Turkish. I was told in the coffee house that there were old ruins, probably rock tombs, at Tschilanemo on the sea.

From Ayios Andronikos one can reach in forty minutes, in a leisurely ride to the northeast across a brush-covered area, the large and prosperous village of Yialousa; the steeple of its church becomes visible already half an hour earlier. The high plateau at first falls down gently toward the sea, which is visible from afar. It then drops down to a gully, which is densely grown-over with bushes and covered with mulberry trees and fields at its foot; its stream is crossed on a stone-built bridge. Having climbed up the far wall of the valley, one already comes upon the first houses of Yialousa; but it takes another half hour from there to the middle of the village with its church of the Archangel. The whole place is about an hour long, because here, as in Ayios Andronikos, the houses stand isolated in the middle of the appertinent well-tended and carefully fenced gardens and fields. In addition to the many mulberry plantations there are also many olive, carob, and fig trees, as well as some palm trees and low pines.

Yialousa still lies on the plateau, which forms the southern border of the coastal plain, which at this point is fairly wide. Below the village the coast leaps far out into the sea and forms, to the northwest, the small harbor of Limenari [Limionas?]; to the east of it is a small hill, called Akamas. This coastal plain certainly was the site of a settlement in antiquity; the location was very favorable, the north coast is not this wide at any other place except Kyrenia, and the soil is very fertile. Indeed, there are many old ruins there. Since we reached Yialousa already at half past two, but could not reach Rizokarpaso on the same day, I decided to stay overnight in Yialousa and utilized the afternoon to descend to the coastal plain, the Jalo [?], together with the son of my host. We walked for a quarter of an hour through the fields of barley, until we reached, in the middle of the plain, a rocky height which was covered with brush and on which a windmill was being built of stone. The whole rocky ground here was cut out into tombs. From there we crossed the fields in a northwestern direction along the sandy beach and at the hill Limenari saw the traces of harbor installations covered by the sand; a colossal block of

---

[282] "Platanisso" is presumed to be derived from πλάτανος = plane tree, and "Tremethusha" from τερέβινθος or τέρμινθος = terebinth tree.

sandstone emerged half-way from the sand. From there we walked back to the village, located half an hour away to the southeast. We passed the ruined chapels of Ayios Georgios and Ayios Yiannis, where there are many old ruins, large blocks of stone, and here and there broken column shafts. In vain I looked for inscriptions. In the yard of the church of the Archangel I saw also a large Corinthian column capital, richly decorated with acanthus leaves.


III. 168–73
Böyükdere, 30 July 1873

Traveling east from Yialousa one gains in one-and-a-half hour, directly at the shore, the site of some ruins with the chapel of Ayios Therizos [Thyrsos]. It is not far from the summer village of the inhabitants of Yialousa; this is called Macherkona (ἡ Μαχερκώνα) [Machairiona] and consists of some twenty miserable shepherds' huts (mandres [μάνδρες]). We did not, however, follow the route directly along the coast, which I already knew, but another one which follows the mountains, here quite low, at half the height; in so doing we had to cross several gorges with abundant vegetation. On both sides of the way—on the right the gently rising mountains and on the left the coast—the land everywhere is well cultivated and fertile. The individual groups of the houses of Yialousa extend far to the east. Half an hour after leaving the house of my host we passed the μαχαλᾶς (quarter) of Aksapoliti [?], which is part of Yialousa. (That part of Yialousa which extends toward the sea is called Kalamnia [?], and the southwestern part, toward Ayios Andronikos, is called Livadhia.) After another ten minutes we came upon another group of houses, which was surrounded by fields and which my guide called Jera [Yera?]. To the right, higher up on the mountain, about fifteen or twenty minutes away, there is a church of Aya Marina, and nearby a ruined chapel of Ayios Pavlos. Yet another twenty minutes further we passed the last group of houses belonging to Yialousa, which is called Melini. Then the way drops down to a broad gorge (ἀρκάκι [?] τῆς Μελίνης) with a stream carrying ample water and a pretty vegetation of cypress trees, carob bushes, wild olive trees, and climbing plants. After another half hour, at the ruined chapel of Ayios Georgios, we left the path which leads along the height and turned southeast, down to the bay of Macherkona. To the southeast above this location, below the ruined chapel of Ayios Dimitri, there are two now almost totally ruined towers, called πύργοι.

From Macherkonas one can reach, in one hour, the ruins of Selenia, which, oddly enough, are not mentioned at all by Sakellarios, who is usually so accurate.[283] They lie a short distance from the sea at the foot of the mountains, which here rise higher again; more specifically below a mountain which my guide called Kavallitschefti [?]. At this point, a little above the church of Ayios Photios, a small gully opens up; in it is a richly bubbling spring, the water of which (νερὸ τῆς Σελενίας) enjoys an excellent reputation. This entire area is remarkably rich in ruined medieval churches and chapels.

Selenia is a fairly spread-out terrain, rising toward the south and full of stones and remains of old buildings, but one cannot get a good view of it because of all the brush. The church of Ayios Photios is built completely of spoils; in its vicinity I saw several column capitals and a plain sandstone sarcophagus. The rocky ground showed many

---

[283] Sakellarios, *Kypriaka,* I 156-57.

traces of rectangular buildings; where the ground consisted of soil—hard as stone—it was dug out in tombs. Among other things I noticed a circular depression, with seven steps leading into it, probably a cistern; this had been discovered only recently by treasure-hunting peasants.

There was an ancient Cypriot city here. This was shown by the excavations which the peasants undertook last summer a little further up near the spring. Apart from the remains of old walls and squared-off sandstone blocks, I saw there, lying around on the ground, many badly eroded statuettes of porous sandstone, thirty to eighty cm. high, left as worthless. Nearly all of them were without their heads, and some without feet as well. All were of the same type: a female figure in a long robe, feet and hands close to the body, the right arm lying across the breast and holding an object, presumably a dove; the left arm hangs down the body and also holds something, a bag or pitcher, in the hand. The technique is entirely ancient Cypriot and exactly the same as that of the statues which were excavated by [Louis Palma di] Cesnola at Athienou and by Lang[284] at Pyla [near Larnaca]; the manner of executing the feet and legs of the statues in high relief which prevails there is also repeated here. At the church there are some stone huts; on the roof of one of them there lay the upper part of a female statue, entirely done in the ancient Cypriot style, with necklaces and bracelets. The head lay next to it.

Our goal today was Rizokarpaso, the last village but also the principal one of the Karpasia peninsula. The shortest way there from Selenia leads by way of the monastery of Eleousa, which is now inhabited only by a single monk. But I chose the way along the coast, in order first to visit the ruins of Ayios Philon with its supposedly ancient temple. At noon, in scorching heat, we continued our ride from Selenia. Cultivation now ceased and the rocky ground is densely covered with brush, which the Cypriots call "woods" (Turkish "orman") and in which herds of wild goats live. The beach is formed here of deep and fine sand, which the mules manage only with difficulty. All around there was deep silence in this lonely wilderness, and our small caravan moved slowly under the glowing sun "with tired pain through the sandy heath."[285] The tall Savas, on his little donkey, was the point man. After an hour and a quarter he led us away from the coast more inland through the "woods" to a single farm. This stands at the head of a small gully which extends down to the sea and is planted with fig trees, mulberry trees, and also grain. The farm is shaded by fruit trees and is called Asprokolymbos ["white pool"]. From its inhabitants I learned that we were close to Rizokarpaso and that to reach Ayios Philon we should have continued along the coast. Ten minutes later we reached the high plateau and saw the first houses of Rizokarpaso and the church of Ayia Triada in front of us. But we had to continue for another good half hour before we reached, in this spread-out village, the house of Savas, the father of our guide Perikles. The latter arranged quarters for us with one of the most prosperous farmers. Here I got my own room, where I set myself up comfortably for several days.

Rizokarpaso (τὸ Ῥιζοκάρπασον) is a large village consisting of 250 to 300 houses and inhabited exclusively by Greeks. It is situated on a high plateau which to the north drops down to the sea gradually and without any precipices, but to the south is set

---

[284] Robert Hamilton Lang (1836–1913), British Consul in Cyprus 1863–1872, collector, excavator, and epigrapher. See *SHC* V (1998) 274–306.
[285] "Mit müder Qual durch die sandige Heide," from the poem "Drei Zigeuner" by the Austrian poet Nikolaus Lenau (1802–1850).

apart from the coast by a very intricate system of mountains. The distance from the northern sea, in a direct line, is about half an hour, while to the southern sea it seemed a little further to me. The village measures about an hour and a half from one end to the other and is divided into three quarters (μαχαλλάδες): 1. Chorio, with about 120 houses and the handsome church of Ayia Triada (where I was staying), lies in the north, from where one can see the sea in the north; 2. Leko, with about eighty houses and the churches of Ayios Arkhangelos and Ayios Synesios, adjoins Chorio in the south and is situated at a lower level; 3. Anavrysi, with about 110 houses and the churches of Ayios Ioannis and Ayios Georgios, joins Leko in the west; it extends to the northwest, following the course of a swampy stream, Potamia, in which many turtles live. This is the lowest and most fertile part of Rizokarpaso, but also less healthy. In Chorio the soil is rocky, yet very fertile, since there is a layer of red earth above the rock. The area occupied by the village is so large because every house is surrounded by fields, vegetable gardens, and orchards. All these gardens were well watered by canals; water is fed into these from a well (λάκκος) or masonry cistern (δεξαμενή) by means of a water wheel (ἀλακατόλλακος or ἀνακατόλλακκος). Every garden has such a water wheel. [Plate 30]

Rizokarpaso is a prosperous village. Its entire appearance compares well with that of other villages of Cyprus, just as its inhabitants do with other Cypriots both in appearance and in character. The main means of support is sericulture; the peasants not only gain the silk from the cocoons of the silkworms but spin it and weave it into material. Cotton is also cultivated and processed, and cattle-breeding is not insignificant. In the gardens I observed besides mulberry and fig trees also orange trees, pomegrenate trees, and vine. Cactus trees are often used for hedges; I also saw some clusters of palm trees (without fruit, of course). The inhabitants are blond and well-built, especially the women. They distinguish themselves by their great industriousness, the women no less than the men. One sees the former busy not only at the loom and in the mill (every house has its own loom, and every reasonably prosperous farmer his own horse-driven mill), but they also work in the fields, just like the men, planting and harvesting. Furthermore the people of Karpasia are very hospitable. Sakellarios rightly says of Rizokarpaso:

Οἱ κάτοικοι τῆς κώμης ταύτης εἶναι οἱ ὡραιότεροι, εὐμηκέστεροι, καὶ ἀνδρειότεροι ὅλων τῶν κατοίκων τῆς νήσου.[286] [The inhabitants of this village are the most beautiful, tallest, and most courageous of all the inhabitants of the island.]

I derived much benefit from becoming acquainted with the school teacher of Leko, a cheerful young man who had previously been a merchant and even had spent some time at Marseilles. He led me around the village, of which he was a native, and acquainted me with the practices and habits of its inhabitants.

Still on the afternoon of my arrival (10 April) I used the rest of the afternnon to make my way down to the ruins of Ayios Philon, together with Perikles' father. These ruins lie directly north of the village on a projection of the coast into the sea. At this point the coast is covered with woods, i.e. low cypress trees and pines, but directly at the sea, where the church is located, there is no vegetation. Even before we reached this church my guide called to my attention a beautiful column of bluish marble, hidden in the bushes. Until a few years ago, he said, there was a second such column here, but the people of Yialousa in 1868 transported it to their own village, having cut it into several parts,

---

[286] Sakellarios, *Kypriaka,* I 157.

to use it in the construction of their church. The ruins of the Byzantine church of Ayios Philon are located directly at the rocky shore, are on the whole well-preserved, are visible from afar, and make, on this lonely stretch of coast, a strong impression on the visitor: one might think to be facing the ruins of an ancient Greek temple, and some have taken the church to be just that.

In any event the church is very old, dates from the times of Byzantine rule, and is entirely built of ancient spoils, which the ruins of the ancient city that once was here offered abundantly. The dimensions of the church are only small; I measured about eighteen paces from the main entrance in the west to the apse. But the pure style of a basilica, the harmony of the individual parts, and the neatness and solidity of the structure, which can be observed everywhere, make a magnificent impression. The church is three-aisled. The nave is higher and wider than the two side aisles and has its own higher roof, above which, in the middle, there is a cupola resting on a cylinder. The main entrance is at the west end; there are two more entrances in the northern and southern side aisles, and between them is the main cupola. The interior is entirely vaulted; the side aisles are separated from the nave by two rows of three columns each, and these are connected one with another by arches. The south side of the church has suffered the most; the entire portal and a part of the wall are missing. The interior is filled with large stone blocks; among them I noticed also several ancient Doric and Ionic column capitals. I think that for the history of Byzantine church architecture it would be important to have the church of Ayios Philon carefully surveyed by architects before it falls entirely into ruin.

In the vicinity of the church the shore is covered everywhere with the remains of an ancient settlement: large sandstone blocks, foundations of walls, many sherds, column shafts and capitals, and a sarcophagus. At this point the coast forms a small bay, which is now not very deep, because of the many large and small blocks of stone which cover the bottom, but in antiquity formed a small harbor. The remnants of ancient harbor installations are worth pointing out. Going north from the bay one can follow for a hundred paces a quay built of mighty blocks which were tied together by iron clamps one to two feet long. For the construction of this mole column drums and entire fluted marble columns were used as well, and this circumstance suggests to me, that this harbor installation does not date from ancient Greek times.

About one quarter of an hour to the west of the church of Ayios Philon a small gorge opens up; it runs from the plateau of Rizokarpaso to the sea, is densely covered with brush, and has a stream (ποτάμι τοῦ καρούλι) flowing through it. At this point there are old quarries and many rock chambers with niches; access is by rectangular vertical doors. From here we first walked for a distance up the gorge and then turned left, back to the village.

The next day was appointed for an excursion to the lonely tip of the peninsula of Karpasia which extends beyond Rizokarpaso. I decided to move along the north coast as far as Cape Andreas and then to return on the south coast by way of the monasterry of Ayios Andreas. I hardly believe that this route has ever been taken by any European since Pococke.[287] To be sure, on Gaudry's agricultural map[288] a red line has been drawn from Rizokarpaso to the monastery of Ayios Andreas, and thus it seems that Gaudry made this

---

[287] [Note from publisher of *Globus*: It has recently been followed by General Cesnola.] On Richard Pococke see *SHC* V (1998) 35–56.
[288] Stylianou, *Cartography*, 151, no. 209.

trip. But he returned by the same route, without having seen the northern coast with the ruins of Aphentrika and the cape.

Cypriots also visit this area only rarely, because there is no village beyond Rizokarpaso. Makrou, which is located there, is not a village, but a depression one hour distant from the monastery and planted in grain; it consists of some rough-built huts (mandres), which serve the shepherds and their flocks during their summer-stay. The only point at which there is still a permanent human presence is the monastery of Ayios Andreas. Its inhabitants travel to and from Rizokarpaso by the path which leads not far from the southern coast by way of Makrou. Other than that, one sees in this remotest and brush-covered corner of Cyprus only now and then some herdsmen and herds of wild goats. But this area is not entirely uncultivated. On the narrow coastal strip at Aphentrika barley is grown; also in the narrow valleys which run parallel to the southern coast and are usually separated from the sea by a series of hills; here olive, carob, and other utility trees are sporadically found. But past Makrou all cultivation ceases, and one sees only "orman." The land is generally hilly, but one really can no longer speak of a continuous ridge or a chain, such as dominates the other mountainous areas. As is already the case between Yialousa and Rizokarpaso, the mountains dissolve toward the south into a system of plateaus and hills; these cannot be considered branches of the ridge of mountains parallel to the northern coast, but are quite independent of them. The mountains turned toward the southern coast are much more varied and complex than those of the northern coast and rise directly from the sea.

At seven o'clock in the morning I started out [on another excursion] in a northeastern direction. I was accompanied by Savas the Levkoniat [from Lefkoniko?] and Savas the father of my guide Perikles; to the latter and to his mule I gave a day of rest. After a one-hour ride I reached the sea at the location called Stilou, having descended from the middle plateau to a deep-cut ravine, which extends further inland, with a stream (τὸ ποτάμι τοῦ ἁγίου Ἀνδρονίκου). While up to this point our way led us only through wild brush, from Stilou to beyond Aphentrika the coastal strip, although narrow, is planted in barley. The name "Stilou" (I noticed only a single uninhabited habitation, to the left of the path) seemed to suggest an ancient settlement, I looked out carefully for any ruins, but discovered only a few squared-off blocks of stone. These, however, suggest ancient foundations, which now probably lie buried beneath the sand, which forms low hills (dunes) just at this point. A small tongue of land extends into the sea; beyond it there is the small island of Levkoniso, which evidently once was joined to that tongue of land. We continued riding for another twenty minutes, skirting the rocky banks which limit the coastal strip to the south, and then, where the coastal strip widens, reached the ruins of Aphentrika. One can see the remains of several buildings still standing upright, but these all belong to the Byzantine Middle Ages. Primarily these are churches. Two of them, that of the Panayia Aphentrikotissa and that of the Asomatos Arkhangelos, are the largest and, because of their architecture, no less noteworthy than the church of Ayios Philon. The cella of the former church has been restored and serves as a church for divine services. Between these two churches, the ruins of which form a disorderly conglomerate of large and small blocks of stone, there are several roughly built huts of stone; all of them were empty at the time.

The churches probably are all built of ancient material, although there are no external signs, such as inscriptions, immured columns, capitals, and the like, particularly to indicate this. The plan of these two churches is the same as that of Ayios Photios (three aisles, each with an apse), but the dimensions of the Panayia are considerably larger. In the restored chapel of Panayia Aphentrikotissa there were two capitals, a Doric one and a smaller Ionic one. Nearby one finds caves cut into the rocky ground; one can climb down into two of them. One of them was quite spacious and had niches on the side walls and a well in one corner; to the left of the entrance there was also an arch of masonry. Nearby there were also, cut fifteen feet deep into the rock, a well, or more correctly a cistern, and traces of waterlines of stone. The two churches are located directly at the foot of the mountain, and to the north of them the coastal plain spreads out. Undoubtedly this plain holds the foundations of many old buildings and tombs, but their traces unfortunately cannot be made out today, because the whole coastal strip is planted in grain. Nevertheless the ground is littered with small stones, while the larger ones have been gathered from the fields and piled up into fences. These fields were vineyards in the Middle Ages, and still today one can find some of the large mill-stones with which the grapes were pressed.

From the church of the Panayia we traveled in a northwestern direction across the fields to the small harbor (τὸ λιμάνι) which on the English navigational map is marked as Exarchos Bay (one of the churches is called ναὸς τοῦ Ἐξάρχου). The name Epiotisa, which one finds written next to it, is entirely unknown in Cyprus, and my guide Savas, who was very familiar with the area east of Rizokarpaso, since he himself had lived for seven years in the monastery of Ayios Andreas, assured me that there was no place and no area by that name. Perhaps the name is only a corruption of Aphentrikotissa. The English navigational map is not at all reliable in matters of the orthography of place names and often even in the location of places. It writes, for instance, Andriako instead of Androniko (also located falsely) and Ghalino for Galinoporni. Yialousa is missing all together, and instead we find a "St. Loudobika," which in reality does not exist. For Rizokarpaso, written "Rizokarpo," a totally false location is given. A "Galatea" on the coast does not exist; where this place is indicated, lies Komajalou [Koma tou Yialou], while Galathia, on the other hand, lies inland near Tavro. Akanthou, Phlamoudhi, and Dhavlos are all placed erroneously; each of these villages lies further to the east.

The name Aphentrika, I suspect, is only a wrong pronunciation of Aphentika (from ἀφέντης, "master," from which also the Turkish "Efendi" is derived) and probably means "rule, dominion." Unfortunately I did not observe whether one says τὰ Ἀφέντρικα, neuter plural, or ἡ Ἀφέντρυκα, as Sakellarios writes.[289] At the harbor I noticed several very thick ancient columns, driven into the ground and having boats tied to them. Aphentrika must have been a significant place in Byzantine times. But that a city stood here already in ancient Greek times is suggested by many indications; especially by the many rock tombs which extend from the harbor to the island of Levkoniso, a quarter of an hour further to the west and in which ancient vessels, lamps, etc. have been found. I crawled into several of these tombs, which are laid out just like those at Ayios Mikhalos, near Akanthou.

The question arises whether the ancient city of Karpasia is to be identified with Aphentrika or with the ruins of Ayios Philon an hour further to the west. The latter has in its favor that it is nearer to today's Karpaso, which has kept the old name. Aphentrika, on the other hand, has in its favor that the ruins are more extensive and the level coastal strip wider. An objection to both locations is the epithet αἰπεινή [high, lofty], which Dionysius [Periegetes], as quoted by Stephen of Byzantium, applies to the city of

---

[289] Sakellarios, *Kypriaka,* I 160.

Καρπασία.[290] One might be tempted thus to accept the opinion of Pococke,[291] who believes to have found the ruins of the ancient city in the modern Rizokarpaso. Antiquities are found there, to be sure (I have seen some of them in a Cypro-Phoenician style), and there are many rock-tombs in the village itself. But Strabo[292] remarks that the width of the Isthmus from Karpasia to the southern sea is thirty stadia,[293] which suggests that Karpasia was located at the sea. In that case, perhaps, ἀπεινή means only that the city was located on a high tongue of land reaching into the sea. Both at Aphentrika and at Ayios Philon the coast is rather steep and almost vertically precipitous.

The old foundations continue from Aphentrika toward the east as far as a group of huts, where the fields of grain cease, while the mountains come quite close to the sea. At this point, called kipos [κῆπος] (garden), I saw to the right of the path, below a wall of rock, two large caves, which one can enter by doors cut in rectangular form. The interior of these caves shows many traces of having been worked by human hands, such as niches, steps, a circular air hole, etc. From there we crossed a ridge and descended on the other side into a gorge, which is called Korakas[294] and where some grain is grown. This gorge opens toward the sea, which we reached again two hours after we had left Aphentrika. Behind this ridge, which rises to a considerable height to the south of this gorge, the monastery of Ayios Andreas is located, as my guide declared. But, staying close to the coast, we continued in the direction of the furthest cape, which the people of Karpasia call Kastron.[295] The land turned more and more desolate and wild; in the woods, in which the low, crooked cypress prevails, we repeatedly saw goats and once also wild donkeys and horses roaming about.

From Korakas we could make only slow progress, since the shore at this point consists of bare rock, washed by the sea and full of holes like a sponge, so that the mules easily stumble here. Where the rock in its crevices holds a little soil, cypress trees are growing; these do not rise above the ground, but creep along like roots and send their many branches across the bare surface of the rock. These pitiful dwarf cypress trees were the second obstacle. Add to that the great heat, which brooded over this hole-riddled, rocky shore at a complete calm. Three quarters of an hour beyond Korakas we came to a small flat bay, which is called Kordilia and the sides of which drop vertically to the sea everywhere.[296] From there it was another hour to the cape, and there were no bays on this section of the rocky shore. The furthest tip of the cape is formed by an isolated high rock, which is impossible to climb, it seems, and is ideally suited to accommodate a fortress or a watch tower ['a' on Plate 31]. This rock is fittingly called the Kastron; there was once an ancient building there, no doubt. I climbed to the top and found there stone ruins. In one place someone, probably a treasure-hunting peasant, had been digging and had laid bare the foundations of old walls built of blocks of stone. Some of the stones were hollowed out like a trough. Also at the foot of the rock there are remains of ancient buildings, such as column fragments, a Doric capital, and squared stones.

---

[290] On Dionysius Periegetes see Müller, *Geogr. Gr. Minores*, II 102 ff. On Stephen of Byzantium see Sakellarios, *Kypriaka*, I 158.

[291] *SHC* V (1998) 35–56.

[292] Strab. 14.682.

[293] Reckoning the stadium at 200 m., this would be six km.

[294] κόρακας = raven or crow.

[295] Schröder must mean Cape Andreas.

[296] But Kordhilia now refers to a group of small islands three miles southwest of Cape Andreas.

Special attention is to be given to a shaft which is driven into the ground like a cellar and at a considerable angle; its interior is of solid masonry ['b']. Stairs hidden in the brush and hard to find (half filled-in; I could still count 10 steps) lead into it. The shaft is vaulted and about four feet wide; it can be followed for about thirty-five feet of its length, but then it is filled in. On the left wall, about mid-way, a niche has been cut out. The whole thing seems to be an old Phoenician tomb; further clearing it would surely lead to the discovery of chamber tombs. Also on a small outcropping of rock on the southeastern coast, to the south of the Kastron and separated from it by a narrow bay, I noticed old ruins: foundations of a stepped building, large square-cut blocks, and stone troughs ['c']. To the Kastron is joined on the northeast a bare rock, steeply and roughly rising from the sea and forming the furthest tip of the island ['d']. It seems to be joined to the mainland, but upon further inspection turns out to be an island; it is, however, separated from the Kastron only by a shallow ford four to five feet wide. At low tide this island can probably be reached dry-shod. Opposite Cape Andreas, which today is also called οὐρὰ τοῦ βοῦ (oxtail), there are the islands ['e, f, g'] which Strabo calls Κλεῖδες [Klidhes = keys];[297] the largest of these, which even has spring water, but is, of course, uninhabited, is today named Kastellatzo ['e']; the smaller island behind it ['g'] is called Platella on account of its low height. In addition to these two islands there are several smaller ones, which emerge from the shallow water as simple rocks and crags. Pliny [the Elder][298] counts four islands; he probably means, in addition to the two which I have mentioned, island ['d',] which lies very close to the Kastron as a continuation of the promontory, and the rock ['f']. [Plate 31]

From the Kastron I could clearly see the Syrian coast, in particular two far-stretched mountains; one of these, at 70–75° east of north, had to be the Jebel Musa [Musa Dag], the other one to the south the Gebel Akrad [Akra Dag], and the opening between them the mouth of the Orontes. Directly to the north the snow-covered Taurus mountains appeared very clearly. Behind me, to the southeast, one could follow both coasts of the peninsula; the northern one for only about an hour as far as the harbor of Kordilia, but the southern one, much more complex and precipitous everywhere, much further. The monastery of Ayios Andreas, gleaming-white and on a rocky promontory which drops vertically down to the sea, was clearly visible.

From the cape we had to ride another hour to reach the monastery, always along the southern coast, where the waves are breaking with deafening noise. I had spent too much time in Aphentrika and on the Kastro, so that we arrived at the monastery only at five o'clock in the afternoon and I thus was forced to stay overnight there, since Rizokarpaso is another four hours distant. The chapel of the apostle Andreas lies in ruins. In its place there is now a very handsome church, which was built only in 1865. Close to the church there are a few houses, which are occupied by the priest who performs the divine service and a few peasants who work the neighboring fields which belong to the monastery. Actually, Apostolos Andreas (not Ayios Andreas) is not a real monastery, but only a church.

IV. 183–86

---

[297] Strab. 14.682.
[298] Pliny *HN* 5.35.130.

The next morning we continued our journey to Rizokarpaso. One half hour beyond the monastery, in the bushes to the left of the path, there are the ruins of the utterly ruined chapel of Ayios Ioannis. Next, also on our left, we came to the bay of Pakhy Ammos [deep sand] (which the English navigational map has made into Pacramo Bay). This bay has been named so rightly, for it is surrounded by deep, yellow sand. Not too far from there, further inland, is the area of Makrou, which we passed. From there the track leads through fields, on which here and there some huts are scattered about. After another hour it crosses a saddle and then at the small bay of Almyrolakkas [? ἄλμυρος = salty; λάκκος = hole] approaches the sea. Continuing, it leads around the high mountain of Pyla, which descends to the like-named cape, and to the plain of Platia, which is planted in barley and has a few isolated, uninhabited summer huts. Next it leads through a narrow, rocky gorge (τὸ στένωμα τοῦ ἀγίου Νικολάου) to the shore, here forming a small harbor, which is named after the entirely ruined chapel of Ayios Nikolaos. Not far from here is the mouth of the river Emetias, on both sides of which there lies a small fertile plain with fields of grain, carob trees, and olive trees. Then we turned inland again, first into the valley already mentioned and then to the left into a gorge called Kusuli [?], steeply rising to the north; there are supposed to be many old tombs and rock chambers there, but I learned about them only after we had already passed the place. When we had reached the watershed we followed it for a few more minutes and then took a detour to the mountain of Rani [?], already mentioned and located to the south of us. From there we had a beautiful view of the southern coast and of Rizokarpaso, now only a quarter of an hour to the west-northwest. The northern sea can also be seen as a narrow strip beyond the village. From the place at which we left the old path in order to climb the mountain of Rani one has to travel for another quarter of an hour to Rizokarpaso; one climbs for a few more minutes until one reaches the high plateau on which right away one encounters the houses of Lekko. At eleven o'clock in the morning we arrived in the village.

There I spent the afternoon of this day (12 April) resting, since the travels of the last two days had very much tired me. Furthermore, there was a humid air and a hot wind from the east, with a thermometer reading of 23° [Réaumur]. I used the free time to visit a clean coffee shop and to collect little folk songs (τραγούδιαι) from the young peasant fellows. There were many congregated there this day, as it was a Saturday, and especially as it was the day before the feast of St. Lazarus (τὸ σάββατον τοῦ Λαζάρου), who is highly regarded in Cyprus. Here is a sample:

Below Rizokarpaso
there is flowing water.
He who bends down to drink of it
forgets Charon.

A cross with four edges
hangs around your neck.
All are kissing the cross
and I your face.

Ten royal physicians,
no matter how learned

cannot heal a heart
that is smitten by love.

He who has been burned by the coals of love
will never be healthy again,
and if the physicians heal him
there will always be an old wound.

There is a large number of rock tombs; some in the village of Rizokarpaso itself, some in the entire area of Ayios Philon, and others finally south of the village toward the harbor of Khelones near the area of Melissakros. Of the tombs in the village itself I visited some near the church of Ayios Synesios. These were natural caves, but with hewn walls and burial niches. These tombs and the antiquities which the people of Rizokarpaso occasionally unearth when tending their gardens or digging a well leave no doubt that on the site of today's Rizokarpaso there must have been an inhabited place already in antiquity. Perhaps this was Karpasia itself (αἰπεινή); if so, then its harbor perhaps was at Ayios Philon.[299]

The next day I was almost sorry to say good-bye to the principal village of the Karpasia peninsula, which is so original and almost completely cut off, and to its friendly and industrious inhabitants. I took the route to the southern sea in the direction of Galinoporni, which is three hours distant from Rizokarpaso. We rode for a quarter of an hour, gradually rising, through the well-tended fields and gardens of the village, until the view of the sea and of the highly structured hill country opened up. The hills are covered with wild bushes; here and there, amidst the green, the yellow-green planted fields, the Kampi, can be seen in the valleys. On our left, toward the sea, there is a valley called Villurgha [Villoures?], and above it to the west there is a high plateau covered with large fields of grain. Perikles' father, who accompanied us for an hour, called this the Kampos tis notias [κάμβος τῆς νοτιᾶς = field of the south wind].

Half an hour beyond Rizokarpaso the path descends into a valley enclosed by bush-covered hills; gradually this valley widens and opens up toward the sea. We followed it almost to the sea and then along the coast, changing our southwestern direction to a west-southwestern one. We were separated from the sea only by a row of hills, which here and there, where there are streams, allow a view of the sea. Our track led us steadily through fields; on our right there were higher hills, and on our left the hills at the shore. This small area used for agriculture can hardly be 300 to 500 feet wide, but widens toward Galinoporni. We reached this village in an hour and a half after we had come upon the sea; the Turks call it Kaleburnu (castle promontory). The distance from Rizokarpaso to Galinoporni is calculated at three hours (we took two and a half hours), and that from Galinoporni to the monastery of Ayios Andreas at six to seven hours, always along the coast. I was already familiar with Galinoporni from a previous visit. It is inhabited exclusively by Turks, and a traveler can tell already from far away that it is a Turkish village by its wretched and neglected loam houses, which are built onto the hill in terraces. The surrounding hills are barren and desolate, consisting of glaring white lime; the houses are not much different in color, which gives an even sadder appearance to the village. A little viticulture is practiced here, but no wine is produced. The village lay to the right of our

---

[299] The ancient city of Karpasia is now believed to have been a short distance north of Rizokarpaso, near the church of Ayios Philon.

path, and, unattractive as it looked, I still took the trouble to ride up to the wretched little place, hoping to find antiquities there. Unfortunately the peasant Mustapha Moro, in whose house I had seen antiquities already in 1870, was not at home.

I used the two-hour stay in the coffee shop to inspect the "Kale." This is what the inhabitants of the village call a man-made, extensive, subterranean structure which has been cut into the limestone on the east side of the ridge, on the western slope of the village, at a considerable elevation above the floor of the valley. The entrance to this "fox warren" is difficult to find and cannot be reached from below, since the wall of the valley rises almost vertically. A path leads from Galinoporni on the height to a spring at the end of the gorge; on its western wall the cave lies a few meters below the path. From this path I climbed down to the entrance of the cave, guided by an elderly Turk. (Across from it on the east side of the gorge, at the same elevation, there is the ruined church of Ayia Anna.) [Plate 32]

As far as its location is concerned, the cave reminded me vividly of the cave of Adullam in the Wadi Ortas [?] (where according to legend David hid when he fled from Saul).[300] But the interior is far different. It is a complex of several man-made galleries cut into the soft limestone, and having vaulted ceilings. The structure has three entrances, which one can reach only on a narrow path barely a foot wide. The main entrance in the middle leads to a corridor 22 m. long and about 4 m. wide. On both sides there are three side galleries eight paces long and less high than the main gallery. It remains unknown whether this whole structure was a fortified position or a tomb chamber. The absence of niches to accommodate sarcophagi argues against the latter possibility; I observed only a small niche (a) in the first side gallery on the left, which, however, is too small to accommodate a body. But in the back wall of the main gallery and in the second side gallery on the right I observed three depressions in the loose soil, which upon excavation would probably prove to be tomb caves; their length and width suggests this. At Elissu and Ayios Symeon there are supposed to be similar caves.


Böyükdere, 15 August 1873


I shall report only briefly about the further course of my travels, lest this letter become too long.

From Galinoporni I followed along the coast, reaching Komajalu [Koma tou Yialou] in four hours. Only unwillingly did my companions follow me, as they were determined to take the northern route by way of Elissou and Vathylakkas to Leonarisso (on the high plateau), a route which I already knew. On this route I did not come upon a single village; only one half hour after Galinoporni I saw on my right, on a height a quarter of an hour away, the village of Korovia. At the place where the stream coming from there empties into the sea our path led us directly to the coast. The latter is extraordinarily desolate; we met no one until we reached Komajalu, and it seems that all prefer the route over the heights. The mountains now come close to the sea and are covered with vegetation, while they are barren at Galinoporni and Korovia. Here and there a piece of arable

---

[300] The cave of Adullam is located 12 miles southwest of Bethlehem in the hill country of Judah. On David hiding there see 1 Samuel 22.1, 2 Samuel 23.13, and 1 Chronicles 11.15. Schröder apparently visited this cave while stationed in Constantinople.

land has been wrested from the narrow, rocky coastal strip ("Trachonen"), but only rarely. After a ride of an hour and a half we came to a place where the coastal strip widens a bit and a stream empties; the hills here retreat more, and between the bushes which cover them entire stretches are planted with grain. These fields belong to the small village of Neta, which itself was not visible. Here, at the mouth of the stream, under some carob trees, we rested for an hour. On the rocks, densely covered with bushes, on the right bank of the stream, there is a ruined chapel of St. George, and all around it there are old ruins: large and small stone rubble, troughs, many sherds, and old foundations, all wildly mixed together, as if the place that once was here had been violently destroyed. Its name now is Selena. In vain I searched for inscriptions, capitals of columns, and architectural fragments with ornaments. In the vicinity there are several large caves. I suspect that the old pots and pitchers which the peasants of Neta claimed to have found in the caves at the sea, as I was told in 1870 at Vathylakkas, came from this site.

The coast, consisting of firm rock, also showed further traces of an earlier settlement in this now so desolate area. For some distance rows of regularly fitted stones cropped up from the ground, which was covered with brushwood and low trees, parallel to the sea; presumably there were once walls here to protect the fields and to break the waves. I also saw along the track round cisterns cut into the rock. About one and a half hours west of Selena a second stream empties, and on the far side of it there stands the ruined chapel of Ayia. Here the rocky ground everywhere shows signs of having been worked by human hands: entire rectangles are cut out in depth, high vertical walls with stairs have been created, and the walls show, in regular rows, holes and niches and the like, just as at Lapithos, Trikomo, and other places. Near the chapel I discovered several natural caves of huge dimensions, which also on the inside and on the outer wall next to the entrance showed many traces of human activity. In one of these caves niches had been cut out in the back, and the ceiling at certain intervals was supported by rough pillars. This cave seemed to be very large; equipped with a light, I ventured about sixty feet into it. It widened further on the inside, but I did not want to expose myself to the risk of losing my way in the cave, and therefore turned back, especially since I could have advanced further only bent over. It would be interesting if in these caves the loose dirt were examined in order to determine whether they were inhabited by human beings as early as in prehistorical times. Three-fourths of an hour further, a quarter of an hour from Komajalu, to the left of the track, there is a site on which I observed, among the squared-off stones, sherds, fired tiles, and the like, also several very large Corinthian capitals. This place is called Ayia Softia [Sophia?].

In Komajalu we stayed overnight. The village is all-Christian and boasts a large handsome church with a high bell tower. There is a large number of chapels, some of them ruined, in and around the village: Ayios Georgios, Ayios Nikolaos, Ayia Solomoni, and Panayia. Nearly all of them are built of ancient materials, and this leads to the conclusion that Komajalu was an important location in the Middle Ages. Among the ruins of the church of St. George I found a Corinthian capital, several column shafts, and a piece of a frieze, all of sandstone. The village is ten to fifteen minutes distant from the sea, at the foot of the "Trachonen" or of the banks of rock which extend on this entire stretch in greater or smaller distance from the sea.

From Komajalu we traveled in one and three fourths hour to Ayios Theodoros, taking the shorter and more comfortable northern route by way of Tavros. Two thirds of the inhabitants of Ayios Theodoros are Turks, and altogether there are about sixty families. From here, and especially from the ridge above the village to the south, one has a good view of the plain of Komi Kebir, and I used it to take numerous compass readings. To travel from Ayios Theodoros to Trikomo, today's (14 April) goal, I chose the route by way of Patriki, Avgalidha (a hamlet with three Turkish families and one Greek family), and Ayios Elias (with forty houses), because I already knew the road by way of Kamares along the coast. From the latter village we rode to Trikomo in one hour across land uncultivated and covered with low bushes, especially small cypress trees ("Trachonenland"). Trikomo is situated right on the border between the uncultivated area and the arable land. It is a village numbering about 150 Greek families but only two Turkish houses; it has many ruined Byzantine churches and several large "chiftliks."[301]

I took lodging with an Englishman whom I already knew, Mr. Philipp M., who is known in Cyprus as Signore Philippos. The latter introduced into Cyprus a number of steam engines for the cleaning of cotton, and these are operated under his supervision in Trikomo. (Cotton is grown in the Mesaoria, especially at Ayios Sergios and at Trikomo.) Since the cotton crop this year had been very poor, some of the engines were used to mill grain.

To the southwest, toward the sea, twenty minutes from the village, there are old rock tombs and nearby the so-called λατῶμαι (quarries), i.e. old rock works similar to the ones at Selena between Komajalu and Galinoporni. I am not sure of their purpose. In any event they were not simply quarries; the vertical walls, as if cut with a spade, the right angles, the man-made niches, and the steps left standing all argue against that.

From Trikomo a straight track leads in a southwestern direction to Levkoniko. On the way, across cultivated land, we passed after one half hour by Syngrasis, a village of fifty to sixty houses, half of them Turkish, where I found antiquities. Another half hour took us past Lapithos, a small and poor village on rocky land, and a further three-quarters of an hour to the prosperous Christian village of Gypsos. From there to Levkoniko took one more hour. The first two of these villages are off to the left of the track and need not be entered, while the road leads directly through Gypsos.

From Levkoniko I returned, heading pretty much south, straight-way to Larnaca, by way of Yenagra (three quarters of an hour), Vatili (an hour and a half), Tremetousha [Tremithus] (one hour), Troulli, and Kellia. From the first three of these places I fixed the location of the surrounding villages. The shortest route from Vatili to Larnaca goes by way of Arsos, Troulli, and Kellia, leaving Tremetousha on the right. The peasants, however, mostly prefer a somewhat longer, but more comfortable route (ἀνοικτὸς δρόμος; i.e. less hilly) by way of Lysi, Pergamos, and Pyla.

From Arsos I turned east to nearby Tremetousha in order to inspect the excavations recently undertaken there and the ancient finds. The latter surpassed my expectations; a whole necropolis had been laid bare west of the village toward Athienou. The tomb chambers are cut into the ground, which is hard as stone, but there is no rock here. Most of the antiquities found here, such as reliefs, lamps, small gold objects, and especially many items of glass ware, had been sold to Mr. Zeno Pierides of Larnaca.[302] Nev-

---

[301] A 'chiftlik' is a large farm.

[302] Zeno Pierides (1839–1911) was a prominent businessman and citizen of Larnaca, the son of Demetrios Pierides (1811–1895), who first started collecting antiquities. The Pierides Collection, now more formally known as the Pierides Foundation Museum, is maintained in Larnaca to this day. See *Cyprus Today* 34:1,2 (Jan.–June 1996).

ertheless I saw still in place several large reliefs. There was one, one and a half m. high, in the form of a stele, which showed a person standing upright, in rich garments and holding the reins of a horse. The art work was of Greek style, but the proportions were not always correct. I also found many sarcophagi and steles with short Greek inscriptions.

Tremetousha (the Turks say Trementesché) was one of the foremost cities of Cyprus in antiquity and in Byzantine times. Of terebinth trees, from which it derives its name, I did not see a single one. Under the Byzantines it was a bishop's see, held by St. Spyridon.[303] The town was destroyed in 1191 by Richard the Lionheart, who here defeated the Greek army.[304] The poor village, two thirds Turkish and one third Greek, which now stands here is built completely from the ruins of the old city. The whole area is littered with stones, and from their mass one can draw conclusions as to the former significance of the city. The necropolis extends to the west from the village, and only its smallest part has been uncovered. The peasants had to give up their excavations because of a prohibition by the Pasha. Most likely the whole area between Tremetousha and Athienou, one and a half hours away, is full of tombs, and it would be worth the effort to undertake here larger systematic excavations, which surely would yield rich results.[305] Although the inscriptions found on the steles are Greek, the sculptures still show the peculiar Cypriot style, modified by Greek influence. Of the heads found here some were entirely in the Greek style, while others were in the Cypriot style: prominent cheekbones, a pointed, smiling mouth, slanted Oriental eyes, and Eastern headdress.[306]

From the roof of the monastery of St. Spyridon, now uninhabited, I fixed the location of the nearest villages. The four neighboring villages of Melousha, Tremitousha, Arsos, and Troulli (τροῦλλοι = hills) [τροῦλλος = dome, cupola] are renowned for their honey. Directly south of Tremitousha, where I stayed overnight, the terrain rises to the limestone hills which separates the coastal plain of Larnaca from the Mesaoria. We ascended the next morning. On our right, in a valley, there are old quarries (λατομεῖα) with a spring, which emerges from a shaft driven into the rock (τὸ ἁγίασμα τοῦ ἁγίου Σπυρίδωνος). Then we came to a small plain planted in grain; at its southern end, between hills and separated from it by the narrow pass of Klisoura [?], lies Troulli. Behind the village the track rises again, until the sea appears in the south, and then continues through the barren and vegetation-less limestone hills. Finally it leads down to a river bottom, called Armyri [Almyros], and to Kellia. Not far from there I made a squeeze of a Phoenician inscription built into the wall of the church of Ayios Antonios. From there it was a fast one-hour ride through Livadhia to Larnaca.

---

[303] St. Spyridon, highly regarded in Cyprus and on the Ionian islands, in all likelihood attended the Council of Nicaea in 325 and certainly the Council of Serdica in 343. His relics are venerated in the Church of St. Spyridon in Corfu.

[304] More specifically the army of Isaac Komnenos.

[305] Excavations at Athienou were undertaken in 1862 and 1865 by the French archaeologists Melchior de Vogue, William Waddington, and Edmond Dutholt, between 1866 and 1873 by Cesnola, between 1969 and 1973 by Prof. Georgios Bakalakis of the University of Thessaloniki, and in 1971 and 1972 by the Israeli archaeologists Trude Dotham and Amnon Ben-Tor. Since 1990 a major archaeological project has been going there under the direction of Prof. Michael Toumazou of Davidson College. The finds have been so rich that a site museum is under construction.

[306] These features can be observed in the large statues from Athienou now in the Metropolitan Museum. Some finds from Athienou are in the Louvre.

# Seiff—1872

Julius Seiff, *Skizze einer Reise durch die Insel Cypern* (Dresden, 1874) 71 and 76–102. Originally a lecture given on 3 January 1873 at a session of the Verein für Erdkunde zu Dresden. Seiff offers a somewhat expanded account in his *Reisen in der asiatischen Turkei* (533 pp., Leipzig, 1875) 76–132. Seiff was a civil engineer by profession. He died ca.1876 at Adana in Cilicia. His name is given in the membership list of the *Verein für Erdkunde zu Dresden, Jahresberichte, 4–14* (1868–1877).

On 11 January of last year, at a time of rather rough winter weather, I embarked at Constantinople on the steamer Apollo of the Austrian Lloyd for the voyage to the island of Cyprus . . .

With Rhodes land gradually disappeared from view. For about 18 to 20 hours we were surrounded by the open sea; then the high, jagged, rocky mountains of Cyprus emerged from the blue sea to the south of us. The ship quickly approached the island, steamed around it on the west side, and cast anchor on the wharf of Larnaca. When I came on deck soon after sunrise, I was greatly surprised and disappointed by the view which offered itself to me. What I saw in front of me corresponded not at all to the image which my imagination had developed of this island, of the lovely shores on which, according to the myth, the goddess of love supposedly rose from the foam of the sea, and which in antiquity was so renowned for its fertility.

Along the flat and bare coast, close to the sea, almost washed by its waves, the irregular mass of the houses of the so-called marina stretches out, while the city of Larnaca as such lies another fifteen minutes inland. No shade-giving tree, no green bush delights the eye; only in the western, Turk-inhabited part of the city do the sorry-looking fronds of a few date palms rise above the flat roofs, and even these suggest that they are intruders from abroad. The area immediately surrounding the marina and the city is essentially flat and bare, although not infertile. A little further into the distance low hills, also bare, limit the view. Only to the west is the view given some charm by the lofty and precipitous cone of Monte Croce, the peak of which is crowned by a monastery [Stavrovouni], and by some other spurs of the island's main western range of mountains, the sight of which was rendered impossible by clouds.

Being the only European going ashore here, I first had to endure a four-day confinement in the quarantine hospital before I was allowed to move freely about the island.[307] The institution of these Turkish quarantine stations is truly outrageous and wholly suited to make even the strongest person sick within a few days. Although the one in Cyprus counts among the better ones I was absolutely stunned when I was led by the official on duty into this wretched prison. It is situated far from the city, close to the shore, and consists of a courtyard surrounded by a high wall and overgrown with wild underwood and weeds of every kind. The courtyard contains two long, one-story buildings with overhanging roofs and consisting of some twenty chambers, more like stables and paved with slabs of stone. One of these was assigned to me as my abode and I was informed that I had to pay 125 piaster for its use if I desired single occupancy. The floor was covered with the most awful debris. When, at my request, it had been cleaned at least

---

[307] Seiff had previously explained that there had been an eruption of the cholera in Constantinople.

superficially, the coarse Greek supervisor, to whom daily I had to pay backschisch, brought a few boards for my bed and the splendid furnishings of the otherwise completely empty room were complete. When I asked for at least a mattress I was told that such would have to be brought to me by my friends in the city; I had none, of course.

Arrangements for feeding the inmates also were totally inadequate. Warm food was not to be had; bread, cheese, and fruit only could be bought at a barred window. Finally, having fasted for a long time, I spoke to the inspector; he was the only one who could speak French, but I had to keep a distance of at least six feet from him. From him I obtained a pot and some eggs, and some of these I then had to cook myself daily for my meal, with the help of the supervisor.

A pair of Turkish mullahs, an officer with his servants, and a number of Greek sailors shared my sufferings. The former, far better equipped for such a stay, took pity on me and daily supplied me with coffee, but repeatedly became a nuisance because of their probing curiosity and disturbed my sleep at night by chanting their prayers. The latter, a rather rough lot, also showed themselves as friendly and helpful towards me and did much to while away the long hours by their cheerful gymnastic games, in which they displayed admirable strength and cleverness.

When the gates of this model health facility finally opened, I called upon the Italian consul, Signor [Riccardo] Colucci, who is at the same time consul of the German Reich. In his house I found the most hospitable and kind reception and also the friendliest advice and the most energetic support with the preparations for my travels through the island.

By area, which Unger and Petermann calculate at 273 [German] square miles, Cyprus is the fourth-largest island of the Mediterranean.[308] It lies below the 35th degree of northern latitude. The longest distance from northeast to southwest, from Cape Andreas to the coast at Paphos, measures 30¼ [German] miles,[309] according to Unger.

The greater part of the island is mountainous, especially the southwestern part, which is occupied by the mighty ridges and summits of the Troodos. Makheras, Adelphos,[310] and Monte Croce [Stavrovouni] are spurs of it; they in turn send lower spurs far to the east, as far as the area of Larnaca. The highest peak of this range of mountains is the so-called Cyprian Olympus; it is rather densely forested and covered by snow during the winter months; Unger determined its height to be 1915 m.[311] In height, massiveness, and extent this range of mountains considerably surpasses the other range, which is completely separate and stretches from Cape Kormakiti along the whole northern coast to Cape Andreas. This latter range gradually descends to low hills on the long Karpas peninsula; being less wide, it drops off rather precipitously both toward the sea and toward the Mesaoria; it offers mostly naked and jagged cliffs, and only occasionally in the more remote places do a few trees provide some cover. Numerous villages and hamlets, surrounded by luscious vegetation, are situated on the lower slopes and at the foot of the range on small streams. These streams run down to the plain mostly in narrow and steep

---

[308] Unger, *Cypern,* 4, apparently by misprint, gives a figure of 173 [German] square miles. 273 German square miles = 3572 statute square miles. Cyprus is actually the third-largest of the Mediterranean islands, after Sicily and Sardinia.
[309] Ca. 140 statute miles.
[310] See Sakellarios, *Kypriaka,* I 15.
[311] Other authors give 1952 m. or 6404 ft.

gorges, between precipitous walls of rock, and then some flow into the Pedieos, while others run out, consumed by irrigation and evaporation.

Between the spurs of the Troodos and these coastal mountains to the north the plain of Mesaoria, broken only by minor unevenness, stretches all the way to the coast. It is fertile, but only in part under cultivation. In its entire length it is crossed by the Pedieos, which comes down from the western mountains, in its course is joined by the Yialias, and finally, between Famagusta and the ruins of Salamis, empties into the sea through several flat estuaries.

According to Strabo (14.684), Eratosthenes has this to say about this plain: "In times past it was so densely forested that because of all the woods the cultivation of fields was not possible. Mining provided some relief from this undesirable condition, since trees were cut for use in smelting copper and silver; also trees were used to build ships for the fleet. Nevertheless the inhabitants did not master the woods, and therefore all who were willing and able were permitted to cut trees and to take possession of the cleared land as tax-free property."[312]

At the present time hardly a single tree can be seen, except near the villages, and, while in the past the whole plain probably was plowed land, the greater part of it is now covered with steppe-like pasture. The latter is covered with fresh green in the winter and spring and provides welcome fodder to the herds of sheep and goats. This is especially true of the southern somewhat higher part of the plain, which, however, judging by the condition of the soil, appears to be less fertile. Nevertheless this part, too, in one way or another, could be exploited for agriculture, if it were not for a lack of the necessary manpower and, where manpower is found, the lack of means, industry, and willingness to work. The lack of the latter may well be the consequence of two factors. One is the tax burden which an uncaring despotic government has for centuries imposed on agriculture and trade without doing the least to support and develop them. The other is the frequent crop failures, which are caused sometimes by an unusual drought and sometimes by the terrible devastation brought on by the locusts.

People repeatedly lamented the steadily worsening drought conditions. These are to be blamed primarily on the foolish waste of the forests, which continues in the mountains even now in truly barbaric fashion. Although there are frequent and long rains in the winter, still the heat of the sun dries up the unprotected soil again too quickly. And the small amount of water which flows down from the mountains in the rivers and streams is barely enough to irrigate the fields located at their foot. During the hot season it rarely or never reaches the coast, so that at the lower elevations of the island the complaint about lack of water is very common. The present Turkish governor believed that he could alleviate the condition by drilling artesian wells and asked me to list places which I thought most suitable for this purpose. But when I declined this and offered the opinion that the intended purpose might be better met by taking care of the woods in the mountains and by planting utility trees, at the proper interval, in the fields, as is the practice in Italy and Spain, he informed me that he already had issued the typically Turkish order that every male inhabitant of the island was, within a year, to plant at least one tree. An order which is not likely to have the desired effect. The main products of the island for export are: wine, St. John's bread [the fruit of the carob tree], madder [a red dye], which is especially

---

[312] For a more accurate text see the Loeb edition by Horace Leonard Jones, or Cobham, *Excerpta*, 3, or *SHC* I (1990) 131.

desirable, some silk, wool, and cotton, as well as sheep, and goat skins; raisins, cheese, brandy, pitch, and tar are exported only in small amounts.

Since the Turkish conquest of the island, once so flourishing and much-desired, its prosperity and accordingly the population have steadily declined, so that the latter now reportedly hardly numbers 100,000 people, the greater part of whom belong to the Greek church. Armenian and Roman Catholic Christians are a small minority, and even the Turkish element is, apart from a few locations, poorly represented. To the extent that I had contact with the inhabitants I always found them friendly, well behaved, and pleasant, in the cities as well as in the country. Their way of life, like the style of their houses, is in general extremely simple and in the country even poor, and cleanliness leaves much to be desired. Since there are no inns anywhere, not even in the cities, a traveler is totally dependent on hospitality, and this is always readily, sometimes indeed amiably, offered.

For transportation people use mules, which are bred on the island, can be rented for a very low price, and are ideally suited for riding, especially on the sometimes dangerous paths in the mountains. For three of them I paid the mucker,[313] who also was a very attentive servant, daily 25 piaster or one Thaler and twenty Neugroschen.[314] It is the local practice, however, not to put saddles on the mules, as is our practice, but pillows, blankets, and bags, on which the rider sits rather uncomfortably, balancing his feet in a pair of loosely suspended stirrups.

There are few horses on the island, and these are small of stature, not much to look upon, and far inferior to those of the Asiatic mainland. Camels are used, as elsewhere, for the transport of freight, especially in the eastern, more level part of the island. Cows are also small and seem to be kept only for plowing; at least for household use goats' milk is used almost exclusively. As for sheep, which populate together with the goats the extensive pasture lands, I heard much praise for their wool, and their meat, along with chicken and goats, is the only one normally eaten.

The city of Larnaca, which I made the base of my excursions through the island, stands on the site of the ancient Kition [Citium], a settlement of the Hivites[315] and the birthplace of Zeno, the founder of Stoicism. It is supposed to have 5000 to 6000 inhabitants, but is rather lifeless and, given its bare surroundings, without charm. Its commerce, most notably the export of the products of the eastern part of the island, is concentrated in the marina. This is also the seat of most of the European consulates, and its bazaars, in part covered with mats, hold European manufactured goods of all kinds. Of the public buildings only one deserves attention, namely the Greek Church of St. Lazarus, more old than beautiful and dating from the 10th or 11th century.

At some distance to the south of the city there is a large salt lake, which is close to the sea, but not connected with it. On its banks considerable quantities of cooking salt are gained and piled up in mighty pyramids, being yet another article for export. The salt has a good taste, but is rather coarse and dirty grey in color.

---

[313] "Mucker" seems to be a corruption of Turkish "mucir" = one who hires himself out. Professor Kemal Çiçek of the Turkish Historical Society, Ankara, kindly confirmed that on Cyprus there were people called "mucir" who guided travelers for pay.

[314] 30 Neugroschen, at 10 Pfennig each, made one Thaler.

[315] Seiff cites Max Duncker, *Geschichte des Alterthums* (Berlin, 1855–1857) IV 498–99. The Hivites (German "Cheviter" or "Hiwiter) were a Canaanite tribe in Palestine and are repeatedly mentioned in the Old Testament.

On the way from the marina to this salt lake one passes a strange, partly underground building which is known as Phaneromene and is supposed to have served once as a chapel. It is an old Phoenician tomb, according to Ross,[316] and consists of a completely destroyed antechamber and two chambers. These are formed of Cyclopean sandstone boulders, on which rests, for a ceiling, a similarly huge flat boulder, also of sandstone and its bottom surface carved out like a vault.

Numerous other tombs of a later period and stone sarcophagi containing vessels of glass and terra cotta have been excavated in the area surrounding the city. Similar excavations have been undertaken especially by the English consul, Mr. Lang,[317] and the American consul, Mr. Cesnola,[318] at various places on the island on a larger scale and with great success. Both of these gentlemen own very valuable collections of statuettes, jewelry, and vessels of glass and terra cotta, although they have already passed the more significant finds on to various European museums. The German [and Italian] consul, Signor [Riccardo] Colucci, also has undertaken several successful excavations in the area of Larnaca.

My first excursion into the interior of the island was to its eastern part and its capital Nicosia or Lefkosia. We left Larnaca in nearly a northeasterly direction, passed first through flat, fertile, and largely cultivated terrain, and then, after a ride of about three quarters of an hour, reached a chain of low, bare hills which consist in part of volcanic rock. Between the naked, rocky cliffs of these hills the way gradually rose to a plateau, along the banks of a flat stream, low in water. On this plain we passed some vineyards and after about three hours reached the fairly large village of Athienou, where a steady and hard rain forced us to make a stop. The population of this village is entirely Christian, and in the midst of the unimpressive, box-like houses, in the walls of which one frequently finds imbedded fragments of ancient sculptures and ornaments, rises a quite attractive church. Here, too, nearby, Mr. Lang reportedly found some larger statues and the traces of a temple.

We continued next morning in a nearly westerly direction, accompanied by bright sunshine and fanned by true spring breezes. The narrow and muddy path wound at first between well-kept fields and then took us behind the village of Petrophani, which we left on our left, to level pasture land covered with dry brushwood. Half an hour south of the village of Pyroi the path crossed the highway which is to connect Larnaca with Nicosia but is not yet finished. Soon it took us across the deep-cut bed of a stream, on the other side of which we rode past the village of Ayios Sozomenos, which lies at the foot of steep hills and is surrounded by extensive olive groves. Then the path descended to an almost swampy but very fertile valley, which turned more and more pleasant the further we got into it. A narrow stream, shaded by dense bushes entangled with climbing plants but unfortunately still without foliage, wound its way, providing nourishment, between the neatly plowed fields, in which the seeds already began to sprout. All manner of trees—olive, carob, orange, lemon, and mulberry—surrounded in irregular, picturesque groups a large estate and were turning green in the gardens of the village of Potamia, which we soon reached. But in the background the imposing, beautifully formed mass of Mt. Makheras rose up, in misty colors, glaring steep and harsh behind its more gently formed

---

[316] Ludwig Ross in (Gerhard's) *Archäologische Zeitung* 9 (1851) 322.
[317] Robert Hamilton Lang, author of *Cyprus: Its History, Its Present Resources and Future Prospects* (London, 1878).
[318] Luigi Palma di Cesnola, notorious plunderer of Cypriot antiquities.

spurs. In the village just mentioned we met in several houses groups of women who were spinning cotton with very simple hand-spindles.

Following the pleasant, lovely valley we finally reached Dhali, a village located on the Yialias River, at about noon. It has a mixed population and therefore both a church and a mosque. Pleasant gardens, in which slender date palms gently move their graceful fronds above shady fruit trees, blend in with the houses, the exterior of which suggests a certain prosperity. Twenty-five to thirty minutes to the southwest of the village, on the slope of rocky hills, lie the ruins of ancient Idalion, which once also included a sanctuary of Aphrodite. In the extensive excavations of Mr. Lang and Mr. Cesnola numerous tombs, the foundations of a temple, as well as statues and statuettes were found here.

Leaving Dhali in a northeasterly direction, we first crossed the river, which was low, but at this time carrying a fair amount of water. On the other side of it we passed along strangely formed, steeply precipitous hills, which leave the impression of being the ruins of a former plateau, their long, perfectly straight ridges lying with such regularity on the same horizontal level. Soon turning more towards the north, we came to a totally desolate valley which is formed by these hills. Its naked faces, consisting of a horizontally stratified conglomerate mass, seem to be broken in some places by volcanic rock.

The closer we got to the Mesaoria, the lower the hills became, and at about three o'clock in the afternoon we had our first glimpse of Nicosia. It is situated in the plain, and the jagged, rocky ridges of the northern coastal range tower above it. With its old fortifications, lofty Gothic churches, slender minarets, and the numerous palm trees, which rise singly and in groups above the confusing mass of houses, it offers a unique and fascinating appearance. At about five o'clock in the evening we entered the city. Just before that we passed a small village of lepers, the unfortunate inhabitants of which are not allowed to enter the city but loiter around the gates, begging and presenting a horrifying sight with their crippled limbs.

Guido [Guy], the first king of the Lusignan dynasty, invested by Richard the Lionheart with the crown of Cyprus in 1192, already had made Nicosia the capital of the island and his residence; his successors fortified it. But the walls still extant today are the work of the Venetians. These had obtained the island in 1489 from Catharine Cornaro, a native of Venice and the widow of James II [1460–1473], the natural son of John II [1432–1458] and last king of Cyprus. When the island had been in the possession of the Venetians for 83 years Nicosia was attacked in 1570 by the Turks under Sultan Selim I; it was stormed, after a siege of almost two months, on 8 September, plundered and laid waste. On this occasion supposedly 15,000 residents, not counting the garrison, were massacred.[319] Since that time it has been uninterruptedly in the possession of Turkey and has declined to its present level of insignificance, although it is still the capital of the island and the residence of the Turkish governor as well as of the Greek archbishop, who bears the peculiar title of "Most Blessed" [μακαριώτατος].

The interior of the city in no way corresponds to the favorable impression which it makes when seen from the distance. Narrow, twisting streets, lined with massive but plain, unattractive houses, wind aimlessly hither and thither, everywhere showing dirt and neglect. Only in the rather extensive bazaars is there much life, and here, in addition to European goods of every kind, local embroideries of gold and silk are offered for sale.

---

[319] Even higher, but unreliable figures are given in other sources; see Hill, *History*, III 984, n. 3.

Of the few monumental buildings which have survived the destruction of the city the beautiful Gothic churches, now converted to mosques, are the most noteworthy, and especially the former Cathedral of St. Sophia, in which the kings of Cyprus were crowned, merits a visit. The archbishop himself, in whose so-called palace I had been hospitably received, did me the honor, together with the bishop of Larnaca, who happened to be present, to accompany me there, preceded by two aides and with a large entourage, since Christians are not permitted to enter without special permission. Although much disfigured by the Turks and left to deterioration, the large, empty space makes a lasting impression by its beautiful proportions. The Emerghé [Omeriyeh] Mosque, considerably older, is also a former church [St. Mary of the Augustinians], but was built in a much simpler and less decorative Gothic style.

From Nicosia I turned towards the eastern coast, crossing the Mesaoria in its entire length and in an almost southeasterly direction (150°). At about eight o'clock in the morning we rode out through the dark gate of the fortress onto the green, sun-lit plain. We kept the rocky coastal mountains, lying in the distance, on our left, and they more and more disappeared in a bluish mist. Only for a short distance after leaving the city did we find the soil under cultivation; after that the uneven path took us across wild, steppe-like pasture land; here sheep and goats found ample food on the fresh green, which was sprouting up among the dry stalks of last year's vegetation. The lower part of the plain, specifically the part between the Pedieos and the mountains, appeared to be under cultivation for the most part, and now and then people were still busy plowing. Everywhere on the island people still cultivate the fields in the same way that they have received from their forebears, just as on the Asian mainland. There is no manuring at all, since the necessary cattle are lacking; the fields are merely allowed to lie fallow on a rotating basis. The plow which is used consists of little more than a trunk grown or shaped to an appropriately pointed angle; the draught animals are hitched to the longer part, while the lower part, shod with iron, breaks up the ground barely hand-deep. Among cereal crops wheat and barley are preferred.

We left the village of Aglanzia,[320] about twenty minutes away, on our right and, after riding for one hour and fifteen minutes, reached the other Rei-Kiu [?]. Another one and three quarter hour after that, near an estate surrounded by flourishing gardens and groves of trees, we reached the Yialias River, which here flows in a northeasterly direction towards the Pedieos. At fifteen minutes after eleven we rode through the Turkish village of Ornithi and fifteen minutes after that through Apanthia [Aphania], which, with its miserable mud huts and without the shade of a single tree, lies rather naked and hopeless looking on the dry plain. After the large Greek village of Asia [Asha], which we reached at noon, we followed a more easterly direction (120°). This took us in one and a quarter hour to the appealing village of Vattili [Vatili], the houses of which—some unusually clean—surround a pretty church with a stately tower.

Beginning with Asha we had again traveled through cultivated land, and now, after a further one and three quarter hour, we passed extensive cotton fields and a few minutes later the small village of Kouklia. Here there is the beautiful estate of a Mr. Montrovani, with its carefully kept and watered gardens and plantations, which show what can be achieved in this soil and with this climate by rational management. Having passed the last-mentioned village I noticed repeatedly by the side of the way, not too close one to the

---

[320] Also Aglangia, Glangia, or Eylenje.

other, short ditches, which, I was told, are meant to catch the locusts. These greedy pests, which so often cheat the farmer out of the fruit of his labor, usually make their annual migration in a tightly closed column, always approaching in the same direction. Thus these ditches are dug, perpendicular to that direction and in the width of the column, and canvas screens are put up behind them. The low-flying pests bump into the canvas screens, fall into the ditches, and there can be killed.

About half an hour past Kouklia we passed though low, almost completely bare hills, which gradually opened up into a small valley containing the poor village of Calopsida [Kalopsidha]. A very difficult ride across low-lying, swampy ground took us from here to the village of Ascheritou [Akhyritou], which is situated on a height and which we reached at sunset. We were most hospitably received by the Italian consular agent who resides here, although our coming seemed to cause considerable disturbance in the somewhat modest household. Simple patriarchic customs surrounded us here. We had barely entered the house, when an old servant woman came with a basin of coals, to fumigate the guests from all sides, as a sign of welcome, and then, together with her master, to provide for their comfort and nourishment. Our host seemed to own considerable land, judging by the draught animals which filled his yard and his stables; also towards evening large herds of sheep and goats came and settled down near the house.

Next morning we left at a good hour, again passed through a low-lying swamp, and came, about one hour away, to the double village of Varosia [Varosha], which lies directly before the gates of Famagusta. This village owns extensive orchards as well as good-size potteries. The vessels produced there show even today almost the same forms as the ancient ones which are so frequently found on the island.

Famagusta was fortified already by Henry II of the Lusignan dynasty, who reigned from 1286 to 1324, and was for a long time one of the most important Christian trading places in the Orient; and here the kings of Cyprus had themselves crowned kings of Jerusalem until the fortress was conquered by the Genoese. At one such coronation [on 3 October 1372], namely that of Peter II, still a minor, whose uncle [John, Prince of Antioch], acted as regent, a dispute over ranking between the resident Venetians and Genoese led to a bloodbath. Consequently on 3 October 1373 a Genoese fleet appeared before the fortress and was able to seize it already on 10 October, thanks to the treason committed by the king's mother [Eleanor of Aquitaine], who was taking her revenge on the regent. Only James II [1460–1473], the last king of Cyprus, succeeded to regain this important place. In the year 1487 Famagusta, along with the rest of the island, came into the possession of the Venetians; they, in turn, were besieged by the Turks and, under their brave commander [Marcantonio] Bragadino, were forced to capitulate on 1 August 1571.

The works of fortification are still in a good state of preservation, but the interior, although it is the see of a Kaimakam [district administrator], is little more than a large field of ruins; it is inhabited by a couple of hundred Turks, including the garrison, whose miserable huts look incongruous next to the unusually large number of ruined Gothic churches and palaces. The beautiful cathedral of St. Sophia, in which the just-mentioned coronations took place, has also been converted into a mosque.

Salamis was once the capital of the most powerful one of the nine small kingdoms in which the island was divided when the Egyptian king Amasis conquered it in 550 B.C.[321] The ruins of this ancient city lie about two hours north of Famagusta, lonely and

---

[321] Actually in 569 B.C.

deserted, next to the sea and occupying several hills, beyond the low wetlands of the Pedieos, which one crosses, like the river itself, on a peculiar old bridge. The foundation of the city is attributed to Teucer, son of Telamon,[322] who landed here after the end of the Trojan War, when his father banished him for having failed to avenge the death of his brother Ajax on Odysseus. In the days of Roman rule the city was destroyed by an earthquake, rebuilt by the successors of Constantine the Great, and named Constantia in his honor.[323] In 647 finally the city was conquered by Muawijah, the general of the caliph Otman, and completely destroyed for the second time.

At present only formless rubble, lying chaotically scattered about wild brush, covers the wide area. The traces of the former city wall, however, can be recognized, also the remnants of a large reservoir, which measured 70 x 20 paces and seems to have been covered; a long aqueduct, of which numerous piers and even some arches still stand upright, brought the water here from the distant mountains.[324]

To the west of these ruins, in the middle of a field, there is a Cyclopean structure similar to the one at Larnaca, also half underground, but consisting of only two chambers. The inhabitants of this area call this the prison of St. Catherine; Ross believes both to be Phoenician tombs. In the immediate vicinity excavations laid bare an underground canal, and at the same time a statue without a head was found. A little further to the west, on a low rise, all by itself, stands the church of St. Barnabas, the patron saint of the island, who in the days of the emperor Caligula [37–41] came to Cyprus with the Apostle Paul to preach the Christian Gospel.

From Varosha I returned directly to Larnaca, traveling in an almost southeasterly[325] direction and crossing a wide, wild plateau. This plateau begins right after the village of Dherima, about twenty minutes from Varosha, and is completely uncultivated and uninhabited; rising slightly towards the southern coast it finally drops off precipitously. We were riding for almost two hours before we sighted a couple of villages on our right. After one further hour we reached some low hills; between these, past the village of Ormidhia, which is located in a narrow valley, the path gradually descends towards the coast. Following the coast, we reached Larnaca after a ride of six and a half hours, first having passed the villages of Bilati and Varoklini in some distance; both of these are situated at the foot of bare hills, which surround the bay but towards Larnaca gradually recede from the coast.

After a short rest I started out again, this time to visit the western and scenically most beautiful part of the island. At about one o'clock in the afternoon we left Larnaca and first passed the salt lake, previously mentioned, on the western shore of which lies the mosque [Hala Sultan] Tekke. We left a second, smaller lake behind us on our left and rode across dry, sandy soil parallel to the coast as far as the village of Menehu, which we reached at about two o'clock. A long aqueduct, carried by arches, carries the life-giving water from the mountains to the nearby fields and the extensive groves of trees. A further thirty-five minutes took us to Kiti with its very old, picturesque, and tree-shaded

---

[322] Lord of Salamis, the island in the Saronic Gulf.
[323] The earthquakes occurred in 342 or 344. The reconstruction was undertaken by Constantius II (337–361); as for his brothers, Constantine II was already deceased and Constans had no part in it. The rebuilt city was named Constantia in honor of Constantius, not of his father.
[324] From Kythrea (Chytroi), ca. 25 miles to the west-northwest.
[325] Surely Seiff must mean southwesterly.

church.[326] Behind that church we crossed a narrow little stream on an equally old bridge. Then we continued again across dry and wild terrain, covered with wild bushes. Among these one notices frequently a small, thorny bush, still without leaves at this time, which is used both as fuel and to make hedges. Often one meets small donkeys which are loaded so high with these bushes that they look like walking pyramids and only their heads protrude from the thorny mass. At a quarter before four the village of Softadhes lay on our left, and forty minutes after that another village, called Aletricot [Alethriko], on our right. The mountains now gradually reach closer to the coast and become scenically more and more beautiful. But the narrow coastal strip remains wild and uncultivated, and only a few olive and carob trees, irregularly scattered about, in a welcome way break the monotony. At four o'clock finally we reached the village of Mazotos, which is situated at the foot of the mountains and at the entrance to a luxuriant valley. Here we found very modest accommodations for the night in one of the rustic houses.

Here, too, the simple housewife greeted us with a bowl of smoking coals and then busied herself to prepare the interior of the house for our reception by vigorous sweeping. But in so doing she stirred up the dust, which had not been disturbed for a long time, so much that for some time we found it impossible to be in the area. Like most houses of the country folk, this house, too, was surrounded by a small yard, was built almost in the form of a cube out of quarry stones, and had only one room, which we had to share with the whole family. The room received a little light only through the open door, since the single small window was without glass and closed with a shutter. A large arch, stretching at the midpoint from wall to wall, supported the beams of the flat roof, which was made of brushwood with packed dirt on top, as is the common practice on the island. These roofs, which in the winter often turn green, like small meadows, have to be rolled again after every substantial rainstorm, if they are to remain tight; therefore on most of them a heavy stone roller is kept permanently in position. Our hosts, while they were not rich, seemed to enjoy a measure of prosperity. Abundant household utensils, consisting of bottles, glasses, and colored earthenware, were put up on a decorative shelf and decorated the simple room; below them, amidst old and smoke-darkened icons, colored plates had been affixed to the wall for decoration. A huge bed in one corner served husband, wife, and daughter; for us beds had been prepared on table-like racks, but the bugs in them deprived us of our sleep. When we moved on the next morning at about eight o'clock, we were again fumigated by our hostess, while the little daughter handed us fragrant flowers, in this subtle way asking for backschisch.

Staying close to the coast, as the mountains got closer and closer to them, we rode this day, too, across wild, uncultivated terrain, which seemed rather bare. Here, as elsewhere on the island, there is no growth of grass at all and the bare ground is to be seen everywhere between the small bushes, green weeds, and dry brush. At least the carob trees were increasing in number and cheered us with their green foliage. We crossed several small streams, which were flowing to the nearby sea amidst oleander and tamarisk bushes, and, at a quarter before ten, also a larger river named Pantachino [Pendaskinos], I was told. No villages were to be seen anywhere; these probably are situated behind the mountains. A few minutes after ten, near Cape Sidion, also called [in French] Cap Carubiere,[327] we passed a group of buildings which announced from far away by their odor

---

[326] The church of Panayia Angeloktistos, renowned for its apse mosaic.
[327] From "caroubier" = carob tree.

211

that they served as magazines for St. John's bread. The latter is stored here during the harvest until it is loaded on ships.

Going on, we crossed the flat bed of the Basilopotamos and, on the other side of it, the rocky spurs of the mountains, which here almost reach the sea. On a very narrow path we rode down to the rock-strewn beach and then along a steeply precipitous wall of conglomerate, only soon thereafter to climb up again on some sandstone cliffs rising just as steeply. From the height of these the coast could be seen far in both directions and offered a splendid view with its rock formations taking many shapes, shining brightly, and rising almost vertically from the blue sea. We stayed on the height for some time and then had difficult going, sometimes in a streambed between sandstone boulders that had rolled down from the hills, and at other times on the floor of a valley made muddy by the rain. Then the path again descended to the coast, and the minarets of Limassol appeared before us.

But before we reached that city we came to the site of ancient Amathus, which originally had been a settlement of the Hivites and later also the capital of one of the small kingdoms previously mentioned. It was renowned in antiquity for its copper mines and its temple of Venus and Jupiter. It was located on a rounded hill and made totally inaccessible on the north side by a steep precipice. Thus its location was not only rather secure but also advantageous and beautiful, thanks to its closeness to the sea, which almost washed the foot of the hill, and to the magnificent mountain background. At the present the hill is partly under cultivation and is covered, apart from insignificant remains of walls, with formless ruins of stone. Among these, at the top of the hill, the fragments of a huge stone vase, almost hidden in the earth, are to be mentioned; a well-preserved counterpart is now in Paris.

A ride of one and a half hour took us from here to Limassol or Limisso, which is located on a bay similar to that of Larnaca. It is smaller than Larnaca, but leaves the impression of being more prosperous; in particular the houses are built in a better way and even have some architectural decoration. Founded by Guido [Guy] of the Lusignans [1192–1194], the city was ceded in 1291 by Henry II [1285–1324] to the Knights of St. John, who expanded and fortified it. The Limassol of today is after Larnaca the most important city on the island. Its commerce handles the export of the products of the western part of the island, notably wine and St. John's bread, and is as significant as that of Larnaca. Through the kindness of the Italian consular agent, Mr. Socrati Francadi, who himself owns a large wine business, I obtained the following statistical data:

There are four different kinds of wine which are produced on the island and are marketed under the names "vin rouge," "vin noir," "Commanderie," and "muskat." Each of these kinds is produced on a special kind of soil, and the following villages are especially engaged in cultivating and processing them: Kellaki, Klonari, Eptagonia, Sanita, Prasto, Vicla, and Akapau; all of these are located in the four administrative areas belonging to Limassol. On the average the island produces annually 80,000 Venetian barils or 4,000,000 Turkish okka of wine: 7,000 barils of "vin rouge," 68,000 to 70,000 barils of "vin noir," and 5,000 barils of "Commanderie."[328] The total value of these comes to

---

[328] The capacity of a baril differed widely from one Italian city to another. The Venetian wine barrel measured 64.4 liter. See Ronald Edward C. Zupko, *Italian Weights and Measures from the Middle Ages to the Nineteenth Century* (Philadelphia, 1981) 22. An okka, accordingly, is 1.28 liter or kg. See also Charles Is-

about 4,175,000 piaster or roundly one million francs; a baril of "Commanderie" is sold for 100 piaster, "vin noir" for 50 piaster, and "vin rouge" for 25 piaster per baril. Appoximately 3,000 wine growers take part in this production, so that each of them gains at most 1,400 piaster or 310 francs on the average. From this amount must be subtracted the not inconsiderable taxes as well as other expenses and losses. The government, for instance, claims ten piaster for the right to produce the "Commanderie;" 10% of the value is imposed as an export duty, and transport to the coast costs eight piaster; thus the wine grower is left, after the subtraction of unavoidable losses, with 56 piaster per baril. In the same way the gain on "vin noir" is reduced to 25 piaster, and on "vin rouge" to 5 piaster at most. Muscat, the finest and sweetest wine, is produced only in small quantities in the villages of Omodhos and Kilani. When they are young the wines of Cyprus have an unpleasant by-taste, due to the pitch-lined skins in which they are initially kept. But in time this disappears, and then the better kinds taste very good.

The second important export commodity is the St. John's bread, of which annually approximately 2,100,000 okka are exported to Russia, Egypt, and Trieste. The monetary gain is on the average 90 piaster per 124 okka or more than 1,500,000 piaster for the whole.

The location of the city is exceedingly advantageous and full of scenic charm: it is situated in a plain watered by an ample stream, close to the mountains, washed on one side by the sea, and surrounded on the other side by gardens, in which lemons and oranges are ripening. In noteworthy places Limassol is as poor as Larnaca; at the most the small citadel is worth mentioning; this was built by the Venetians and the center of it is well preserved.

Immediately to the west of the city the flat peninsula of Akrotiri, with Cape Gata, the southernmost point of the island, stretches far into the sea and encloses a salt lake. But to the north of it [of the peninsula] the village of Kolossi lies, pleasantly surrounded by shade-giving groups of trees, on a cheerful stream. It boasts an old castle of the Templars, supposedly their first commandery on the island. From the flat roof of the tower-like building we enjoyed a far and beautiful view: to the north were the mountains and to the south the sea and the peninsula of Akrotiri; the latter was spread out before us like a map, with the villages of Asomatos, Phasuri, and Akrotiri. All around the land seemed extraordinarily fertile and showed fresh vegetation such as we had so far not encountered anywhere on the island.

Hardly twenty minutes past Kolossi we crossed the broad bed of a river, the name of which my companions were unable to give me.[329] And a few minutes later we reached the substantial village of Episkopi, the houses of which, scattered among luxuriant vegetable gardens, situated in a picturesque way on the slopes of the mountains, and surrounded by fresh green vegetation and fruit-laden lemon trees, offered the most cheerful appearance. The population is part Turkish and part Greek; with a poor weaver of the latter nationality we found modest accommodation.

Early the next morning we left, guided by a Turk who knew the area, for the ruins of ancient Kourion [Curium]. These are located a short distance west of the village on the ridge of a hill which drops off steeply on the east side. At the foot of the hill we passed a cave tomb which had been cut into the soft sandstone, was half filled with rubble, and offered nothing of importance. At another vertical rock wall I noticed a row of square

---

sawi, *The Economic History of Turkey* (Chicago, 1980) 375, and Halil Inalcik and Donald Quataert, *An Economic and Social History of the Ottoman Empire 1300–1914* (Cambridge, 1994) 991.
[329] The Kouris.

holes, which had been chiseled [into the rock] in a regular pattern and apparently had served to receive a system of beams. A difficult path led us to the summit of the hill, the uneven ground of which slopes strongly toward the south. Here we found above ground the remnants of a small walled water basin. This probably was connected by means of clay pipes, parts of which are still enclosed in the wall, with a subterranean cistern only a few steps away. Further inland, on somewhat higher ground, and hidden by bushes, lies a small theater in a semicircular field of rubble, with numerous fragments of columns, among which I noticed several of grey-black marble with spiral fluting. But a short distance to the west of these, the remnants of walls, a little above ground, allowed us easily to see the whole extent of a stadium.

From here a ride of about a quarter of an hour took us to another place also thickly covered with ruins but situated at a higher level; here in antiquity was Hyle with a temple of Apollo Hylates [of the woodlands]. But here also in the course of a long investigation I found among the innumerable, hardly recognizable fragments of architectural components nothing of importance, save the remains of a large foundation. Here various drums of columns lie about in the midst of wild bushes and formless pieces of stone, and nearby a large water cistern has been cut into the rock. These remains of a foundation gain some interest from the fact that they probably once belonged to the temple of Apollo.

Only reluctantly did our animals leave the juicy food which grew abundantly amidst the old stones. But we remounted and continued in a westerly direction, at a considerable height above the sea through a pathless wilderness, passing huge clefts in the rocks, probably created by earthquakes. From the edges of these we looked down into the dizzying depth of narrow and dark gorges, but also ranged without hindrance and widely over the deep-blue surface of the sea, from which the whitish sandstone crags of the coast far and wide rose steeply and brilliantly. The southernmost point of this part of the coast has been called Capo Bianco.[330]

After a short time we found our path again, and it took us down into a small valley full of gnarled old olive trees; on the far side of that it rose again steeply along a high face of rock. So it went for hours in a constant alternation of mountain and valley. Gradually we had moved further and further away from the coast and at times found ourselves surrounded by a wild, magnificent mountain landscape. But the nature of the wholly untrodden path also forced us repeatedly to dismount and lead our animals by the reins. Only in one of the valleys through which our path took us did we again pass a couple of villages, having first crossed a small river overgrown with oleander bushes, about three and a half hours after Hyle. One village, Avdimu [Evdhimou], we left on our right; the other, Pissouri, high on the mountain to our left.

Only after two more long hours of traveling up and down did the view towards the coast open up again, and when we finally had crossed the last ridge we reached at sunset the village of Kouklia, which occupies the site of the ancient Palea Paphos. Here, that same evening, 4 February, we had opportunity to observe a gorgeous northern light of such brightness and color as I had never seen before.

The next morning a sharp cold wind was blowing down from the mountains, and under the gloomy rain clouds, which had gathered during the night, the miserable village, with its pitiful huts scattered about the bare and hilly terrain, made the saddest impression. Led by our host I wandered through the village on my way to the ruins of the once so famous

---

[330] More commonly Cape Aspro.

temple of Paphian Aphrodite, which was believed by the ancients to be the most significant sanctuary of the goddess on the island. According to legend, King Kinyras built this temple and was the first to introduce here the cult of the Syro-Phoenician Asherah.[331] Representations of the temple on ancient Cypriot coins show the idol of this goddess, a twisted, cone-like stone, set up between two columns. Of the ancient structure only the corner of a wall still stands upright; it is without decoration, built of Cyclopean boulders and believed to have been a part of the cella. Nearby a cistern has been cut into the rocky ground.

To the south of these unimportant remains rises the ruin of a medieval castle, presently inhabited by a Turk and disfigured by modern additions. But at some distance to the east of the village my guide took me to a flat, rocky hill full of cave tombs, of which, however, only a few are still accessible. The largest of these consists of three chambers which are reached through a ruined antechamber; the two larger ones measure 5½ m. long and 4½ m. wide, with two burial niches on each of its long sides; the smaller one, behind them, measures 3 m. square.

When I had returned to our quarters and had inspected a large number of objects brought in by the villagers but totally worthless, we departed at about noon for Ktima, which is situated about three hours to the west of Kouklia near the ruins of Nea Paphos.[332] Immediately after the village we crossed a stream [the Dhiarizos] on an old bridge supported by pointed arches, and then rode across an only partly cultivated plain which stretches at little width from the sea to the foot of the mountains. About 35 minutes out of Kouklia we left the village of Mantrika [Mandria], which is surrounded by gardens, on our left, and after another 25 minutes Timi on the right. Twenty minutes later we rode past nearby Archelia [Akhelia], 25 minutes after that we passed Koloni, and finally, after 35 minutes, Hieroskipos [Yeroskipos], where an abundant spring, which formerly watered a grove sacred to the goddess, rises from the rocky ground.

Ktima is a small city with a partly Christian and partly Turkish population and is the residence of a Kaimakam [district administrator] and also the see of a Greek bishop, who received us most hospitably. The city lies stretched out on the rocky edge of a plateau which drops off sharply towards the lower level; this forms the coast and on it, close to the sea, lie the extensive ruins of Nea Paphos. Of the latter Strabo [*Geographica* 14.683] reports that it was a foundation of Agapenor,[333] with a harbor and richly decorated temples, 60 stadia by land from Palea Paphos, and that annually men and women, some even gathering here from other cities, go there in a procession.

The city was destroyed by an earthquake during the reign of Augustus, but was rebuilt by him. It was already deteriorating, however, at the time when the Lusignans took possession of the island.

The Italian consular agent, Mr. Hadschi Smith, who already has kindly rendered the same service to many a fellow-countryman, became my charming and knowledgeable guide as well when I rode down to the lower plain next morning. The steep cliff on which Ktima is located is riddled with graves; we also found graves, but almost all of them filled up, in the flat, rocky soil to the east of Paphos. The actual ruins of the ancient city are at present a veritable desert of stone. Here, among the unimportant ruins of medieval

---

[331] Seiff cites Max Duncker, *Geschichte des Alterthums* (Berlin, 1855–1857) I 345.
[332] More correctly northwest.
[333] Leader of the Arcadian contingent in the Trojan War.

buildings, rise the wretched huts of a small village; only occasionally a few mutilated columns rise up among the formless fragments.

The ancient harbor, formed by two half-submerged quays and defended by a small fort, is now totally unused and probably not able to be used as well. A large foundation on a nearby hill seems to have belonged to a temple. Broken column shafts lie about in large numbers. To the north of the city we came to a large rock grotto, which formerly served as a chapel and was dedicated to St. Salome.[334] Even now the small altar niche shows traces of Christian paintings. Adjoining this grotto is a series of rocky hills which extend rather far to the west, consist of sandstone, and almost all contain cave tombs of different size and arrangement.[335] Some of them are located around an open rectangular court enclosed by columns or pillars which support an entablature with a frieze of triglyphs. Many of these tombs seem to have been destroyed by earthquakes.

From Ktima I turned to the mountains, crossing in almost northeasterly direction (40°) the narrow but fertile plain which lies in front of them. After we had passed on our left the villages of Petrida (40 minutes) and Tremithura [Trimithousa] (25 minutes) and traveled for a distance along the foot of the mountains, we reached eight minutes later the village of Messoia [Mesoyi], which is surrounded by vineyards. Behind it the path led along the slope of a narrow gorge enclosed by bare mountains and began to rise so steeply that we were forced to dismount.

But with every step forward the laborious hiking rewarded us with an increasingly free and beautiful view over land and sea; and when we finally had climbed the summit of the first ridge a panorama of surprising uniqueness and splendor was spread out before us also in the opposite direction. Deep valleys extended below our feet between long, steep, and only thinly overgrown faces of rock. Behind them towered dark mountains, and behind them, in turn, even higher ones, and above all of them the snow-covered summit of Mt. Olympus was shining brightly.

Only a few small villages could still be seen on the steep slopes; the one closest to us, on our left, is named Zada [Tsadha], I was told. Every new turn brought new important views and took us higher and higher. The narrow, exceedingly difficult path sometimes descended into one of the more level valleys, but always soon led us upward again that much more steeply along another face of rock and often along dizzying precipices. We passed a few villages, nearly all of them looking impoverished. The first one, one hour and 25 minutes past Messoia and located amidst vineyards, was named Polemi; it was followed 30 minutes later by Letimbou, which operates both vineyards and olive groves, and then, in a fertile valley, Gurdaka [Kourtaka] (20 minutes). An hour and 25 minutes further on we rode past Hula [Khoulou], which is next to the path, and after yet another two hours through the village of Stados [Statos]. By now we had reached such altitude that, over the low ridges next to the coast, the sea was visible almost in a semicircle. Beautiful old oak trees delighted us with their picturesque growth, and denser brush than before covered the faces of the mountains, on the summits of which occasionally a few pine trees are growing. But repeatedly we found the shrubs burned over large stretches, which can hardly be attributed to chance, as my companions are wont to do, since the purpose of this destruction is not evident. Finally, after a very tiring ride of almost eight hours, we reached the Greek monastery of Chrisoroghiatissa [Khrysorroy-

---

[334] Mk. 15.40 and 16.1.
[335] The so-called Tombs of the Kings at Paleokastro.

iatissa],[336] which lies 816 m. above sea level and in loneliness below the high wall of a valley. The more venerable than clean fathers of the monastery kindly welcomed us in their airy abode and, as is the custom of the country, treated us to fruit jelly and coffee.

The monastery, on the age of which I was not able to obtain any information, consists of an irregular complex of poorly maintained buildings with the church in the middle and seems to be very poor. In spite of the high and therefore rough location even the windows of the domestic quarters are not provided with glass panels but are usually closed with fragile wooden shutters, save one which admits the necessary light. These shutters provide so little protection against wind and weather that we were bothered during the day, in the half-dark rooms, by an uncomfortable draft and during the night by sharp cold, while in the morning we found our beds quite moist from the fog, since heavy rain clouds had gathered on the mountains. Only a few monks now inhabit the rambling buildings, from the windows of which one has the most wonderful view. In the distance, toward the west, the view ranges over fertile valleys and boldly formed rocky mountains, the dark masses of which with their sharp contours contrast with the bright surface of the sea. The latter is visible almost in a semicircle and stretches without limit to the horizon, reflecting the deep blue of the sky in one place and glowing like silver under the rays of the sun in another. At the foot of the monastery, in an almost westerly direction, a trough-like valley descends to the coast. Several villages are to be seen in this valley, and their names were given to me as follows; next to the monastery, only a little to the east of the northern approach [?], Mamundali; further down in an almost northwesterly direction Asproia [Asproyia], west of the latter at an even lower elevation Kritou, and at the end of the valley toward the east Panayia.

When we started out again the next morning the monastery's entire impoverished looking service staff, including the unclean mistress of the kitchen, appeared to receive their bakschisch for the services which they had rendered us. After they had been taken care of we rode, accompanied by their blessings and a cold drizzle, around the east end of the valley and through the village of Panayia. Unfortunately the dense clouds, which surrounded us and at times turned into rain, deprived us of any view. Just past this village we came into another valley of wild beauty. The steep walls of this valley were densely covered with tall bushes. Between these the red, corral-like branches of the Oriental strawberry tree[337] were abundantly shining forth, while on the summits slender pine trees were hiding their crowns in the dark clouds. For hour after hour we rode along the steep walls of lonely wild valleys up and down, frequently changing direction, but not a single human habitation came into sight on our long trek. The mountains seemed at this point entirely uninhabited, and we sighted only a few goatherders with their herds wandering about on the slopes between the young bushes. Our route, although considerably better than yesterday's, was still at all times very difficult, diminished at times to the narrowest of paths, and led along precipices which caused even my native dragoman to suffer an attack of vertigo.

At one time we passed a rather extensive, but sparse pine forest with magnificent old trunks. But a large number of these, and always the most beautiful ones, had been cut into a few feet above ground and singed, while others, already fallen, were apparently not put to use and left to rot. All these trees become victims of the production of pitch, which

---

[336] Our Lady of the Golden Pomegranate.
[337] The *arbutus unedo*, an evergreen tree native to the Mediterranean and bearing strawberry-like fruit.

thus far is in no way regulated by the government and is the long-lasting cause of the regrettable devastation of the forests previously mentioned.

We climbed higher and higher and finally found ourselves, after a ride of about six hours, exactly opposite the rounded top of densely forested Mt. Olympus, from the snow fields of which an icy wind was blowing down. A few hundred feet below us, to the right of a flat ridge, was the village of Milikwi [Milikouri]. Half an hour later we rode through the gates of the monastery of Kikko [Kykko], which is situated 1159 m. above sea level on a saddle separating two valleys.

The monastery possesses an icon of the Madonna supposedly painted by St. Luke. This makes it one of the most famous and most often visited places of pilgrimage, and consequently it enjoys considerable income. The pious fathers within its walls lead a far more comfortable and pleasant life than their colleagues at Chrisoroghiatissa. Extensive and carefully tended vineyards and fields surround the spacious, well-kept buildings, the living quarters of which are all provided with glass windows. A comforting fire of coals warmed the quarters assigned to us, and a passibly set and carefully attended table offered us welcome nourishment. The small church which holds the icon of the Madonna, is overloaded with valuable lamps, vessels, and silver-framed icons to the point that it resembles a treasury more than a house of God.

When we prepared for our departure next morning the sun was again smiling upon us from a blue sky, warm as spring and giving light and color to the magnificent panorama of mountains surrounding us. Here, too, a whole troop of black figures, but better clad and cleaner than those at Chrisoroghiatissa, eagerly expecting their bakschisch, awaited our departure. Accompanied by the father guardian and some of the older fathers to the gate of the monastery, we there mounted our animals, and off we were again into a brilliant morning.

Initially we descended for a while in a valley sloping toward the northeast, but then we rode on the excellent pilgrimage road, high along a steeply precipitous wall. From there, 800 to 1000 feet below us, I suppose, we looked down upon a fertile valley and, beyond low ridges, on the Bay of Morphou with Cape Kormachiti [Kormakiti] and the northern coastal mountains, which were clad in a blue mist and beyond which the shiny surface of the sea was spreading out.

We continued to enjoy this view and climbed up to a narrow ridge which separated two deep and wild valleys. Then the path descended steeply into the eastern one of these, and we reached its well-cultivated floor after a ride of one and a half hour and there watered our animals at a tree-shaded spring. A quarter hour later we passed the village of Zakistra, and twenty minutes further another, called Kambos. From here we rode along a narrow and often rather pleasant valley, on the floor of which a cheerful stream in a stony bed was rushing toward the plain. Extensive vineyards and occasional plantations of mulberry trees covered the slopes, and a special charm was given to these by splendid clumps of old walnut trees, unfortunately still without foliage. Soon the walls of the valley—the way followed the southern one at changing heights—moved together more closely, as far as the mouth of a side valley; this brought new influx to the stream, which was here shaded by mighty plane trees. But gradually the height of the mountains now decreased, the valley became broader and flatter, and the brook, now having grown into a small river [the Kambos], hastened by in a wide bed. Finally, after a ride of about five hours, the sea appeared brightly before us, the last low hill was crossed, and we were again in the plain. We soon passed a group of houses located on the shore of the Bay of

Morphou; my dragoman called it Karavostasi[a] and identified it as store houses. From here a little less than an hour brought us to the monastery Xeropotamos, which is situated in the plain, not far from the coast, completely isolated. It appeared to be exceedingly poor and delapidated and to have only two residents. But the surroundings of fruit-laden lemon trees and the beautiful view of the mountains gave even to these unclean quarters not a little charm.

When we started out again the next morning at about eight o'clock, the air was so pure and clear that above the horizon we could clearly see the giant mountains of Karamania,[338] their snow fields illuminated by the sun and gleaming across [the sea] in the most delicate coloration. We moved on in an exactly easterly direction across the monotonous plain, leaving the village of Pendeia [Pendayia] about half an hour distant to our right. At a quarter before nine we passed Kasivera [Ghaziveran], close to our route, and five minutes after nine Brasiko; then, twenty minutes later, we had the large, city-like Morphou at some distance to our left. At 10 minutes after nine we rode through the village of Sodies, behind which, on the right, at most five minutes away, lies Gadosodia [Kato Zhodia]. An hour later we had Astromerides to our left and at 10:45 we passed through Kadokopia; a quarter hour away, also on our left, we sighted the village of Masari. At 11:15 we made a brief stop at the banks of the Pedieos,[339] and at 12:08, on the move again, we reached Avlona, to the right of which lies Agatzi [Akaki]. The plain all about is covered only by wild pasture land.

At 12:45 the village of Denia [Dhenia] appeared on our right in a hollow; at 1:25, also on our right, Mammaria, after which Nicosia came into sight before us. Twenty minutes later we rode through the spread-out Jerolakos [Yerolakkos] and at about three o'clock through the pleasant Ayios Demetis [Dhometios]. There we stopped at the monastery of Ayios Prokopios and found excellent reception and hospitalty. It is an appealing place surrounded by well-kept fields. The clean and rather new church rises in the center of the yard, amidst green lemon trees, and from the balconies of the monastery buildings a distant view over the fertile plain, the rocky coastal mountains, and nearby Nicosia with its palm trees and minarets opens up.

From here we rode on in the morning, leaving Nicosia on our left and the village of Ayios Molostari on our right, towards the great highway which eventually will link Nicosia with Larnaca. Crossing the Yialias on this highway, we reached the village of Piroi [Pyroi] in a three-hour ride. From there we returned to Larnaca, to please our mucker by way of Athienou, his home village. We were in time to allow me to embark only two days later for Syria.


## Ritter zur Helle von Samo—1874

[Plate 33]

Alfred Ritter zur Helle von Samo, *Das Vilajet der Inseln des Weissen Meeres, das priviligierte Beylik Samos und das selbstständige Mutessariflik Cypern* (Vienna, 1878) 74–76. Alfred Ritter zur Helle

---

[338] The southern coastal region of Asia Minor, facing Cyprus and comprising Caria, Lycia, Pamphylia, and Cilicia.
[339] Seiff is in error. The stream must be the Akaki.

von Samo (1834–?) was the military attaché at the Austro-Hungarian Embassy in Istanbul. He gives a negative account of the island.

*Die Insel Cypern*, by Dr. Unger and Dr. Kotschy (Vienna, 1865) contains a detailed description of the physical and organic nature of this island, "the birthplace and chosen abode of the goddess of beauty and love." Therefore I believe that here I need only to supplement this rich work by the pertinent statistical, military, and a few other data which have escaped the notice of the natural scientists just named or have been prompted by changes that have occurred since then.

Sixty years ago [Edward Daniel] Clarke [1769–1822] wrote these less than flattering words about Cyprus in his *Travels*,[340] vol. I, p. 315: "Agriculture neglected, population almost annihilated, pestiferous air, indolence, poverty, desolation." These words can be confirmed as correct even now by any traveler who must decide on a longer stay on the island and especially in its southern and eastern part. These impressions are, if anything, made even worse by the harsh conditions to which one is exposed in exploring the interior: unbearable heat, a lack of regular and clean accommodations, the plague of innumerable insects of all kinds, etc.

One travels in Cyprus by horse, mule, or donkey. The numerous camels are employed only for the conveyance of goods. The beautiful mules of Cyprus are, like those of Crete, famous for their excellent qualities; at the time of the Abyssinian War [1867] a large number of these were bought by the English.

Most of the owners of transport animals (kiradschi) live in the village of Athienou (Atina), which is, so to speak, the center and hub of the lines of communication of the island. On the most commonly traveled routes, from Larnaca to Lefkosia and from Lefkosia to Famagusta, Athienou is usually chosen as a stop and lay-over. While the traveler will find the best accommodation and good food in the homes of the well-to-do kiradschi, this arrangement allows the latter in the course of each journey to spend a few hours in their own village and to tend to their affairs and their families. Athienou, now called Kiradschiköi,[341] counts today about two-hundred families. The rental price per animal per day varies between ten and thirty piasters. Between the two major mountain ranges of the island lies the central plain of the Mesaoria. Through it, from west to east, flows the major river of the island, the Potamos or Pedikos [Pedieos], the headwaters of which are at Mt. Olympus (6168 [6404] ft. high). This insignificant body of water is joined on its right side by the Satrachos.[342]

The inhabitants produce some grain, and some vegetables, also cotton, hemp, alizari or Levantine madder, linseed, and tobacco, as well as olives, citrus fruits, dates, St. John's bread, and spices. Severe droughts and devastating swarms of locusts are frequently recurring disasters in Cyprus, and a surplus in one year is followed immediately in the next year by a severe shortage, since prudent planning in the export of grain is often neglected here. The forests, consisting of cedars, pines, and cypresses as well as oak and beech trees, provide good timber. Cattle-breeding is insignificant, and so are apicul-

---

[340] *Travels in Various Countries of Europe, Asia and Africa.* 11 vols. (Cambridge and London, 1810-1823). Excerpts Cobham, *Excerpta,* 378-94 and *SHC* V (1998) 121ff.

[341] See also Jack C. Goodwin, *An Historical Toponymy of Cyprus* (5th ed. Nicosia, 1985) I 77.

[342] The author is mistaken here. It is the Yialias which joins the Pedieos from the right side. The Satrachos or Setrachos originates on the northern slope of the Troodos Mountains and empties into the Bay of Morphou.

ture and sericulture. Cypriot wines are highly esteemed even today, and the Commanderia is the best of them.

The capital in the interior, Lefkosia (Nicosia, Lefkotscha), is the see of a Greek archbishop and of an Armenian bishop. The population is 12,000 to 13,000. The most important coastal cities are Larnaca (Tuzla), with its European consulates and 6,000 inhabitants, Famagusta, and Kyrenia.

A rebuilding of the ports of Kyrenia and Famagusta would require only a thorough dredging to accommodate the biggest war ships and to replace the poor wharf of Larnaca. This would considerably enhance the military value of the island of Cyprus, situated as it is off the southern coast of Asia Minor, either as a base and collection point for undertaking operations against the ports of Alexandretta [Iskenderun], Mersin, Alanya, and Antalya,[343] or for the defense of the continent against any kind of attack. And the economic and commercial development of the island would similarly be enhanced.

The old fortifications of Tuzla, Lefkosia, Kyrenia, Famagusta, and Limassol are of value today almost only to photographers. In order to guard and maintain them two battalions of fortress artillery exist on Cyprus, each comprised of two companies.

Of zaptiye [police or gendarmerie] the island has about 350, 50 of them mounted; of these 200 foot and 25 horse are stationed in Lefkosia, 12 foot and 8 horse in Larnaca, 20 foot in Limassol, and the rest are distributed in other towns of the island.

Although military conscription on Cyprus annually provides not only the necessary quota for the island's fortress artillery but also a small contingent of recruits for the regular army, there is no reserve center here; maintaining the roster of the reserve soldiers is handled by the military command in Lefkosia.

Note: the capital of Lefkosia has about 13,000 inhabitants, 12 mosques, 8 churches, and 8 baths. Famagusta has within the fortifications 150 houses, 1 mosque, 1 bath, and 650 Turkish inhabitants, while the Christians live in the suburb of Varosha, a quarter of an hour away. Limassol has 2 mosques, 3 churches, and 2 baths. Larnaca has 3 mosques, 4 churches, 3 baths, and 2 monasteries.

## de Crenneville—1876

Count Victor Folliot de Crenneville, *Die Insel Cypern in ihrer heutigen Gestalt, ihren ethnographischen und wirtschaftlichen Verhältnissen* (Vienna, ca. 1879) 1–44 and 46–49. The author was the Austrian vice consul in Smyrna. The translator has not been able to correct all of the numerous errors in this account.

### Introduction

In the fall of the year 1876 I had the privilege, in the company of Consul General R. von Zwiedinek and starting out from Beirut, to visit Cyprus and to learn more about its major points. The notes which I took at that time during a one-month stay on the island, guided by the experienced hand of the superior just mentioned, I have now collected and now present to the public. The new fate of Cyprus encourages me in the hope that this modest effort will be read with some interest. I have endeavored especially to devote

---

[343] The latter three on the coast of Karamania.

great care to ethnographical aspects. It is the purpose of the present study to describe Cyprus as it now is and its inhabitants as they now have been met by their new English lords.

V. C.

Smyrna, December 1878

## The Origin of the Name

Historians in antiquity and in modern times have explained the origin of the name Kypros in various ways. I will cite only the most common ones, namely:

I. Semitic

"Chitim," derived from the capital of the Hittites, today's Larnaca.

II. Greek

    a. *Kypron, cuprum*, copper, because numerous copper mines were known on the island in antiquity.

    b. *Krypton*, hidden, because seafarers see the island only when they are immediately upon it.

III. Roman

    a. *Cornutis*, horned, because of the island's many pointed promontories.

    b. *Cypris*, Venus, as the birthplace of the goddess of love.

IV. Modern Explanation

This will also be the most convincing one and derives the name from that of a plant which has been known since antiquity, grows abundantly on Cyprus, and is important in the practice of medicine: *Kypros*, Kopher (from which the dye "Henna" is obtained).

## Historical Survey

The first inhabitants of the island mentioned in history were Semites, specifically Hittites, who founded their capital Chittim, which then gave its name to the whole island. Following them, Phoenicians from Tyre settled the island and marketed its natural products, such as the timber of its mighty forests and the copper of its mines, in all the world.

At that time Astarte ruled on the island. But already Homer tells in his Trojan rhapsodies how Hellenic princes ruled on Cyprus, such as Teneros [Teukros, Teucer], brother of Ajax, at Salamis [Pind. *Nem.* 4.46–49].

The cruel goddess Astarte and her repulsive cult were replaced by that of the goddess of sweet love, who had been born from the foam at Paphos. However many kingdoms or principalities were formed on the island, Aphrodite presided over all of them.

At the end of the 13th century B.C. Cyprus was conquered by Belus, king of Tyre.

In the seventh century it came under Egyptian rule, until Cambyses [529–522 B.C.] snatched it from the Pharaohs.

Under Darius Hystaspes [522–486 B.C.] the Cypriots tried in vain to free themselves of Persian rule.

Diodorus [Siculus 11.44.1–2] reports that ca. 473 B.C. the island was conquered by the combined forces of the Athenians and Spartans under Aristides and Pausanias. Having been taken again from the Greeks, it was regained in 455 B.C. by Cimon, son of Miltiades.

Greek and Persian rule now alternated, until Alexander of Macedon in 344 B.C. [correctly 333 B.C.] gained Cyprus as booty from the Persians.

After the death of Alexander the Ptolemies and the Seleucids contended for his realm, until M[arcus Porcius] Cato in 58 B.C. took the island from Ptolemy [XII] Philauletes [Auletes].

Julius Caesar gave the island to Arsinoe, the younger sister of Cleopatra, but Mark Antony caused Arsinoe to be murdered and made Cleopatra queen of Cyprus.

In A.D. 40 [correctly A.D. 46], from nearby Palestine, by way of Damascus [correctly Antioch], Paul and Barnabas, the latter himself a Cypriot, came to Cyprus, and with them Christianity. But the cult of the goddess of love was so firmly established among the Cypriots that they called the mother of Jesus Aphroditissa.

With the end of the West-Roman empire Cyprus fell into the hands of Byzantium.[344]

From the middle of the seventh century to the end of the twelfth century Cyprus was held at some times by the Arabs and at other times by the Greek emperors.[345] Emigration and desolation diminished the population of the island.

Under Isaac [II] Angelos, emperor of Byzantium, Isaac Komnenos seized the island,[346] and his cruelty prompted many Cypriots to emigrate.

In the course of his crusade and after the capture of Sidon, Richard the Lionheart of England conquered Cyprus, and in 1190 he sold it to the Order of the Templars for 25,000 Mark silver. The templars, however, paid only 10,000 Mark and after a year and a half returned the island to the king.

In 1192 Richard sold the island a second time, this time to Guy de Lusignan, the last king of Jerusalem, who had lost his kingdom and his throne to Saladin, on condition that Guy should renounce all claims on Jerusalem.

Of all the principalities which the crusaders founded in the lands of the East, the kingdom of Cyprus maintained itself the longest (1192–1489).[347]

These Lusignans were strong rulers, and Cyprus owes to them its second flowering, which, with its Gothic churches and castles, offers a fine counterpart to the time of the first flowering, when the cult in honor of the native goddess was still active.

Guy de Lusignan (1192–1194). He built the first works of fortification around Famagusta. By bringing in Syrian Christians he sought to repopulate the island, which, as just mentioned, had been depopulated. More than 600 knights were invested by him. After a reign of two years this first ruler from the Lusignan dynasty died and was buried in the cathedral of Nicosia.

Aimery [G. Amarich], Guy's brother (1194–1205). During the eleven years of his reign Cyprus was elevated to the rank of a kingdom by the German emperor Henry VI [1190–1197], son of Frederick [I] Barbarossa [1152–1190]. He was succeeded by his son Hugh I (1205–1218). He in turn was followed by his son Henry I (1218–1254).

The Lusignan dynasty proper died out with Hugh II (1254–1267); he was followed by his nephew Hugh of Breyne [Brienne] and Tarentum (1267–1284), who took the name of Hugh III de Lusignan. It is to him that St. Thomas Aquinas [ca. 1225–1274]

---

[344] At no time was Cyprus part of the West-Roman empire.

[345] The Arabs undertook numerous raids on Cyprus, but did not establish permanent control of the island.

[346] Actually under Andronikos I Komnenos, 1183–1185. Isaac II Angelos, 1185–1195, was unsuccessful in his attempt to dislodge Isaac Komnenos.

[347] For a complete genealogical table of the Lusignans see Hill, *History,* III 1156–58. See also David Hunt, *Footprints in Cyprus: An Illustrated History* (London, 1990) 225.

dedicated his *De Regno* [or *De Regimine Principum*]. His son John I reigned only two years, 1284–1285. He died single and bequeathed his kingdom to his brother Henry II, who reigned from 1285 to 1324 and thus longer than all other kings of Cyprus.

He was followed by his nephew Hugh IV, 1324–1361 [–1359]. Boccacio [1313–1375] addressed to him his *Genealogy of the Gods*.[348] Hugh's son Peter I, who married Eleanor of Aragon, reigned in 1361–1372 [1358–1369]. Whereas all his predecessors had distinguished themselves by their preference for the peaceful pursuit of the arts and sciences, Peter had a warlike bend of mind. He equipped 150 ships, undertook raids along the coast of Syria, conquered and plundered Alexandria, and devastated the Turkish settlements of Cilicia. During his absence he appointed Count Rochas [John de Morphou, Count of Roucha] as regent. Upon his return he learned that the latter had had an illegitimate relationship with the queen. He had charges brought against both of them before the highest court in Nicosia, but the judges acquitted the queen, while they condemned the disloyal vassal.

Peter, dissatisfied with the judgment, vented his anger against the Cypriot nobility. The decline of the kingdom begins with him. His arbitrariness and cruelty brought about his fall, and he was murdered in 1372 [1369].

Peter II, the Stout, 1372 [1369]–1382, married [Valentina, or Valenza, Visconti] the daughter of [Barnabò Visconti] the Duke of Milan [in 1378].

For a long time already the Republic of Genoa had attempted to establish a foothold in Cyprus. It took advantage of the weak rule of Peter II to take possession of Famagusta, which it transformed into a strong harbor for its navy. In vain Peter formed an alliance against Genoa with Milan and Venice. Genoa proved, thanks to Turkish assistance, too strong. Rather, at this time the island republic[349] began to assert its influence on Cyprus.

James I, Peter's nephew [correctly, uncle] ruled 1382–1398. He was followed by his son John II [correctly Janus], 1398–1432. The latter's marriage to Charlotte de Bourbon produced his son and successor John and a daughter Anna, who married Louis II, Duke of Savoy, son of Amadeus VIII.

During the reign of John II [correctly Janus] the troops of Saifodin Tuman, Sultan of Egypt,[350] landed at Limassol, which they devastated together with Paphos and Nicosia. They then made themselves masters of the island, except for Kyrenia and the strip of land occupied by the Genoese. The king was taken prisoner and brought to Cairo [1426].

On payment of a ransom of 100,000 Thaler, raised by his vassals, and on condition that he pay tribute to the Sultan of Egypt, John [Janus] returned [1427], but died soon thereafter [1432].

He was succeeded by John III [correctly II], 1432–1458. The latter's second wife was Helena, daughter of Andreas Palaiologos, despot of the Morea, who by her evil character estranged the hearts of all from the court. Of the children of this marriage only one daughter, Charlotte, was alive when the king died. This daughter married first John of Portugal and after his death [her cousin] Louis of Savoy.

---

[348] In 15 books, the most exhaustive work on Greek mythology up to this time.

[349] Genoa at one time controlled both Corsica and Sardinia.

[350] Saif ad-Din of the Ayubid dynasty.

After the death of John III [II] the hatred of the Cypriots against the queen was carried over to his successor; she was to reign for six years only (1458–1464) as Charlotte I.[351]

A natural son of John III [II], James, landed in Cyprus, supported by the Sultan of Egypt and the Venetians. Queen Charlotte resolutely defended her castle at Bellapais, but he forced her and her husband to leave the island; he also, with the help of Andrea Cornaro, took Famagusta from the Genoese.

James II ruled 1464-1473. He married Catherine Cornaro [or Caterina Corner], the daughter of the Doge of Venice.[352] Having been given a dowry of 100,000 zechini[353] by the Republic, the young, beautiful queen arrived in Famagusta with a flotilla of Venetian galleys amidst pomp and splendor.

After a reign of nine years James II was succeeded by his posthumous son James III, 1473–1475. With James II the Venetians had actually become masters of the country, even if they allowed the shadow kings James II and James III to retain their royal titles. Incensed by the arrogance of the Venetians who had come to Cyprus with Catherine and Andrea Cornaro or with Mark Bembo to divide offices and honors among themselves, the nobles of Cyprus formed a conspiracy against the frivolous queen and her child. The archbishop of Nicosia (Louis Perez Fabregues) took the first place among the malcontents. His natural son, married to an illegitimate daughter of James III [II], was supposed to be raised to the throne. In the night of 13 November 1474 Andrea Cornaro [the queen's uncle] and Mark Bembo [the queen's cousin] were murdered by the conspirators, the royal palace occupied, and the queen and her little son taken to a secure place.

The young bastard, proclaimed king, now aimed at seizing the whole island. But a Venetian fleet, appearing already early in 1475, awakened him from his dreams of royalty and gave him the sleep of death. Most of the conspirators met a similar fate, exile, or incarceration.

Meanwhile James III, last king of Cyprus, died.

1475–1489: Catherine Cornaro was now for fourteen years the royal regent of the Republic [Venice] on Cyprus, which did not belie its Aphrodisian power over the queen. Finally, tired of loving and of ruling, Catherine yielded to the urging of her countrymen and, in 1489, presented the island to the Republic of Venice, in recognition of which a marble tablet in the city of St. Mark honors her memory to this day.[354]

In vain ex-queen Charlotte in Italy had sought help from the Pope and the princes in her efforts to assert her valid claims to Cyprus. Her husband, Louis of Savoy, died, and at that time she voluntarily quit all claims to the island in favor of the Duke of Savoy.

Even this declaration, which was solemnly read at Bologna at the time of the coronation of Emperor Charles V [1519–1556] before Pope Paul III [1534–1549] and the College of Cardinals, in no way disturbed the Venetians in their secure possession of Cyprus; it merely added to the titles of the regents of Savoy the title of a king without a country.

---

[351] There was no Charlotte II. Charlotte did not formally abdicate until 1485 and died two years later in Rome.

[352] Catherine's father was Marco Cornaro, a Venetian nobleman, but not a doge. The family had commercial interests in Cyprus.

[353] A zechino (or zecchino) is a Venetian gold coin.

[354] This is a reference to the queen's monument, by Bernardino Contino, in the south transept of the Church of San Salvatore. In the central relief of this monument Caterina is surrendering her crown to the Doge. She died in Venice on 10 July 1510. Her body was laid to rest first in the Cornaro Chapel of Venice's Church of Santi Apostoli but at the end of the 16th century was transferred to the Church of San Salvatore, where a marble slab at the foot of her monument marks her tomb.

During the Venetian rule (1489–1571) nothing special is to be noted in Cyprus. Frequently the muslims attempted to seize the island, both Egyptians (Mamelukes) and finally, successfully, the Turks.

Like other possessions of the Republic in the Levant, the island was administered without regard for the welfare of the native inhabitants and simply to the advantage of the ruling cliques of Venice, who divided offices and honors among themselves without doing much for the real recovery of the island, which once had been so rich.

Under the first Latin rulers the island had gotten a good boost, and soon a relatively free class of peasants had formed in the lowlands, and burghers and merchants in the ports and cities. But the dynasty, steadily growing weaker, could not prevent upstarts at the court and the clergy, which had been powerful since the times of the Templars, from bringing strife and discontent to the island. The monarchy kept losing power to the haughty vassals, and individual energetic rulers, such as Peter III [Peter I], did not know how to practice moderation and their strength turned to cruelty, which then alienated the people as well.

The trades and commerce declined, and the peasants, who alone were still productive, did not know whether they preferred the Genoese or the Venetians as masters.

With the Venetians better order came into the administration, but the primarily agrarian population was disappointed in most of its expectations, since Venice considered Cyprus a milch cow. At the end of the 16th century the Republic of Venice was so weakened by internal and external feuds that, apart from Nicosia and Famagusta, there was hardly a garrison that might defend the fortified places and thus the island itself against eventual enemy attacks.

When in Europe religious unrest fully occupied France and Germany, when the power of Poland had been broken by the last unhappy war and the Battle of Varna [Bulgaria, 1444; death of king Ladislaus III], and when the Republic of the Lion itself had been weakened by disputes in Italy and by accidents, such as the fire of the arsenal, then the Jew John Miches or Vassy [Joseph Miquez] took his revenge against Venice, which had refused to take him in when he had been driven out of Spain, and planted in the mind of the Sultan in Istanbul the thought of stealing Cyprus, the jewel in the Doge's crown.

Already a favorite of the palace under Suleiman the Magnificent [1520–1566], Miches gained extraordinary influence under Suleiman's successor Selim [II, 1566–1574]. Supported by Mustafa, Selim's Capudan-Pasha,[355] Miches knew how to convince the Sultan that he should demand the surrender of the island, on the grounds that it had been conquered by Selim I of Egypt [1512–1520].

But it was not only the [island's] political and strategic importance which influenced Sultan Selim. He only too often indulged in sweet wines, notwithstanding the Koran, and Vassy cleverly employed the circumstance that Cyprus could provide the noblest of all wines, the Hyacinth-colored Commanderia.

Then, when Venice refused the Sultan's demands, the Sultan dispatched Mustafa Pasha to Cyprus with a considerable fleet. On 1 July 1570 the Turks landed with 60,000 infantry men, 3000 pioneers, an equal number of cavalry men, and 5000 horses. Their artillery consisted of 55 culverins[356] and 35 field-pieces of 50 to 100 pound. The Venetians had a defensive force of barely 7000 men on the entire island.

---

[355] Famagusta's Lala Mustafa Pasha Mosque, the former Cathedral of St. Nicholas, was named after him in 1954.

[356] A culverin or "Feldschlange" is a kind of heavy cannon used in the 16th and 17th century.

Nevertheless the struggle for the possession of the island lasted thirteen months. In a month and nine days the Turks stormed the capital of Nicosia, and 20,000 inhabitants were cut down. In the month of October the Ottomans began to lay siege to Famagusta. In the meantime the Venetians had been able to bring in by sea a reinforcement of 7000 men, provisions, and ammunition. Also, the man in command here was not a weak and incompetent captain, but the noble Venetian [Marco Antonio] Bragadino and the engineer [Count Hercules] Martinengo. The siege lasted until August 1 [1571]. Only then, when ammunition and food had been completely exhausted and the number of men fit for combat had dwindled to nothing, was the white flag raised on the tower of Famagusta, and the commandant surrendered the city on condition of free departure for all. But the Sultan and his generals violated the terms of surrender, Bragadino was flayed alive, and 20,000 people were massacred. But when the Turkish fleet, laden with costly booty, gold, and jewels, and taking along Cyprus' most beautiful women with blond hair, as in Titian's paintings, was about to leave the harbor of Famagusta, one of the captive Cypriot women laid fire to the Capudan's ship. Most of the stolen treasures and the living booty sank to the bottom of the harbor, with thousands of the captors and the burning wrecks of the galleys; ever since the harbor has been ruined and silted up. History has not recorded the full name of that heroic woman, who preferred certain death to life in a Turkish harem; her first name was Maria. All in all the Turks lost 50,000 men before Famagusta, and the siege cost the republic nearly 5,000,000 zechini.

The treaty of 15 March 1573 confirmed the loss of Cyprus for Venice, which now began its decline. The Turkish rule lasted more than 300 years (1571–1878), without ever losing the character of alien rule. The jewel of the Mediterranean was laid waste and desolate when the Turks took possession of it, and it is no better now, only poorer in population, as Victoria Britannia takes it to her protecting breast.

Two phenomena are peculiar to the history of Cyprus because of their constant recurrence. One is the great influence exerted on the island by women. Beginning with Aphrodite, who came ashore at Paphos, and with her temples and erotic mysteries, which made Cyprus a unique Hellenic sanctuary, right down to our days when the queen of England has again erected the banner which Richard the Lionheart first planted on the fortress of the Komneni, women have played a role in the history of Cyprus as hardly in the history of any other country. This is not the place even to list the names of those cities which especially enjoyed the patronage of the goddess of love, built temples and altars in her honor, and put up works of Hellenic art in sacred groves. The entire southwestern part of the island was, after all, dedicated to the cult of Aphrodite.[357]

But even when the old Greek gods had been defeated and expelled from Olympus and a new faith was building new altars, Cytherea's [Aphrodite's] land remained an "island of women."

Arsinoe, Cyprus' first queen, for the sake of this possession, had to die by the hand of an assassin, to leave the kingdom to her sister Cleopatra. Under Justinian [527–565] the island was given the name Justiniana in honor of that emperor's wife

---

[357] In a footnote the author refers to the excavations undertaken by Luigi Palma di Cesnola (whose name he misspells) and surmises that future excavations will bring to light many important finds.

65] the island was given the name Justiniana in honor of that emperor's wife [Theodora], who hailed from Cyprus.[358]

When Richard the Lionheart and his wife Berengaria of Navarre received only violence and insult instead of hospitality on Cyprus from Isaac Komnenos, the king swore to avenge the insult to Berengaria and conquered the island [1191]. The sons of the beautiful nymph Mélusine gained Cyprus.[359] Eleanor of Aragon, wife of Peter I de Lusignan [1358–1369], by her faithlessness, laid the groundwork for the alienation of the dynasty from its vassals.

Helena of the Morea, wife of John III [II, 1432–1458], by her cruelty prepared the fall of the Lusignans.

In vain did her daughter Charlotte [1458–1485], a noble figure of a woman, attempt to preserve the realm for her husband Louis of Savoy. After a heroic defense of Bellapais she had to go into exile, and another woman, the typical, sensuous, beautiful daughter of the city of gondolas, with the easy mores of the times and the patrician families, Catherine Cornaro, moved into the palace at Nicosia as wife of a weak bastard king [James II], mother of the last king [James III], and herself the last sovereign in Cyprus.

The second fateful phenomenon is the hatred with which the Israelites have persecuted the islanders.

According to Xiphilinus[360] the Israelites under Artemion devastated the island in the early years of Christianity and supposedly massacred 240,000 Cypriots.[361] Since that time the Israelites have been forbidden to set foot in Cyprus, and to this day not a single confessor of the Old Testament is found there.

Finally Cyprus has to thank Spanish Jews [i.e. Miquez] for 300 years of Turkish rule.

## Topography

The most important cities in Cyprus in antiquity were about twenty in number.

1. Paphos. Old and New Paphos (now the place where, according to the legend, Aphrodite came ashore ca. 1980 B.C. [?]). Herodotus [?] tells that the first temple in her honor was erected by the people of Paphos. The image of the goddess consisted of a cone. According to Tacitus [*Hist.* 2.3] it was Kinyras of Cilicia who brought the cult of Venus to Paphos, and for this reason the office of her high priest was hereditary in his family. The reputation of these priests was so strong into Roman days that Cato of Attica [Utica!], before he, on behalf of the Senate, took Cyprus from the Egyptians [58 B.C.], sent his legate Canidius [*RE* III.2, 1475 (1)] to King Ptolemy[362] to persuade him to turn the island over to the Romans without striking a blow, in return for being given this of-

---

[358] More accurately Justiniana Secunda, also Nova Justiniana. To this day the archbishops of Cyprus are officially styled "Archbishop of New Justiniana and All Cyprus." The correctness of the title is questioned by Hackett, *Orthodox Church,* 45 and 261.

[359] The Lusignans traced their line back to the fairy Mélusine, "la mère de Lusignan," whose oldest son supposedly became king of Cyprus. She was the subject of a Romance by Jean d'Arras in the late 14th century.

[360] Dio Cassius 68.32.2–3 in the epitome of Xiphilinus.

[361] Artemion led the Jews of Cyprus in the revolt which erupted in 116 A.D.

[362] Ptolemy, King of Cyprus, son of Ptolemy IX and younger brother of Ptolemy XII.

fice of high priest.[363] The city was often afflicted by earthquakes. Seneca mentions that Paphos was destroyed by an earthquake (ca. 840 B.C.).[364]

2. Kourion (today Episkopi), founded by Kinyras' son [Koureus]. Herodotus [5.113] mentions this city and its king Stesenor in the context of the Persian Wars. There are remains of the aqueduct leading to the ancient baths.

3. Kition (today Kiti), according to Diogenes Laertius[365] founded ca. 1300 [B.C.] as a colony of Tyre, is the birthplace of Zeno, the founder of Stoicism (A.D. 362 [335 B.C.]), and was known and famous for its salt works.

4. Amathus (now Amathonta), not far from Limasol. According to the legend founded by Amathus, the son of Herakles (1335 B.C.) [?]; here Adonis especially was venerated.

5. Lapithos was built by the "Luidanonier" [Laconians], according to Strabo [14.683].

6. (Aipeia) Soloi. Plutarch tells in his biography of Solon [26] that this city on the banks of the Klaris was founded by Demophon [or Demophoon], the son of Theseus. Solon, on his journey from Egypt, was hospitably received by its king Philokypros and counseled him to extend his city further toward the plain. The king, following this advice, named the new city Soloi, in honor of Solon (596 B.C.) The city was one of the island's most important ones, and Herodotus [5.115] mentions it in the Persian Wars under Darius Hystaspes.

7. Kytros (now Kythrea), famous for its honey.

8. Golgion (now Golgi), founded by colonists from Sikyon, supposedly venerated Venus even before Paphos.

9. Karpasia (now Karpassos [or Rizokarpaso]), built by Pygmalion, the sculptor and husband of Galatea, had a small harbor, thanks to its location on the promontory of Sarpedon [Strabo 14.683].

10. Tamassos, rich in copper mines.

11. Arsinoe. There were three cities by that name; they were founded by Ptolemy [II] Philadelphus ca. 285 [B.C.].

12. Marion (now Arsinoe).

13. Idalion (now Dhali), between Larnaca and Nicosia, famous for its temple of Venus.

14. Kyrenia (now Kerynia), famous for its olive trees.

15. Additionally Pliny, Vergil, and Valerius Flaccus mention the city of Lefkosia (now Nicosia) and

16. Chidos, the native city of Ktesias;[366] also

17, 18, 19. Aphrodisia [Aphrodision][367], Alexandretta, and Argos.[368]

We now come to the most important city of Cyprus in antiquity:

20. Salamis. Teucer, expelled by his brother [father] Telamon because he had not avenged the death of his brother Ajax, landed in Cyprus at Koronea, a small village,

---

[363] Plutarch, *Vit. Cat. Mi.* 35.2.

[364] Seneca the Elder mentions earthquakes at Paphos in *QNat.* 6.26.4 and in *Ep.* 91, but does not give specific dates.

[365] Diogenes Laertius, in his biography of Zeno, 7.1–160, repeatedly refers to Kition, but not to its foundation.

[366] This appears to be an erroneous reference. Ktesias, 5th c. B.C. Greek physician and author of a history of Persia, was a native of Knidos in Caria.

[367] On the northern coast, ca. 25 miles east of Kyrenia.

[368] These seem to be erroneous entries.

which he enlarged. Thus Salamis came about in 1271 B.C. [?]. Here there was a temple of Zeus; another altar was erected to the semi-deity Argulis [Aglauros or Agraulos], the daughter of Cecrops. Lactantius reports [?] that human sacrifice was practiced here until the days of Hadrian (117 A.D.).[369]

At the time of the Persian Wars Salamis under Evagoras I gained the hegemony over the nine kingdoms of Cyprus by its courageous uprising against Artaxerxes [II] (ca. 449 B.C. [ca. 390 B.C.; Diod. Sic. 14.98.2, 14.110.3, and 15.2.3]).

Among the later rulers of Salamis Nicocreon the Cruel is noteworthy: he, in 324 B.C. [323 B.C. or later], had the philosopher Anaxarchus crushed to death in a mortar [D. L. 9.58-60].

According to Dionysius of Halicarnassus Salamis was the native city of the historian Aristides [?], who wrote a history of Alexander.

An earthquake destroyed the city in the 28th year of the reign of Constantine the Great [333 A.D.].[370]

## Topographical and Geological Conditions

Cyprus is the fourth-largest of the islands of the Mediterranean. From Paphos to Cape Andreas, its greatest length, it measures 30.27 geographical miles, and from Cape Kormakiti to Cape Gata, is greatest width, it measures 12.8 geographical miles. Its circumference is 80.5 geographical miles, and its area 172.97 [correctly, 273] geographical square miles.[371]

The island lies between 34° 33' 30'' and 35° 41' 18" north, and between 32° 15' 42" and 34° 35' 48" east of Greenwich, in the upper corner of the bay formed by Asia Minor and Syria, i.e. in the so-called Pamphylian Sea.

Geographically the island can be divided three ways: in the north the Kyrenia [or Pentadaktylos] range, in the south the Olympus (now Troodos) massif, and between them a large plain [the Mesaoria], stretching from west to east.

The Kyrenia mountains stretch along the Sea of Karamania[372] and, with a small southeasterly divergence at Kormakitis and at Buffavento, end at Komi [?]; they are 28 [geographical] miles [ca. 125 statute miles] long and 2–7 [geographical] miles [ca. 9–30 statute miles] wide. This northern range is formed by compact and multicolored limestone (mostly Jurassic limestone with Vienna sandstone in the foreground. Its cental height is up to 1000 m. (St. Hilarion = 960 m.; Buffavento = 980 m.; Pentadaktylos = 960 m.).

The Troodos mountain massif, which begins in the southwest and soon rises to lofty Mt. Olympus, is as far as its eastern continuation (Adelphos and Makheras) and also in the south at Larnaca (Stravovouni or Monte Croce) of Plutonic origin. This mountain massif takes up more than half of the island and its height varies from 1000 m. to 2000 m. (Troodos or Olympus = 1895 m.; Adelphos = 1610 m.; Makheras = 1450 m; Stavrovouni = 700 m.).

---

[369] Porph. *Abst.* 2.54; Euseb. *Praep. Evang.* 4.16 and *De Laudibus Constantini* 13.7.
[370] Another major earthquake occurred at Salamis in 342 or 344; the city was rebuilt by Constantius II (337–361) and renamed Constantia in his honor.
[371] Cyprus is actually the third-largest island in the Mediterranean, after Sicily and Sardinia. Converted into statute miles, the measurements given by the author are 138, 59, 371, and 3572, respectively.
[372] The southern coastal region of Asia Minor, facing Cyprus and comprising Caria, Lycia, Pamphylia, and Cilicia.

The ridge of the Olympian mountains consists of greenstone, while its slopes in the south are formed by tertiary limestone and marl. Spread out between Kyrenia and Mt. Olympus lies the great plain [the Mesaoria], the rich soil of which is up to 5–6 m. deep and forms the breadbasket of Cyprus.

Cyprus has two major rivers; the Potamos of Morphou [?] and the Pedieos. Both of them leave their banks during the rainy season (October to February) and flood the land far and wide. The same thing happens with numerous other rivers which, flowing down from the mountains, irrigate and fertilize the gentle slopes and small plains all around. When the water is evaporated in February it leaves behind in the fields [a deposit of] mud which in its chemical effect is quite similar to the mud of the Nile; this is particularly true of the Pedieos.

Of the smaller rivers which have their source in the Troodos Mountains let me mention two in the north which flow parallel to each other: the Xero [Karyotis], which irrigates the Evrykhou valley, and the Klarko [Setrakhos], which irrigates the district of Lefka;[373] of those in the east, west, and north let me mention the Krysokhou [emptying into the like-named bay].

The Karapotamos [Dhiarizos], coming from the Amodos [?], empties into the sea at Kouklia. In the south the third largest river of the island, the Likos [Kouris[374]], irrigates the fields of Episkopi, Kolossi, and Akrotiri.

Of lakes Cyprus only has a few. Para [Paralimni] Lake in the Famagusta district is a sweet-water lake rich in fish. Also there are the salt lakes of the Scala [Larnaca] and of Akrotiri; there, too, are the best salines. Mineral springs are hardly known; there is merely the bitter spring at Bii [?], near Kouklia.

## Bays, Harbors, and Wharfs

In the north: the harbor of Kyrenia, in the like-named district; the harbor-wharf of Komi [?] in the district of Karpas; the bay of Exarkos [?] in the same district.

In the east: the wharf of Sarakino[?] in the district of Karpas; the wharf of Eftakomi [?] in the same district; the bays and harbors of Salamis and Famagusta in the district of Famagusta.

In the south: the bay and wharf of Larnaca (Scala) in the district of Larnaca; the bay and harbor of Limassol in the district of Limas; the wharf of Pissouri in the district of Ardion [?]; the harbor of Paphos in the district of Paphos.

In the west: the bay of Krysokhou and in the district of Krysokhou; the open wharf of Pyrgos in the district of Lefka; the open wharf of Morphou in the district of Morphou.

The formation of bays is far more important in the south and east than in the north and west.

The commercially most important bays are located on the southern coast:

1. The bay and wharf of Larnaca, in the like-named province; this bay is formed by two promontories, that of Pyla and that of Chiti [Kiti]. Indeed the wharf of Larnaca is the one which is used by most commercial ships, especially by the ships of the Austro-Hungarian Lloyd, the only steamers which carry mail to Cyprus. Therefore all importation of goods to Cyprus is handled here only, as well as most of the exportation from the island.

---

[373] The Xeros is actually a third river in this group; it flows a little west of the Setrakhos.
[374] Formed by the Kryos and the Limnatis.

Since nothing has been done by the government to build a harbor or at least to improve the wharf, the latter is, like the landing places of Syria, exposed to the wind and the weather, and landing, because of the shallow water, must be done at a distance of 15 minutes by barques. In the winter this is so difficult that often the Lloyd steamer cannot anchor but must go on. Even small boats cannot land then, because of the strong surf, and goods must by carried by porters wading ashore.

At little expense it would be possible to create from the wharf, now mostly open because of the shallow water, a spacious harbor, by dredging and by building a mole against the surf and the winds from the north. And it could be done more easily here than at the Syrian landing places.

The so-called Scala forms a suburb of the city of Larnaca proper and under an enlightened and energetic government would soon merge with it.

Although the city is only one m. above sea level, the sea never rises above it. Together with the construction of a harbor, lighthouses would have to be built, of course, on the promontories of Pyla and Chiti [Kiti]. The Scala is 6 1/2 [geographical] miles [ca. 30 statute miles] distant from the present capital of the island [Nicosia], but will soon surpass the latter metropolis in importance. There is no shortage of building stone, since this can be found in the hills surrounding the city in the north. The city is nine [geographical] miles [ca. 40 statute miles] from Famagusta and sixty miles [actually 108 nautical miles] from Beirut by sea.

While the Scala is inhabited almost exclusively by Europeans (Greeks, Italians, Englishmen, Frenchmen, Germans, and Austrians), mostly merchants and numbering 4000, in Larnaca proper there are 16,500 inhabitants, about 6,000 of them Turks.

Larnaca is the only city with half-way good warehouses. One quarter of a mile east of the Scala, towards Ormidhia, there is a hospital after the European manner and the quarantine station. The city has Catholic and Greek schools and churches and a French boarding school run by the Sisters of St. Joseph.

The climate is rough in the winter and hot in the summer, but on the whole rather unhealthy.

2. Limassol. The city is built in a valley. The hills surrounding it are planted in vines, St. John's bread, olives, figs, and mulberry trees, which give a pleasant character to the generally fertile area. The location is healthy, and the average temperature through the year is moderate. The rather closed wharf is formed by the promontory of Gata and by Moni and is exposed only to the winds from the east. The harbor itself is now the deepest of the island and can accommodate ships of 200 tons; it could easily be converted into a large harbor, especially by blowing up the reef of Zevgari. A harbor mole from north to west would hold back the winds from the west.

Two small forts of Venetian times lie in ruins.

Limassol is the center of the trade in Cyprian wine, the better varieties of which grow in the district of Limassol, in the Commanderia vineyards which are named after the Templars.

During the hot season drinking water is scarce and is drawn primarily from cisterns. But it would be possible to gain good water by employing artesian wells. Of 7500 inhabitants hardly 2000 are Muslims, and all others Greeks.

3. Famagusta. We now come to the port which was the most important at the time of the Latins and the Venetians and will be the most important also for England. The har-

bor of Famagusta, now called Ammochostos, is formed by the peculiar development of the coast in the eastern part of Cyprus. The same formation continued at Constantia (Salamis), only richer in bays. The harbor of Famagusta was at the end of the 16th century so deep and spacious that the entire fleet of the Republic of Venice could dock there.

In a word, Famagusta was until the beginning of the 17th century a first-rate war-harbor. Today the ruins of the old lighthouse, sand, and mud, which accumulated first around the sunken ships of Mustafa Pasha, have buried the living and the dead ornaments of the Lion of St. Mark. Only small ships of ten to twelve tons capacity can enter the harbor today.

If this harbor were restored and the fortifications rebuilt, it would be a war-harbor and a sea-fortress of the first rank. Its fortifications are not threatened by nearby heights and themselves control land and sea; the moat of the fortifications can be filled with water. Being close to Larnaca and only a short distance from Nicosia, it will become for the English the center of their operations on the mainland of Asia Minor, just as Limassol will be for Syria and Egypt.

The rebuilding of the old harbor will quite naturally lead to its connection with the harbor of Salamis. A recently laid-out railroad line will connect the new capital of the island with the old one.

The city of Famagusta itself will then soon recall its old splendor, when at the time of the last Lusignans it counted three hundred churches, while today it barely houses two hundred inhabitants.

Famagusta must become the capital city of Cyprus for England, and all those speculators who have acquired real estate around Larnaca at a high price will soon regret their error.

4. In the north Cyprus possesses only one anchorage. This is the Bay of Kyrenia. This wharf, exposed only to the winds from the north, today offers shelter to ships of up to 85 tons only, but could easily be converted to an excellent commercial harbor.

The lovely northern slopes of the Kyrenia range, with Bellapais in the east and Lapithos in the west, give to the bay a peculiar charm, while the area's rich production of carobs, olives, wine, and silk for the mainland of Caramania, only twenty miles [correctly: ca. 50 nautical miles] away, provides significant activity for the harbor. Now most of the production goes on mules at high prices to Nicosia.

The city is small and surrounded by works of fortification still rather well preserved. From a historical perspective it is of interest as the scene of the last battles of the troops of the German empire of Frederick II against the knights of the assizes (1232–1234).[375]

5. In the south there is Paphos (Kouklia). For England this will be of importance because of the archipelago. Now but a good small harbor, the coast offers the best location for a larger shipyard, for which the nearby forests could furnish the timber.

If the harbor were enlarged, a lighthouse would be indispensable. Two miles from Ktima (the old Paphos)[376] is New Paphos with its venerable ruins of classical Greek times. Not far from the coast of New Paphos is the small island of Paphos, which has given its name to both cities.

---

[375] In the course of the so-called Lombard or Longobard War.
[376] Not to be confused with Palea Paphos or Kouklia, sixteen km. to the southeast.

## Cities and Places in the Interior of the Island

In the northern half of Cyprus, surrounded by a fertile plain, which is watered by the Cypriot Nile [the Pedieos], lies the present capital of the island: Nicosia (once Leoteon [Lefkontheon?], in Greek Lefkosia).

This is the largest city in Cyprus and gives even today a faithful picture of the rich, fortified cities of the Middle Ages, although the Turks in their usual way have here, too, allowed the old to go to ruin and created nothing new. The cathedral, recalling that of Famagusta, is built in the most beautiful Gothic style, and even the two plump minarets added to it cannot detract from the beauty of the slender towers or of the noble vaults and arches.

Destructive rage has done a lot of damage here. As Bragadino was at Famagusta, so the marble Lion of St. Mark at the old palace of the Lusignans was butchered and mutilated. A number of palaces and churches serve as warehouses and barracks. But the column with the escutcheon of Venice, where, perhaps, one of Shakespeare's principal heroes once stood, still stands proudly in the same place in the city.[377] Here also is the plane tree, from the strong branches of which the Greek bishops and many notables were hanged at the time of the Greek uprising [1821].

## Monuments of different peoples and their customs.

After the palace of the Lusignans that of the Templars is the most beautiful one.

The fortifications are rather extensive and in the best state of preservation. The walls, armed with old Venetian cannons, and a few Genoese ones, are more of interest as remnants of the past than suitable for defense.

The city of Nicosia has a population of 20,000, of which 11,000 are Turks, 5000 Greeks, and the remainder Armenians, Maronites, and Catholics. The Turkish Pasha, Governor des Livas of Cyprus,[378] presided here until 4 June 1878, in the palace of the Lusignans. The Greek archbishop and autocephalous metropolitan of Cyprus also resides in Nicosia.

The original streets are well laid out and the squares spacious.

The surrounding plain is rich with its river, the Pedieos; the trade routes for the commerce of Nicosia are established by custom; there is a not inconsiderable cottage industry of silk and leather (cordovan). Considering these factors, the English surely will create from Nicosia a city of the second class, even if its administrative importance must decline because of its interior location.

A road only built ten years ago leads from Nicosia to Larnaca; but it is, thanks to the winter rains and Turkish mismanagement, in total disrepair, and a wretched diligence carriage requires seven hours to cover the distance.

After Nicosia, Lefkoniko is without doubt one of the most important towns in the interior. Located in the Mesaoria, it is, with its neat homes, like a European market town. It has about 3000 inhabitants and is the island's most important grain market. There, too, one finds a fairly good school.

---

[377] The allusion must be to Othello, who is also associated with the so-called Tower of Othello at Famagusta. The column here referred to is not the one which stands in Ataturk Square today. That column was taken down by the Turks after their conquest of Cyprus and not re-erected until 1915.

[378] A liva was an administrative area or province. The last Turkish governor was Besim Pasha.

Here one has the best opportunity to become acquainted with the type of free and prosperous Cypriot peole.

The expanded harbor of Famagusta-Salamis would be the natural emporium for Lefkoniko and a railroad, therefore, between these two places of the utmost importance.

Between Lefkoniko and Nicosia, about 1½ hours distant from the latter, lies Kythrea, one of the most charming places of the whole island.

About twenty small villages are situated in a lusciously green narrow valley on seven different streams which join to form a larger stream, the Kythron. The crosses of twenty-seven Greek churches are seen between the groves of fruit and willow trees. Whole forests of splendid pomegranate bushes beautify countless gardens with their purple blossoms and fruit, the largest and best of the island.

Cheerful mills are working along the stream, and under colossal plane trees the peaceful farmer is smoking his narghileh, the soft gurgling of which is drowned out by the foaming water at his feet ...

The most important promontories of Cyprus are [counter-clockwise from the north]: Cape Kormakiti [west of Kyrenia], Cape Suino [?], Cape Epiphani [or Arnaouti, Akamas Peninsula], Cape Gata [Akrotiri Peninsula], Cape Kiti [south of Larnaca], Cape Pyla [the eastern limit of Larnaca Bay], Cape Greco [southeast of Famagusta], and Cape St. Andreas [Karpas Peninsula].

In the mountains a temperature like that of central Europe prevails, the coastal districts resemble Syria, and the great plain in the summer is like the land of the Pharaohs.

During the reign of Hugh [IV] of Lusignan (1330), due to abnormal rainfall, all the rivers rose to such level that their waters created much suffering in both the cities and the country. During the reign of Constantine [the Great, 306–337] there was supposedly no rain in Cyprus for 36 years, so that most inhabitants had to leave the island.

From the end of October to February it rains as in the tropics. In March, April, and May it is spring, which adorns its green coat with thousandfold blossoms and gives new beauty even to the evergreens, which have remained faithful through wind and rain. In the middle of June the hot summer begins, at once causing the flowers to wilt and the fruit to ripen. The broiling sun gives to the grapes that sweet flavor which pleases us in the wines of Cyprus, but by the middle of September one is tired of such dry heat.

On the whole the climate of Cyprus is very healthy, even if at the lower elevations close to the coast fevers are common after rains and during the first heat. The temperature varies in the winter between 10 and 15° Réaumur and in the summer between 25 and 30° Réaumur.[379]

The surface area of Cyprus can be categorized as follows:

34% arable, but now uncultivated land
18% cultivated land
16% forest land
11% wetlands, salines, streams, rivers, lakes, and roads.[380]

Partly mountainous and partly flat, Cyprus enjoys a very varied climate. One might almost say that the island possesses the qualities of the three continents which surround it. Artificial irrigation and a rational management of the forests would be able to turn Cyprus into a veritable Eden.

---

[379] On the Réaumur thermometer the freezing point of water is 0° and the boiling point is 80°.
[380] That leaves 21% unaccounted for.

Among all the agricultural products cereals occupy first place. Primarily wheat, barley, and oats are grown. The Greek authors and Pliny [the Elder, *HN* 18.67] mention Cyprian wheat, and Stephen de Lusignan[381] reports that much grain was exported from Cyprus to other lands.

The main area for cultivating grain is the central plain (the Mesaoria), which is rich in humus, the plain of Morphou, the valleys which are watered by rivers and streams, and almost the whole coastal area.

Since the farmers are unfamiliar with fertilizer, as is the case in the entire Levant, crop rotation and letting land lie fallow must take its place, whereby, of course, almost one third of the arable land is made to go without harvest.

Early sowing is done from the end of September to the middle of October, late sowing in January, and harvest falls into May. The plow is of the same kind that the ancients had and entirely of wood; it is drawn by cows which are scarcely able to draw the wooden tip through the soil.

The entire population rushes to the harvest, in order to protect it from the locusts. This plague on the land must now be described.

The species of these locusts is the *stauronotus conciatus*,[382] which also devastates Anatolia, Asia Minor, and the islands of the archipelago in the same way and there, too, has its breeding ground. This species (ἀκρίδια) deposits its egg capsules not in cultivated but in unproductive land. In Cyprus its main breeding ground is probably in the Karpas peninsula and in the Trachaeotis [?]. In the last third of the month of March the young insect crawls out of its egg, grows rapidly, and sloughs its skin four times. After four weeks the insect acquires its wings and, driven by the wind, flies across the land. Throughout April, May, and June the locusts are on the move, since they have quickly devoured the available feed; thus they descend upon the whole island. In the month of July, August, and September the locusts die, and their carcasses spoil the air with their stench along the mountain streams and even more along the beaches.

There are several ways to fight this ugly plague on the land, but the government hitherto in power has applied almost none of them, and it is also likely that not every means can be employed. The most recommendable means of protection would be a rational and universal management of the soil. By digging up and plowing the soil the eggs of these orthoptera are exposed to the wind and the weather, and with their breeding grounds the brood itself is destroyed. With the elimination of the locusts the island could again become what it once was as far as its agriculture is concerned.

Just as in the past wheat was the preferred cereal crop, so it now is barley, because it ripens earlier and thus has a better chance to escape the locusts.

As soon as the grain has been cut with a sickle it is brought in sheaves to the storage. This is located, away from the dwelling places, on stamped dirt under the open sky. The sheaves are stacked according to their owners, and then the grain is thrashed, and that, too, under the open sky and in a manner which would elicit laughter if it were not so unfortunately stupid. The sheaves are spread out on the thrashing floor, and the thrashing machine consists of a wooden sled the bottom of which is curved and equipped with

---

[381] Of the royal house of Cyprus, Dominican, and author of three books on the history of Cyprus; born in 1526/27. See *SHC* X (2001), par. 582.
[382] Perhaps identical with the *stauronotus maroccanus*, which is distributed throughout the Mediterranean countries.

strong stone glides. A man sits on the sled and drives the team of oxen or donkeys. Through the friction, when the sled is driven over the sheaves, the ears are shelled, but at the same time squashed. The pulp that is created by this kind of thrashing is cast to one side, the straw to the other. It is self-evident that the draught animals have a good deal and devour a good part of the harvest.

The instruments of the period of the lake-dwellers are superior to the agricultural implements of this Christian nation of the 19th century! Only with difficulty and gradually will the English government succeed in persuading the Cypriots to manage their agriculture in a rational manner, because they cling with incredible blindness to their antediluvian agriculture. Private attempts at innovation, most recently by an Italian farmer, who even brought Italian workers with him, were frustrated by the meanness and resistance of the peasants.

After cereals, the cultivation of legumes, namely peas, lentils, beans, sweet peas, and chick-peas, is of some importance. Here, as well as in Anatolia and Syria, the cultivation of oil-rich sesame would have much to offer; it is now limited to the area on the north and west coast and around Dhali.

Brought in from Egypt, colocasia[383] is grown in the mountainous areas as a substitute for potatoes; its large tubers are a very popular vegetable.

Cotton: The cotton plant, once, in the 16th century, grown to excess, is now grown very little. It demands a better soil than grain does, the so-called βαμβάκιον. Before sowing the cotton seed is soaked in liquid manure, which causes it to sprout more quickly. The young plants are watered and hoed every two weeks. Flowering occurs in early September, and the bolls are harvested in October. Of course, just as in Asia Minor, the wool is not plucked from the boll and the boll left on the bush, but the whole boll with its wool is torn off. This very much diminishes the value of the wool, which takes on a brownish color. The best cotton comes from the districts of Soli and Evrykhou. At the time of the Lusignans and the Venetians close to 30,000 bales were exported [annually]; now the island exports barely 4000 bales.

Madder: Until recently Cyprian madder [*rubia tinctorum*] was excellent both in quantity and quality; unfortunately it has become almost entirely worthless with the invention of the chemically equivalent artificial alizarin.[384]

Tobacco: The cultivation of tobacco is insignificant and brings little profit.

Sugar cane: Once, at the time of the kingdom of Cyprus, sugar, too, was a considerable export commodity; the best sugar cane fields were at Limasol, Kouklia, Kolossi, and Lapithos. Even in 1825 Ludwig Ross still found sugar cane at Kolossi.

Hemp: The cultivation of hemp is insignificant, but could bring good results. On the other hand, since the devaluation of the alizarin plant [madder], Indian hemp, *canabis indica*, has been introduced and is cultivated in quantity primarily near the coast. It is very profitably exported to Egypt, where it is used in making hashish.

Fruit trees: Cyprus was once famous for its fruit trees, and even if the number of orchards in Famagusta of which the historians tell, is probably as exaggerated as the city's 300 churches, the orchards of Cyprus, nevertheless, may once have been ten times as important as today.

---

[383] A giant, tuberous herb of the family of the Araceae.
[384] A dye, C14H804.

Very appropriate for the island of love is the pomegranate tree (*Punica granatum*), supposedly Aphrodite's gift, which thrives best at Kythrea. Apart from the pomegranates the orchards of Varosha, Kythrea, Episkopi, Bellapais, etc. produce figs, oranges, lemons, almonds, cherries, apples, walnuts, pears, and medlars. Outside Nicosia even dates will ripen, which does not happen in nearby Syria. Bananas, still doing well here at the end of the 16th century, are no longer found here now.

Sericulture: Among garden trees the most important one for Cyprus is the mulberry tree, because of sericulture. Sericulture seems to have been introduced in Cyprus already before Justinian [527–565]. Cyprian silk and velvet cloth were famous in the 13th and 14th century. Under the Turkish government sericulture soon declined. Over the last forty years, especially since the silkworm disease appeared in Syria almost constantly, it has again somewhat increased, and during this time ca. 300,000 new trees were planted, mainly two types of the *morus alba*. These grow best at Paphos, Kythrea, Varosha, and on the Karpas peninsula. The island produces ca. 30,000 kg. of spun silk [annually]. The silkworms are strong and healthy.

Forests: Not only the oldest Greek authors who mention the island but even later Roman authors, such as Pliny [the Elder, *HN* 16.203], tell of the mighty forests which with their trees, mostly evergreens, adorned hills and mountains. Originally the whole island was surely covered with forests, and, from the Semites and Phoenicians to the Byzantines and Latins, its slim trunks served in the construction of ships and the operation of mines. So gradually, first along the coast, especially in the south, and then in the interior plains, the beautiful forests have disappeared and have survived only in the higher mountains. Now free forest maintains itself only on the summits and in the gorges of the mountains, while everywhere selfish man, mindless of future generations, has converted the ground into fields and pastures, but mostly into bare wasteland. The description, given above, of the total surface and its distribution will provide sad evidence with dry figures of how the wanton devastation of the forest with iron and fire has harmed the island. Where once the sacred groves of Aphrodite stood, now bristling underwood covers the impoverished soil and offers only poor food to the herds of goats, the third enemy of the trees.

Naturally the destruction of the forests had a negative impact also on the climate, and every summer, there being no rain, adds to the dry wasteland and even the springs dry up little by little. The only still forested areas of the island are the mountain ranges of Olympos, Kyrenia, and the Akamas peninsula.

The forest trees of Cyprus are:

Various kinds of oak, especially the "Steineiche," laurel trees, and needle trees (cedars, Scotch pines, Karaman, *pinus laricio* [Corsican pine], costal pines, junipers, and cypresses), pines, plane trees, alders, and terebinth (pistachio) trees.

Of these trees the pine of Karamania is the most handsome; only under the cover of its broad tops do eagle ferns [*pteris aquilina*] surround the purple-red peonies, which blossom at the end of spring between the rocks and moss. The densest growth of Karamania pines, not unlike the virgin forests of America, covers the heights of Olympos, Adelphos, and Makheras; The coastal pine and the black pine also grow there. The cypress does best in the Jurassic limestone mountains of the north. Of the junipers the *juniperus phoenicea* occurs the most frequent. The light-green Cyprian oak is found mostly in the district of Lefka. On the northern slopes of the mountains of Kyrenia the strawberry tree, *arbutus Andrachne*, grows; the cultivation of this tree could be of great advantage to Cyprian export, because of the utilization of its fruit in the distillation of spirits.

The most beautiful plane trees one finds around Kythrea; there, too, in the mountains of Kyrenia, at Morphou, and at Paphos are the most luxuriant olive trees. Of the many forest bushes I mention only the myrtle and the mastic bushes. Finally I should mention the bush to which Cyprus owes its name, the Kopher plant [Kypros], from which ladanum (henna) is gained. Of the other useful plants growing wild especially the caper bush deserves to be mentioned.

Horticulture: The olive tree came to Cyprus from Greece. It does well up to 1000 m. above sea level, and especially well near springs. The loveliest olive groves are found at Kitti, Moni, Kolossi, Episkopi, Lapithos, Bellapais, and above all at Kythrea. For the Cypriots olives are the preferred fruit, and at the time of strict fasting, together with bread, their only nourishment. The care given to the olive trees on the part of the people is almost nil, and only thanks to its toughness does the tree thrive on the island. With violent roughness the olives are beaten off the trees, and in the process the trees are injured and mutilated. Furthermore there is the wholly primitive way in which the oil is pressed from the olives. At least 60% of the oil is lost in the process. Nevertheless ca. 4600 hectoliters are produced annually.

The carob or St. John's bread tree is autochthonous and peculiar to the island, but does well only when grafted. Carob trees abundantly cover the south and north coast of Cyprus. Further inland St. John's bread finds little use, except for the extraction of a kind of syrup and as fodder for cattle; it is, however, a significant commodity for export and thus, logically, traded at Kyrenia in the north and Limassol in the south. Since an okka [of St. John's bread] barely brought in a few paras,[385] the peasants often cut the carob trees down. In recent years Trieste obtained a fair amount of St. John' bread for the distillation of spirits.

Cyprus' main export commodity today is wine, famous from the days of classical Greece to the present for its fire and praised by Greek and Roman poets, monks, and laymen for its exquisite taste. Viticulture reached its zenith at the time of the Templars and the Lusignans. Even if Sultan Selim [II, 1566–1574] conquered Cyprus for the sake of its wine, viticulture, nevertheless, has declined since the Turkish conquest.

Vines do well up to 1000 m. above sea level, but best in the area south and southeast of Olympos, in the districts of Orini [?], Tillyria [between Khrysokhou Bay and Lefka], and Limassol. The noblest [of Cyprian wines] is the Commanderia wine, from the area south of Proodos and Avon.

Of 14,000 Joch[386] of arable land barely 1/124th is now given to viticulture. How much more wine could be produced on Cyprus, given the island's excellent soil conditions![387]

Game: As for game, we find in the mountains the deer and the mountain sheep (moufflon, Greek *agrinor*),[388] the latter on the peninsula of Akamas and in the Troodos mountains. In the plain and in the wetlands there are many rabbits, hazel-hens, rock par-

---

[385] A para is an Ottoman monetary unit. For the Ottoman monetary system see Halil Inalcik and Donald Quataert, *An Economic and Social History of the Ottoman Empire, 1300–1914* (Cambridge, 1994) 947–80.
[386] The Joch is an obsolete German measure of land: the area which one man with a team of oxen can plow in one day; varying between 3000 and 6500 square meters.
[387] For a guide to more recent and more complete literature on the fauna of Cyprus one should consult David G. Frodin, *Guide to Standard Floras of the World*, 2nd ed. (Cambridge, 2001) 698.
[388] The moufflon is found in the mountains of Corsica and Sardinia; *agrinor* by error for προβατάγριον = wild sheep?

tridges (francolins),[389] quail, and snipes. An especially sought-after, although very small, wild bird is the so-called "beccafico" or "Feigenschnepfen" [a kind of snipe].

As for harmful wildlife, there are the polecat, the jackal, and the fox.

Although Cyprus was also called the island of snakes, of such dangerous reptiles only one kind of asp, called Coupli, is found, and even that only rarely.

## Pits, Mines, and Quarries

Although there are no mines in operation today, the island's wealth of metals gives reason to hope that the English government will put new life into this important branch of industry. The following would be especially productive:

1. For copper, the areas of Tyrria [?], Khrysokhou [north of Paphos], Thinhussa [?], Kornos, Lefkara, Lythrodhonda [these three west of Larnaca], and Solea [south of Lefka].
2. For iron the areas of Lisso [?], Hai-Herakliti [?] and Monte Croce [Stavrovouni].
3. For sulfur the mountains behind Paphos.

Strangely enough older authors speak of deposits of zinc, but no traveler in modern times has been able to find these. The limestone mountains offer the best building stone, almost similar to marble. The range of hills northwest of Larnaca offers an excellent kind of gypsum; quartz and rock crystal are found at Monte Croce [Stavrovouni]. Jasper is fairly abundant in the districts of Karpas, Orini [?], and Limassol; and there, too, agate and chalcedony are found. Also one finds in Cyprus three kinds of ochre and umber which are renowned in trade and industry; the yellow, light-brown, and dark-brown. These are obtained primarily at Mavro Vouni, in the district of Larnaca, and at Strullos, in the district of Mesaoria, and for the most part exported to Holland, and at a relatively low price. Amicant and alaun are also found, although only in small amounts.

The salines of the island produce annually 7,600,000 kg. of salt from the sea. The best salines are those of the Scala, in the district of Larnaca, and those of Akrotiri, in the district of Limassol. During the hot summer months the salt crystalizes after the water has evaporated. In August the salt is piled up along the salines, and in March it is shipped. It is quite white and mild and was shipped primarily to Syria, Cospoli [?], and Smyrna.

## Domestic Animals

Of domestic animals we find on the island all those of southern Europe and also a large number of camels. Cattle are usually kept in stall-feeding, sheep and goats on the open pasture. Sheep (mostly fat-tails) are the major source of meat, along with poultry, which thrives very well. Turkeys, ducks, and black hens, which lay eggs with two yolks, are sought after far and wide and form a considerable export item. In the Mesaoria pigs are raised and excellent ham produced.

Especially in the valleys there are many bee-keepers, who produce honey and wax of excellent quality.

Because of their strength and good nature Cypriot donkeys and mules are especially famous. Egypt imports from Cyprus its snow-white "Pasha-donkey," and almost the entire Orient its mules. The latter, although stocky of body, are not inferior to the

---

[389] A game bird of the genus *phasianidae*.

splendid mules of Kentucky. Horses are few in number and small; most of them are imported from Syria. The camel will carry burdens up to 350 kg., the mule up to 250, and the donkey up to 150.

The goat is a domestic animal which does more harm than good and must receive special mention. Cyprus' herds of goats come close to the locust plague in the awful damage which they do. Thousands upon thousands of goats are herded across field and meadow, forest and vineyard. What does the goatherd care that his herd destroys tender young plants with the roots or feeds upon the best barely formed grapes? It does not affect him directly; so what does it matter? He has to pay taxes without seeing that the government does anything useful with the money forcibly taken from him. What the goats leave is enough for his neighbor, farmer or winegrower. The latter, too, if it seems good to him, will cut the young grapes of his neighbor to season his meal.

## Means of Transport and Traffic Routes

Up to the present time, because of the complete absence, already mentioned, of roads and highways, beasts of burden are the only means of transportation: camels, mules, donkeys, and horses. Products and wares are transported in caravans of 10 to 50 animals, and this means of transportation is not only slow but also expensive. Thus, for instance, from the Mesaoria (Lefkoniko) to Larnaca camel freight, in the case of cotton, is 45 piasters for two bales, and in the case of grain 40 piasters [for ?]. From Nicosia to Larnaca the corresponding rates are 39 and 34 piasters, from Morphou and Solea to Larnaca 60 and 50 piasters, and finally from the villages of the Karpas (Leonarisso) to Larnaca 60 and 70 piasters. All these are camel loads. Because of the bad paths the products of the southwestern districts can be transported by mules only, which further adds to the price of transportation.

Excepting the road which leads from Nicosia to Larnaca, there are on the entire island no roads other than narrow paths, which in the winter can be used only with great difficulty. Although there is more than enough material to build roads, absolutely nothing was done in almost three centuries to improve communication. The major obstacle to rapid road constuction, the noticeable lack of indigenous labor, could have been overcome.

## The Population

The present population of the island divides into two communities, the Islamic-Turkish and the Greek. The Turks live primarily in the cities and in only a few villages of the plains. Once, in the Greek pagan period and the Latin Christian period, the island counted more than 1½ million inhabitants and thrived in proverbial prosperity. But since the beginning of Turkish rule forced emigration has steadily diminished the island's Christian population, while, nevertheless, the Ottomans on the island were not able to increase and to establish themselves.

Egypt, Greece, Lebanon, and especially since 1860 even the Syrian seaports, being closer to the protection afforded by the partners of the treaty, took in the fugitive Cypriots. The cities were left to the Turks, who were neither willing nor able to cultivate the plains. More than half of the once flourishing island of Aphrodite turned into a desert, and the remaining Christians, barely numbering 200,000, owe it only to the blessing of the naturally rich soil and to their own tough character that not all of Cyprus became a desert.

The Christian inhabitants of Cyprus are a peaceful, quiet population, extremely moderate and content in all their practices. Violent crimes occur very rarely. Through centuries of servitude the Greek character has remained fairly pure, but has lost many of its good qualities. There is a continuous withdrawal, an eternal illusion and lie, which demeans the Christian inhabitants of the island. There is a strictly moral family life, with harem-like seclusion, which is broken only at ecclesiastical feasts, especially the feast of the Virgin Mary, the so-called "Panajiri."[390] This strictly moral family life marks the industrious rural population, which is, unfortunately, totally inadequate for the available land surface.

But the Greek spirit of speculation also dwells in the Cypriots, and it is an admirable phenomenon that, in spite of oppression and indolence, a close-knit and free class of peasants developed and maintained itself in Cyprus as on no other island of the archipelagos. Every rural resident owns his own land, which he works, and his own house, in which he lives with his family. As if following instinct, the oppressors, facing this enduring work ethic, withdrew into the cities. This keen spirit of speculation manifests itself also in the trades and in commerce, which is entirely in the hands of the residents along the coast. In this circumstance lies also the main reason for the otherwise unjustified importance of Larnaca and the Scala; particularly so, since the only European mail steamer, that of the Austro-Hungarian Lloyd, regularly stops here, thus connecting Cyprus with the rest of the world, and since here also the consuls of the European powers reside.

It is easily understood that the means by which the Cypriots make commercial gain are not the most honorable and only too often come into conflict with the Turkish laws. Among the Christians of Turkey, unfortunately, the sense of justice and honesty has long been badly corrupted. A well-ordered judicial system will serve directly to ennoble the people, and the free development of a national culture in school and church must go hand in hand with it.

## Religion

The religions practiced in Cyprus are the following:
1. Islam, claiming ca. 60,000 souls.
2. Greek-Uniate, claiming ca.11,000 souls.
3. Maronite, claiming ca. 3000 souls.
(The latter two are in communion with the Roman-Catholic Church.)
4. Armenian, claiming ca. 700 souls, and finally
5. Greek Orthodox, claiming ca. 200,000 souls.

The two Catholic sects, the Maronites and the Greek-Uniate, are few in numbers and bear the same character as their fellow-religionists in Lebanon, whence they immigrated. The main religion of the islanders is the Greek-schismatic confession. Hierarchically the Greeks of Cyprus and their clergy are different in that their ecclesiastical head, the archbishop of Nicosia, is completely independent [autocephalous] of the patriarch in Constantinople, the supreme head of all other Greek churches in the East. This independence of the Cypriot metropolitan has its roots in antiquity.

---

[390] The feast of the Assumption or Dormition is observed on 15 August.

The archbishop is chosen, theoretically, from among the 36 arch priests of the island by the people; in practice the choice is made by a few influential Greeks, who usually know how to place a weak man in this important post, in order to advance their personal interests through him.

The metropolitan resides in Nicosia and is called "Most Holy" [μακαριώτατος] and his decretals are signed in red ink.[391] The archbishop has at his disposal considerable pomp for ceremonial occasions, and the Russian government has recently, through its consuls in Cyprus and Beirut, given much money and many valuable objects to the Orthodox churches of the island. The sympathies of the Cypriots gravitate toward Athens. In the palace of the rich Greek banker as well as in the wretched hut of the Greek peasant one sees next to the icon of the Panayia (Mother of God) the pictures of the Greek royal couple and the heroes of the Greek War of Independence. When some enterprise in Athens and Greece is at stake, every Greek in Turkey as well as in Cyprus pays a voluntary contribution according to his means. Cypriots not only send goods and money for peaceful works of art, science, commerce, and the trades to the ideal homeland; their sons have fought on Crete and in Thessaly in the front ranks and given their lives.

The Greek clergy of the island is not numerous. It is extremely poor and ignorant, so that the majority of the priests can hardly read the religious books and even less fill out a certificate of baptism or death. It is usually the younger sons of the peasants who dedicate themselves to the priesthood. The first thing that they have to do to attain this dignity is to enter the house of a "papa" as a servant; then they let their hair and beard grow long, after a year or two are permitted to put on their master's dirty old suit, and wait for the death of a priest in their district, to take over his post. This is a good-natured kind of priest, who for the most part are occupied in agriculture, from which they really live, since their clerical salary seldom exceeds 300 Austrian florins per annum.

Like the whole rural population, so the priests, in their dress and their habitat, are ragged and grossly dirty. The same wretched condition prevails in the churches and monasteries. Although the most beautiful of the former Christian churches were converted to mosques or storehouses, churches and monasteries are still extraordinarily numerous; but neglect and misery can be observed in these houses of God in a pitiful way.

The other bishops of Cyprus also reside in the monasteries. Most of these are probably abbeys from the time of the crusaders, Templars, and Lusignans, apart from a few which date from the oldest period of early Christianity, since there were many Christians in Cyprus already at the time of Paul and Cyprus-born Barnabas. Like the abbeys of our countries, these monasteries take the form of mighty fortresses, and the monks are occupied in both divine service and agriculture. In contrast to European monks they seem, strangely, to have had little to do with science or the arts, since nowhere are there libraries or archives. Therefore, also, all accurate information on when the monasteries were founded is unfortunately lacking.

Even in the monasteries the number of monks is small, and, except for the monastery of Khrysomatissia [?], scarcely five or six monks live in the mostly very large buildings. The appearance of these servants of God is truly pitiful. In a robe torn and faded by sun and rain, the hair and beard hanging down in filthy locks under a cap riddled with holes, with a lifeless stare which announces his being tired of life, the Cypriot monk slinks along, mentally wasting away in unbelievable ignorance.

---

[391] Hackett, *Orthodox Church,* 258.

In the churches there still prevails the old spirit of Byzantium, which decorates them with dark, heavily gilded icons, while in other ways the temple of God abounds in filth. The Panayia almost ranks higher than Christ, and to her, too, the place of honor is assigned at the altar. She glories in much richer make-up in the icons and is especially often licked [kissed] by the faithful. Above the Panayia there is at times a gift of pious Russians, a Russian eagle. Next to the Mother of God St. George is venerated the most. The icons of these three are usually covered by an age-old layer of saliva and dust.

Just as once the priests of Cybele contended with those of Athena, so now frequently various monasteries contend one with another over who might possess the more powerful saint or whose relic of the cross might be the more authentic.

A particularly comical example of religious confusion might be seen in the competition in which two monasteries not so far from Larnaca engage over their patron saint. Both possess the same St. George; only his icon in one monastery shows him long and his icon in the other shows him short. Georgios megalos and Georgios mikros now fight bitterly over who merits more veneration and more contributions.[392] The monasteries of Monte Croce [Stravovouni] and Lefkara are at odds with each other over the authenticity of their particles of the cross.[393]

In general the monks are hospitable, and, since there are no inns in Cyprus, travelers find monasteries the best place to stay.

Among the previously mentioned peculiarities of the Cypriot clergy there is one which I must not fail to mention and which is shared with the whole population; this is the great frugality, which at the time of fasting turns into unreasonable asceticism.

I shall next offer a description of some of the island's most characteristic monasteries; this is based partly on the excellent works of Professors [Franz] Unger and [Theodor] Kotschy and partly on my own observation.

## Monasteries

Bellapais. On the north slope of the mountains of Kyrenia, three and one half hours east of Kyrenia and on the same elevation as Fungi [or Funji, an estate near Kyrenia], we find the monastery of Bellapais. All around, right to the tip of the mountain, one is greeted by lovely, fertile land. Luxuriant fields of wheat alternate with light-green vineyards and gray olive groves with dark stands of carob trees.

I had visited this charming place at a time when a multicolored carpet of flowers stretched down to the mirror-smooth, blue sea below and the clear air granted a view even of the highlands of Caramania, commanding the entire northern part of the island at the same time. Like a true picture of Crusaders, the walls of a pure Gothic structure greet us; unfortunately they are falling into ruin more and more, from one day to the next. They hail from those days when the monks' cups were filled with hyacinth-colored wine, but they did not disdain to fight, sword in hand, for cross and prince.

Hugh III of Tarentum [1267–1284] built this fortified abbey around the middle of the 13th century.[394] Then it was named Abbey of Peace—de la paix. The language of the

---

[392] Hackett, *Orthodox Church*, 365 gives the names of the two monasteries as Georgios tou Kontou and Georgios tou Makri. Gunnis, *Cyprus*, 118, gives a more reasonable explanation.
[393] Hackett, *Orthodox Church*, 453–54.
[394] Hugh was a benefactor of the monastery, but not its founder. See Hackett, *Orthodox Church*, 611–15.

people changed the name to Bellapais, and not without justification: the area in the center of which the Gothic monastery rises on the outcropping rocks is magically beautiful. It was turned over by Hugh to the knights of the Premonstratensian Order. And there, too, this king, who came to be called "the Great" because of his efforts for art and science and also for the welfare of his small country, lies buried. Of the whole complex, which is built of blocks of white sandstone, the refectory is preserved in its entirety; it features a delicate pulpit at a pointed window toward the sea. Also preserved, with their high vaults, is the greater part of the corridors of the cloister, which on the inside surrounded the living quarters of the clerics.

Of the three-story high main building even the lower vaults have collapsed, and in the large hall of knights wild roses are blooming. Here once stood the heroic figures of knights and surrounded the last daughter of the Lusignan dynasty, Queen Charlotte, who heroically defended herself at Bellapais against the bastard prince James II (1464), who was to become the last shadow king of Cyprus and shadow husband of Catherine Cornaro.

The monastery church outside of the quadrangle has now been converted into a poor Greek church, in which crude Byzantine icons form a sharp contrast to the pure lines of Gothic architecture. Above the great entrance portal, which leads from the cloister into the refectory, the escutcheons of the Lusignans and of Jerusalem can be seen well preserved, carved in stone. Outside of the cloister there is a well-preserved open sarcophagus of white marble, with a beautiful floral relief and a genius in the center.

Thus this proud building, erected by human hands, goes to ruin, while surrounded on all sides by new springs with new blossoms.

Akhiropiitos: To the northwest of Bellapais and north of the new Lapithos lies one of the largest and best preserved monasteries, that of Akhiropiitos ['Αχειροποίητος = "built without hands"]. It is situated on a rock close to the sea. Below this rock there is a grotto, from which good spring water flows abundantly. In the yard rises a church dedicated to St. Pantaleon [or Panteleimon].[395]

From the lofty refectory one overlooks one of the most charming landscapes of Cyprus: on the left the high mountains, on the right the blue sea, and between them a veritable garden of nature, the fertile plain. Next to the monastery lie the ruins of the old Lapithos (now Lampusti [Lambousa]), and half an hour away from there the new Lapithos, built from the stones of the old. The icon of the Panayia reportedly contains a piece from the sudarium of Jesus Christ [the *mandylion*] and hence the name of the monastery.

The modern Morphou developed from the ancient Greek city of Limenia, and on the ruins of the ancient city the Byzantine monastery of St. Mamas stands in the middle of Morphou.[396] The manner in which this monastery was built is peculiarly irregular: there are in the nave of the church sixteen columns on the right side and eleven columns on the left side; the capitals of these columns are quite different one from another, and some are monotone while others are painted. The supposedly miracle-working saint is depicted on the sarcophagus which contains his bones; he is riding on a fierce lion and himself looking fierce. The monastery is one of the more affluent ones, and the monks engage in sericulture.

---

[395] The dedication to this saint is questionable. For a different account see Gunnis, *Cyprus*, 315.
[396] The author erroneously speaks of a female St. Mama. On St. Mamas see Hackett, *Orthodox Church*, 415–18.

The pilgrimage monastery of Kykko is visited even by Russian pilgrims. This monastery is built on a lonely plateau, on an almost impassable rock, in the district of Lefka. The icon of the Panayia is believed to have been painted by St. Luke himself, like the one in Bologna with the help of the archangel Gabriel;[397] it says nothing for the great artistic talent of the Evangelist. Isaac Komnenos is supposed to have brought it from Byzantium. The monastery was once inhabited by 170 monks of the Order of St. Basil.

Because of its lofty location (nearly 1200 m.) the monastery of Troodhitissa deserves mention; it is located on the south slope of Mt. Olympos, 12 m. lower than Prodhromos, in a narrow wooded canyon. Almost ruined today, its Alpine-like vegetation offers tourists a peculiar charm.

## Industry and Commerce

To speak of art and science under these cultural conditions would be ironical. We have seen how certain trades and agriculture are conducted in the manner of lake-dwellers. Nevertheless there exist in Cyprus some branches of industry which would easily be capable of development. Wool and woollen fabrics especially, but also calico are produced. Apart from the usual offerings of Turkish bazaars, such as lace-work, cloth, leather, and saddlery, there are special branches of Greek Cypriot industry. To this class belongs the domestic weaving of silk in Nicosia, Larnaca, Kilani [ca. 15 miles northwest of Limassol], Ritima [?], and Paphos; the girls of the household do this on very primitive looms, but with great skill and good taste.

Likewise tanneries and dye-shops have established themselves in Nicosia and other major locations, especially since the Franco-Prussian War has made the importation of leather from France more difficult. These establishments offer a fully competitive product, especially saffron and cordovan, which is already exported to Syria and Egypt. In the areas rich in [olive] oil good soap is produced, and brandy is distilled in wine-growing areas. Both products, particularly the latter, given the juicy grapes and abundant carobs, will play an important role in the future under English administration.

Even though all the trades which are necessary for daily life are carried on in Cyprus, this is only at a very primitive level. The irregularly built houses and huts witness to the shortage of master builders, just as the primitive boats witness to the lack of shipyards. The latter, absolutely necessary and very profitable, will surely be built by the new owners.

Now, in discussing actual trade, it is to be observed that the data which hitherto have been made available on commercial activities in all the trade centers of the Ottoman Empire, whether in consular reports or in special studies of national economists, are highly inaccurate and even have to be so, given the conditions under which they are produced. A literature of monographs in the field of trade policies developed only beginning with the World Exhibition of 1873. This literature, although derived from often most heterogeneous sources, has acquainted the educated public of Europe with the countries and peoples of the Orient. The difficulties with which such studies had to contend is, by the way, easily understood if one knows how they had to be undertaken. Especially in Turkey the collection of data is far more difficult than in our countries, since authentic state records are in most cases entirely lacking and one is thus dependent on one's own observation.

---

[397] In the sanctuary of Madonna di San Luca, in the hills above the city.

In the present study I have endeavored to draw the necessary information, as far as possible, from my own perceptions and observations on the spot, while I have used other persons' conclusions, when offered to me, only with great reservations, not to say mistrust.

In the north Cyprus is only 25 miles [correctly ca. 50 nautical miles] distant from Caramania, and thus all of Asia Minor is open to it; similarly in the east Syria and Palestine lead to Persia, India, and Arabia, while Egypt controls the southern routes. This fortunate strategic location of the island should be equally fortunate for its trade.

At the present time the export trade of Cyprus is very insignificant and represents a total value of barely 4,000,000 florins, while the value of imports amounts to 1,500,000 florins, given the few and truly primitive needs of the island's people.

Apart from silk textiles, which can really be called finished products, and wine and brandy, which can be called half-finished products, all exports from Cyprus are raw materials. [The statistical tables given on pp. 44–46 are here omitted.]

The government will have to pay attention above all to agriculture. A free class of peasants already exists, and European farmers in Cyprus will set a good example with model operations. Cyprus could soon regain its material prosperity, mainly by the introduction of practical agricultural implements and machines and by the acclimatization of new utility plants of which the English colonies possess so many and which are suited to the soil and climate of the island; and also by the management of the forests, initially handled with Draconian severity. The products if Cyprus will then be of importance also for export.

## Life

Daily life was in general exceedingly cheap until the arrival of the English, just as in the coastal cities of Syria. For the moment the prices for foodstuffs and real estate may have risen out of proportion. This is especially due to the fact that initially the entire English occupation was limited to the Scala and to Larnaca, where even the most sanguine English speculators found that everything was as expensive as the climate was bad and life miserable. Thus most of the accounts which give a negative picture of the island of Cyprus have come about, since their authors have judged the entire island by Larnaca, with which alone they were familiar.

Based on what I have said about the development of a free class of peasants, it is my impression that there are very few day-workers on the island, and these are hired only against high wages. A day's pay is normally as much as 1½ florins; women hired for the year receive per year 100 florins, men 150 florins, plus maintenance and clothing. The Turks cultivate their fields mostly with slaves, which they buy in the markets of Tanta in Egypt, Damascus in Syria, or Magnesia in Anatolia. The price of a male slave ranged from 200 to 500 florins, that of a female from 300 to 1000 florins.

## Political Organization

Prior to the Convention of 4 July 1878 and since the year 1870 Cyprus formed its own liva. This was divided in eighteen districts or cazas as follows:

Larnaca, capital Larnaca
Limassol, capital Limassol
Piscopi, capital Episkopi

Kilani, capital Kilani
Avdimou [Evdhimou], capital Avdimou
Paphos, capital Paphos
Kouklia, capital Kouklia
Lefka, capital Lefka
Morphou, capital Morphou
Orini, capital Lithrodonta
Piliria [?], capital Pera
Kythrea, capital Kythrea
Lapithos, capital Lapithos
Kyrenia, capital Kyrenia
Mesauria [Mesaoria], capital Atpeniou [Athienou?]
Famagusta, capital Famagusta
Karpas, capital Trikomo.[398]

The liva was governed by a governor [pasha]; a cazas was administered by a kai-makam; the latter, in turn, appointed the village heads. Public security and police were the concern of the mudir and the kadis.

In reality security was owed to the indolence of the people, for gendarmerie or police were non-existent.

## Language

The dominant language on the island is, naturally enough, modern Greek. The country folk speak a broad dialect heavily seasoned with Arabic and Italian phrases. But good Hellenic Greek is generally understood by the Cypriots and fluently spoken by the upper class. In the few locations of the plain in which Turks live next to Greeks, even they prefer to speak Greek, just as in the interior of Anatolia there are Greeks who can speak only Turkish. Cypriots will quickly adopt the language of Athens, especially since they have a definite talent for modulation and rhyme. I have witnessed how at festive occasions women and men indulge in improvised verses which in form and contents in no way reflect badly on the descendants of Homeric rhapsodes.

With what devotion the Cypriot people cling to their language is borne out by the fact that the first collective request addressed to the new English government was that Greek be made the official language.

## The Significance of Cyprus

What the possession of Cyprus means for England and its position in the East, for the Oriental-Indian question, and for Egypt can be summarized in a few words. Whoever holds Cyprus and has a fleet controls Asia Minor and Egypt, and the Bay of Alexandretta as well. Iskenderun or Alexandretta, we know, is going to become the terminus of the Euphrates railway. This port lies only forty miles from the valley of the Euphrates and only seven miles from Aleppo, which the new railway line will again make the central point for Persia-Mesopotamia and India. Cyprus and Iskenderun with the Euphrates railway will give to the English the sole control of Asia Minor, Palestine, Arabia, and Persia,

---

[398] For a complete account of the administrative organization see Hill, *History,* IV 5–8.

and at the same time a defensive position against possible attacks on India. Thus, for trade as well as strategically, Cyprus is for Great Britain the key which secures the treasures which she already holds and opens up immeasurable new ones.

In recognition of the importance of Cyprus, efforts are now being launched in Turkish circles to develop other islands of the archipelago, especially Mytilene and Rhodes, into places which will compete with Cyprus. Mytilene shall become a free port with great warehouses and the residence of the vali of the archipelago.[399] Sadik Pasha, an eager supporter of Midhat Pasha[400] and one of the most competent administrators, reportedly will be entrusted with the implementation of these reforms. The world has become accustomed, however, to viewing such reform projects of individual enlightened Turkish statesmen with considerable skepticism. In this case it is an additional factor that it would be a struggle against two much stronger cultures, the British and the Greek; and these, furthermore, would enter the arena under far better conditions, so that the result of such competition leaves no room for doubt. Waged with the weapons of peace and competition, the battle may yet ensue; in that case it will not be a total loss even for the loser.

---

[399] A vali is a provincial governor.
[400] On Midhat Pasha see Stanford J. Shaw, *History of the Ottoman Empire and modern Turkey* (Cambridge, 1976–1977) II passim.

# APPENDIX:
## Biographical Sketches[401]

In 19th century Europe it was fashionable for men, and sometimes women, of means and standing to travel extensively beyond the limits of their respective homelands. They might undertake such travel as an indispensable part of their education, in the pursuit of scholarly objectives, in line of official duties, or as adventurers. Such travel was encouraged, too, by the colonizing and commercial activities of the great European powers. And also during this century archaeology emerged as a serious scholarly discipline. As for travelers to the Near East, one may think of the Anglo-Swiss explorer John L. Burkhardt, the German theologian Constantin von Tischendorff, or the romantic and eccentric Lady Hester Stanhope. And already in the 18th century there had been Bishop Richard Pococke.

Cyprus was frequently included in travelers' itineraries, not uncommonly as a convenient stopping place on the way to or from the Levant. Many of the European states maintained consulates in Larnaca. Of French scholars active in Cyprus in the 19th century only a few shall be mentioned here. Louis de Mas Latrie (1815–1897) was a distinguished scholar primarily interested in mapping the island and in the history of the Lusignans. Albert Gaudry (1827–1908) deserves to be remembered as a map maker. Melchior de Vogüé (1829–1916), William Waddington (1826–1894), and Edmond Duthoit (1837–1889), going far beyond the casual copying of inscriptions practiced by earlier visitors to the island, put Cypriot epigraphy on a sound scholarly basis.[402] The British took an interest in Cyprus well before the island was ceded to them by Turkey. Robert Hamilton Lang, British consul at Larnaca in 1863–1872, was active as an excavator, collector, and epigrapher. Some years later, Claude Delaval Cobham, district commissioner at Larnaca in 1879–1907, made fine scholarly contributions to the field. And, of course, Luigi Palma di Cesnola should not be passed over.

It is the purpose of this article to give an account of selected German travelers and archaeologists in Cyprus during the first three quarters of the 19th century.[403] The period of British rule in Cyprus is thus not included. I shall endeavor to show who these men were, what they came to accomplish, what they experienced, and how they responded to their experiences. I shall proceed in chronological order.

**Freiherr Joseph von Hammer-Purgstall** [Plate 1] (1774 Graz–1856 Vienna) was an Austrian civil servant, scholar, and poet. He had spent ten years studying Oriental languages, especially Persian and Turkish, at the Orientalische Akademie in Vienna. He

[401] The kind assistance given by Prof. Andreas Mehl of the University of Halle is gratefully acknowledged. An earlier version of this chapter was published as "German Travelers on Cyprus in the 19th Century," *Epiterida* 30 (2004) 361–391 (Cyprus Research Centre, ed. Dr. Nicholas Coureas).
[402] Olivier Masson, " Les archéologues et voyageurs du XIXe siècle" / "Archaeologists and Travelers in the XIXth Century" in *Kinyras: L'Archéologie française à Chypre / Kinyras: French Archaeology in Cyprus* (Lyon: Maison de l'Orient, 1993, and Paris: Bocard, 1993) 17–22; Lucie Bonato, "Melchior de Vogüé et alii and Cyprus," in Veronica Tatton-Brown, ed., *Cyprus in the 19th century AD: Fact, Fancy and Fiction* (Oxford, 2001) 189–97; Rita C. Severis, "Edmond Duthoit: An Artist and Etnographer in Cyprus, 1862, 1865," *ibid.* 32–49, with 60 figs.
[403] Several of these men were German only in the sense that German was their native tongue; six were Austrians, one a subject of the Czar, and another the subject of the King of Denmark.

held government appointments in Istanbul, Moldavia, and Vienna. In 1847 he founded the Österreichische Akademie der Wissenschaften and became its first president. In 1958 the Österreichische Orientgesellschaft or Hammer-Purgstall-Gesellschaft was established in his honor.[404] His numerous publications include *Geschichte des osmanischen Reiches*.[405]

In the present context another of his publications needs to be examined: *Topographische Ansichten gesammelt auf einer Reise in die Levante*.[406] In Cyprus von Hammer-Purgstall visited sites at Limassol, Paphos, and Larnaca. He came well prepared; he had read Pococke and compared his own observations with Pococke's descriptions.[407] One will observe that he had studied not only Oriental languages, but also Latin and Greek. There are quotations from *Homeric Hymn* 5 (to Aphrodite), Sappho, Vergil, Ovid, Horace, Martial, Tacitus, and Pliny. He waxes romantic when he imagines Aphrodite rising from the sea or her rites being performed at Paphos or at Amathus, or when he tells the myth of Pygmalion.[408] He was amazed at the two colossal stone vases at Amathus, both still *in situ* then.[409] His fascination with the Phoenicians led him to assert that the tombs of Paphos were Phoenician and that the Doric order of architecture was invented not by the Greeks but by the Phoenicians.[410] He was interested in the dress and the speech of the local people. He observes, strangely enough, that most Muslims on Cyprus speak both Greek and Arabic. Did he mean Greek and Turkish? Surely he knew the difference. He was aware of the unhealthy climate prevailing at Larnaca. The most valuable part of his account is probably to be seen in the inscriptions which he copied, transcribed, and translated, but not without some mistakes.[411]

**Johann Adam Bergk** (1769–1834) was a "Doctor beider Rechte und der Philosophie" (doctor of canon law, civil law, and philosophy) and a "Privatgelehrter" (independent scholar) in Leipzig.[412] His interests and publications ranged widely across several disciplines, such as philosophy, especially the philosophy of Kant, political science, history, and geography. He has been called a "Popularphilosoph" and does not receive

---

[404] Karl Goedeke, *Grundriss zur Geschichte der deutschen Dichtung*, 2nd. ed. (Dresden, 1884 ff.) VII 747–70; Wilhelm Bietak, *Gottes ist der Orient, Gottes ist der Okzident: Eine Studie über Joseph von Hammer-Purgstall* (Vienna, 1948); *Österreichisches Biographisches Lexikon 1815–1950*, fasc. 7 (1958) 165–68; Sepp Reichl, *Hammer-Purgstall: Auf den romantischen Pfaden eines österreichischen Orientforschers* (Graz and Vienna, 1973). See further *The Catholic Encyclopedia* 7 (1910) 124–25; *Neue deutsche Biographie* 7 (1965) 593–94; *Deutsche biographische Enzyklopädie* 6 (1996) 362; *Austrian Information* (New York: Austrian Consulate General; also online) LII, no. 6/7, July 1999; Online AEIOU* Österreich Lexikon in either English or German.

[405] 1st ed., 10 vols., Pest, 1827–1833. 2nd ed., 4 vols., Pest, 1834–1836.

[406] Hammer-Purgstall, *Ansichten*, 121–55 and 176–84 are concerned with Cyprus.

[407] Pococke, *Description*; *SHC* V 35–56.

[408] Hammer-Purgstall, *Ansichten*, 121, 135, 147–49, and 155–56.

[409] Hammer-Purgstall, *Ansichten*, 128. The intact one of the two vases was removed to the Louvre in 1865/1866. See Antoine Hermary, *Catalogue des antiquités de Chypre: Sculptures* (Paris: Musée du Louvre, Département des antiquités orientales, 1989), no. 918.

[410] Hammer-Purgstall, *Ansichten*, 140 and 155.

[411] *CIG* II 2613–15, 2618, 2620, 2628–29, 2637, 2640–44, 2648–49, and 2652.

[412] See further *Allgemeine deutsche Biographie* 2 (1875) 389; *Meyers Konversationslexikon*, 4th ed., 2 (1888) 737; Robert S. Bledsoe, "Harnessing the Autonomous Work of Art: Enlightenment and Aesthetic Education in Johann Adam Bergk's *Die Kunst, Bücher zu lesen*," *German Life and Letters*, n.s., 53 (October, 2000) 470–86.

much attention today. More attention has been paid to his son Theodor Bergk (1812–1881), a noted classical scholar.

**Otto Friedrichs von Richter** [Plate 4] was born in 1792 on a country estate near Dorpat (Tartu in Estonian, Yuryev in Russian), Estonia, into a noble family of German extraction. He was privately tutored and also studied in Moscow, Heidelberg, and Vienna, taking a special interest in ethnography and languages. In Vienna, much to his advantage, he made the acquaintance of Joseph von Hammer-Purgstall. Posthumously published writings include *Rekonstruktion und Geschichte der römischen Rednerbühne* (64 pp. Berlin, 1884) and *Über antike Steinmetzzeichen*, etc. (51 pp. Berlin, 1885). In 1815–1816 he traveled extensively in the Near East, including Cyprus; he died in 1816 at Smyrna before he could complete his intended itinerary. His diary and letters were edited and published in book form by his former tutor, Johann Philipp Gustav Ewers.[413] The inscriptions which he had gathered were published by Johann Valentin Francke.[414]

Von Richter reached Cyprus on 12 March 1816, landing at Famagusta. He had spent the previous few months in Egypt, Nubia, and the Holy Land. What he saw at Famagusta seems to have filled him with sadness. There were few houses amidst the ruins, and only some three hundred Turkish inhabitants were "slinking about." Formerly beautiful houses were once the abode of knights, but now only of donkeys. Surveying the surrounding plain from the walls he observed flocks of sheep alternating with cemeteries.

At Larnaca von Richter, being a Russian subject, enjoyed the hospitality of the Russian consul, a Greek named Peristiany. Of the consuls at Larnaca in general he reports that they were regarded as greedy as they were smart, and that they fully replaced the Jews, who had not been permitted since the days of Trajan to live on the island.[415] The ruins of ancient Kition did not impress him, nor did the Hala Sultan Téké, which he did not even identify by name. The salt lake seemed more interesting to him. Meeting a French traveler and the French consul prompts him to remark that "no government does more for the exploration of the Orient than the French government and sends there men better prepared."[416]

On the journey from Larnaca to Nicosia von Richter stayed overnight at Athienou, the village of the muleteers, as was the practice. He noticed the beauty of his Greek hostess.

As he approached Nicosia it seemed like a beautiful city to him from the distance. Once inside he observed poorly built houses and narrow, dirty streets. He called on Archbishop Kyprianou, with whom he conversed in Turkish rather than in Greek and on whose extravagant life style he comments. Little did he know that in 1821 this same archbishop would be hanged from a tree by the bloodthirsty Turkish governor Küchük Mehmed.

---

[413] *Wallfahrten im Morgenlande* (Berlin, 1822); pp. 298–326 and 566–69 pertain to Cyprus. Ewers was born in 1781 in the village of Amelunxen (now part of Beverungen; Kreis Höxter, Westphalia). Having studied at Göttingen, he obtained an appointment as tutor in the household of the "Landrat" Otto Magnus von Richter, Otto Friedrich von Richter's father, in 1803. He was appointed professor at the University of Dorpat, then a purely German institution, in 1810 and served as rector of the university from 1818 until his death in 1830. He was the grandfather of the renowned Adolf von Harnack. See *Deutsche Biographische Enzyklopädie* 3 (1996) 200; Lea Leppik, "Ein deutscher Professor im russischen Reich: Über Leben und Werk des Historikers Gustav Ewers," in Helmut Piirimäe and Claus Sommerhage, eds., *Zur Geschichte der Deutschen in Dorpat* (Tartu, 1998) 111–39.

[414] *Griechische und lateinische Inschriften gesammelt von O. F. von Richter* (Berlin, 1830).

[415] Richter, *Wallfahrten*, 307.

[416] Richter, *Wallfahrten*, 310.

Next von Richter visited the monastery of St. John Chrysostom. He complains about the icons in the church being blackened and about the church being so dark that he could not tell whether the ceiling decorations were painted or mosaics. He did enjoy the entertainment that came with his dinner. From the monastery he took the strenuous climb up to Buffavento Castle at an altitude of 954 m. The sight from there, in both directions, very much impressed him.

On the way back he stopped at Kythrea, staying with a well-to-do Greek named Petraki. He listened with sympathy to his host's complaint about being harassed by the government. He was aware of the heavy taxation imposed on the people, the mindless depletion of the forests, and the general mismanagement apparent everywhere.

In the course of his travels he took time to copy five inscriptions, four of them Greek, the fifth one Venetian.[417] These inscriptions had not been previously recorded by von Hammer-Purgstall.

On 21 March at Larnaca he boarded a ship which got under way only with some delay, passed Limassol and Paphos, and took him to Alaja, now Alanya, on the coast of Caramania, where he debarked on 25 March. In nine days he had seen about as much of the island as he could, given the difficulty of travel on the island. He had observed carefully and intelligently.

**Ludwig Ross** [Plate 5] was born in 1806 on an estate near Bornhöved in Schleswig-Holstein (then part of Denmark). He graduated from the University of Kiel in 1829 and undertook a journey to Greece in 1832. There he was appointed conservator of antiquities, first at Nauplia in 1833 and then at Athens in 1834, by King Otho. He is best remembered for his discovery of the substructure of the Parthenon and his reconstruction of the Nike-Temple on the Athenian Acropolis.[418] He was also an excellent epigrapher.[419] Appointed professor at the University of Athens in 1837, he lectured in Modern Greek, in which he had become fluent. In 1841 he published a handbook on archaeology in Greek, Ἐγχειρίδιον τῆς ἀρχαιολογίας τῶν τεχνῶν. Dismissed from his post in 1843 for political reasons, he was appointed professor in the University of Halle. But he did not assume his duties there until the fall of 1845, having spent the intervening time traveling in Greek lands. Embroiled in a bitter academic dispute and suffering from a painful and incurable disease, he ended his life by suicide in 1859.[420]

Ludwig Ross is currently receiving much attention. He was the subject of a conference at the German Archaeological Institute in Athens in the fall of 2002. In December 2002 Prof. Andreas Mehl of the University of Halle gave a lecture on him at a collo-

---

[417] For the Greek inscriptions see *CIG* II 2617, 2627, 2645, and 2647.

[418] Ludwig Ross, *Die Akropolis von Athen nach den neuesten Ausgrabungen* (Berlin, 1839).

[419] Ludwig Ross, *Inscriptiones Graecae ineditae*, 3 vols. (Nauplia, 1834–1845).

[420] *Allgemeine deutsche Biographie* 29 (1899) 246–53; Carl Robert, *Zum Gedächnis von Ludwig Ross. Rede zum Antritt des Rektorats der vereinigten Friedrichs-Universität Halle-Wittenberg am 12. Juli 1906* (28 pp. Berlin, 1906. Microfilm at the University of Cincinnati); Olivier Masson and Antoine Hermary, "Le Voyage de Ludwig Ross à Chypre en 1845 et les antiquités chypriotes du Musée de Berlin," *Cahier* 9 (1988) 3–10; Christoph Schwingenstein in Lullies and Schiering, *Archäologenbildnisse*, 27–28. R. Ross Holloway, *The Hand of Daedalus* (Providence, R. I.: Brown University, The Center for Old World Archaeology and Art, online publication, 1999) Chapter II, "The Fateful Year 480 in the History of Greek Art," 1–21 at 6.

quium at the University of Salzburg. For the 200th anniversary of Ross's birth in 2006 the University of Halle and the University of Kiel are planning a joint exhibition.[421]

Ross traveled extensively throughout Greece and also in Cyprus. He reported on his experiences and activities in the first three volumes of *Reisen auf die griechischen Inseln*.[422] In 1852 he added a fourth volume to the set, titling it *Reisen nach Kos, Halikarnassos, Rhodos und der Insel Cypern* (Halle, 1852). In his preface he modestly refers to this work of VIII+212 pp. as a "Bändchen" (little volume). Pages 83–212 pertain to Cyprus. The value of this report was recognized by Claude Delaval Cobham, who translated it into English and published it under the title *A Journey to Cyprus, February and March 1845*.[423]

Ross arrived at Larnaca on 16 February 1845, having left Smyrna four days earlier on an Austrian steamer. He stayed on the island five-and-a-half weeks, traveling tirelessly and never complaining about the hardships associated with his travels. He came well prepared; he knew what Homer, Thucydides, Strabo, Ovid, Pliny the Elder, Tacitus, Plutarch, Pausanias, Aelian, Stephanus Byzantius, and Constantine Porphyrogenitus had to say about Cyprus; he had read Lusignan,[424] "Meursius,"[425] Pococke,[426] Mariti,[427] von Hammer-Purgstall, Ali Bey,[428] Müller,[429] Engel,[430] and Movers.[431] He recorded a wealth of geographical, topographical, and archaeological observations. He copied a fair number of inscriptions, which he later published in the *Rheinisches Museum* or in *Gerhards Archäologische Zeitung*. He acquired several ancient statuettes for the Berlin Museum. He is rightly numbered among the pioneers who established archaeology as an academic discipline.

We can share in the grief which he felt over the loss of what today is called cultural property. He tells of villagers who found a life-size bronze statue, but hacked it to pieces and sold the fragments for the value of the metal; of other villagers who dragged a large inscribed stone to the shore to load it onto a ship, but then, when the ship did not appear, simply abandoned it to be lost forever; and of a man, a consular agent at that, who routinely broke up ancient inscriptions because he believed that there was money inside the stones. Both of the colossal stone vases at Amathus were still intact at the time of the Turkish conquest, he thinks. Ancient ruins, of course, in Cyprus as elsewhere, were used for quarries, and anyone taking an interest in antiquities was believed to be a treasure hunter.

Ross does not limit his interest to matters of history and archaeology. He has much to say on socio-economic conditions, the administration of the island, and on religious practices. Like von Richter he finds the view of Nicosia splendid from the distance, but once inside the city he is appalled by shabby houses and narrow and dirty

---

[421] Information courtesy of Prof. Mehl.

[422] (Stuttgart and Tübingen, 1840–1845). Later editions under slightly different titles.

[423] (Nicosia, 1910). A microfilm of this rare title exists in the library of the Royal Commonwealth Society at the University of Cambridge.

[424] Steffano Lusignano, *Chorograffia et breve historia universale de Cipro* (Bologna, 1573). See *SHC* X.

[425] Johannes van Meurs, *Creta, Cyprus, Rhodus* etc. (2nd. ed. Amsterdam, 1675).

[426] Pococke, *Description*. *SHC* V 35–56.

[427] Giovanni Mariti, *Viaggi per l'isola di Cipro* etc. (10 vols. Lucca, 1769–1776). An English translation by Claude Delaval Cobham, first published in 1909, is available.

[428] Ali Bey, alias Domingo Badia y Leblich, *Travels in Morocco, Tripoli, Cyprus* etc., 2 vols. (London, 1816).

[429] Karl Otfried Müller, *Handbuch der Archäologie der Kunst* (2nd. ed. Breslau, 1835).

[430] Engel, *Kypros*.

[431] Franz Carl Movers, *Die Phoenizier*, 2 vols. in 4 (Bonn, 1841–1856).

streets. He observes poverty generally prevailing among both Turks and Greeks, exorbitant rates of taxation, and the steady loss of population and decline of prosperity. All of these he attributes to the "wretched Turkish rule,"[432] and what little prosperity remains is simply a left-over of Frankish times. He knows about the Turkish excesses of 1821, and he calls Küzük Mehmed, the Turkish governor at the time, a "Wüterich" (raging madman).[433]

His impressions of the religious life on the island are quite negative: "It seems indeed that for the peoples of the Near East, who like to think and to feel little, the Greek church and Islam are the most suitable religions, since these, in their intellectual stupor, place all religious merit in mechanical, external exercises. The Catholic Church makes too many demands on their [the people's] mind and heart. As for Protestantism, since it has almost no symbolism or external forms of devotion at all, it is for the Orientals no religion at all."

He has learned about the intrigues which accompany the election of the archbishop, the secret Christians (Linobambakoi), and the ignorance of both people and clergy.

On 26 March, by invitation of the French consul, he boarded a French warship; on 7 April he arrived in the Piraeus, where he had to endure a 17-day quarantine before he could continue his travels.

**Julius Heinrich Petermann** [Plate 7] (1801–1876) was an orientalist with a special interest in ancient Armenia. He completed his studies at the University of Berlin in 1829, was a "Privatdozent" there in 1830–1837, and was then appointed professor of oriental philology. In 1852–1855 he traveled throughout the Near East, including Cyprus, and in 1868–1869 he served as consul general of the North German Confederation in Jerusalem. His collection of no fewer than 1532 Near Eastern manuscripts is held by the Staatsbibliothek in Berlin (Unter den Linden). The library also owns the author's copy of his *Grammatica linguae armenicae* (Berlin, 1837).[434]

Of his numerous books the one of the greatest interest in the present context is *Reisen im Orient* (2 vols. Leipzig, 1860–1861). In this work pages 41–43, 344–45, and 358–74 of Volume I pertain to Cyprus. In the preface (p. VIII) he announces that, following the advice of Alexander von Humboldt, he will not take the travels and researches of other scholars into account, but will report only what he himself has seen and experienced. And, indeed, there are no citations or quotations.

On 16 July 1852 Petermann spent a few hours at Larnaca, while the ship on which he was traveling lay off shore. Having occasion to call on the Prussian consul, an elderly gentleman named Giovanni Mattei, he inquired about the possibility of buying ancient coins and manuscripts. He was told that he might find a few coins but that there was little hope of finding manuscripts. Later, on board his ship, he made the acquaintance of another passenger who opined that indeed it should be possible to find some manuscripts on Cyprus. Petermann resolved to return. On a second, again very brief, stop at Larnaca on 1 October 1853 he managed to acquire some coins.

---

[432] Ross, *Reisen*, 175.
[433] Ross, *Reisen*, 93.
[434] Meyers *Konversationslexikon* 12 (1888) 911; Joseph Karst, *Geschichte der armenischen Philologie* (Heidelberg, 1930) 3–4; *Neue deutsche Biographie* 20 (2000) 238; Deutsche Staatsbibliothek, *Armeni syn die menschen genant* (Exhibition catalog. Berlin, 2000) 235–36.

Petermann took time for a third, longer visit, arriving at Larnaca on 22 October 1853. Two days later he left on the first of two excursions inland. His travel arrangements are interesting: leaving some of his belongings with his host in Larnaca, he required "only" three mules to carry his bed, kitchen utensils, and food supply. He had trouble communicating with his "mucker" (muleteer or guide), whether it be in Greek or in Turkish.

This first excursion took him to Famagusta and Salamis. Observing the city of Famagusta, he says that "the city . . . like everything that has fallen into Turkish hands, is ruined and desolate," and the "maniacal destruction wreaked by the fanatical Turks" filled him with sadness.[435] At Salamis he saw the so-called prison of St. Catherine and the monastery of St. Barnabas. He also had been able to buy some more coins.

The second excursion took him, with the usual overnight stop at Athienou, to Nicosia. He, too, was impressed by the splendid view of the city as he approached it; he took quarters at the Franciscan monastery. Continuing from Nicosia to points further north, he suffered a fall from his mule, striking his chest on a stone; this was to give him considerable pain for the rest of the excursion. He visited Bellapais Abbey, Kyrenia, and Akheropiitos (Ἀχειροποίητος) Monastery, where a relic of the famous mandylion was kept. Some ninety years ago, he reports, this monastery was plundered and burned by Turkish robbers from Caramania, but the relic survived, while the monastery's library went up in flames. His interest in all things Armenian prompts him to tell the legend of King Abgar and the mandylion at length.[436]

He returned to Larnaca by way of Nicosia and on 5 November embarked for Beirut, where he hoped to get some medical assistance. Of manuscripts he had found none.

**Theodor Kotschy** [Plate 8] (1813–1866) was a botanist at the Botanisches Hof-Cabinet in Vienna. For more than twenty years he traveled extensively in the Balkans, North Africa, and the Near East. Cyprus was part of his itinerary three times: in 1840, 1859, and 1862. He reported on his second visit to Cyprus in "Reise nach Cypern und Klein-Asien, 1859," in *Petermann's geographische Mittheilungen* 8 (1862) 289–304.[437] On the third visit he was accompanied by Franz Unger (to be considered next), with whom he then joined in co-authoring *Die Insel Cypern, ihrer physischen und organischen Natur nach, mit Rücksicht auf ihre frühere Geschichte* (Vienna, 1865). He was an indefatigable collector; on one journey alone, in 1837, he sent home 80,000 botanical specimens, and the toal number of specimens collected by him exceeds 300,000! Quite a few plants are named after him. He is regarded as the founder of the tradition of Oriental research still carried on at Vienna's Museum of Natural History.[438]

Kotschy arrived for his second visit to Cyprus on 29 March 1859 and lodged with the Austrian consul in Larnaca. As a natural scientist rather than an archaeologist or historian, he was keenly interested in the natural environment of the city. He comments on the flowers, trees, and gardens, all at their loveliest at this time of year, on the petrified conchylia (mollusk shells) in the hills, and on the foam which forms on the salt lake. He

---

[435] Petermann, *Reisen*, 362–63.

[436] Petermann, *Reisen*, 372–73.

[437] August Petermann, not Julius Heinrich Petermann.

[438] *Allgemeine deutsche Biographie* XVI (1882) 763–64; K. H. Rechinger, "Theodor Kotschy, ein Pioneer der botanischen Orientforschung," *Taxon* 9 (1960) 33–35; *Österreichisches Biographisches Lexikon* 1815–1950, fasc. 17 (1967) 160; *Deutsche biographische Enzyklopädie* VI (1997) 54; Christa Riedl-Dorn in Wilfried Seipel, ed., *Die Entdeckung der Welt, die Welt der Entdeckungen: Österreichische Forscher, Sammler, Abenteurer* (exhibition catalogue, Vienna, 2001) 257–60.

was aware also of the unhealthy climate of Larnaca and advises visitors to spend as little time there as possible.

On 1 April he set out for his first excursion, to Nicosia, by way of Athienou, and from there to the monastery of St. John Chrysostom. Along the way he took plenty of thermometer, barometer, and compass readings and took detailed notes on the vegetation. He was, in modern terms, environmentally conscious when he noted the damage done not only in Cyprus, but elsewhere in the Near East as well, by the ubiquitous herds of goats.[439] He, too, found the distant view of Nicosia very pleasant; but as he approached the gate to the city, he was moved by the sad sight of the lepers begging there for alms. The most impressive buildings in the city, he remarks, are leftovers of an earlier, higher culture, and most of the buildings are quite rickety, as is Turkish practice. The streets, as in most cities in the Levant, are narrow and dirty.[440]

At the monastery of St. John Chrysostom he was well received. The monastery takes its name from a preacher at the time of Constantine, he tells us.[441] And he misinterprets the icon, in the monastery church, which depicts Maria di Molino.[442] His knowledge of history is less impressive than his knowledge of botany. He recommends the icon to future visitors for more detailed study.

In the course of the second excursion Kotschy climbed Mt. Olympus, collecting specimens as he went up. He did not take time to visit Kykko Monastery and erroneously refers to the monastery's most famous icon as having been painted by St. Mark.[443] Later that day, as he was sorting and packing his specimens, he was bothered by curious villagers who hampered his work until he firmly bade them leave. Passing through Limassol on his way back, he notes the city's commercial activity, especially in wine and St. John's bread.

On 10 April he reached Larnaca and congratulated himself on having visited the most important places of the island comfortably in less than two weeks. He had seen neither Famagusta nor Paphos. He appended to his account a table of metereological data.

To the book jointly published with Franz Unger (Unger and Kotschy, *Cypern*) Kotschy contributed nearly half: most of Chapter 5, on the vegetation of Cyprus, and an appendix surveying the animals of Cyprus.

**Franz Joseph Andreas Unger** [Plate 10] (1800–1870) was a native of Styria. He studied medicine, botany, and paleontology at the universities of Graz, Vienna, and Prague. Having practiced medicine for a number of years, he was appointed professor of botany at the Joanneum of Graz in 1835; in 1849 he was called to a professorship in Vienna. In the 1860s he traveled widely in Greece and the Levant. He was the author of 170 scientific publications and co-author with Theodor Kotschy of the book just mentioned. In his younger years he professed liberal political ideas and had to endure a seven-month

---

[439] Kotschy, "Reise," 295b–296a.

[440] Kotschy, "Reise," 294b.

[441] St. John Chrysostom, much more than a "Kanzelredner" but one of the Doctors of the Greek church, lived well after Constantine, namely c. 347–407; he was Patriarch of Constantinople in 398–404.

[442] Kotschy, "Reise," 296b. She was a noble lady and benefactress of the monastery, but not a queen, and she is attended by her son, not her daughter. See Hackett, *Orthodox Church,* 357. The icon is now lost.

[443] Kotschy, "Reise," 299b. The icon is attributed by tradition to St. Luke. See Hackett, *Orthodox Church,* 339–44, and Athanasios Papageorgiou, *Icons of Cyprus* (New York, 1970) 42–43.

imprisonment in 1823–1824. In his later years, in Vienna, his scientific ideas, sometimes anticipating the Darwinian concept of evolution, made him suspect to clerical circles.[444]

In May 1862 Unger and Kotschy spent twelve days in the village of Prodromo in the Troodos Mountains to pursue their botanical studies. In the penultimate chapter of Unger and Kotschy, *Cypern*, pp. 474–501, Unger describes his work and also his impressions: primitive houses, abject poverty, unscrupulous despoliation of the forests, and a less than dignified wedding. He observes "innate idleness" among the people, and their laziness keeps them powerless, needy, and miserable, he concludes.[445] Nearby Trooditissa Monastery he found to be a "filthy junk room."[446]

The last chapter, "Historisch-Topographisches," pages 502–69, also by Unger, will be of the greatest interest to most readers. Unger has arranged his material not in the order of a travelogue, but in topical order: churches and monasteries, forts and castles, and ancient buildings.

He begins with a complaint: it fills him with sadness and anger, he writes, to see that sacred places in Cyprus are with unbelievable carelessness surrendered to deterioration and neglect. There is no church or monastery on the island which is not to some degree delapidated. He has seen only one monastery where new construction was going on. The monks make it their business to know nothing about the foundation of their respective monastery, and nowhere are there libraries or archives.[447] On this last point, however, he is not entirely correct.[448]

Unger is sharply critical of Greek orthodox religious practices as he observed them in Cyprus. The appearance of the monks he found repulsive, and their ignorance appalling. "Diese gottgeweihte Schar" ("this God-dedicated flock") he calls them sarcastically. Much gold is wasted on the framing of icons, it seems to him, while the rest of the church is neglected. The interior of the churches "leaves the heart cold and contributes nothing to the elevation of the spirit," he finds. The constant coming and going during services and the practice of osculation offend him. He ridicules a dispute about the authenticity of a relic of the True Cross, and, as he does so, erroneously calls St. Helena Constantine's wife rather than his mother. The table manners of even a bishop are lacking, and the invocation of a saint against lice and roaches amuses him. He does credit the monks with being generally good-natured and hospitable.[449]

Unger was given at times to sentimentalism and romanticizing. Describing his visit to the Monastery of St. John Chrysostom, he writes that he envies Maria di Molino for having "such a peaceful and quiet resting place, where the screech-owls are not prevented from singing their melancholy funeral dirges even in broad daylight." The deso-

---

[444] Alexander Reyer, *Leben und Werken des Naturhistorikers Dr. Franz Unger* (Graz, 1871); *Allgemeine deutsche Biographie* 39 (1895) 286–89; Joanna Enslein, *Die wissenschaftliche Untersuchung und Wertung der anatomischen, physiologischen und ökologischen Arbeiten von Franz Unger* (Vienna, 1956); *Dictionary of Scientific Biography* 13 (1976) 542–43.

[445] Unger and Kotschy, *Cypern*, 477 and 499.

[446] Unger and Kotschy, *Cypern*, 498.

[447] Unger and Kotschy, *Cypern*, 502–503.

[448] Akheropiitos Monastery once had a library, as we have seen. So did Kykko Monastery and the Monastery of St. John Chrysostom. The foundation rules of two Cypriot Orthodox monasteries are extant. Those of Makhairas Monastery are still in the monastery; those of the Hermitage of Neophytos are now in the library of the University of Edinburgh. See Nicholas Coureas, *The Foundation Rules of Medieval Cypriot Monasteries: Makhairas and St. Neophytos* (Nicosia, 2003) 13.

[449] Unger and Kotschy, *Cypern*, 504–13.

lation of Bellapais Abbey and the view from Akheropiitos Monastery made a deep impression on him. The piers of an aqueduct he compares to ghosts, and a lone tree in a grain field to a steadfast soldier maintaining his post.[450]

The principal building in the town of Morphou is the Monastery of St. Mamas. Accounts of St. Mamas are highly unreliable, but the saint certainly was a male. Unger, nevertheless, speaks of a female St. Mama;[451] in this he apparently followed Richard Pococke.[452] Unger did not visit Kykko Monastery, although he was aware of the famous icon kept there. Of the three castles in the Pentadaktylos mountains, Buffavento, St. Hilarion, and Kantara, Unger visited only the first. But he failed to reach the very top, while Kotschy, his companion, succeeded. Nevertheless, Unger, always the scientist, took a reading with his hypsometer and got a reading of 2892 ft. above sea level.[453]

Today's readers will be dismayed to learn that the castle of Kolossi was used by its owner for the storage of grain.[454]

In his survey of ancient sites Unger describes Larnaca, Salamis, Idalion, Paphos, Palaipaphos, Amathus, Lapithos, and Lamnias (Akrotiri), in that order.[455] He includes two Phoenician inscriptions already published by Heinrich Ewald of Göttingen[456] and an Assyrian stele already removed to Berlin.[457] In an unfortunate error he confuses Zeno of Kition with Zeno of Elea.[458] The effort to explain the name of "Aphrodite" leads him to indulge in a long digression on the foam which forms on the salt lake of Larnaca.[459] Another unfortunate error occurs as he discusses the cone-shaped idol of Aphrodite: he writes κοινον κυπριων instead of κῶνος Κυπρίων.[460] His reconstruction of the temple of Aphrodite at Palaepaphos is rather speculative.[461] At Amathus the colossal stone vase was, of course, the center of his interest.[462]

A year after the publication of the Unger-Kotschy book Unger gave a lecture in Graz, titled, like the book, "Die Insel Cypern einst und jetzt."[463] In beautiful words he succeeds in relating the history of the island to its natural features. Again there is a measure of sadness as he reflects on the continuing ruination of the island's natural resources, on the primitive methods of agriculture, and on the lack of progress and initiative. And on Turkish rule he passes judgment thus: "A numbness of death followed the catastrophe

---

[450] Unger and Kotschy, *Cypern*, 514, 516, 518, 534, and 538.

[451] Unger and Kotschy, *Cypern*, 518–19.

[452] Pococke, *Description*, II. 1, 223.

[453] Unger and Kotschy, *Cypern*, 522.

[454] Unger and Kotschy, *Cypern*, 526.

[455] Unger and Kotschy, *Cypern*, 527–69.

[456] Unger and Kotschy, *Cypern*, 530–32. *Nachrichten von der Georg-Augusts-Universität und der Königlichen Gesellschaft der Wissenschaften zu Göttingen.* 5 November 1862, no. 23, pp. 457–70. Ewald (1803–1875) was a distinguished professor of Hebrew and the Old Testament; one of the "Göttingen Seven."

[457] Unger and Kotschy, *Cypern*, 532–33. A stele of Sargon II. Pergamon Museum, inv. VA 968. Acquisition by the Vorderasiatisches Museum of Berlin had been arranged in 1846 by Ludwig Ross. See Gerhard Rudolf Meyer, *Altorientalische Denkmäler im Vorderasiatischen Museum zu Berlin*, 2nd. ed. (Leipzig, 1970), p. 26, no.130, and ill.130; Jutta Börker-Klähn, *Altvorderasiatische Bildstelen und vergleichbare Felsreliefs* (Mainz, 1982) I, no. 175, and II, no. 175a–b.

[458] Unger and Kotschy, *Cypern*, 533.

[459] Unger and Kotschy, *Cypern*, 542–48.

[460] Unger and Kotschy, *Cypern*, 548.

[461] Unger and Kotschy, *Cypern*, 555–60.

[462] Unger and Kotschy, *Cypern*, 562–63.

[463] (Vienna, 1866), 21 pages.

[the conquest of Cyprus by the Turks in 1571]. No matter how significant the time that has passed since those unhappy days, the country never did rise again to its previous greatness, prosperity, and moral strength; it felt the weight of the iron chains and little by little became used to it." "And now a heart-felt farewell to the native country of the goddess of beauty and love," he concludes. "I shall never forget the hours which I spent in intimate touch with the splendid nature and with the good, pitiable people." One can feel the sincerity of his emotions.

**Carl (also Karl) Friederichs** [Plate 28] (1831–1871) studied at the universities of Göttingen and Erlangen. He became professor at the Royal University in Berlin in 1859 and director of the antiquities department at the Royal Museum in Berlin in 1868. In 1869 he was sent by the museum on a journey to various Mediterranean and Near Eastern countries for the purpose of acquiring antiquities. The lengthy and descriptive letters which he sent home to his wife were published posthumously, with only private matters omitted.[464]

In September and October 1869 Friederichs spent four weeks in Cyprus, the first two in Larnaca as guest of Luigi Palma di Cesnola and the second two traveling with him across the central and western parts of the island. On 11 October, the day before his departure from Cyprus, he wrote to his wife. Although the more private portions of the letter are not given, one can sense that he missed his family. He also felt isolated. The boat carrying mail and newspapers calls at Larnaca once every two weeks, and there is no news from the German homeland. He appreciated the things which he had seen, but, he exclaims, "thank God, that this first station, Cyprus, will soon be behind me." He admits to having had "an incredibly rich and interesting time," but also complains about the "hardships, deprivations, and adventures" which he experienced in the course of his journey. He grumbles about poor accommodations, inedible food, dreadful Cypriot wine, the heat, and bumpy roads.

Larnaca seemed to him to be a desert of sand, a treeless, waterless, and sad desert, but Dhali he found to be a lovely, wonderful place, a green oasis. Dhali, rather than Athienou, was his overnight stop on the way to Nicosia, since Cesnola had a country home there. We learn that Cesnola opened some 3,000 tombs at Idalion![465] Of Turkish rule Friederichs had formed a very low opinion; "to this day it kills everything."[466] He was courteously received by the Pasha, Mehmed Said Pasha; nevertheless: "The pasha is a very elegant, fine man, whose Turkish barbarism is thinly covered by French refinement, but comes to the fore now and then."[467] He was not slow to fault the Greeks either; the common people and the clergy are equally ignorant.[468] Having acquired enough antiquities for the Berlin Museum to fill fifteen boxes, he is happy to leave the island; all the more so, as he is looking forward to seeing Jerusalem.

---

[464] Carl Friederichs, *Kunst und Leben: Reisebriefe aus Griechenland, dem Orient und Italien* (Düsseldorf, 1872) pages 30–51 pertain to Cyprus. *Allgemeine Deutsche Biographie* 7 (1877) 391–92; Meyers *Konversationslexikon* 6 (1889) 690; Lullies and Schiering, *Archäologenbildniss*, 57–58; Helmut Prückner, "Carl Friederichs," in Bernhard Forssman, ed., *Sie waren Uttenreuther: Lebensbilder einstiger Erlanger Studenten* (Erlangen: Uttenreuther Blätter, 1993) 26–31.
[465] Friedrichs, *Reisebriefe*, 36.
[466] Friedrichs, *Reisebriefe*, 38.
[467] Friedrichs, *Reisebriefe*, 39.
[468] Friedrichs, *Reisebriefe*, 40, 45.

**Louis (Ludwig) Salvator [Plate 14]** (1847–1915) Archduke of Austria, was the son of Leopold II, grandduke of Tuscany. Somewhat of an eccentric, he devoted himself to travel and scientific studies rather than to affairs of government. He wrote fifty books, all but four on the Mediterranean and some published anonymously. He lived mostly on the island of Mallorca or on his yacht "Nixe." In 1867 he was decorated with the Order of the Golden Fleece; a regiment of the Austro-Hungarian Army was named after him.[469]

**Paul Schröder** (1844 Elsterwerda–1915 Jena) graduated from the University of Halle in 1867. In 1869–1882 he was the dragoman of the German Consulate General in Constantinople, and in 1885–1888 of the German Embassy in Constantinople. In 1882–1885 he served as the German consul in Beirut, and in 1888–1909 as consul general, again in Beirut.[470] He was a distinguished scholar of Phoenician and had published *Die phönizische Sprache;*[471] also "Über einige Fragmente phoenikischer Inschriften aus Cypern."[472] He was also knowledgeable of Turkish and Arabic. He spent several weeks on Cyprus in the spring of 1870 and returned for a second visit in the spring of 1873. In 1878 he published "Meine zweite Reise auf Cypern im Frühjahr 1873," from letters to Prof. Heinrich Kiepert in Berlin.[473] The latter (1818–1899), the author of numerous books, atlases, and maps, used the data provided by Schröder in producing a map of Cyprus in 1878.[474]

After he had returned from Cyprus to Constantinople, Schröder reported to Kiepert in three long letters dated 30 May, 30 July, and 15 August 1873. These letters provide a wealth of geographical, topographical, and meteorological data, based on many readings taken with compass, thermometer, and barometer. As far as possible Schröder avoided places which he had already seen on his first journey, in order to provide as much new information as possible. Thus he ventured into the district of Tylliria, in the northwestern part of the island. He found the inhabitants of this district to be indeed backward: they wear tattered and filthy clothes; they have no furniture of any sort in their huts and sleep on the floor like dogs, he reports; he could not understand them.[475] He did not stay long.

He was a man of many interests. He had come well-prepared. He cites Pliny, Strabo, Diodorus Siculus, and Stephanus Byzantius; also Engel,[476] Ross, and Sakellarios. He was familiar with Gaudry's agricultural map of Cyprus.[477] He copied inscriptions, even correcting one previously published.[478] At Paphos he purchased two inscriptions which looked interesting to him, only to find later that they were forged. "So fraud and

---

[469] Leo Woerl, Erzherzog Ludwig Salvator aus dem österreichischen Kaiserhause als Forscher des Mittelmeers (Leipzig, 1899); Österreichisches Biographisches Lexikon 1815–1950, fasc. 24 (1971) 350–51; Helga Schwendinger, Erzherzog Ludwig Salvator: Der Wissenschaftler aus dem Kaiserhaus: Die Biographie (Vienna, 1991); Horst Joseph Kleinmann, Erzherzog Ludwig Salvator: Mallorcas ungekrönter König (Graz, 1991); Online AEIOU* Österreich Lexikon, in either English or German.

[470] *Wer ist's*, 7th ed. (Leipzig, 1914) 1528; *Deutsches biographisches Jahrbuch*, Überleitungsband I, 1915, p. 340.

[471] (Halle, 1869; repr. Wiesbaden, 1979).

[472] *Königliche Akademie der Wissenschaften, Berlin, Monatsberichte*, 1873, pp. 330–41.

[473] Schröder, "Reise," 135–39, 152–56, 168–72, and 183–86.

[474] Stylianou, *Cartography*, 153, no. 216, and 416, fig. 200.

[475] Schröder, "Reise," 136–37.

[476] Engel, *Kypros*.

[477] Schröder, "Reise," 170. On this map, see Stylianou, *Cartography*, 151–52.

[478] Schröder, "Reise," 136.

deception have found their way even into these regions which are cut off from all culture and contact with strangers," he laments.[479] He examined ancient sites, sometimes providing carefully done site plans.[480] He was not always able to tell whether some ruins were ancient or medieval.[481] At one location, Selenia on the Karpas peninsula, he found that the local peasants had illegally dug for antiquities and had left behind many votive figures, deeming them worthless because they were fragmentary.[482]

Like other visitors to Cyprus he was horrified by the systematic and reckless destruction of the island's forests. And he appreciated the scenic beauty of which Cyprus has so much to offer; the view feom Buffavento Castle he found inspiring.

He collected folk songs (τραγούδια) on his way. In the district of Tylliria he was denied success, because of the backwardness of the inhabitants. At Rizokarpaso he was more successful. One of these folk songs he passed on to Kiepert.[483]

Schröder left Cyprus at some time after 12 April; the exact date is not given.

**Julius Seiff** spent four weeks in Cyprus in January and February 1872 in the course of a journey to Asia Minor and Syria. He recorded his experiences in *Skizze einer Reise durch die Insel Cypern* (Dresden, 1874) and in *Reisen in der asiatischen Turkei* (Leipzig, 1875). In *Reisen* pages 76-132 pertain to Cyprus.

Seiff began his visit to Cyprus on an unhappy note. His first view of Larnaca was disappointing. Worse yet, because of an outbreak of the cholera in Constantinople he was restricted for four days to a Turkish quarantine facility, which was most primitive and uncomfortable. "A model public health facility," he called it sarcastically.[484]

Much of what Seiff reports on the geography, economy, and history of the island is not new. He, too, was appalled by the reckless destruction of the forests,[485] the primitive methods of agriculture,[486] the recurring locust plague,[487] the lepers at the gate of Nicosia,[488] and the narrow and dirty streets of that city.[489] There is a general lack of cleanliness in people's homes; he tells of one housewife who upon the arrival of her

---

[479] Schröder, "Reise," 139.

[480] Schröder, "Reise," 154, 169, 172, and 184.

[481] Schröder, "Reise," 152–53.

[482] Schröder, "Reise," 168.

[483] Schröder, "Reise," 183. Readers might be pleased by the last two strophes:
> Ten royal physicians,
> no matter how learned,
> cannot heal a heart
> which has been smitten by love.
>
> He who has been burned by the coals of love
> will never be whole again.
> And if the physicians heal him,
> the old wound will always remain.

[484] Seiff, "Reise," 77–79.

[485] Seiff, "Reise," 81–82, 125.

[486] Seiff, "Reise," 94.

[487] Seiff, "Reise," 96.

[488] Seiff, "Reise," 90.

[489] Seiff, "Reise," 92.

guests sweeps the floor so vigorously that she stirs up enough dust to drive them out.[490] Two of the monasteries at which he stayed he also found unclean.[491]

Seiff identifies two causes which underlie the deplorable conditions which he has observed. The first is a lack of means, industry, and willingness to work on the part of the people.[492] The second is the oppressive Turkish rule: "Since the Turkish conquest of the island, once so flourishing and much-desired, its prosperity and accordingly the population have steadily declined."[493]

Seiff reveals little about his person, status, or family. From the title page of his book we learn that he was a civil engineer by profession. He is listed in the address books of Dresden for the years 1865–1875. He was an active member of the "Verein für Erdkunde zu Dresden." The Jahresbericht issued by that organization in 1877 reports, without giving a specific date, that he died at Adana in Asia Minor.

**Alfred Ritter zur Helle von Samo** [Plate 33] was born in 1834 in Namiest (Moravia), entered the Austrian army as a sub-lieutenant in 1855, and attained the rank of Major in the course of a 20-year career. He saw action in the Austrian-Italian War of 1859 and in the Austrian-Prussian War of 1866. In the latter conflict at the Battle of Königgrätz he suffered three head wounds and was taken prisoner. His service record is extant in the Österreichisches Staatsarchiv, but does not record his death. He served as the military attaché at the Austro-Hungarian Embassy in Constantinople in 1870–1875 and and visited Cyprus in 1874.[494] He published *Die Völker des osmanischen Reiches* (Vienna, 1877). More pertinent to the present article is his *Das Vilajet der Inseln des Weißen Meeres, das priviligierte Beylik Samos und das selbstständige Mutessariflik Cypern* (Vienna, 1878). Pages 16–19 and 74–79 pertain to Cyprus; pages 16–19 are available in an English translation in *The Geographical Magazine* 5 (1978) 168.

In the first segment, pp. 16–19, a very brief historical summary is followed by a statistical table taken from the description of Cyprus by Lacroix[495] and some additional statistical data. Lacroix's table, dating from 1853, shows the island divided into 13 districts with 610 villages and a population of 108,600, of whom 33,300 are Muslims, 73,200 Greek Orthodox, 1400 Maronites, 500 Roman Catholics, and 200 Armenians. The same table shows a count of 610 villages. From another source, not identified, we learn that in 1571 there were 860 villages. These figures confirm what we have already learned about the loss of population. But at the time of his visit in 1874 Ritter zur Helle learned that the population was ca. 144,000. which is at variance with the earlier figure, as an increase of 35,400 over a period of 21 years is highly unlikely.

The second segment, pp. 74–79, provides information on military and economic matters and reads almost like a handbook for diplomats and intelligence officers. Ritter zur Helle declares that he means only to supplement and update the Unger-Kotschy book. His overall impression of the island is very negative. He quotes an earlier English observer: "Agriculture neglected, population almost annihilated, pestiferous air, indolence,

[490] Seiff, "Reise," 104.
[491] Seiff, "Reise," 111, 128.
[492] Seiff, "Reise," 82.
[493] Seiff, "Reise," 84.
[494] Service record, *Kriegsarchiv, Österreichisches Staatsarchiv*.
[495] Louis Lacroix, *Les Isles de la Grèce* (Paris, 1853) 88.

poverty, desolation."[496] And he heartily agrees. As a military attaché he recognized the value of Cyprus for defensive purposes as well as for offensive operations against the coast of Syria and Asia Minor. Military planners of Greece, Turkey, and Great Britain to this day appreciate this military value of the island. The old fortifications of Cyprus' cities, on the other hand, he remarks, are of value to photograpers only. He concludes with a report on the volume and value of Cypriot agricultural exports. One might wonder where he obtained his information.

Nowhere does he voice a criticism of the Turkish administration.

**Victor Graf Folliot de Crenneville** (1847–1920) was the son of Franz Graf Folliot de Crenneville (1815–1888), who had distinguished himself in both the military and civilian service of the Austrian government. He served as the Austrian vice consul in Smyrna.[497]

It remains now to make some observations on these thirteen men as a group. Some emerge as personalities more strongly than others, depending on the richness or meagerness of our sources. All came to Cyprus not with the casual interest of the modern tourist, but with serious objectives. All were of the upper middle class or of the nobility, and all were very well educated. All had broad "interdisciplinary" interests, but also had developed an academic specialty. Thus Ross and Friederichs were primarily archaeologists, and Kotschy and Unger botanists. Von Hammer-Purgstall, Petermann, and Schröder were philologists studying Near-Eastern languages such as Turkish, Arabic, Phoenician, or Armenian, being interested at the same time in the Greek-Cypriot dialect. Ritter zur Helle was a military man. Young Otto von Richter, had he lived, would probably have continued his studies in languages and ethnography. Kotschy and Schröder also contributed to the geography and topography of Cyprus. Seiff remains largely an unknown.

Among the people of Cyprus von Richter, Ross, Unger, Schröder, Seiff, and Ritter zur Helle observed poverty, indolence, ignorance, and lack of cleanliness. Ross and Unger are both sharply critical of the Cypriot church, finding that monks and priests are largely ignorant. But the sharpest criticism is aimed at the Turkish rule; Ross, Petermann, Kotschy, Unger, Friederichs, and Seiff speak as if with one voice on this subject. None of them, however, encountered any difficulty on the part of the Pasha or other Turkish officials. There is some grumbling about poor accommodations, bumpy roads (or no roads at all), and the discomforts of travel in general, but the hospitality offered by villagers or monasteries and the general friendliness of the people are gratefully acknowledged. Except when they stayed with one of the consuls in Larnaca, these travelers must have experienced first-hand the lack of sanitary facilities, but good taste apparently bade them to remain silent on this point, and on matters of personal hygiene as well.

None of these travelers stayed in Cyprus much longer than four weeks; what they saw is by necessity limited. They never discovered the wonderful painted churches in the Troodos mountains.[498] But they observed intelligently and recorded diligently. They were keenly conscious of being Europeans, while the people of Cyprus, whether Greek or Turkish, were "Orientals." The cultural differences could not be ignored. What they report on the economy of the island tells us that the industrial revolution had not reached it. Archaeologists will note with sorrow that some antiquities seen by these travelers are

---

[496] Edward Daniel Clarke, *Travels in Various Countries of Europe, Asia, and Africa* (11 vols. Cambridge and London, 1819–1823) I 315. Excerpts in Cobham, *Excerpta*, 378–94 and *SHC* V 121–134.
[497] See further *Neue deutsche Biographie*, 5 (1961) 287.
[498] Stylianou, *Painted Churches*.

now irretrievably lost, but some antiquities now removed to museums were seen and described in situ. Anthropologists and sociologists can learn much about 19th century Greek-Cypriot society. Much less can be learned about the Turkish-Cypriot community, with which there was only minimal contact.

# INDEX

Footnotes and the appendix of biographical sketches, pp. 250—265, have not been included in this index.

PLATE 1

Freiherr Joseph von Hammer-Purgstall
Photo Österreichische Nationalbibliothek, Vienna, NB 502942-B

PLATE 2

Colossal vase
*(Bergk)*

PLATE 3

Limassol
(*Bergk*)

PLATE 4

Otto Friedrich von Richter
Frontispiece, *Wallfahrten im Morgenlande*

PLATE 5

Ludwig Ross
Photo Institut für klassische Altertumswissenschanften, Universität Hall

PLATE 6

Statuette
(Ross)

PLATE 7

Julius Heinrich Petermann
Photo Universitätsbibliothek der Humboldt Universität zu Berlin, Portätsammlung

PLATE 8

Theodor Kotschy
Photo Österreichische Nationalbibliothek, Vienna, NB 503833-B

PLATE 9

Larnaca
(Kotschy)

PLATE 10

Franz Joseph Andreas Unger
Photo Landesmuseum Joanneum, Graz

PLATE 11

Bellapais
(Unger and Kotschy)

PLATE 12

Old Paphos
(Unger and Kotschy)

PLATE 13

Temple of Aphrodite
(Unger and Kotschy)

PLATE 14

Archduke Ludwig Salvator of Austria
Photo *Levkosia, The Capital of Cyprus* (Trigraph: London, 1983)

PLATE 15

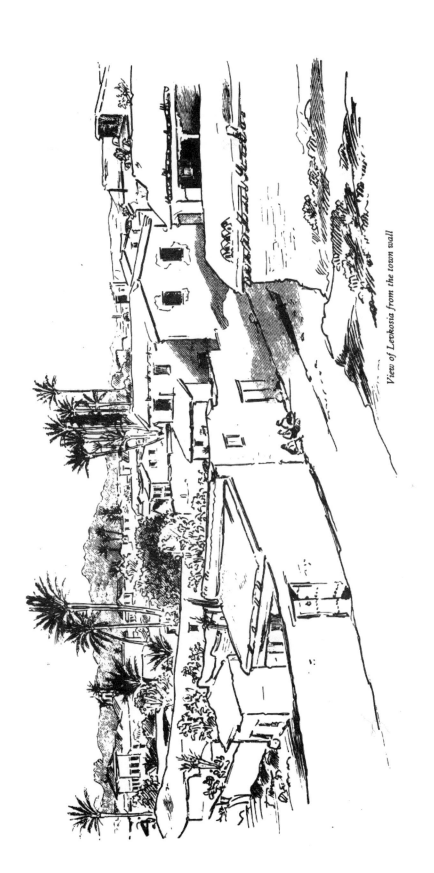

*View of Levkosia from the town wall*

Levkosia
(Ludwig Salvator)

PLATE 16

Tahta gala from Famagosta Gate

Famagosta Gate
(Ludwig Salvator)

PLATE 17

*View in Tripiodis Street*

Tripolis Street
(Ludwig Salvator)

PLATE 18

Hall in a private house

Private house
(Ludwig Salvator)

PLATE 19

*A fountain near the Tahta Calá Djami Si*

Fountain
(Ludwig Salvator)

PLATE 20

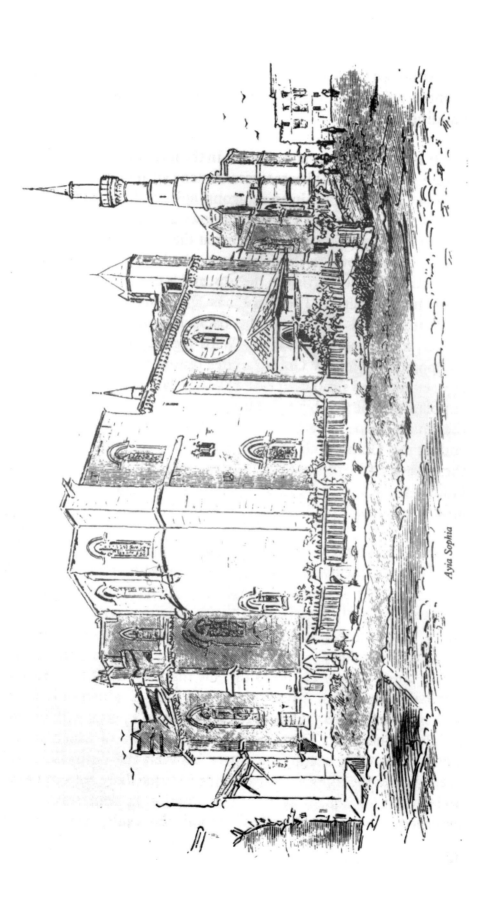

Ayia Sophia

Ayia Sophia
(Ludwig Salvator)

PLATE 21

*Porch of the Baptistery*

Porch of Baptistery
(Ludwig Salvator)

PLATE 22

*Haidar Pascha Djami Si*

Haidar Pascha Djami Si
(Ludwig Salvator)

PLATE 23

Yegni Djami

Yegni Djami
(Ludwig Salvator)

PLATE 24

*The Venetian Column*

Venetian column
(Ludwig Salvator)

PLATE 25

Bejuk Khan

Bejuk Khan
(Ludwig Salvator)

PLATE 26

*Wells in Bazaar*

Wells
(Ludwig Salvator)

PLATE 27

*Mehemmed Veiss, Governor of Cyprus*

Mehemmed Veiss
(Ludwig Salvator)

PLATE 28

Carl Friederichs
Photo Deutsches Archäologisches Institut, Berlin

PLATE 29

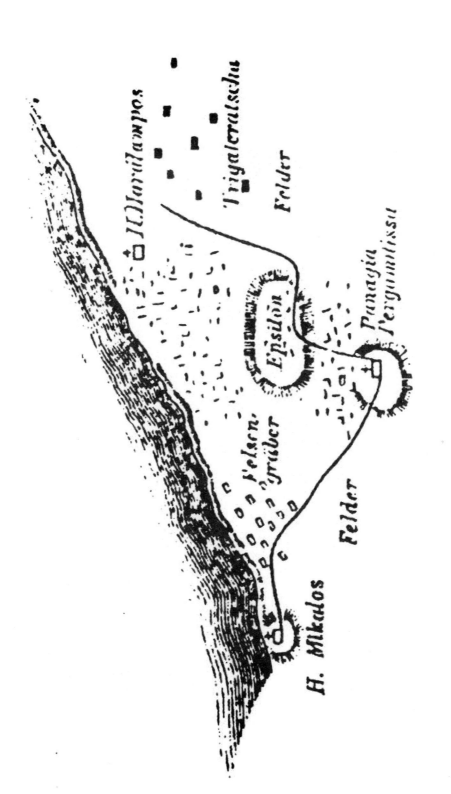

Panayia Pergaminiotissa
(Schröder)

PLATE 30

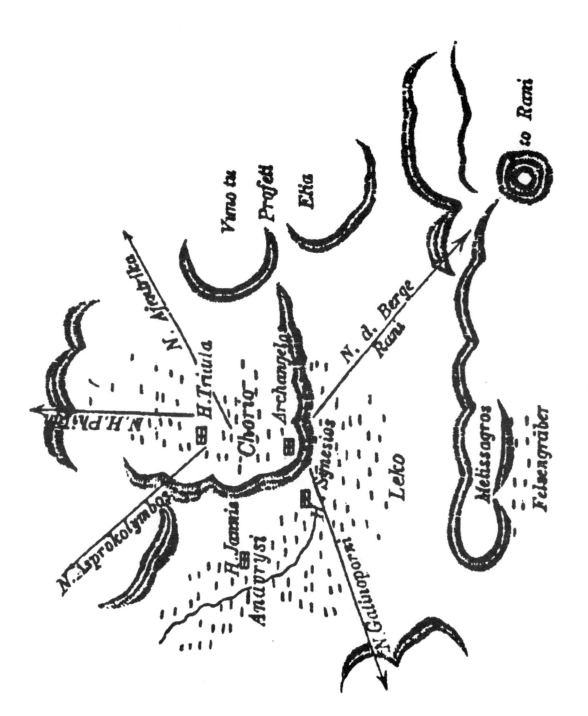

Chorio
(Schröder)

PLATE 31

Kastro
(Schröder)

PLATE 32

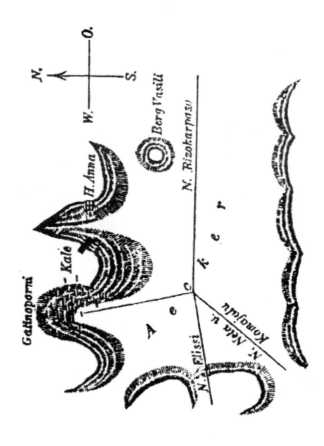

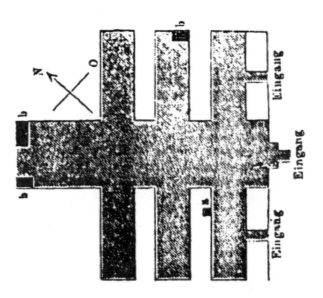

Galinoporni
(Schröder)

PLATE 33

Alfred Ritter zur Helle von Samo
Photo Österreichisches Staatsarchiv—Kriegsarchiv, Vienna